THE ORAL HISTORY OF
Admiral Thomas H. Collins U.S. Coast Guard (Retired)

INTERVIEWED BY
Jim Dolbow

U.S. Naval Institute • Annapolis, Maryland

Copyright © 2019

Preface

Thomas H. Collins served in the U.S. Coast Guard for an eventful 38 years from the time he entered the Coast Guard Academy in the summer of 1964 until his retirement as the 22nd Commandant of the U.S. Coast Guard in May 2006. From the Cold War to the War on Drugs to protecting the U.S. homeland, Collins held six different major commands.

Recorded between January and April 2016, these 25 hours of interviews reveal that Admiral Collins was a change agent and process-oriented leader skilled at implementing organizational change in a dynamic and large institution like the U.S. Coast Guard. This was a skill he honed throughout his entire career and one he put to good use as he achieved greater responsibility in the U.S. Coast Guard. One of many examples of him being a change agent was his vision that led to the establishment of Coast Guard Sectors during his tenure as Commandant. Today, these sectors are hailed as one-stop shopping by all of those impacted by an emergency.

As Commandant, Admiral Collins oversaw an aging Coast Guard fleet of cutters, aircraft, and communication systems and an active duty force that was about the same size as the New York City Police Department. Despite the chronic underfunding of the Coast Guard, which readers are made well aware throughout the interview, given Collins' budget expertise, the Coast Guard lived up to its motto of *"Semper Paratus"* and prevented a terrorist attack in our nation's 361 ports and 95,000 miles of waterways. No small feat considering the attacks on the aviation sector on September 11, 2001, and the concerns that the maritime sector was the next target. Moreover, Collins deployed Coast Guard personnel and platforms overseas in support of Operation Iraqi Freedom in March 2003. Finally, as if guarding the U.S. homeland against a maritime 9/11 attack and deploying forces in support of DOD's combatant commanders weren't enough, Adm. Collins also oversaw the transfer of the U.S. Coast Guard from the Department of Transportation to the newly created Department of Homeland Security in March 2003 followed two years later by the Coast Guard's rescue from peril of 24,145 lives and the evacuation of 9,409 medical evacuations in the aftermath of Hurricane Katrina.

Thanks go to Rick Russell, Tom Cutler, Annie Rehill, and Eric Mills of the Naval Institute staff for their support and guidance throughout the course of this important project. Special thanks must go to Adm. Collins for being a great interviewee. He was well prepared for each interview and edited the transcripts in a prompt manner. History will show that Adm. Collins' tour as Commandant was the most action-packed of any Coast Guard Commandant since that of Adm. Russell R. Waesche, 8th Commandant of the U.S. Coast Guard from 1936–1946. I am confident Admiral Collins' oral history will make a significant contribution to knowledge about the U.S. Coast Guard for many, many years to come.

Jim Dolbow, interviewer
March 2019

The U.S. Naval Institute Oral History Program

Researchers and authors have been drawing on the Naval Institute's Oral History Program since 1969, the year it was established by Dr. John T. Mason Jr. He and his successor, author and historian Paul Stillwell, sought to capture, preserve, and disseminate a permanent record of the stories of significant figures in naval history. In recent years, the program has expanded, with increasing numbers of historians conducting more interviews.

These oral histories are carefully fact-checked and reviewed by both historians and interview subjects before being made available. The Naval Institute is known for this high level of editorial intervention and polishing. The reader is reminded, as with all oral history interviews, that this is a record of the spoken word.

The Naval Institute wishes to acknowledge the many donors who make this program possible, in particular the generous support of the Pritzker Military Foundation of Chicago and the late Jack C. Taylor of St. Louis.

ADMIRAL THOMAS H. COLLINS
UNITED STATES COAST GUARD (RETIRED)

Admiral Thomas H. Collins served as the 22nd Commandant of the United States Coast Guard from May 30, 2002 to May 25, 2006. As Commandant, Collins served as the senior uniformed Coast Guard officer responsible for the organization, training and equipage of more than 100,000 active-duty, Reserve, Auxiliary, and civilian forces serving in the United States and overseas. He also managed an $8.1 billion budget and a fleet of more than 220 ships, 230 aircraft, and 1,800 boats stationed at more than 160 shore facilities.

Highlights of his tour as Commandant of the U.S. Coast Guard included the:

- Transfer of the Coast Guard from the Department of Transportation to the newly created Department of Homeland Security
- Deployment of Coast Guard forces in support of Operation Iraqi Freedom
- Development and implementation of national and international strategies, policies, and operations designed to mitigate security risk in the 361 U.S. ports and 95,000 miles of waterways, and beyond
- Design and implementation of "Sectors," a new, unified/integrated operational field structure and organization throughout the Coast Guard for enhanced command and control, information flow, and operational performance
- Award and recalibration (due to revised 9/11 related program requirements) of the largest capital asset (cutters/boats/aircraft) modernization program in Coast Guard history.

Prior to becoming Commandant, Collins served as the Coast Guard's Vice Commandant from 2000 to 2002, creating the Innovation Council, spearheading service-wide process improvement initiatives, and directing system enhancements as the Coast Guard Acquisition Executive. From 1998 to 2000 he served as Commander, Pacific Area and Eleventh Coast Guard District, where he developed the successful Coast Guard response to the increase in illegal drug and migrant smuggling traffic in the Eastern Pacific. His other flag assignments included serving as Commander, Fourteenth Coast Guard District in Honolulu, Hawaii, and Chief, Office of Acquisition at Coast Guard Headquarters, where he managed the acquisition of twelve major systems worth nearly $3 billion and laid the foundation for the Integrated Deepwater System project. The project will modernize the ships, aircraft, and sensors that the Coast Guard uses to perform its many open-ocean missions. Prior to his promotion to Flag Officer in 1994, he served as the Chief, Programs Division at Coast Guard Headquarters.

Admiral Collins began his Coast Guard career in June 1968 as a deck watch officer and first lieutenant aboard the cutter *Vigilant* (WMEC-617). Following that assignment, he served a two-year tour as commanding officer of the cutter *Cape Morgan* (WPB-95313), a patrol boat homeported in Charleston, South Carolina. His shore operational assignments included Deputy Commander, Group St. Petersburg, Florida, and

Commander of Coast Guard Group and Captain of the Port, Long Island Sound, in New Haven, Connecticut.

Admiral Collins graduated from the Coast Guard Academy in 1968 and later served as a faculty member within the Humanities Department. He earned a Master of Arts degree in liberal studies from Wesleyan University and a Master of Business Administration from the University of New Haven.

Since his retirement from the Coast Guard after 38 years of service in 2006, Admiral Collins has served as a maritime consultant, providing strategic-level vision and strategies associated with maritime safety, security, and environmental processes, systems, infrastructure, and organizations. He has provided guidance and advice to both corporate and governmental entities in the areas of strategic planning, port and facility master planning, maritime risk management, waterways management, and emergency preparation and response systems, processes, and organizations.

He also currently serves as a member of the board of directors of SureID Inc. (a security credentialing company); Terma North America Inc. (a defense/security services and systems manufacturer); and the Armed Forces Benefit Association (AFBA—a provider of insurance products). He also serves as chairman of the board to NTT Data Federal Systems Inc., an information technology company.

A native of Stoughton, Massachusetts, Admiral Collins is married to the former Nancy Monahan of New London, Connecticut. They have two daughters, Christine and Kathryn, and two grandchildren, Hadley and Jack.

EDUCATION

1968   Bachelor of Science, U. S. Coast Guard Academy, New London, Connecticut

1972   Master of Arts in Liberal Studies, Wesleyan University, Middletown, Connecticut

1976   Master of Business Administration, University of New Haven, New Haven, Connecticut

1994   Capstone Program in National Security, International Affairs, and Joint Defense Operations, National War College, Washington, D.C.

ASSIGNMENTS

1968–1969, Deck Watch Officer and First Lieutenant, USCGC *Vigilant* (WMEC-617), New Bedford, Massachusetts

1969–1971, Commanding Officer, USCGC *Cape Morgan* (WPB-95313), Charleston, South Carolina

1971–1972, Full Time Duty Under Instruction (DUINS), Wesleyan University, Middletown, Connecticut

1972–1976, Professor, United States Coast Guard Academy, New London, Connecticut

1976–1980, Deputy Chief Planning and Programming Staff, Office of Research & Development, U.S. Coast Guard Headquarters, Washington, D.C

1980–1983, Deputy Commanding Officer Group St. Petersburg, and Commanding Officer, Station St. Petersburg, St. Petersburg, Florida

1983–1987, Program Analyst, Programs Division, U.S. Coast Guard Headquarters, Washington, D.C

1987–1990, Commander of Coast Guard Group and Captain of the Port, Long Island Sound, New Haven, CT

1990–1992, Chief, Administrative Division, Fourteenth Coast Guard District, Honolulu, Hawaii

1992–1994, Chief, Programs Division, U.S. Coast Guard Headquarters, Washington, D.C

1994–1996, Chief, Office of Acquisition, U.S. Coast Guard Headquarters, Washington, D.C.

1996–1998, Commander, Fourteenth Coast Guard District, Honolulu, Hawaii

1998–2000, Commander, Pacific Area and Eleventh Coast Guard District, Alameda, CA

2000–2002, Vice Commandant, U.S. Coast Guard Headquarters, Washington, D.C

2002–2006, Commandant, U.S. Coast Guard Headquarters, Washington, D.C.

MAJOR AWARDS AND DECORATIONS

Department of Transportation Distinguished Service Medal

Department of Homeland Security Distinguished Service Medal

Coast Guard Distinguished Service Medal

Defense Distinguish Service Medal

Army Distinguished Service Medal

Legion of Merit (three awards)

Meritorious Service Medal (two awards)

Coast Guard Commendation Medal (three awards)

Presidential Unit Commendation

CG Unit Commendation

CG Meritorious Unit Commendation

CG Meritorious Team Commendation (2 awards)

Global War on Terror Service Medal

Humanitarian Service Medal

Argentine Coast Guard Distinguished Service Medal

EFFECTIVE DATES OF PROMOTION

Ensign	June 4, 1968
Lieutenant (junior grade)	December 4, 1969
Lieutenant	December 4, 1971
Lieutenant Commander	November 2, 1977
Commander	July 1, 1983
Captain	October 1, 1989
Rear Admiral (Lower Half)	September 29, 1994
Rear Admiral (Upper Half)	June 1998
Vice Admiral	June 30, 1998
Admiral	May 30, 2002

BOARD POSTIONS/COMPANY AFFILIATIONS:

Director, Board of Directors, SureID Inc.

Director, Board of Directors, Terma North America

Director, Board of Directors, Armed Forces Benefit Association

Chairman of the Board, NTT Data Federal Systems (NDFS)

PAST PROFESSIONAL AFFILIATIONS/ASSOCIATIONS:

Director, Board of Directors, Spatial Data Analytics Corporation

Director, Board of Directors, Altegrity Corporation

International Maritime Organization—IMO Assembly, head of delegation

North Pacific Coast Guard Forum—Annual summit, head of delegation

Executive Office of the President, National Drug Agency Control Policy—The Interdiction Committee, Chair U. S. Interdiction Coordinator, (one year)

American Bureau of Shipping American Society of Naval Engineers, Council, honorary member

Committee on the Maritime Transportation System—Coordinating Board member and subcommittee chair

United Seaman's Service—Council of Trustees, honorary member

Deed of Gift

The U.S. Naval Institute is hereby authorized to make available in any format it chooses, from bound-book hard copy to electronic/digital Internet access and as part of videorecordings, the audio recordings, transcripts, and videorecordings of the oral-history interview series conducted concerning the life and career of the undersigned. Disposition, repositories, and access shall be at the discretion of the Naval Institute. The undersigned shall be offered the opportunity to review the transcribed oral history prior to its finalization, and to make any corrections thereto that the undersigned deems necessary.

The undersigned does hereby release and assign to the U.S. Naval Institute the rights and title to these interviews, with the exception that the undersigned and heirs retain the right to use the material for personal, noncommercial purposes. The copyright in the oral, transcribed, and videorecorded versions shall be held by the U.S. Naval Institute. All recordings, transcriptions, and videorecordings of the interviews shall remain the property of the U.S. Naval Institute.

Signed and sealed this __14__ day of __January__ 2015. 2016

Signed name __Thomas Collins__

Printed name __THOMAS COLLINS__

Interviewer: Jim Dolbow (JD)

Interviewee: Admiral Thomas Collins, USCG Ret. (TC)

Begin audio file Collins1.1.Dolbow.USNI.1.11.16

JD: January 11th in Arlington, Virginia. I'm Jim Dolbow. I'm here interviewing Admiral Thomas Collins for the US Naval Institute's Oral History program. Admiral, it was a pleasure to meet you earlier today, to get acquainted a little bit. The intent here is to cover your entire life and Coast Guard career for the benefit of history. So, if you could begin at the beginning, please—something about when and where you were born and your parents.

TC: Well, that's a good place to start. I was born in Quincy, Massachusetts in 1946. I didn't spend much of my life there. Most of childhood life was spent in Stoughton, Massachusetts from about 1955 to 1964. I was the middle child of a hardworking middle-class family. I had an older brother—two years older than myself, and a sister—ten years younger. My father, Harley Collins, worked for Liberty Mutual in Boston where he headed up their data processing center. My mother, Inger Collins, was a full-time housewife and mother, and was very, very good at it. My family environment growing up was very warm and supportive. I was very fortunate.

JD: What values would you say you learned from your parents? Were there things that they especially stressed?

TC: Hard work, quality work. That you don't get anything for nothing. I can remember my father always saying to me, "anything worth doing is worth doing well." It was a matter of working hard and earning your pay, so to speak.

Other values which were stressed were focused on treating people like you would like to be treated. They preached the "golden rule" and they lived the "golden rule" and that's always stuck with me along with having respect for people of all types, shapes, and sizes. Along with honesty and integrity, were an essential set of values that they not only preached, but lived. So, they were very good examples for me. They engendered values that have remained with me throughout my life.

JD: Going back, what was it like being the middle child?

TC: I thought it was pretty cool. It was great having an older brother. My older brother looked out for me, paved the way for me in many respects—at school, at the part-time workplaces we shared as teenagers. We had a very good relationship growing up. He was very tolerant of me and frequently included me in activities with his friends, all older than me. We both, I think, benefited from having a much younger sister that was ten years my junior. When she was a baby we helped our mother in all the babysitting tasks. It helped us learn what family is all about.

JD: What kind of student were you growing up and what schools did you attend?

TC: I attended kindergarten through third grade in Waltham, Massachusetts. We lived there for a short period of time. But, most of my schooling was in the Stoughton, Massachusetts school systems where I attended elementary, junior high, and high school. I was a pretty good student frequently attaining advanced placement in most classes. Stoughton was a small, old mill town home to the Corcoran Shoe Company and other factories that are no longer in business, but that's what that town had been all about historically. When I was growing up it was a bedroom community for metropolitan Boston. It was a comfortable small town atmosphere and it was a very positive experience going to school there.

JD: What were some of your favorite subjects in school?

TC: During junior high and then high school, I was stronger in the quantitative subjects than I was in the verbal subjects. I was in advanced placement class during high school so I had plenty of competition from my classmates. We had subjects like advanced math and advanced calculus and so forth in high school. I can remember my algebra teacher, Mr. Vogel. He was a piece of work. He was ethnically German and very exacting. But he was a great teacher and I learned a great deal from him.

JD: Were there any other teachers that were role models for you or inspired you?

TC: Mr. Vogel is the one that stands out in my mind. He was low-key and down-to-earth, but held people accountable and so forth. He was a model of sound analytical thinking. He understood young kids and really knew how to draw the best out of students. So, he was probably the best instructor that I had during high school.

JD: Did it help to have a brother go before you by two years in some of these classes and teachers? Did they compare?

TC: I had a great brother to follow. He was a good—but not great—student. He was, and is, an extrovert and was very popular in school. My brother also had a good reputation among the faculty. But I think—in many ways—we were our own folks and we just plowed our own trail. But it was good to have him in the same school that I was in.

JD: How about your sister? Did she ever come back from school and, say, talk about stories from teachers about you or your brother?

TC: Yes, there was a little of that. More now, than then. We reminisce now, when we get together. For example, I was invited back to Stoughton High School in 2006 while I was Commandant for induction into the Stoughton High School Hall of Fame. I went back and addressed the student body. It was a kick. It was a lot of fun and, of course, the intent of the program and my message to them was, "You can be everything you want to be and here are some of the things you've got to pay attention to, in order to make that happen."

It was a very warm gathering, a great reception. They had a high school jazz band that had gained national recognition to play during the ceremony. They were terrific. My sister and her daughter attended, so it was a lot of fun and I was quite honored to be included in the program, and to help out their Hall of Fame. They created the event to get successful graduates back as role models for the students. I think it's a great program for the school, and for the kids in the school.

JD: Definitely. Growing up as a kid, did you have any hobbies you pursued or activities?

TC: Yes, my brother and I were very active kids. We did all of the neighborhood sports with the neighborhood gang of friends. We had a big field in the back of our house where we played baseball and football nonstop. We also had a pond about a mile away that froze over during the winter to provide us with a good ice hockey venue. I can remember my mother saying, "Okay, well, just make sure you get home when the lights come on." When we weren't in school, we would get underway in the morning and wouldn't be back until dark. I suspect most kids and parents are not that way now, in today's society. I think, now, most are a little more guarded—a little more cautious, given all the risks of our present-day society. But then—for my brother and I—there was a long, long leash that our parents gave us. We took full advantage of it.

I was involved in school activities: I was in the student council, and I was president of my senior class—I had to give a fancy speech at graduation, which I was very nervous about and, thankfully, my English teacher and my father helped me prepare for that. But I also was in junior varsity sports and I stress "junior" varsity.

When I became old enough to work, I worked a number of jobs. My father and mother believed in us earning money and buying the extra things we wanted. Not everything—but enough to show us the value of money and work. I had a paper route and I caddied at the Blue Hills Country Club in Canton, Massachusetts. My brother and I would hitchhike up to that golf course during the summer and caddy for several rounds of golfers. When I became sixteen, I worked at the Brockton Public Market with my brother and that's where I really benefited from him, because he had such a good work experience. The management thought he just walked on water, so he paved my way into that job. I worked the rest of the way through high school so I was busy in the work front, busy on the social front, and busy on the academic front.

That was important—looking back on it—because the Coast Guard Academy's selection process put a heavy premium on not only on your academic record, but also your extracurricular record. *Are you an activist? Are you involved in things? Do you reach out in the community?* and so forth. That's a very, very important part of that selection process, and the type of young person that the Coast Guard looks for—so that wide-ranging experience I had as a teenager was, I think, good for me. Again, hats off to my parents for shaping the boundary conditions for me, and encouraging me to be an activist in my "growing up" years. They were very, very supportive.

JD: Talking about your family, what part did religion play in the life of your family?

TC: That's an interesting question. My mother and father operated within the framework of Christian values and associated spirituality. But they weren't avid, ardent churchgoers. I clearly bought into the value structure associated with religion. All of the Christian values were practiced and talked about in the home environment. Every Sunday, my brother and I went to Sunday School. Then, when we get a little older, we went to student youth programs in the church. So, it was, "Okay kid, dip your toe in that pond. This is a good thing for you. When you get old enough, make your own decisions on how active you want to be in religion as an institution."

JD: Did you read much as a kid? If so, what did you like to read?

TC: There was always books in the house from a very early age. For example, Hans Christian Andersen. I can remember the old padded book that got a lot of mileage as a very young kid, listening to those stories that my mother and father would read to us. As a very young boy, I would devour the Hardy Boys series. I can remember reading every one of those Hardy Boy books. And then, of course, during high school, I read adventure stories and more sophisticated and classical types of readings. I would say I was an average reader—a moderate reader.

JD: Did you read any books about the Coast Guard?

TC: My exposure to the Coast Guard started with my grandfather and my brother. My brother started looking at the Coast Guard before I did, and I don't know where he got the seed planted—maybe with my grandfather. My grandfather was a Danish sailor who migrated to the US during World War I. He had been in the Danish Navy and the Danish Merchant Marine. In the US, he was a Chief Engineer for the Mystic Lines, which was primarily an east coast shipping firm. He ended up being the Chief Engineer of the company before he retired. So, you know, he frequently talked maritime to my brother and me. Because of that influence, my brother looked at both Merchant Marine and Coast Guard Academies—but ultimately focused on the Coast Guard Academy.

That was at the time when you had to travel to New London, Connecticut and take an entrance exam to qualify for the Academy. The day my brother was supposed to travel to New London and take the exam, he came down with the flu and never made it there. But I had all the material around and I dug into it. What really was the big draw for me was the mission set of the Coast Guard. I quickly came to realize that the Coast Guard does some really good things for our nation every day, and that I would like to be a part of that. So, I went through the application process. Prior to that decision, I was going to be a dentist. I was accepted to a pre-dent academic program, and had a deposit down to go to Bowling Green in Ohio. Meanwhile, I got accepted to the Coast Guard Academy and I signed on the dotted line.

JD: How did you find out that you were accepted into the Academy? Did they send you a letter or give you a phone call?

TC: It was by letter. It notified me that I was accepted as a primary candidate. As I recall, I had to respond back and, in my case, prepare to report to base in Boston for a physical exam and a final interview. It was part of the process. I think at that time, you were given a preliminary appointment, subject to an interview and a physical, and then all of those things had to come together, and then you were given a final appointment.

JD: What did your parents say when you got the letter?

TC: They were very proud. But, quite frankly, I don't think they truly understood all the specifics of the Academy program and Academy life. They had a general idea but they didn't know the inner-workings and hidden mechanisms of the US Coast Guard Academy. They would soon learn. I think they were recognized that it was difficult to get accepted and recognized I had succeeded in a very competitive process. I had an excellent high school academic record, had all of the extracurricular activities, and so forth. Overall, they were proud parents.

JD: What did your grandfather say?

TC: Well, my grandfather was thrilled. By the way, he wasn't an extrovert. He wasn't a real talkative guy but he had a great smile on his face. When my grandfather and my step-grandmother lived in Ft. Lauderdale during the winter and traveled north to their place on the Maine coast every summer, they would stop with us for two or three weeks. During their late spring visit in 1964, concurrent with my acceptance to the Academy, I discuss my upcoming adventure with them. A couple of years later—on a long summer cruise onboard *Eagle*—one of the *Eagle*'s ports of call for the cruise was Miami and I had three day's liberty there. My grandfather showed up at the dock to pick me up on liberty and he was as proud as a peacock to see me in uniform disembarking from the *Eagle*. Those few days with him was worth a million bucks.

JD: After high school graduation, what did you do between graduation and reporting to the Coast Guard Academy?

TC: It was a short time. I recognized the Academy would be physically demanding. I wasn't in bad shape—I weighed 148 lbs. dripping wet at that time—but I worked out every day. I wanted to be up to the task when I got to the Academy, and to be prepared to deal with all the physically demanding activities. As I recall, I was in pretty good shape when I got there. I was probably not as emotionally prepared as I was physically, for some of the stresses and the strains and the differences in lifestyle that the Academy entails. That took a little more getting used to. It was a little bit of a shock that first summer.

JD: I can imagine. How did you get to New London for induction day?

TC: We drove. My parents drove me down to New London via old Route 1. At that time, I-95 didn't exist. The trip seemed to take forever, I was anxious to get there. We had to drive through Providence, via one-way streets, at a snail's pace. Some of my classmates travelled from as far away as California and Washington state. Because I didn't have to travel so far, I traveled and reported in during the last day of the reporting period. By the time I reported in, most of the other cadet swabs had already reported in. So, I got the last company to be formed—Zulu Company. It was an interesting day. You just kind of waved goodbye to your parents and you don't see them for about three months.

JD: Can you talk a little bit about Swab Summer?

TC: Again, it was a demanding period. Looking back on it, clearly, the intent there is to put stress on your system. The service's goal is to attract, develop, and retain the very best of our country's young men and women. Very early in this process, it is trying to ascertain if the incoming cadet has what it takes to serve in the US Coast Guard: *Does this person really have it? Does the new cadet have the temperament? The fortitude? The focus? The commitment that we want?*

There is no better time to put that to a test, you know, right up front—and that's what the first summer and year is all about. The first summer and/or year, there is a significant attrition of new cadets. My class—the great class of 1968—had well over 300 reports in July 1964. As I recall, we ultimately graduated 154. So, there was a significant attrition and a lot of that happens in the first year. Some of the new cadets saw that it was not the experience that they had expected. They would rather have been in a college frat house and the Academy was clearly not a college frat house environment. As a new cadet, you lived, ate, and slept that whole lifestyle 24-hours a day, seven days a week. Although, I did escape during the weekends when I finally got liberty in the fall. I met a local, lovely girl—Nancy Monahan. We dated and I ultimately married that girl, and am still married to her, by the way.

JD: So, if you went to dental school, you might not have met your wife.

TC: That's right. I wouldn't have met my wife of some forty-eight years. I wouldn't have had the two children I had. I wouldn't have had two wonderful, fantastic grandchildren that I now have: a six-year-old and a two-and-a-half-year-old. So, things did work out.

JD: Outstanding.

TC: New London was good to me, and for me.

JD: Was this your first time away from home?

TC: No. I had one other time. My brother and I went to Eastwood Ho Country Club. It's still there, in Chatham Massachusetts on Cape Cod. It was a caddie camp in which you spent the entire summer, from school closing to school opening. It was sponsored by the Boys Club of Boston for inner city kids. It was a program designed to get kids out of the inner city and get them exposed to something different—a leadership experience. They even took us suburban kids. So, we spent that whole summer away from home in a barracks-like environment. The counselor we had was an ex-Marine. It was good. As one of the older camp goers, my brother found out how to wiggle his way up to work in the country club. He worked in the kitchen and so forth, and got tips and everything else. We were all envious of him but we enjoyed caddying.

JD: Do you recall what an average day was like for a swab? What time it started?

TC: Our day started around six a.m. and typically entailed the entire platoon being led in exercises by our very demanding upperclassman. It might include assuming the green bench which required that your back was against the wall in a sitting position without a chair for an extended amount of time. You did that before you formed up—before you went to breakfast. You formed up before you went to lunch. You formed up in your barracks area, before you went to dinner, and you hated to do that because you were going to get some kind of pressure— something that wasn't particularly, you know, friendly, prior to those formations.

The swabs were also responsible for the upkeep and cleanliness of their barracks area. The day might also include standing watch, and some form of professional training, or sailing, or athletics, or military drilling. That first summer, we also experienced a short training cruise on the *Eagle*. The first summer was the most intense in terms of military discipline and physical endurance, but it moderated some as we went into the academic year in the fall. It was all part of the process of academy indoctrination. And I acclimated to it and learned a great deal from it.

JD: Did you encounter anything that would now be called hazing?

TC: There was but, as I recall, there was no abuse. But there was a lot of demands on you— testing of you, both physically and mentally. Most were practiced on the entire platoon as a group, not just on the individual. One of the major Academy's goals that summer was developing the concept of teamwork.

In the disciplinary process, there were a number of enforcement techniques used. An example of upperclassmen exerting discipline on you might include being ordered to go back to your room and get your mattress, putting it over your head, and then doing laps with your mattress around the third or second deck of the barracks, wherever you lived. Again, all of it was a continuous mental, emotional, and physical test. I didn't like it at the time, but I wasn't going to bail because I wasn't going to fail. It was one of those things. They were interested in who were the people that don't want to fail, who could handle stressful situations and work as a team.

JD: Do you remember any of the other names of the upperclassmen at this time? And did you run into them later on in your career?

TC: The class of 1966 was the class that indoctrinated my class, the class of 1968. My Zulu 1 Platoon Commander was a big, ethnically Russian guy by the name of Leskanovich and, to me, he was a very big guy. He was very demanding and his PPO [Platoon Petty Officer] was a guy named Alejandro and I really thought they were very ugly people. Not ugly in appearance, but ugly dispositions. They were never happy. They were always grouchy. All of the other swab platoons and members of those platoons would never go through our barrack area. They would always go up and over and they would go to the next deck and across. They would never come into our area because, if they ran into Leskanovich or Alejandro, they would get the business. So, everyone avoided our barracks area.

Our platoon had a reputation as a real tough one and looking back on it, you know, to be finally a non-attrit from Zulu 1, you were pretty good. Over half the members of my summer platoon did not make it through swab year. But in retrospect, I must salute the upperclassman that ran me through my paces. They prepared me well for my future as a Coast Guard officer. I never served with them through my career—they had different career tracks. One trained and served as an aviator.

JD: Did being at the Academy live up to your expectations?

TC: It exceeded them, I think. I didn't recognize the total comprehensive nature of that experience. It was more than academics. It was a lot of things designed to make well-rounded individuals—to make leaders.

Were there better academic institutions in the United States of America? Yes. But were there those that cared about what kind of person you are? What you stand for? What kind of values you have? All that? There's not too many that compare to our service academies in that regard. So, I think the service academies do a tremendous job. They are a great value to the nation. While I was in active duty, there were periodic proposals or considerations on Capitol Hill about service academies being too expensive, or we shouldn't have academies, or we should change academies. Every time that was looked into, the answer was always the same—that is, our country is fortunate to have great institutions such as our service academies. I think they provide a great value in terms of cost/benefit, and they perpetuate the kind of personal and professional values and traditions that we want in our military.

I spent eight years of my life in the Coast Guard Academy, four years as a cadet, and later in my career, as an instructor. And, as such, I have a great warm spot in my heart for the institution and what it stands for. On net, I think it was a great experience for me and a cherished institution for the American public.

JD: We talked a little bit about military aspects, such as drilling. How easy did you adapt to drill and ceremony, and other functions?

TC: That wasn't a problem, but you wouldn't call me a military fanatic in terms of all that stuff. There was an event called drill down where the best cadets with the rifles and movements and all—port arms and all of that—competed. I was never into that. I didn't mind regimental drills. I thought the pomp and circumstances were kind of neat. I loved the music and participating. In many ways, it involved activities that required the cadets to function as a team—a clear overall goal of the academy. I did it because that was part of the trappings and traditions of the organization.

JD: What do you remember about the atmosphere in the barracks and the comradery with your classmates?

TC: I think, as I eluded to before in previous comment, it was not a college frat house. That's what it wasn't. The barracks were an extension of the Academy. It wasn't a refuge. There were extensive rules and regulations. You had to have your room the right way. You had to have your underwear stenciled with your name on it and it had to be folded a certain way and it had to be in the drawer in a certain position. Your bed had to be made in just the right kind of way. That type of culture—that kind of life—permeated everything. When you went to bed, how you went to bed, how you woke up, how you ate, how you conducted yourself at the table—for all of those things, there was a procedure. There was a process. There was a format. There was an architecture for all that stuff.

Looking back, it was very good for me. I wasn't a totally structured guy when I was in high school. I was kind of footloose and fancy free, but the Academy gave me structure. It gave me focus and a sense of responsibility that has served me well. And the barracks life was very much a part of that. The platoon that you were in or the company that you were in—you developed very, very strong bonds with those other cadets because you were all in the same boat and you depended on each other. We helped out each other.

I can remember, if someone was caught doing something that wasn't exactly according to the rules, you might be given a special inspection that occurred on a Saturday at 13:00, when everyone else was going on liberty. You would have to stay behind with other folks that got the same type of deal and a special inspection. You would form up before upperclassmen and they would order you to go back to your room and get into a certain uniform within so many minutes. When you reported back, you were ordered into a different uniform, sometime more than one type at the same time. Then between, you'd be given butts, and muzzles, and laps around the barracks. Well, who helped you change and do all of that stuff? Your classmates. We had all of the uniforms laid out. We helped undress and dress the special inspection classmate so he would make it back to the upperclassmen on time, because if you were late getting back there were additional penalties. And we helped clean up his room in the aftermath of the inspection. This is a very graphic example of how you helped each other out.

That type of teamwork and support allowed you to survive all the disciplinary stuff. In the course of everything you learned that teamwork is really important. In the end, you tend to develop strong bonds going through that. I suspect it is not unlike the experience of those going through the various services' boot camps.

JD: Can you talk about the transition from the end of swab summer to the start of your fourth class, as a cadet in the fall?

TC: It was a little sigh of relief.

You've made it through the swab summer and the academic year is not as tight a little box as you are painted into before. There was some liberty granted and then you started the academic year. It was clearly a change of pace, but the routine and the environment didn't change much. You were still the lowest of low, as a swab. You were still the lowest of low and upperclassmen assumed you didn't know much—that you were dumber than a box of bricks. That stayed through the whole year—but as you move toward the end of the academic years, it really moderated. Then, when you got to be a third classman—oh my god, you really have arrived. It's an interesting culture that's created there. With the start of the academic year came additional challenges because on top of the military discipline, you had a very full academic plate. It all made for long days.

JD: Who were some of your instructors? Were they mostly active duty officers or civilians?

TC: I think it's still true today—typically one-third active duty military, one-third permanent military staff, and one-third permanent civilian professors. I thought that combination of faculty was really good. When I came back to teach at the Academy in 1972, I was the rotating military part of that three-part faculty. That faculty construct helps ensure that the cadets have currency and familiarity with real-world Coast Guards—that cadets had contact with those that had very recently been in the operational Coast Guard, as well as being an instructor. That is the structure that was created and I think it has served the institution well.

JD: What was the curriculum like at the Academy? Any favorite courses?

TC: While I was there, there was what was called a two-track curriculum. The first two years everyone took the same course with very few electives and a heavy emphasis on quantitative subjects. Two years of chemistry, two years of physics, two years of calculus, mechanical engineering, and so on. The last two years you opted for engineering or humanities. That divide happened at the end of the third-class year into your second-class year. Today, the Academy has around thirteen majors and it's much more diversified.

I struggled a bit during the first couple of years, academically. One reason was that I think it was just a lot of pressures on you and, by the end of the day, as a swab, you were a tired puppy—too tired to open a book and start to study, or study at length. I found the combination of all of those things conflicting at times. I was just interested in surviving. So, getting the studying done so that I could excel in academics sometimes took a back seat. The first two years, I didn't do well. As I recall, I had a cumulative average of 2.1, or something like that.

At the end of third-class year, I opted to go into engineering. After about a week's worth of engineering—differential equations and thermodynamics classes, I and my roommate, football quarterback Ron Sharp, came to the realization that maybe we were not cut out for the engineering track of study. We both appealed to the Dean, Captain Paul Foye, for a switch to the Humanities track. To our amazement and our great fortune, he allowed us to change. My point average subsequently went up to 3.7 the last two years.

I guess I had found the subject matter that was right for me. In fact, I even got an academic award at graduation when the Daughters of the American Revolution awarded me a sword for excelling in history. So, I blossomed academically in my second- and first-class year. It was due to the fact that I took more naturally to the course offerings within the humanities track. And also because I had a little more discretionary time to put into academics, realizing a better balance between academics and the military barracks life.

JD: During this time at the Academy, how did you keep in touch with your siblings and your parents?

TC: Mostly through letters and telephone calls, here and there. I would try to call them once a week. There was a parent's weekend once a year. They came down for that and visited me and, of course, you had an opportunity to visit during the last three summers at the Academy. After the long cruise, we had about 21-days' leave or something like that, and we went home for a much-waited-for break from the Academy. It was great to see them.

I can remember going home for the third-class summer and I said to my dad, "You really need to buy a new car." He said, what do you think I should look for? I said a Buick convertible, and we went to the dealer and to my amazement me he said, "Okay, let's get it." He bought it. He knew I was going to spend a weekend on Cape Cod with the girl that I had been dating from New London, who was vacationing there with her family. My dad said, "Why don't you go pick up the car from the dealer? You can take the car on your Cape Cod weekend." I couldn't believe it. I suspect he was proud of his cadet son and wanted to do something special. Well, he clearly made a special leave period for me that summer. I picked up the new Buick from the dealership and was off to the Cape. I thought I was hot stuff in this shiny, silvery blue, big Buick. I didn't tell my girlfriend—now, my wife—in advance, and showed up with new car, top down. It was a big hit.

JD: How did you keep in touch with your future wife at the Academy?

TC: When I did get liberty on weekends, I escaped to her family's home in New London. I didn't have overnights, but on the weekend, I'd go over to her house, was able to do laundry, and enjoy home cooking. You know, her parents were gracious and supportive. They made me feel part of the family. Nancy's father was Comptroller for the Naval Underwater Sound Lab in New London, so he was not a stranger to the military sea services. Nancy and I frequently had access to the family car to use on weekend activities. So, I had access to a car, good company, good food—and being with beautiful young girl. I said, this is…

JD: What a country!

TC: What a wonderful country this is.

So, it was a way of balancing things going on during the time at the Academy, you know. And maybe that's why—I mean, I wasn't high in the cadet regimental structure and I wasn't actively into all of the barracks administration things because I had this outlet. It was a way to create a diversion from the day-to-day at the Academy and a better balance in my life during that time. When I look back on it, I can't help but think it was a very positive thing. You know, mentally, emotionally, it was a very positive thing.

JD: I should have asked this sooner. How did you two meet? If it's not classified.

TC: I roomed with a fellow swab named Ray Dimmick. Ray was from Waterford, which is right outside New London. His father had a dairy farm and. when we could, we would go out to Ray's home and enjoy the environment of farm life—quite different from barrack life at the academy. Ray had a sister that was about two years younger than him. His sister and my soon-to-be girlfriend—now my wife—Nancy, were good friends. They both went to St. Bernard's High School in New London.

One day, early in the fall of my fourth-class year during our first liberty after swab summer, Ray and I went to pick up his sister at her place of employment, Michael's Dairy on Montauk Avenue—a very popular local ice cream joint. My wife also worked at the Dairy. When I first saw her, she had her arm and half her head down in the ice cream bin scooping—had chocolate all over her arms and so forth. That's where I met her and then I met her again out at Ray Demmick's farm.

I subsequently asked her to the first formal Academy dance in the fall, to which you had to attend. I figured she was a perfect invite. And she laughs to this day about my invite technique. I mean I called her up with great anxiety. At that point in my life, I was not very good regarding my sophistication with women. I didn't know what to say or how to act around females. As a young guy, I wasn't very suave. But I called her up and I said, "Oh, Nancy, we have a formal on such-and-such a day. Would you be willing to go with me?" And she said, "Sure." I was so relieved that she accepted, I replied "Okay. Thank you very much. I will call you later." She laughs to this day. Oh, how uncool I was with all that. But that's how we met and we dated through my time there in New London.

I graduated on the 4th of June of 1968 and I was married on June 7th at the Coast Guard Chapel, then went on to New Bedford for my first assignment, which was aboard the CGC *Vigilant*. So, you can see how much the Academy has figured in my life, you know, as a cadet, as a faculty member, and getting married there, living in New London—all of that. It's so very, very much a part of who I am.

JD: Can you go into detail about your first cruise onboard the CGC *Barque Eagle* [WIX-327]?

TC: Well, as I recall, the first cruise was to Bermuda. My memory is a little vague on that but what you did back then was, in your first year—as a fourth classman—you would deploy on a short cruise, supervised by selected second classmen, for about two weeks. Then you went the following third-class year on a long cruise, which was about eight to ten weeks. Then another short second-class year, and then a long cruise the last summer.

Typically, the long cruises took cadets to Europe. But at that time, there were budget problems so we didn't go to Europe, and we stayed domestic instead. We went to the Caribbean and ports within the US They were still great experiences. Looking back, I can compare domestic versus foreign ports because, when I was an Academy faculty member, I was deployed on a long cadet cruise to Europe in the mid-seventies to oversee cadet professional training. It was part of my collateral duties as an Academy professor.

My perspective is that the domestic ports of call were every bit as enjoyable as the foreign ones. The people in the US ports of call were even incredibly friendly and hospitable, and they poured out in welcome. They invited you into their homes. There usually was some kind of big dance or something that they sponsored. I can recall one that was held down at the Francis Drake Hotel in

San Francisco. I can remember, on their top floor, they had the big social thing for us and all the beautiful young ladies of San Francisco were there because they wanted to date cadets. It was terrific. For a young cadet, it was a very enjoyable experience.

Of course, the primary reason for the summer cruises was professional training—from seamanship, to navigation, to signaling, to ships-in-formation evolutions, and so forth. We got plenty of exposure to all the necessary maritime skillsets during the cruises, most of which were accomplished as a squadron—the *Eagle* and two other Coast Guard Cutters. Of course, as fourth classmen, we were charged with many of the basic seaman level duties—chipping paint, working in the scullery, etc.

JD: Was that your first time underway at sea?

TC: My grandparents had a place in Maine on the water. They had a little 15-foot boat with an outboard on it and my brother and I lived on that thing all summer long. So, I was in or around the water extensively as a youth, but the *Eagle* was my first time underway on a seagoing platform with assigned duties. It was an interesting experience.

The *Eagle* is a great national treasure. It is a wonderful training ground for young folks because it teaches them about the elements and forces of the sea. You've got to learn about the sea. and about currents, and wind, and all of those things. The operation of *Eagle*, as a large sailing vessel, is dependent on the sailors' understanding of those elements. And, the other incredible thing it teaches is teamwork because you do nothing by yourself on the *Eagle*. I mean, you can't grab a hold of a line and hope to do something with it all by yourself. It's about working together and teamwork. When you set sail, that's an all-hands evolution. When you go aloft, that's a whole gang of people laying out across the yardarm—over 150 feet above decks—which gets your attention the first time around. But it's a magnificent thing and—not only that—a great training platform.

It's also a wonderful public relations asset for the Coast Guard. I mean, what could be better? It epitomizes professional seafaring folk—with a big red stripe on it, pulling into port. Cities around the country compete to get the *Eagle* visit. So, today it's an old classic sailing vessel that keeps chugging—better than ever, with improved modernized propulsion, and other systems and enhance habitability.

Of course, the *Eagle* had a couple of sister ships. The Danmark was one. USCGC *Danmark* [WIX-283] spent time in the US during World War II because it escaped the Germans with its Danish crew. It served to train Coast Guard Academy cadets during World War II. And of course, the *Eagle* was a war reparation, so it has just an amazing history and, again, it's a national treasure.

JD: Do you remember your first time going up on top of the mast?

TC: Yes.

JD: What was that like?

TC: I think some of my fingerprints are still on the jackstay—a little metal bar that runs across the side of the yard. The main yardarm is over a foot in diameter, but as you get up to the gallant and the royal, the yardarms themselves get smaller and there is a jackstay across the top of the yard that you can hold on to. That's where you used to bring in the sail and tuck the sail in between two jackstays and you tie them off, so there's only one hand for you and one for the ship. You stood on a little foot rope. Your belly was on the yard and you inched your way out. The first time up, you are a bit apprehensive, but the view is so spectacular. The vantage point up there is so spectacular, that the apprehension quickly disappears. It was just so amazing to be up there, you know—especially underway, when the ship is working and in motion in a seaway. And you get the rolling and pitching of the ship accentuated aloft. The ship looks about a couple of inches long when you look down. It's quite a spectacular adventure for a young man.

JD: What was it like becoming a second-class cadet at the Academy?

TC: You know, you just get a little more latitude in your day-to-day life at the Academy. You experience less constraints, a little more flexibility, and increasingly think of yourself as a coastie. You are more seasoned as a cadet and in the ways of barracks life and the Academy—and you have made life-long friends in your classmates. You are always expected to take on additional leadership and training responsibilities, as you now have responsibility for oversight of the new fourth-class cadets.

JD: You were at the Coast Guard Academy during a turbulent time in the sixties. Do you recall hearing about that on the news, or were you pretty much just worrying about survival?

TC: I think, as cadets, we were pretty isolated from that. I mean, certainly, we saw the news and recognized the give and take on the national and international scene. It was a contentious time which continued into the early seventies, especially with Vietnam, and so forth. But, again, we were very much part of the military establishment by that time, so we thought in those terms. So much of your focus was on war-related issues and citizen reactions to them, rather than the social issues of the day. You tended to perceive things from a military perspective and you saw some citizenry behavior as anti-American and thought, "Why don't those folks pony up to their responsibilities in living in this great country?" There clearly were some dramatic differences of opinion at that time in our socio-political landscape—but divisive issues persist in our current political/economic world, don't they?

JD: Did you get to march in the 1965 Presidential Inauguration Parade in Washington, DC?

TC: I did.

JD: What was that like?

TC: It was darn cold. The whole regiment went down by train. We arrived at the Washington Railroad Yard and got off and stomped through mud. Trying to get your uniform squared away for the parade was a chore. It was very cold that day—I remember that. And when we passed, eyes right, by the President he did not appear to be watching us since he was preoccupied with other things, including his dog. It was a bit disappointing. Having said that, it was a once in a lifetime experience and quite an honor to be involved in it.

JD: Fast forward. Did you ever think you would be in the reviewing stand with a president, forty years later?

TC: No. Inaugurations are spectacular events. It never gets old. And, years later as Commandant, I was privileged to participate in another one, including standing on the reviewing stand alongside the President.

It was hard at the cadet part of my career to project that far ahead. I mentioned earlier some of the values that I was brought up with—that is, anything worth doing is worth doing your best. That was my philosophy and I worked hard at every job I had. I sought the most challenging, interesting job I could compete for, and it didn't necessarily have to fit into a certain stream. I just wanted a competitive and challenging job, to work hard at it, and—very importantly—have a good time at it. Good things happen when you follow that course. I never had a grand design or grand plot, you know. My focus was to try to excel, one job at a time. Do it as best as I can and let the chips fall where they may.

JD: You did pretty well.

TC: It worked out.

JD: Finishing up your first-class year and getting ready for graduation, when do you find out your first assignment after you are commissioned? What is that process like?

TC: I'm not quite sure how it is done today, but at that time you had assignment night. You all got together in the first-class lounge. Then it was done by combined academic and professional standing. You get graded on both. You had a combined precedence in your class and that's the order by which we chose our assignments. There may be slight variations for each class. Office of Personnel from Headquarters would send down all of their available billets, all sea-going. Everyone had to go to sea. I forget where I stood in the pack. I may have been about third of the way down in the priority list. A 210-foot Medium Endurance Cutter—the *Vigilant* [WMEC-617], out of New Bedford—became available when it was my turn. A classmate and good friend had already picked an engineering assignment on the vessel, so I opted for a deck watch officer assignment on that vessel as well.

JD: What was graduation day like? Do you remember your commencement speaker?

TC: Vice President Hubert H. Humphrey was our guest speaker at our graduation. In fact, I've got a picture of him giving me my degree and shaking my hand. Oh, there was a great feeling of excitement during graduation because everything seemed to be coming together after four long and demanding years. And an adventure lay ahead. It was a special feeling. My parents were there to share in the event and, in a couple of days, I was going to get married. And I was about to embark on a brand-new job at sea. You know, life was good. They paid me all of $5,400 a year to do all of that. That was an ensign's base pay at that time: $5,400.

JD: That was pretty good.

TC: Nancy and I got married several days after graduation. I went off to New Bedford with the need to find quarters that could fit within my ensign's pay. We found a rental in Mattapoisett, Massachusetts—which is a couple of towns out of New Bedford, to the east towards Cape Cod—on the second floor of a two-family home for a whopping $125 a month.

It was an exciting time. It was another one of those transition points in your life. And what, to me, was so attractive was that that there was a framework for what you were going to do—a generally defined career laying ahead of you. There was a structure about how you were going to live your life, where you are going to work, how you are going to work, and what it all stood for. A military career took a lot of uncertainty out of the job process, which was a nice thing for young folks trying to find out and nail down what they want to do when they grow up.

JD: Who from your family attended the graduation?

TC: My mother, father, brother, and sister all attended. It was terrific to have them in attendance. It was a big day with a great deal of good memories. My brother is a teacher. He graduated from Bridgewater State University in Massachusetts and, as soon as he did, he moved up to Vermont. And he's never left. He has been a justice of the peace, insurance salesman, a teacher in Chester, Vermont—and now he's a principal of a high school just across the border in New Hampshire, and has a great family. My sister has never left my hometown and has a wonderful family as well.

JD: Then, three days later you got married. How long after was it until you had to report for your first assignment?

TC: Yes, graduation was soon followed by another party—my wedding on June 7th—a great affair held at the Academy Chapel with classmates as ushers and my brother as best man. The reception was held at the sub base officer's club across the river. I had to report to the *Vigilant* by the end of the month, as I recall, so Nancy and I did have time for a honeymoon—a week's trip to Bermuda. It was a wedding gift from my in-laws. After a spectacular time as newlyweds in Bermuda, we made our way to Mattapoisett and moved into our second-floor apartment.

JD: What was it like becoming an ensign?

TC: Well, it was a little humbling because, you know, there was a greater cross-section of rank and seniority and everything else when you go aboard a ship. It's not a whole bunch of cadets in a relatively isolated Coast Guard Academy. There are different people from different backgrounds, different levels of society, different rank and structure, and so forth.

So, going aboard, I said to myself, "It's time to be humble." and, you know, "Don't walk aboard like you know everything because you don't." Go aboard to learn and contribute to the team. That's how I went aboard. One of the first things I did was try to reach out to the Chief's Mess as much as I could. I was First Lieutenant on the *Vigilant*. Chief Boatswain Mate Jerry O'Neill, from Massachusetts, was my number two. By the way, he had a good Irish tenor singing voice. I humbly reached out to the Chief and his fellow chiefs for their guidance and assistance. Soon I was invited to the Chief's Mess once or twice during patrol for dinner. I started a double-deck pinochle and cribbage competition between the Chief's Mess and the Officer's Mess. It was all about how to develop trust and respect.

I think my relationship with the Chief's Mess, while still respecting rank difference, served me well. I would always ask their opinion on things, and have them involved. If it was an operational deal or a particular event that we went through, we talked through the event with the whole team to seek their ideas. Let them feel that they are part of the deal.

JD: Just want to wrap up your time at the Academy. Is there anything else you want to mention about your time there as a cadet?

TC: No. I think we covered the general nature of it. Like I said, it's more than an academic institution. It's about a lifestyle. It's about integrity. It's about values. It's all of those things and

I have great respect for the Academy as an institution. I feel honored to have been selected to attend it. I feel honored, later in my career, to be a part of it as well.

You know, I went back as Commandant as frequently as I could. Every time I met cadets, I was so impressed with their maturation and everything else, and particularly the females at the Academy. They are awesome. I can remember talking to a number of them that had participated in an inter-service debate team that went to Europe and debated folks from a wide variety of top universities. They were the leading folks on the inter-service team. I was so impressed with their poise. The institution is doing a great deal of things right and it has gotten better and better over time. You go in as young swab and you come out as a better, more capable person.

The Coast Guard's Officer Candidate School, by the way, is a great institution as well and having them co-located up at the Academy makes a heck of a lot of sense.

JD: I agree.

JD: Did you have many interactions with any of the superintendents that were there during your time?

TC: The only interaction I had was with Captain Paul Foye, the Dean. The reason I did was because I had met him very briefly while on liberty at Nancy's parents' home. He was a good friend of her parents. They were sailors together—they sailed together at the Thames River Yacht Club. So, he knew who I was. I didn't relate at that time to any superintendent. They were too many levels above me.

JD: Can you talk a little bit about the class of 1968? What was it like to be a member?

TC: It was a very cool bunch of guys. They still are. You know, our fiftieth is not that far away and that's kind of a big deal. They are already planning that, so that will be a must do. But, there were folks from all parts of the country—different perspectives. But the one thing that I think is a constant is, you know, when you are all in the same boat in a demanding environment. you get ahead by working together and you help each other out. And, because of that, you develop really strong bonds and that remains for a lifetime.

JD: Before moving on to your first assignment, what advice would you give to someone who is considering applying to the Coast Guard Academy?

TC: I would say you, number one, you have to be academically, emotionally, and physically prepared to go. You need to know that the Academy—and the Coast Guard—is what you want to do. Don't say "I think I want to do it." You need to thoroughly research what it's all about and you need to talk to people that have already been there. The AIM Program, the Academy Introductory Mission Program is a great way to do that. I mean, you go there as a high-schooler during the summer and you dip your toe in the pond, so to speak.

And, if you really want to be there, then you've got to tend to your academics and you have to also be participating in extracurricular activities. It's a two-way thing. You can excel academically while being a wallflower and you won't get in. In the selection process, first there is an academic threshold that you have to meet, and then your whole record gets reviewed by not one officer, but three. You get three separate look-sees, and then you're graded, and then you're compared, and then you're interviewed. If you want to be competitive, you have to understand the selection process and understand the institution.

JD: Any advice for these same high school students that get an appointment to the Academy on how to survive swab summer?

TC: Yeah. Just have a thick skin—a very thick skin. Don't take things personally. There are going to be things said to you, and done to you, and put stress on the system. Just suck it up and keep the end-goal in mind.

JD: Now you've graduated and you are reporting to your first assignment to the cutter *Vigilant*. Can you tell us a little bit more about the *Vigilant*?

TC: Yes. The *Vigilant*, a Medium Endurance Cutter with helo flight deck; 210-feet long; had a crew at that time of about 55. It's up to about 70 now for those types of cutters. But, most of them, of course, are decommissioned and now have been replaced. Homeported in New Bedford, Massachusetts, its missions at that time were largely offshore search-and-rescue (SAR) and fisheries law enforcement with a mission of patrolling George's Banks, which is a famous fishing grounds off of New England. Its efforts were to ensure that foreigners were not fishing within our EEZ. The vessel had frequent offshore law enforcement patrols and also had SAR standby responsibility while moored to a harbor buoy at Provincetown. Most of our search-and-rescue calls were assistance to distressed fishermen in the George's Banks area.

JD: Any memorable SAR cases?

TC: One patrol was very memorable, during a storm that involved the distressed Bluenose II and other vessels.

There was a huge storm during the winter of 1968—a real nor'easter-type storm. A research vessel from Woods Hole went down and it was rescued by the tanker ESSO Christina—relatively empty at the time with really high freeboard, on its way to Europe. It picked up the distressed researchers, and we were diverted from our patrol on the banks to go about 150 miles and rendezvous with the Christina. The mission was to take these researchers off the Christina. It was cold. It was unbelievably rough. Despite the huge freeboard on the tanker, waves were breaking over its bridge, which was over 65 feet in height. The XO, Ensign Collins, said "Get the boat crew ready to launch. Get in wetsuits, launch, and go alongside the Christina for personnel transfer." This was a Maalox moment, since launching our small boat, coming alongside a tanker with a high freeboard, and breaking sea in winter conditions would be a great challenge and high risk. The Exec and I discussed the risks involved. I offered that the risk was too great, that the rescued researchers were safe where they were and that the best course was for them to continue the voyage with the Christina. Both my leading chief and first-class petty officer supported me. Fortunately, at the midnight moment, both the Christina's CO and the rescued personnel aboard the Christina elected not to be transferred under such adverse conditions.

Shortly thereafter, we were diverted to the Bluenose II—a sailing vessel of America's Cup fame. It was a famous Canadian America's Cup sailing vessel, owned by the Oland Brewery in Canada. In the winter storm, it had lost its rudder, broken its steering quadrant, and lost a couple of people and life rafts overboard. It had lost pumps and it was taking on water. We had to go another 250 miles in this weather, rendezvous with the Bluenose, get dewatering pumps aboard in very high seas, dewater it, and then escort it all the way to Bermuda. The only great thing about the trip was a big party—when we arrived in Bermuda, the owners of the brewery had a big party to thank us for saving that ship. So, it was an incredible, eventful patrol, all told, in some horrific weather. Just horrific weather. Plenty of adventure for a new ensign!

JD: Are there any lessons learned from that incident that stayed with you for the rest of your career?

TC: Yes. Manage risk. Our business—the Coast Guard business—is about managing risk. That's what it's about. Whether it's making a programmatic decision in Washington or operational risk, we had better have risk management awareness and processes be front and center. And, fortunately, over the years our organization has gotten very good risk management. We got so good at that.

JD: Going back to your fisheries patrol, what countries were the violators? And, what types of fish?

TC: The Russians, the Germans, and the Poles. That is my recollection. They had huge stern trawlers and big factory ships. They would dwarf our little fishing vessels out of New Bedford and Gloucester. They were fishing machines and they would come right up in pairs to the EEZ boundary, steam up there and be scooping up everything. It would be hake, and cod, and haddock, and all the lower ground fish and so forth—but they were after our fish. So, we were there to ensure the protection of our resources.

JD: Did they ever ram you?

TC: No. The only really contentious event—and it happened after I left for ship—was the Simas Kudirka incident where you had a Lithuanian sailor jumping to the *Vigilant*, off the Soviet merchant ship, Sovetskaya Litva, during a Russian/US meeting at sea, and then allowing them to come aboard the *Vigilant* to take him back. That incident spawned a lot of case studies that have been done on what not to do in those types of situations.

JD: Yes. What not to do.

TC: What not to do.

Most of the wardroom, including the CO Phil Griebel and the XO Paul Welling, had changed over by the time of the incident. But, I always thought to myself, the Kudirka incident would not have happened if those two people were still there. In the end, it was violation of US sovereignty as a US public vessel in US territory. In the end, it entailed poor communication up and down the chain of command, including government organizations outside the Coast Guard. There has been plenty written about the incident since it happened.

JD: Right. What was it like standing watch for the first time underway?

TC: I loved it. I qualified on the first patrol as Underway OD. Chief Boatswain was a great help in my training, as was our chief quartermaster—a guy named Benten. I think they were hurting for qualified ODs and they didn't want to be standing one in three.

I can remember coming in off my very first patrol—coming in at night, to New Bedford—going through a narrow passage in a structure known as the hurricane dike, and then proceeding onto our dock. I advised the XO of our position well before entering the harbor area. The XO came up to the bridge as we were approaching the hurricane dike opening. I had never docked a 210 and kept looking for the XO to relieve me. No relief. He said, "Ensign Collins, you can take this to the dock." This was at night, and a little windy with an offshore wind. Our dock space was wedged in between the 95-foot patrol boat, Cape George, and CGC Escanaba. Ultimately, I successfully moored the vessel.

I must say that whole experience made me feel really good. I was trusted to do it and I pulled it off without killing anybody or ramming the dock. I was elated.

JD: Did you feel that the Coast Guard gave you more responsibility as a Junior Officer than, let's say, if you had been in the Navy?

TC: You know, it's hard to say. I haven't experienced the Navy onboard experience—but, hey, I qualified very quickly for evolution. I mean the philosophy of Phil Griebel and Paul Welling was, if you're a qualified OD and there is something happening during your watch, you are going to do that evolution. You don't usually get relieved by someone more senior. If you can't do it, then we are not going to make you a qualified OD. That was their philosophy.

So clearly, on the *Vigilant*, there was a wide range of opportunities for everything—and we weren't relieved when we entered piloting waters. We weren't relieved when we entered the harbor. Then, here I am, a young ensign—and after ten months on the Medium Endurance Cutter, the *Vigilant*, they are giving me my own boat as Commanding Officer. Wow! "Hey, you're not even a JG yet, and here you are a CO. You are a Commanding Officer of a 95-foot patrol boat, the *Cape Morgan* in Charleston. You will be responsible for your crew and for the missions that the boat was supposed to perform."

Yes, I don't think you get that elsewhere. It applies to our enlisted force as well. You've got a young enlisted petty officer—eighteen, nineteen years old. And he's got a near million-dollar boat—a 47-foot motor lifeboat (MLB), for example—that he is responsible for, along a crew, the people you are rescuing, and all of the laws you are supposed to know. Where else would you get that kind of responsibility?

JD: Can you talk a little bit about the qualification process to be an Officer of the Deck and standing watches? What did it involve?

TC: There was a lot of preparation. You had a ship's qualification book that you had to go through. During the patrol, they always set aside time for training, for launching small boats, for running man overboard drills, for docking drills. You had to know all of your ship's systems—that's part of the checkoff—more, if you were a student engineer than a deck officer. But, still, as a deck officer as well. Overall, it was pretty rigorous and I think it's even getting better today on some of the procedures used to qualify.

JD: What was an average day like while on patrol?

TC: You were dominated by your watch schedule. You stood watches and you did things in between. I was the department head and I was first lieutenant, so I was responsible for operation of deck equipment and boats, managing and training the people associated with the equipment, and maintaining our equipment. So, you had plenty to do while off-watch. Between those two responsibilities, it's a pretty full day—especially if you were standing the mid-watch or four- to eight-watch, or if you had a particular evolution that you were involved in.

JD: How was the food onboard the *Vigilant*?

TC: It was pretty decent. One officer onboard would be mess treasurer as a collateral duty. That person was responsible for organizing overseeing the menu, supervising the mess attendants, and governing the mess. Of course, the XO was the head of the mess and the CO had his own dining up at his cabin, but there was a mess treasurer that did the day-to-day, nitty-gritty oversight of it. At that time, we had TNs. They were mostly Filipinos and were great cooks. They made some great stuff. Chicken adobo I can remember. The sauce was outstanding. So, it was not gourmet dining all the time, but it was fairly reasonable.

JD: Can you talk about the military capabilities the ship had?

TC: It was very rudimentary compared to today. You know, today's systems are much more sophisticated and that ship in particular was not equipped with high-end weaponry. We had the .50-caliber, an 81mm mortar, and a three-inch gun up. The new National Security cutters are much better equipped, given today's threat environment.

JD: Right.

JD: *Vigilant* was relatively new when you reported.

TC: I would have to back and look at that. It might have been approaching ten years old.

JD: Did you ever think it would still be around when you were the Commandant?

TC: No. Hey, the taxpayer, if they only knew what a deal the United States Coast Guard of America is. We run ships that are old enough to collect social security. They are so old. We decommissioned ships, fifty and sixty years old, and we run them hard. They are fully-employed ships. We spent a lot of time caring for them and maintaining them right. Those old platforms have served us well.

JD: You talked about this little bit before, but I want to go into greater detail for the purposes of this history, and for future general officers to learn. They say it's a wise ensign who learns from his petty officers. What did you learn?

TC: A lot of practical things. I always consulted with them and they had great ideas. They were part of the decision-making process. I wanted their input and their constructive criticism, but all the while, I had the final decisions. I've always practiced this approach and I think managing, building, and nurturing the team is one of the top things that a good leader should do. And, you want a diverse team, by the way. Not everyone thinks the same, which you can leverage. You want multiple inputs—you want a lot of lines of position. You get a very good fix, the more and different lines of position you have.

JD: How was the morale on the *Vigilant*?

TC: It was pretty good. There were always the one or two folks that didn't get with the program and there might be some disciplinary action taken. I remember one guy had a problem with alcohol. We don't know where he got it. He must have hidden it on the ship somewhere. But, all-in-all, for a crew that size, I thought that the problems were very, very minimal. If you set high standards and hold people accountable for things, and you build a team environment, that spawns higher morale. You avoid problems when you don't stick your head in the sand. A good leader doesn't.

JD: What do you recall of the comradery with your fellow junior officers in the wardroom?

TC: I think it was pretty good, especially with my classmate and long-time friend. It was very good. He was an engineer, a student engineer—and there were several OCS ensigns onboard and we got along very, very well, sharing both work and liberty experiences. We were underway well over 50% of the year, so we were together quite a bit and learned to respect and depend on each other.

JD: When you were out to sea, what did your wife do?

TC: She pined for me, Jim. She pined away.

She had a job at the New Bedford Chamber of Commerce. As I already noted, the ship was deployed well over 50% of the time during the eleven months I was assigned to it. As newlyweds, we missed each other but the reunions were terrific. It was an "absence makes the heart grow fonder" type of deal. She acclimated. She's done exceedingly well over my career with home responsibilities. I've moved her around seventeen times or so, and, in fact, of the two of us, she has probably handled it the best.

JD: I should have asked this sooner. Did you do a better job at asking her to marry you than going to the social?

TC: I did. I did.

Welling was a very good sailor with a solid experience at sea as well as ashore. He clearly, of the two—and this is no hit against Commander Griebel—he had the stronger personality.

I think by the time we were getting into the third year, it was almost like an unstated thing. We got along so well, that we both, without even saying it, thought that was what was ultimately going to happen.

JD: I apologize for the rabbit trail, but that was a question I meant to ask sooner. Back to the *Vigilant*. Anything else you want to mention about the captain's personality or the leadership style? You covered some of it.

TC: A little bit. Phil Griebel was a buoy tender sailor and a capable sailor. Paul played the XO role to the hilt. By that I mean, he was a very strong XO. And that was to the ship's benefit. But it was a little bit of an extension of the Coast Guard Academy, due to the fact that he was my tactics officer while I was at the Academy. Both officers gave their JOs a good deal of responsibility, gave high priority to JO training and development, and did not micro manage.

JD: Does that cause you to have any flashbacks?

TC: One patrol, I came on bridge watch wearing non-regulation shoes—a pair of these little high-top boondocker-type shoes. You know, the ones with the light-colored leather. While on watch when you are standing up on your feet for hours on hard decks, your feet take a beating so I resorted to more comfortable footwear. The XO didn't let that happen for very long. He had me report around to his stateroom telling me I was out of uniform and that it was totally inappropriate. I felt I was back at the Academy. Anyway, he was right, you know. But it was a bit of a flashback. I got in the right uniform shoe. He was a very professional, capable XO.

JD: What were the berthing spaces like?

TC: I had a great single-person stateroom with its own head. I thought it was one of the best. The first lieutenant was typically the one on that ship that was down below the main deck, down below the wardroom—right up the centerline, mid-ship. The 210 is not the greatest riding boat in a seaway. It had a lot of high freeboard with a lot of wind impact and a lot of rolling. So, to have that below decks, centerline, mid-ship stateroom was a gift.

JD: In a few months, the class of 2017 is going to graduate from the Academy. What advice would you have for them as they prepare for their first assignment?

TC: Wow. Be humble. But, at the same time, lean forward. Go for it and hit the decks running. Don't be afraid to take advantage of things that you learned at the Academy. At the same time, be humble when you are doing it and you can't—especially as a new ensign—you can't go aboard ordering people around. Take it in. Understand the immediate environment that you are in. Get to know and understand the people that work for you—that's probably one of the most important things. *Who are they? What makes them tick? How can I make them successful? How can I show them I care about who they are, what they are doing, and how to get ahead?* Focus on building the team. I think those things are the recipes for success.

JD: How did you find out about your next assignment as a Commanding Officer?

TC: Oh, I, you know, put my assignment request sheet in and waited for a chance to speak with my Headquarters assignment office. It was funny. The guy that was in the Office of Personnel at that time was a guy named LCDR Bill Wilkins. Bill was my summer ensign back during my Swab Summer. During Swab Summer, they keep a few newly graduated ensigns around through the summer before they go to their first ship assignment to help run the cadet summer program. Each one is assigned a company and Bill was my company officer at the Academy that first summer and he remembered me. I don't know why. Maybe I did something wrong. I don't know. But he remembered me and said, because I was in Zulu 1, that he had a good assignment for me. He had a 95-foot command for me. Of course, that is the unit type I had requested. At that time, you served on a patrol boat—either an 82-footer or a 95-footer—state-side for one year and, after a successful tour, you went over to Vietnam to run patrol boat operation off the coast of Vietnam. That was the sequence of events.

Well, Bill Wilkins had been my company officer, summer ensign. He also had been a prior CO of the *Cape Morgan*. He offered me the *Cape Morgan* because it was in great condition, had a good crew, and Charleston was a good place to be stationed. He noted that it's not the geographic area that I requested, but it was the best boat for me. I said, "Sign me up." And so, that's how I got my orders, and it was a great boat—great place to live. I lived in Charleston, about ten minutes from the boat in a garden apartment. And my first child was born there in Charleston. It couldn't have turned out better.

JD: I think we are at the two-hour mark. I think this is a great place to stop if that's okay with you.

TC: That's fine.

End audio file Collins1.2.Dolbow.USNI.1.11.16

Interviewer: Jim Dolbow (JD)

Interviewee: Admiral Thomas Collins, USCG Ret. (TC)

Begin audio file Collins2.1.Dolbow.USNI.2.4.16

JD: Good afternoon, Admiral. This is Jim Dolbow. I'm here with Admiral Tom Collins in Arlington, Virginia. It is February 4th, 2016 and we are about to begin our second interview session.

Admiral, we are ready to go on the next phase of your career, which was your first command tour as commanding officer of USCGC *Cape Morgan* [WPB-95313]. Can you tell us how it felt, as a junior officer, to be selected as a Commanding Officer of a Coast Guard cutter?

TC: Well, Jim, I was obviously thrilled. I was a young ensign and they were about to give me command of my own vessel, at such a young age, and at a place that seemed like a great place in terms of living conditions. So, I was very, very excited about it. I was fortunate to have a detailer at Coast Guard Headquarters that had been my summer ensign, when I was at the Coast Guard Academy as a young swab. He knew me. He called and filled me in extensively about what my options were. He said, "Look, my recommendation is for you to go to the *Cape Morgan*. It's not number one on your list, but I'm telling you, it's a great boat in great condition with a wonderful crew. You would love being there in Charleston, South Carolina and I think it should be really a good go for you." So, I signed up and didn't look back.

JD: Did they send you a telegram? Or how did you find out? What was the official notification?

TC: Ultimately you do get message traffic about your next assignment. Initially, he told me over the phone that this was the decision and then obviously, subsequently, you do get message traffic that details the terms of your transfer.

JD: Did you do anything to celebrate your new assignment?

TC: Well, I think my wife was excited about moving away from New Bedford. Not that she hated New Bedford, but it was not the garden spot of the world. At that time, one would probably describe it as an economically depressed city. I think she was eager to get to warmer climates and a different venue. And we were footloose and fancy-free. We didn't have any children at that time and so we both saw it as a great adventure that we were off on.

JD: How did you prepare to become a commanding officer of a US Coast Guard Cutter? Is there a textbook or a school for perspective commanding officers?

TC: At the time, there was no pipeline training as such. You didn't go to commanding officer's school. But, I drew on my experiences in my first assignment on a larger ship. You cut your teeth on that and then apply that experience to that command assignment. I was a department head for only 10 or 11 months on a Medium Endurance Cutter prior to assuming command of *Cape Morgan*. But, I did get exposure to a wide variety of challenging operations aboard that cutter that I could apply to my new assignment.

I also gained leadership and management experience as first lieutenant. There was a personnel management dimension of being a division officer onboard *Vigilant*, and there was a professional development part and sea-going part. All of those blended together to help you be prepared—as well as reading professional publications, such as the *Deck Watch Officer Guide,* and some specific Coast Guard publications, before I assumed command. For example, I knew that I was going to have to oversee a commissary and I was going to be the only officer on board. So, I read the controller's manual, and got up close and personal to some of the requirements. You can do a lot without having specific pipeline training by aggressively diving into a task and getting yourself prepared.

JD: How much time did you have in-between?

TC: Well, typically, you get notified in the spring and then you report in the June/July timeframe. I don't recall the specific date that I reported. It was probably in the July timeframe.

JD: What was the change of command ceremony like?

TC: Compared to subsequent changes in larger commands that I've had, it was a very low-key affair, as I was at the low-end of the totem pole. I don't even remember the exact location. It might have been on the fantail of the cutter. After all, it was my second assignment after having been on active duty for only ten months. Since I was a lowly ensign, the district commander was not going to come running to Charleston to attend my change of command ceremony. So, being realistic, that was fine with me. It was just good enough and it was formal. You read orders and did all of those kinds of things that are the mandatory parts of a change of command ceremony.

JD: Do you remember who you relieved as CO of USCGC *Cape Morgan*?

TC: I do. I relieved a LTJG named John Ebersole. He went to Vietnam upon being relieved of command, as that was a common sequence at that time. You cut your teeth on a stateside WPB, and then you were rotated after that to a WPB in Vietnam. I mean you don't want to send total rookies over there in that theater. Incidentally, he was the very last person to be rotated over to Vietnam because the WPB deployments tailed off after that.

JD: What was the transition like between you and Ebersole?

TC: It was about five days, and that's all we really needed.

There are mandatory and specified items that must be addressed in any change of command. You need to go through certain documents, and you need to go through classified material accounting. You need to go through the status of anything like the commissary that deals in money and accounting. You want to make sure all of those books are in order before you relieve so things don't come back to haunt you. You didn't want to take over a mess. If there was a mess, you want it documented so that there is, for example, accountability of property and all of those things. So, that's what we spent time on. And, then we went through operational drills, most of them underway. You wanted to get some sense of the operational readiness of the unit. So, it was a combination of going through those "got you" type accounts that you needed to be cognizant of and having your pulse on the operation of the units. Fortunately, as my detailer had foretold, the unit was in superb material condition—everything done well.

My great fortune was that my executive petty officer, John Hebert, a senior chief quartermaster, had been on the boat for seven or eight years before I got there. He knew the boat inside, outside, and around. Before he was a quartermaster, he was the boatswain's mate so he knew how to maintain boats. He knew the boatswain's mate rating. He knew the quartermaster rating, and he was attentive to details, and always wanted to do things the right way. He was a huge help to me. I drew on him a lot during that relief process. John was part of the noted Hebert family in Louisiana. His uncle was Congressman F. Edward Hebert, a longstanding congressman from Louisiana. But, John was just a talented Louisiana guy.

JD: Did his uncle ever come to visit?

TC: He did not. You know, which was fine with me as a young ensign. The distance between the congressman and me, in terms of official standing, was substantial.

JD: Can you tell us about the *Cape Morgan*?

TC: *Cape Morgan* was a 95-foot patrol boat or Cape-class of cutter. It wasn't the speediest thing on the planet. It topped off at 18 knots with a following sea, maybe. But, it was really a powerhouse—a towing machine. It had four Cummins VT-600 diesels. It also put out an incredible wake. You had to be careful going by yacht clubs and boat basins so you didn't create a damaging wake.

Cape Morgan was a great boat and I think the other part about it was, unlike the 82-footer which came subsequently, the 95-footers had a crew of 14, including yourself, thirteen enlisted, and one officer. The 82-footer had a crew of 8. So, you had much more depth and more professionalism onboard the *Cape Morgan*. For example, I had a chief engineman that ran the engineering division. I had a senior chief quartermaster as XPO. I had a first-class boatswain's mate, first-class electrician, first-class engineman, third-class gunner's mate, and the rest were seamen and firemen. That's a pretty good spectrum of talent on that small unit so it was a capable platform for coastal missions. Its primary missions were SAR, port safety and security, and law enforcement.

JD: How did you balance between being a relatively new officer—with ten months of experience—with some of your new crewmembers that had been in there for a while?

TC: It's interesting because it's a situation where you are the only officer on board, the thirteen others are enlisted, and you really have to depend upon and draw on them. I think it's all about respecting their talent and drawing upon that, and building a very successful team. You can't be too rigid in terms of rank. You've got to be friendly and respectful, but not "a friend," as such. As CO, you can't be a buddy. I tried to keep a very informal, respectful environment where they felt free to comment and discuss and add value. I wasn't going to go on liberty with them and I wasn't going to be their buddy. And I held them accountable to high standards of professionalism and personal behavior. That's the balance that you've got to strike. Some JOs have been good at that on WPBs, some haven't. Some of them have gotten into a little bit of trouble because they didn't know how to balance that out.

JD: Okay. Can you tell us about some of the lessons you learned from your crew?

TC: Well, for one thing, I learned how to maintain the hull of the boat—mostly from my XPO who used the trick of tinting white hull paint to make it pop. The technique is not in the Coast Guard paint and color manual, but you tint white hull paint with a little blue, just a little bit, and it really sparkles. It's just little things that you can draw on to make a difference. He was very good at paper management and requirements, and we acted as a team. It was a partnership and that's how I approached the XPO, and, to a lesser extent, all of the Petty Officers. I asked their opinions on things. It was group decision-making in many ways. Although, sometimes you can't have group decision-making. The buck stopped with you, and you make a final decision, but everyone had a voice, particularly in operations. When it became a difficult operation, it was: *Let's talk through this. Where do we want people positioned? What equipment do we want broken out? How do we approach this?* All of those things make up part of a team and, most importantly, that approach resulted in good risk management. It's essential for success. In a nutshell, I respected their views and drew on their experience.

JD: To what extent was the *Cape Morgan* armed?

TC: Oh, it was with little pea shooters. It had what they called a piggyback mount, up forward. It was an 81mm mortar and you could rig a .50-caliber machine gun with it in a piggyback type of arrangement. We also had .45-caliber pistols and 12 gauge shotguns. That was the extent of it, but that was enough for our purposes at that time.

JD: Can you talk about the mission of the *Cape Morgan*?

TC: Yes. In port, we did harbor patrols to support Sector Charleston's Captain of the Port's port safety and security mission. The Officer in Charge of Marine Inspection was a separate organization. We conducted harbor patrols three days a week. We would go all the way up to the Naval Weapons Station Charleston, up the Cooper River. We would record all of the vessels; we would look at load lines; we would look for potential pollution problems, etc., and we would compile it in a specified reporting format and provide it to Port Ops.

Of course, search-and-rescue standby was the main priority of our mission set. We were on standby readiness status—Bravo-0, Bravo-2—almost all of the time. Very rarely did we go to Bravo-6, Bravo-12. We were almost always on Bravo-2.

Responding to overdue recreational boaters was a frequent occurrence. The group would be doing communications checks and running overdues down, and when that effort did not produce results, *Cape Morgan* would get notified by the group to recall its crew and get underway to locate the overdue or missing boater. Typically, I would get a call at 22:30 or 23:00 to get underway. Most of the SAR was offshore. The Gulf Stream is a magic place for pleasure boaters. They want to do one thing: fish (marlin, etc.). So, there were numerous 25-35-foot pleasure boats that go out in the Gulf Stream. The edge of the Gulf Stream was about 40 miles off Charleston.

The other aspect of our operations was being deployed on scheduled patrol mostly down to the Florida Straits. These deployments lasted three to four weeks. Typically, we would sail to Miami get briefed in the district office on current ops in the Florida Straits, and then conduct the patrol in a patrol area that basically went from Key Largo to Dry Tortugas, which is 60 miles west of Key West. During the patrol, we were responsible for search-and-rescue, interdicting Cuban migrants, and logistics support of the lighthouse on Dry Tortugas. At that time, it was manned. It hadn't been automated yet and so we would take the relief crew and assorted supplies out to the light. So, logistics, search-and-rescue, and law enforcement/security were the mission there.

JD: Do you remember the first time you went underway as Commanding Officer and what was that like?

TC: You know, I don't. Of course, we got underway several times during the relief process to conduct drills including going offshore drills. So, that was really my first time to get underway with the vessel, and that was with the LTJG that I was about to relieve. My Senior Chief was my biggest aide in honing my skills at sea. I will tell you, he was a terrific guy. We would do things as a partnership. For example, whenever we came alongside another vessel at sea, or were preparing to take a distressed vessel in a tow, etc., either he or I would be on the bridge and the other on the bridge wing, and we would be talking to each other all of the time regarding the evolution at-hand. It was a great way to do it. It was a wonderful risk management thing because you had two sets of eyes on the issue. And I would have to give him a great deal of credit because, during the first several operational mission, he extended a great deal of faith in me even though he was not totally convinced, yet, that I knew my stuff operationally—that I was a capable sailor. He was apprehensive at first, but after I performed well during several challenging operations, his apprehension eased substantially. Performing operationally in a competent way in front of the crew was very important because it brought instant credibility and confidence. There's nothing like gaining respect by doing—and doing well.

JD: Can you go into greater detail about your night patrols and riding it out in heavy storms?

TC: Yes. A lot of our SAR work was done at night. A lot of our work in the Florida Straits was done at night, in bad weather, and, again, you just had to work through the events very very carefully.

There was one offshore nighttime case early in my tour where I learned a great deal. The mission was to remove an injured sailor from a fairly large tank vessel. The tank vessel's cargo had been offloaded at a previous port call and, accordingly, the vessel had a very high freeboard, making the crew member transfer more challenging since there was a pretty good drop from its main deck to the *Cape Morgan*. Because the vessel was so light, and the sea was pretty rough, there was a lot of rolling and pitching of the vessel. I had the conn and was at the helm. I learned a great deal from that evolution. Number one, I didn't realize the suction factor of coming along a vessel that size. It will suck you as you approach from astern and it was so light that some of its prop was out of the water. I got a bit too close in my stern approach and started to get sucked in, but I quickly backed off. So, I made a second, more cautious try, and it came off really well. Overall, it was a good learning experience regarding how our two respective vessels react at night, in challenging sea conditions, while coming alongside. Heavy weather offshore operations are always challenging for a patrol board the *Cape Morgan*'s size. In addition to more challenging maneuvers, there are safety and fatigue factors for the crew that come into play.

JD: Can you talk about Hurricane Camille?

TC: We were on one of our deployments during 1969 in the Florida Straits when Hurricane Camille came through. Hurricane Camille was one of those big, fierce hurricanes that our country has experienced—thank goodness, not too often. Hurricane Camille was the second of three CAT-5 hurricanes to come ashore in the United States in the twentieth century. Our patrol area was from Key Largo down to the Dry Tortugas area. We were just watching and watching Camille as it moved and we plotted every position report on the eye of that storm. One of our concerns was that the *Cape Morgan* had a jammed rudder. *Cape Morgan* was a twin-screw, twin-rudder vessel, and we had just come out of a yard period where the shipyard had installed a new rudder. But, after a short period of operations underway, it was apparent that they had not gotten the clearance right between the new rudder and the rudderpost. The bottom line was, I had reduced maneuverability with a CAT-5 hurricane approaching. Camille plotted along the southern coast of Cuba and then flipped up north around the western end of Cuba, destined to go fairly close to Key West, which was where the district insisted we go as the hurricane passed. I was nervous about getting into Key West, which was right along the projected track of that hurricane. And, because of its low topography, it did not offer much protection. So, I maneuvered within the patrol area, in keeping with patrol area ops orders, but proceeded toward the extreme eastern and northern edge of my patrol area, which was up closer to Miami. That's where I wanted to go—as far away from that storm as I possibly could—and that's what happened. We sailed up toward Miami and concurrently District 7 operations and naval engineering staffs finally decided the *Cape Morgan* needed to make port for rudder repairs. Since at that point, we were closer to Miami than Key West, we proceeded at best speed to a shipyard in Miami, a good distance from menacing Hurricane Camille. The entire crew breathed a sigh of relief. Camille was a beauty. Although we had to deal with heavy weather during that patrol we did not have to face Camille up-close and personal.

JD: Did you have to do anything in the aftermath of Camille?

TC: No. The decision was for the *Cape Morgan* to go back into a shipyard in Miami to get dry-docked and get the rudder fixed.

JD: How long were you at the shipyard? Do you recall?

TC: It was about a week by the time we got hauled out and put on blocks, and they squared away the rudder. And then we were back to Charleston.

JD: When you were out on deployment, were you and the crew able to keep in touch with family members?

TC: Not really. We didn't have all of the connectivity our cutters have now. So, only if there was an emergency or when we made a port call.

JD: How was the food onboard *Cape Morgan*?

TC: As a small cutter, *Cape Morgan* had the smallest mess classification, which meant that it had the highest funding allowance per crew member. Because we had a healthy mess budget, we could purchase quality rations, and most from the local super market, Piggy Wiggly. In port, for those on duty, crewmembers could go into the galley and pull out a TV dinner, or whatever. They made their own type of thing for breakfast, for those very few who lived aboard. But while in port, lunch was the only meal prepared by our assigned cook. Underway, of course, we had three meals per day. When we were in port, every Friday was a big seafood day because Chief

Hebert was from Louisiana, so we had to have all of the Louisiana fare. And he was always bragging that it was so much better than all of the stuff from New England, where I'm from. So, we had a little competition going—one Friday was Louisiana-type seafood (oysters, and shrimp, and such), the next Friday would be New England seafood for lunch—and then we would see what the crew liked best. And, as I'm from New England, we frequently had Maine lobster. So, we ate well and enjoyed the friendly competition at the same time. By the way, most of the time, the competition resulted in a draw between the two seafood types.

JD: Did the cook like to make you something special as the CO or anything like that?

TC: No. I wasn't too fussy. I approved the menu for the mess and I ate whatever was on the menu. I ate on the mess deck with everyone else. There was no ability to have CO's mess.

I can remember we had one cook that wasn't terribly good but the first-class boatswain's mate was a pretty good cook. So, I assigned him as a special detail to assist in the galley for a short period to teach the cook seven to ten basic, but good, meals. Because of the work of first-class BM, the cook finally knew how to make at least make ten good meals. The crew is a happy crew when they are well fed, especially on a small unit.

JD: Is there anything else you would like to add about the logistical support you received?

TC: It was pretty good. We did our own procurement. We did our own commissary purchases. We prepped for our yard periods. There were several shipyard haul outs that we had. One was up the Wando River in Charleston, another was in Miami—but we'd prepare for that. We did most of the upfront preparatory work ourselves. We worked closely with the engineering folks in the seventh district staff in Miami.

The Coast Guard did not have maintenance/logistics commands at that time, so the engineering functions and a lot of the support functions were embedded in the district staff. So, we dealt directly with them—copy to the group and that kind of thing. Fortunately, we had the onboard talent and technical skills needed to plan for and conduct the proper maintenance of the vessel. When we needed help ashore, the group had various engineering support functions ashore that were available. They were especially supportive when it came to maintenance and repair of electronic equipment. There an electronic shop ashore at the Base Charleston that was terrific.

JD: Speaking of the group, did you have a lot of latitude in your patrol area?

TC: Most of the Charleston area patrols were prescribed harbor patrols, in support of port operations at the group COTP. That was a patrol with prescribed procedures and reporting. The Florida straits patrols were governed by a lengthy 7th District operation order, which detailed communications protocols, area boundaries, patrol procedures, SAR procedures, and the like. A great deal of our time while in Charleston was involved with SAR standby and responding to SAR issues or other emergencies. Along with the group's small boats, we were the maritime fire department for the port and coastal area, and the type of emergencies can be quite varied.

One time, an emergency involved the USS *George Washington* [SSBN-598], a ballistic missile submarine. It ran aground while transiting the seaward entry to Charleston Harbor in fog, and got stuck in the mud and silt at the edge of the entrance channel and they couldn't get out. So, the COTP, for the safety of the sub and other ships, closed the port to shipping until tugs could extract the sub, and detailed the *Cape Morgan* to go out and enforce the closure and ensure the safety of any traffic. I remember that day, while transiting to the sub, that the navy base admiral became lost in his barge in the very heavy fog. I came to the assistance of the admiral's barge and got him safely to the *George Washington*. I know how to, you know, support an admiral. It took several large tractor tugs to pull the sub out of the mud. The navy didn't brag about that one too much but those kinds of things happen. It is a sample of the non-scheduled emergency events that Coast Guard units get. That's why they maintain a Bravo-2 or Bravo-0 readiness status to respond to those kinds of events.

JD: Let's say you were in port. How would they track you down in the middle of the night? Because it seems bad things never happen during the day.

TC: You always have your beeper on—there were no smart phones at that time. When beeped, you called into the group for details. It was usually someone or something in trouble. And it was frequently at an awkward time when you were at a movie, or you are taking your wife out to dinner, or it was in the middle of the night. That's when you would usually get called or beeped. You didn't get called or beeped, it seemed, at a convenient time. But that was part of the job that we signed up for and enjoyed.

JD: Were there certain days or times of the year you knew there was going to be a SAR case?

TC: If there was bad weather coming in, you knew you were liable to get a call. If there was a holiday weekend, you knew you were likely to get a call because that's when a lot of the pleasure boaters were out on their time off, and the first thing they wanted to do is jump in their boat and go out to the Gulf Stream. So, those were the very predictable times when you knew you were likely to get a call. When you didn't get a call, it was like, *Wow, good. We can enjoy the weekend.*

JD: We talked a little bit about the weather with Hurricane Camille, but can you talk about the weather forecasts that you would receive and the accuracy of the predictions?

TC: It was pretty good even then. While underway, we frequently got the forecasts by radio-telephone. There were weather broadcasts all the time and with 2182 kHz and Channel 16 VHF, the Coast Guard was always sending out weather broadcasts all the time on the distress-calling frequencies. So, most pleasure boaters monitored that stuff. And, we did too. If there was a special issue that we needed to know, the group would pulse into us and either our group, or another group, or another station would pulse into us and let us know. So, it was pretty good and that's why the electronic shop at the base was so important. I wanted to make sure that all of my electronics were always in good operations. I made friends with those folks or I had the crew, particularly my chiefs, cozy up to them because they were so important information.

JD: Can you talk about the radio traffic? How heavy of a message traffic did you receive?

TC: We received the standard message traffic. I would do situation reports during any SAR cases. You get some basic underway orders and then you get updated underway orders. The group would have certain communications protocols, and so if you were deployed on a SAR case, you had a certain regime under which you communicated—including how often you sent situation reports, what should be in them, and all of those kinds of things. Some were just standard format.

JD: Can you tell us a little bit about the *Cape Morgan*'s homeport of Charleston, South Carolina, and what was it like? And was this your first time to Charleston?

TC: It was my first time. I'm a northerner so I'm down south, well below the Mason-Dixon line in Charleston. It's a terrific city—great if you are a history buff. There's all kinds of history up, down, and sideways in Charleston. If you like fine dining, some of the best restaurants in the entire southeast are in Charleston, some of the best hotels, too. So, it's got a lot to offer. The people are incredibly friendly. *Gone with the Wind* was filmed there. If you want to see what a plantation looked like, you can go do that. So, it was a really wonderful city—a great place to work and live. We lived just ten minutes away across the Ashley River in a one-bedroom garden apartment, and that was great for us. My first child was born in Charleston.

JD: What was that like to become a new father?

TC: We didn't know enough to be dangerous. They don't issue any books on how to be parents. So, it was exciting and scary at the same time. My first daughter Christine was born in the Charleston Naval Hospital. The doctor that ran the OB-GYN maternity ward was a Marine and she ran the ward like a Marine. The baby had to be delivered to you, and first had to be wrapped a certain way, and you couldn't take the wrapping off. My wife's like, "I can't even look at the baby's little legs and stuff." It was funny. But it was good care. It was just a different experience. The second daughter's birth, a few years later, was a little different. But that made quite an experience. Becoming parents changed our lives there in Charleston. It was a very exciting time for Nancy and me.

JD: I guess you were present for the birth of both your daughters?

TC: Fortunately, I was.

JD: So, you weren't out to sea, getting a message or anything?

TC: No, no.

JD: Did you go out to sea later, just to get some rest?

TC: Well, while my wife was in the hospital, I recall that I had a search-and-rescue deployment but I got into port again before my wife came home with the baby. I did take a couple of days off to help her get settled with the new baby.

JD: Outstanding. That's good news.

Another question about Charleston. They had a big Navy base back then. Besides the incident involving USS *George Washington* [SSBN-598], can you talk about any interaction you had with the Navy?

TC: Not a heck of a lot. We went up the Cooper River by the Navy base on our harbor patrols, which were just another layer of security associated with the weapons depot where they loaded and off-loaded missiles from submarines. But, other than that, there wasn't a lot of day-to-day interaction with them from my mission set.

JD: Going back to the Coast Guard base in Charleston, what was the base itself like?

TC: It was in the historical part of town, on 196 Tradd St. and there was a set of piers there. There was also an old rice mill that had been transformed into support spaces. That's where the ET shop and a number of other things were. There was a three-story brick building housing administrative and operations spaces/ops center along with the COTP staff. There was also a small barracks on the base. We had a dedicated finger pier that the *Cape Morgan* tied to, which was perpendicular to the historic district's seawall, called the Battery. We were in a great part of town.

JD: On this period, while you were in command, the US was heavily involved in the Vietnam War. Were there any demonstrations in the Charleston area that you recall?

TC: I don't recall any protests at all in the Charleston area. You've got to remember Charleston had a huge military presence at that time and a lot of the congressional folks that had been in their roles for many years.

JD: Like Congressman L. Mendel Rivers?

TC: Absolutely. Mendel Rivers.

JD: Senator Strom Thurmond.

TC: Absolutely. And those folks had a huge presence in Charleston. So, you had the Air Force base in north Charleston which was huge, and you had the Navy base which is a significant presence. So, there was a large military population throughout that area. Maybe that had something to do with it. But, I don't recall any protest actions.

In terms of the personal impact of Vietnam, I was under the understanding that I was going to Vietnam to a patrol boat after a year aboard the *Cape Morgan*. As it turned out, that was not the case. As I noted before, John Ebersole—the LTJG I relieved—was the last officer to be rotated from a US patrol boat to one in Vietnam.

JD: How far into your command did you find out that you were not going to Vietnam next?

TC: It was toward the end of my first year on the *Cape Morgan* when they said Ebersole was the last one and "Oh, by the way, you've been selected for post-graduate school." I had put on my assignment wish sheet that I had wanted to go to post-grad school and Wesleyan was one of my choices. Officer Personnel indicated that I'd been selected for Wesleyan and, because of that, their plans were to keep me on *Cape Morgan* until I started school. I said to myself, *Hallelujah!* I got the post-grad school I wanted, and I got a two-year tour on a stateside WPB. *I just died and went to heaven!*

JD: And, in Charleston.

TC: And, in Charleston. So, I guess it's better to be lucky than good sometimes. This was being at the right place at the right time and all of those things fell into place and so it was a terrific sequence for me.

JD: I was doing some research on the Coast Guard historian's website and they mentioned on March 16, 1970—and you talked about this earlier—that the *Cape Morgan* medevaced a crewmember from M/V Mobilgas off of Charleston, and on October 2, 1970 you towed a disabled pleasure craft, *Miss Carriage*, to Charleston. Is there anything else that you would like to add about those incidents?

TC: I believe the Mobilgas incident was the one I talked about earlier where I came alongside in heavy seas and I had to make two approaches because the first approach didn't cut the mustard.

The *Miss Carriage* is vaguely familiar, but there were so many of those—you know, those small pleasure boat assists—that I just don't recall that one. Typically, in a year, we'd do anywhere between thirty to fifty direct assists that ended in a tow and that kind of thing. When we would tow them in, in fact, usually most of them were going to a boat basin that was just to the north of the base. We would tow them in, shorten tow coming into the harbor, and then standoff the boat basin in a 40-footer from the base would come out, relieve us of the tow, and bring them into the small boat basin.

But most of the pleasure boats, by the way, were really happy to see us because they would typically run out of gas, and they were getting bounced around, and they were hungry and looked like tired little puppies by the time we got to them. So, they were very thrilled to see us.

JD: So, I guess the Coast Guard had good relations with the people in the area?

TC: Yes. It was wonderful. It was a very friendly place. Had a good rapport with the local first responders as well.

JD: Did you ever have to coordinate with the Charleston police on anything?

TC: Usually it was a drunk boating type of incident. We would coordinate a sobriety test and so forth. If an arrest was called for, they would step up to the plate. We would coordinate boating safety efforts with them when there was a large sailing event in the bay or rivers.

JD: Is there any incident in your two years as CO that was either the most difficult or terrifying, or most memorable?

TC: Yes. There is one that stands out. I remember it like it was yesterday. We were group ops directed via telephone at about 23:00 to get underway and proceed offshore off of Edisto Beach. We were to arrive at first light and assist a shrimper that had gone aground. Edisto Beach was a little south of Charleston, half-way to Savannah. That particular area has a great deal of shifting shoals. So, the chart would say one thing—you know, so-many feet—and there would be a footnote indicating that the area is subject to shifting sand, and the exact depth can't be confirmed. When we arrived, we found the shrimper completely out of the water sitting high on the beach between two jetties about an eighth-mile apart. There was also a strong longshore current to the south, along with breaking surf. After evaluating the on-scene conditions, I reported back to the group. I noted that we were on-scene, that the shrimper was high and dry, and detailed wx and sea conditions. I recommended that this was a salvage operation and not a search-and-rescue operation, and that the vessel was safer sitting on the beach rather than trying to pull him off, and perhaps damaging him and taking on water in the process.

The message response from the group was to pull the shrimper off. The Senior Chief and I looked at each other in disbelief. Number one, we couldn't be sure of the depth of the water and we were going to have to get in real close to get a line on him. There was a good surf running onto the beach and the long shore current made positioning difficult. So, I messaged back recommending not preceding, that it was a high risk to our vessel, and that we will only proceed with a direct order from the Group Commander. We got a message back a little bit later: "Group Commander sends, take the shrimper off." I think it was, to this day, a very very bad call. No hits on the Group Commander—he was a capable professional—but he was an aviator and not a surface sailor. And, in this particular instance, I don't think he made a good call and/or his staff gave him bad advice.

Anyway, we had a direct order so I looked at the Senior Chief and said "Let's go for it." We talked at length about it at from a risk management perspective. We decided to proceed toward the beach through the surf bow first, so as to keep our props in the deepest water, and then use a line throwing gun to get a messenger line ashore which would be attached to a tow line. We ran the messenger-tow line from astern forward and outward of the lifelines. We had one our crew constantly sounding with a lead line. We fired the line-throwing gun as far forward on the bow as we could. Meanwhile we were rocking and rolling in the breaking surf and getting set down toward the southern jetty by the longshore current. Maintaining the vessel's position perpendicular to the beach in these conditions was difficult. We fired one projectile. It didn't get to the shrimper and its crew. We had to go in a little closer and use a heavier projectile on the line throwing gun. In the process of all this, the surf rode the *Cape Morgan* up and, when we came down on the backside of the surf, our bow struck bottom. When it did, the whole boat shook like someone shaking you in a shoe box.

I immediately directed Chief Smith, my chief engineman, to check out the spaces below decks—every space, the bilges and everything—to make sure there was no damage to the hull and or signs of water intrusion. We then quickly and successfully fired the heavier projectile and messenger line and backed astern full to gain deeper water. We finally got the towline ashore. The fisherman secured it to the shrimper. We moved to even deeper water and pulled the darn thing off the beach. We maintained constant communication with the shrimper to make sure that they remained intact as we were pulling it off. My worst fear was pulling it off and, in so doing, putting a hole in the bottom and seeing it sink. It turned out—apart from the *Cape Morgan* hitting the bottom and having a lot of anxious moments—that we got the boat off with no casualties.

But, overall it was a very high risk evolution. It was the wrong call. It was a classic case of the group ops folks not doing the right risk assessment, but it ended well.

JD: That's good. Would you say that was something that stayed with you throughout the rest of your career?

TC: Absolutely. You know, it's the kind of thing that leaves such vivid impressions in your mind and any one little thing could have happened that would have made that a total disaster.

JD: Speaking of leaving vivid impressions for the rest of your career, can you just talk about the Simas Kudirka case and its impact?

TC: Of course. The incident involved the CGC *Vigilant*, homeported in New Bedford. As we discussed earlier, I was only assigned to the *Vigilant* for about ten months, my first assignment after graduating from the Academy. I had transferred to the *Cape Morgan* well before the Kudirka incident, so I can't offer a firsthand account. Both the CO, Phil Griebel, and the XO, Paul Welling, had also transferred. So, it was a fairly significant change in the wardroom when the incident with the Russian vessel occurred. During the fall of 1970, the *Vigilant* was part of a fisheries discussion with the Soviets off Martha's Vineyard, nested with a Russian vessel offshore in US waters.

During the discussions, Simas Kudirka, a Soviet seaman of Lithuanian nationality, defected by jumping to the *Vigilant* and the *Vigilant* had him for a while. After much deliberations, going back and forth, the Russians indicated that they wanted him back, accusing him of stealing money from their vessel. They were allowed to come onboard a US flag vessel—to use their Russian authorities—to forcefully get him. The incident has been used as a case study of what to do and what not to do; what sovereignty means; what authorities you have and how you deal with them; and how to deal with defections.

There were communications issues at the heart of the matter—between the vessel back to the district, and to other governmental entities. There was clearly confusion over US policy on defections, associated asylum issues, and untimely and incomplete guidance back to the vessel from higher-ups. The 1st District commander, Rear Admiral Ellis, directed Commander Eustis, CO of *Vigilant*, to permit a KGB detachment to board *Vigilant*, and return Kudirka to the Soviet ship. As a result of the incident, the district commander and his Chief of Staff were given administrative punishment under Art 15 of the UCMJ, and the *Vigilant* CO was given a letter of reprimand and reassigned ashore. From my view, one of the lessons is: when in doubt, when you don't have a clear mandate for action, wait until you do. So, bottom line, the Soviets should have never been allowed to come aboard and use force. The Soviets had to beat Kudirka up to bring him back and did it all on a US vessel, which not was consistent with the *Vigilant*'s status and authorities as US territory.

Since this case, more detailed and robust intra-governmental protocols have been put in place, which deal with international incidents. I read about this incident with great interest from the *Cape Morgan*. It's a great case study and has subsequently been used in the professional studies department at the Academy and other places to study decision-making in a high-impact crisis environment. An award-winning book about the incident, *Day of Shame*, was published in 1973 and a television movie about the incident starring Alan Arkin was made in late-1970s.

JD: Can you talk a little bit about the administrative duties of a Commanding Officer?

TC: Well, on a smaller vessel like the *Cape Morgan*, the CO has more administrative tasks than on a larger cutter given the lack of a wardroom. But the CO does share a lot of that with the XPO, and you look to the XPO to deal with many of the administrative details. One area I wanted direct oversight of was those administrative tasks involving anything that had to do with classified material. I didn't have an officer-type ops officer, or a communications officer that you might have on a larger ship. You have to get the administration of classified material right. The other thing that you don't want to mess up is property control and accountability. So, I considered classified material, property control, and also commissary, priority administrative matters for a patrol boat CO. With larger, current-day patrol boats with a larger, more senior crew, the CO is able to delegate administrative tasks to a greater degree.

JD: Right. Just a few more questions about your CO tour. Is there any such thing as a typical day as a Commanding Officer? If so, can you describe your day?

TC: Other than the administrative things, I would come in and get briefed by the outgoing OD of any issues overnight. *What is the status of the plant, etc.?* Some standard things. You're the chief readiness officer, you're the chief safety officer. I mean, those are the kinds of things you are always focused on. If there was a harbor patrol, we had a certain routine for harbor patrol day. I would arrive at the vessel at a certain time, the propulsion plant would be lit up at a certain time, etc. So, we tried to standardize a lot of those events.

If you were down in the Florida Keys, there was a certain routine we had, all keeping with the patrol orders that we were operating under. On our Florida deployments, we were underway most of the time during the day. During nighttime and/or sloppy weather or sea conditions, we would occasionally seek a sheltered position. For example, we might anchor for the night in the vicinity of an inner channel that ran south of the Keys—all allowed by our operations order. We would drop the hook and let the crew have a good night's sleep and be ready for business the next day.

At times, we would even show movies on the fantail for the crew. We weren't supposed to have access to movies because of our vessel size. At the time, it was all film that you got from the Navy, a motion picture exchange at the Navy base in Charleston. The reason we were able to gain access was because my first-class electrician, Tom Hessler, lived next door to the warrant officer that ran the Navy motion picture exchange, so they were a bit flexible. And, when we deployed to the Keys, we were able to add to our crew's morale with movies. So, little things could really add to the morale, spirit, and productivity of the unit.

JD: Do you recall any of the movie titles?

TC: I tried to get adventure stuff that the crew would like. We worked them hard and held them accountable to the hull maintenance, operations, and making the boat look spit-shined. The boat looked brand new all of the time. We worked the crew hard and we did good ops. But, at the same time, we found ways to make it as enjoyable as we could for them. So, among other things, we had the movies while deployed on a lengthy patrol.

JD: What would you say would be the satisfaction of command at sea?

TC: Well, there was high satisfaction and, to some degree, a bit of independence as a CO. Here, I was an ensign and they trusted me with this 95-foot Coast Guard cutter, a 105-ton vessel. So clearly, there was a lot of gratification and satisfaction that went well beyond the pay. The pay wasn't terribly great, by the way. I mean, as I recall, base pay for an ensign back then was like $5,400 per year. So, the biggest payoff was a great feeling of accomplishment and satisfaction in the missions that you did. That was the great allure for me. That's the great attraction about service with the Coast Guard. The missions are incredibly self-gratifying.

And the other thing that I enjoyed was seeing the progress—the professional development—of the young kids under my command. To see them get ahead. I was always urging them to take the courses necessary to get advanced. Showing that kind of interest in them pays dividends, as well. So, to see them get ahead was a great and satisfying thing.

JD: What advice would you give to a Junior Officer that is about to become a perspective Commanding Officer of a Coast Guard cutter?

TC: Prepare yourself as much as you can. Understand the job. Try to attract and develop quality. Talk to detailers about the needs of your unit. Help develop your people. Develop the team. Have everyone contribute to the team. You want your crew to feel that they are part of contributing to something important. Once you crack that nut and once people understand that they are valued and respected—even the most junior, the FA, the SA—I think that's the magic. So, preparation, build a team, nurture the team, and focus on risk management. Think through those things and, when in the relief process, make sure you check and double check, and that you are comfortable with the condition of both the material condition and the operational readiness of the unit—two very, very important things. Every unit is not going to be perfect. But, make sure you know where the holes are, and where the priorities are regarding the first, second, third things that you should tackle. And hit the decks running!

JD: What was it like giving up command of the *Cape Morgan*?

TC: I was not anxious to leave Charleston—to leave that boat and its great crew. I think we had established a solid relationship built on respect in that crew. I think we executed all of our operations incredibly well and the material condition of the boat made it one of the standout WPBs in the district.

When we worked with the district staff to prepare for a yard period, I remember the engineering staffer that we dealt with up there, Lieutenant Ed Harless. He was a warrant-to-lieutenant type. He handled and supervised all of the WPBs for their yard periods. He was very flexible regarding optional yard work items for us, and I think it was because he recognized that, since we kept the boat in such a great condition, extra work items included in the yard work list for us were justified.

The bottom line here is that I thoroughly enjoyed my assignment. I did meaningful things and had fun doing it.

JD: Did you ever come across the *Cape Morgan* the rest of your career at all?

TC: Not really. I don't recall exactly how it got disposed of as excess. It was a fairly old boat when I got it. But then again, it was one of the ones that was in really great shape. But, they were wonderful boats for the times—for the missions required of them. The Coast Guard got its money's worth out of them.

But, you look at the Coast Guard's new patrol boats now, Jim, and you look then—two different boats. The new patrol boats are much larger platforms, have bigger crew size, better sea-keeping and habitability features, better boat launching capabilities, great communication equipment and sensors, more capabilities in a higher sea, etc. It's just a whole different generation, as it should be. But, for their time, it was a great platform. And in terms of a platform to develop on and mature in the organization, it was a great platform for me.

JD: Is there anything else you would like to add about the *Cape Morgan* before we move on to your next assignment?

TC: No. Just that my hat is off to the crew that supported me there—from the Senior Chief, all the way down to the seamen/firemen. Again, I feel very fortunate that my detailer directed me to the right vessel in which to continue to develop professionally. It worked out very well and it was a very satisfying tour.

JD: Okay. Now you are going to graduate school and you mentioned how that came about. Were there other Coast Guard officers with you at Wesleyan University?

TC: There were. It was one of the reasons I put in for that particular school. It was a prelude to coming back to the Academy to be an instructor in the Humanities Department. The faculty at the Coast Guard Academy was a three-pronged, three-structured faculty. One-third permanent military staff, one-third rotating military, and one-third civilian. So, after Wesleyan, I was going to be part of the rotating faculty for four years, and then back to the operational Coast Guard. The Coast Guard Academy did that so that the officer corps would have some tie and connection back to the operational Coast Guard. I think it was a great arrangement.

Anyway, that was my sequence. That particular year up at Wesleyan there were four Coast Guard officers—all slated to become instructors at the Coast Guard Academy following graduate school. I was a history and government student; another officer was an English lit student; the third was a math student; and the fourth studied physics and chemistry. The three other students were classmates of mine at the Coast Guard Academy: Rich Asaro, George Perreault, and Dan McKinley. We had a built-in fraternity at Wesleyan, if you will, based on those four years at the Academy. And, we were really older than the rest of the students on campus.

I took maybe 60% undergraduate courses, and then the rest post-graduate courses. I was glad to be selected and to be extended on the WPB a year. I wanted to go back to the Academy. My wife was a lovely local from New London; her parents still lived there. They now had a grandchild and it was nice for them to have us be close for a few years. It was a great fit family wise and it's something that I wanted to do. While at Wesleyan, we lived on the second floor of a two-story university-owned home fairly close to the university campus. So, that's how it all kind of fit together.

JD: Can you talk about your courses you had to teach at the Coast Guard Academy, as well as the courses you had to take as a student at Wesleyan?

TC: I approached Captain Ron Wells, head of the Humanities Department at the Coast Guard Academy, on the matter of my course selection at Wesleyan. Ron was an English literature professor who had his doctorate from Columbia or NYU, as I recall. He recommended that I take courses where he had holes and/or needs regarding the composition of his existing faculty members: basic US history and government; political science; East Asian history. But he also suggested that I make some room for courses that I didn't have available to me at the Academy when I was a cadet—ones that I would enjoy intellectually. He was wonderful to be that flexible.

I ended up taking a great deal of political science, history, along with Japanese and Chinese history courses—mostly modern history, from the Opium Wars forward. I even took a course on the history of music in western civilization—from the Gregorian chant onward. It was a two-semester course. Frankly, it was the best course I'd ever taken because it was co-taught by the chairs of the music department. One was a noted playwright and one was an accomplished classical pianist, and they were awesome. It was a fantastic course to take, and I thank Ron Wells for giving me license to do that. It was a great experience. So, that's a quick snap shot of my course load.

One thing I should note is that the faculty at Wesleyan University was excellent. They were almost exclusively PhDs. Even the basic courses were frequently taught by the chairmen of the departments. So, you had the best, even for the core courses. It was an outstanding institution. I thoroughly enjoyed my time there. I was in Wesleyan's Master of Arts in Liberal Studies program, which was designed for Connecticut schoolteachers who were enrolled there part-time during the summer, to meet job advancement requirements. The initial summer involved classes with teachers from all over the state; the following fall and spring classes included mostly graduate and undergraduate students that were enrolled full-time at Wesleyan. This summer/fall/spring sequence was a special arrangement with the university configured for Coast Guard graduate students ultimately destined for the Academy. And, when I became an instructor at the Academy, I worked for Ron Wells and taught US history, political science/government, and modern East Asian history courses.

JD: Did your courses in East Asian history come in handy when you were the Pacific Area Commander, and later on as Commandant?

TC: I think it gave me better context for a lot of things. People like to try and put China in one box. It's impossible to view China from one dimension. It's a complex country, with a complex history, and a complex culture in a society vastly different from our own. And to understand that is hugely helpful when you are developing policy and relations, or conducting operations with China's maritime services. We achieved huge advances with them in selected mission areas and I was personally involved in that. I think there is a connection. I think that helped me have a different—more informed—perspective on it than I would have had otherwise.

JD: Did you have to write a thesis there? If you did, what was your topic?

TC: I did. I wrote it under Professor Jim Millinger. He was an ex-navy lieutenant who had served in China and was an instructor for one of my courses. The thesis focused on how China dealt with modernization, especially as related to maritime development, in comparison to Japan. How one modernized more successfully than the other, and what factors were involved in that success.

Luckily for me, Jim spoke and read Chinese, and a lot of the material that I had to use in my thesis was written in Chinese. He translated selected parts of that material for me. The thesis was entitled *Maritime Development in the People's Republic of China,* covering the period from the time Mao came to power in 1949 to the present. It was about what the development was and what it wasn't, really—why it wasn't as far along as it could or should have been. It examined the historical, economic, cultural, and political factors that influenced maritime development. It also included a biographical sketch of their Navy maritime leadership, and how their experiences shaped the direction of modernization. That's where I especially needed Jim's help in translating the research material.

JD: Did you do anything for fun while you were in school? I mean, you just came from two years as CO and you were a new father.

TC: Studying took a great deal of my time. I never did so much reading and writing in all my life. For example, one course I took was entitled Urban History. It was a history of the evolution of the modern city in western society. I had twenty-six books in that course. I never before had that kind of reading, along with a lot of writing. I was fully engaged as a student.

Needless to say, during the first eight months or so, I didn't have extended periods of free time. But the workload eased up a bit as I entered the last semester. I had just about met my core requirements for the degree and I could create some holes in my schedule. I purposely loaded up my schedule in one part of the week so I would have the last part of the week open. That schedule was helpful in preparing to relocate to New London.

I bought a fixer-upper house in New London at the beginning of my last semester. It was in a great neighborhood, but it definitely needed work. With the last semester schedule I had, I had an opportunity to get down there and do some work on the house, and have visitation time with my wife and daughter, and their parents and grandparents.

JD: How did they prepare you to be a Coast Guard Academy professor? You took all of the classes. Did they teach you teaching methods?

TC: No. That's one thing that wasn't readily available after the initial summer period. I would have benefited from that kind of preparation because it was a baptism under fire. It went pretty well after I got rolling and gained some momentum. But the first semester of the first year was like staying one step ahead of the cadets all the time, and trying to shape the courses that I wanted to teach, and how I wanted to teach them. I think it eventually came out right, but a teaching methods-type course would have helped.

JD: Is there anything else you would like to add about your time at Wesleyan?

TC: No. It was, it was a great experience. I learned a lot. Like I said, great faculty and I think it was good preparatory work for the Academy.

JD: Did your experience at Wesleyan inspire you to encourage others to seek post-graduate education?

TC: Yes. I was always high on post-graduate school. When I was Commandant, we had an ability to expand that availability and we did. It means more money, right? Overall, the Coast Guard—even back then—was very out in front on post-graduate education. We send people to some of the best places all over the country, like Purdue, Harvard, Sloan School at MIT, Michigan, and California.

For a relatively small agency, I think the Coast Guard was out in front in offering post-graduate education, and I think that's a positive reflection on service leadership—that the development of our personnel is a priority. Accordingly, our personnel become much better prepared to handle future jobs. They know how to analyze, write, and comprehend. All of these general educational benefits make them more worldly, in a way. They understand things in a larger context. So, post-graduate education is high on the Coast Guard agenda, and should continue to be.

JD: Now, have you been back to Wesleyan at all?

TC: I have attended several social events held for alumni but most of the time my job requirements and travels have taken me far away from Connecticut.

JD: You are finished with your studies at Wesleyan and now you are back at the Coast Guard Academy, as a professor. What was it like going back to the Academy, especially being on the other side?

TC: It was very different from being a cadet, obviously. And it was a great opportunity for me to get back there and see it from another angle. The cadets were refreshing. You know, some are not so, some are, but the really good cadet is just so great to deal with. And, as an instructor, I was in a super department. I had good people to work with. I was in a bullpen office. There were four or five of us in there—all lieutenants or lieutenant commanders. The atmosphere was enjoyable. We solved all of the world's problem in the bullpen.

I also had a great department head in Ron Wells—and a long leash. The department had a very competent faculty. Several of the long standing civilian staff were particularly sharp—like the history professor Irv King, who was originally from Maine. For years, he taught Russian and US history at the Academy and his courses were always very popular with the cadets. I learned a lot from him. The other thing the Academy allows you to do is get involved in the Academy in a multifaceted way. Not only are you an instructor, but you are involved in other aspects of cadet development and life, like helping with athletics, professional development, the summer training program, and cruises, etc. In many ways, the entire faculty is an extension of the professional studies department especially during the summer program.

JD: What subjects did you teach?

TC: I taught a few semesters of US History, but most of the courses involved the study of US government. It was basically Government 101. It was a required course. The class was usually comprised of twenty to twenty-five students. A lot of them were engineers who made up the majority of students at the Academy. I also taught electives involving modern East Asian history and political science courses—Political Parties and Interest Groups, for example. There was a two-track curriculum when I attended the Academy as a cadet—humanities and engineering. Then, when I went back as an instructor, the academic program included about seven to nine different tracks. There are even more offerings today.

But, everyone is required to take a government course. For me, the electives were most rewarding and enjoyable. For those electives, the students really wanted to be there and put in increased effort for the class. And for the first time, I introduced females into one of my electives—Political Parties and Interest Groups. I taught the first coed class at the United States Coast Guard Academy. I solicited students from Connecticut College up the street, on Mohegan Avenue, which was an all-girls school at the time. Now, it's coed. But it was a girls' school at the time, and they were very good students. The attraction to the course was to have former Congressman Bob Steele [CT-02] co-teach the course. That was the hook, so to speak, for the ladies to join the course. It was a great experiment. First, the Conn College females were very capable students. Second, the cadets were overwhelmed, as it was a great challenge for them academically. But the environment pressured them to up their efforts, academically.

Then, the other elective I taught was an East Asian elective. We studied East Asian history from the Opium Wars forward, with a heavy focus on how both Japan and China had reacted to the West's increasing presence and intrusion—why they reacted the way they did; where one was relatively successful and where the other wasn't; why there were problems and crisis in one and where there wasn't in the other; and how that all unfolded. It was about only nine to ten cadets in the course, max. I had a cut-off at ten because I wanted a lot of interaction.

JD: How did you get engineers interested in Government 101?

TC: One, they didn't have a choice. But, to get them interested, I tried to make it as real world as I could. I just didn't stand up there and lecture, lecture, lecture. I tried to have a dialogue on issues. I tried to bring in current events. One textbook that I used was *Government by the People* by Professor James McGregor Burns. He was the Woodrow Wilson Professor Emeritus at Williams College. It was the classic textbook of government courses. That's what I used.

But, that's not all. I required cadets to read the newspaper so they will know current events. I tried to use real world things happening as they were taking the course, and would fold them into our discussions about various elements of how government works and how it doesn't work; why it doesn't work just smooth and hunky dory; why it isn't just this well-greased machine. Well, it was a shock for some to learn that the Founding Fathers meant for it to be cumbersome. They meant it to be complex. They meant for it to have checks and balances because they were afraid of power.

The other thing that I required was an analytical paper. I stressed to them that there are many shades of gray on many public policy and government issues. I wanted them to take a public policy issue, tear it apart, and take a certain position. They had a tough time getting their arms around that because they thought, *Well, there's only one position on things*. So, I think it was incredibly good for them to do that, because many of the engineering courses did not lend themselves to that approach. My counsel to them was that it didn't make any difference if you are a mathematician, or a physicist, or a mechanical engineer—in any job going forward, you are going to have to express yourself by arguing a position in an analytical format of some type. You are going to have to convince management of a specific issue. I felt strongly that the government course offered an opportunity for that type of thinking, and that it would serve them well. I think I got through to most of them. Some of them, I might never have gotten through to, but I think I got through to most of them.

JD: How did you prepare for a class?

TC: Long and hard, particularly the first iteration of the course. *How did I want to approach it? What did it constitute? What are the readings in addition to the text?* There was a lot of prep work. Initially, I would be one step ahead of the cadets. Three or four hours preparing each night was typical, and then I kept refining the courses. I tried to continue to improve them for the next semester, and the next semester.

For my elective on East Asian history, I had varied readings. I had a couple of texts from Dr. John King Fairbank who was noted for establishing a center for East Asian research at Harvard. To mix things up, I even included the famous novel *The Good Earth,* by Pulitzer Prize-winning author Pearl Buck. It is a pretty good book to try to understand the Chinese culture and what the peasant was going through in 1920s China. The novel had also spawned a movie, *The Good Earth* with Paul Muni, and I required my students to read the book. I also invited the class over to my house to watch this old black and white movie. We had pizza and soda, and then showed the movie. Then, we talked about it.

I tried to mix different things into the course to make it a little different—to make it real.

JD: Did you ever have like flashback of your Government 101 class later on in your career? Like when you had to deal with the Executive Branch and the US Congress?

TC: Well, yes. There's the text version, then there's the real-world version. You can read about it in the newspaper, but until you are immersed in the process, I don't think you have a true appreciation for it. You understand the machinery of the whole thing. There is a lot of personalities mixed in that you have to take into account, which drive a lot of things in Washington. In my subsequent jobs, I had many dealings with the OMB [Office of Management and Budget], the White House, and the congressional committees. That was eye-opening. Sometimes it was like going to the dentist, but it was eye-opening and, obviously, my earlier academic pursuits helped in understanding it all.

JD: You mentioned your department head, Ron Wells. Is there anything else you would like to add—just for the historical record—about him? It sounded like he was a great individual.

TC: He was a really good boss and colleague. He gave me a very long leash. In other words, he gave me latitude and flexibility. He was a very intelligent guy. His doctoral thesis focused on epistemology—the study of words, origins, and all of that matter. It sounds arcane or stuffy, but really, in studying origins, etc., you have to understand humankind, societies, culture, and history. He knew all of that. He was a gentleman, an upfront guy. It was a pleasure working with him.

JD: What advice would you have for Coast Guard officers being assigned to the faculty of the Coast Guard Academy today?

TC: I think, treat the cadets with as much respect as you want to be treated. Don't come across as the heavy-handed authoritarian. It's a learning experience for them, so be a role model. Be a good officer and be open. Encourage a give-and-take atmosphere. Challenge them intellectually. Spend time pondering how to create a good learning experience.

By the way, from my perspective, cadets have become more and more talented academically over the years. I made several visits later, as Commandant, and came away terribly impressed with their capabilities and poise. I would hate to compete with them myself now.

JD: Did you have any memorable cadets in your classes?

TC: There are so many of them. I can remember faces but names are a blur. One cadet that I had in my class, Gary Blore, was in one of the HQ Chief of Staff divisions—the Programs Division—with me later in my career. We'd had this staff meeting every morning that we called "round room." We'd report to the boss on what issues we were working on and that kind of thing, and have an open discussion on them to get everyone's input. Well, Gary noted at one of the meetings that he had a complaint. In a tongue-and-cheek way, he said he had been working through some of his files and he came across one of his essays he wrote for an exam, and that I was the instructor who graded the essay, and that he was not given an honors or "H" mark, but should have been. He actually produced the essay document. Jokingly, he added he wanted his grade corrected because it was such outstanding work. So, I offered to have copies made of the essay, distribute it to everyone in the staff, and have them grade the paper; and, depending on what they came up with, we would correct the record accordingly. With that offer, he quickly withdrew his objection to the mark he had received. We all had a good laugh about it. Gary was one of many very talented cadets that it was my pleasure to assist, in a small way, in their academic and professional development.

JD: Your second daughter was born at the Academy while you were a professor and you were doing an MBA from the University of New Haven. How did you manage everything?

TC: I attended the University of New Haven MBA program at night. The facility they used was Fitch High School and the program was developed to attract officers from the subbase in Groton, executives from General Dynamics, and officers from the Coast Guard Academy. So, all of your fellow students were more mature than the average graduate student, and they were from similar environments. I did it over two and a half years, at night. I would go a couple times a week. There were several other Coast Guard officers attending, as well. We would carpool from the Academy. Looking back, I would say that it was very well worth the effort. But, it did take a lot of my time between teaching and family life.

JD: I'm guessing the MBA came in handy for the rest of your career.

TC: It did. I thought it was a good thing to have on my resume and for my brain cells to have exposure to that field of study.

JD: Was that something that you sought out on your own, or were you encouraged to pursue an MBA?

TC: It was something several of my fellow instructors and I had researched and talked about and, together, we made the plunge. I felt that I should check that box. It just would give me more options going forward.

JD: What do you think your students would have said about you if they were able to rate you as a professor?

TC: You know, that's in the eyes of the beholder. But I don't know, I think I would get fairly positive reviews. Although, you always wish you could have been more of an expert than you were. We arrive at the Academy as instructor without a great deal of experience under our belts. But, given the road I travelled, I think I did a fairly decent job.

I can remember, later in my career, I was assigned to Group Long Island Sound and there was an Earth Day event at the Academy where they were having a special program with speakers. Since I was local and available, they asked me to come and talk about environmental protection which was a big part of the Long Island Sound's mission. After addressing the cadet corps, three or four current faculty members who had been cadets when I was teaching at the Academy approached me and reflected a bit about being in my classes as cadets. They said that, at first, when I started my talk, it was a bit rocky but after five minutes, they felt like they were right back in their class with me as instructor. They were very positive about their experience with instructor Collins. That was fun to hear. Maybe that's a positive endorsement, I don't know. But, it's hard to self-evaluate.

JD: Speaking of teaching Government 101, Watergate occurred during your time on the faculty of the Coast Guard Academy. How did you incorporate current events into your classroom?

TC: Again, it was one of those present-day things that you try to keep tabs of, and I would actually incorporate them into the class discussions, exams, and essays, to make sure they were staying in touch with the media and current events. *What is the role of the media in politics and in government? What's too far? What's isn't too far? Why are they important in our society, etc.?* There were a lot of different angles you could explore with Watergate. So, I tried to incorporate that into the course.

JD: Before we go on to your next assignment, can you talk about the importance of mentoring junior officers?

TC: Yes. I think it is terribly important to have role models and be coached. And to serve as an example for others. Quite frankly, I can't say I had real strong mentors until I served in the R&D office, largely because up to that point in my career I was on independent ops, in terms of the type of assignments I had. Captain Bob Platt was head of our division in the Office of R&D—the planning staff—and he was a good role model. He was a solid citizen. Captain Ed Gilbert, my CO at Group St. Petersburg—and later Rear Admiral Gilbert—was always very supportive of me and watchful of my career progress.

The real strong mentors for me were when I went to the Programs Division in the Chief of Staff office, especially Dick Herr who, years later, retired as Vice Commandant of the Coast Guard. He was a deputy division chief at the time, as a lieutenant commander. He was incredibly helpful to me and continued to be so. If I had an issue, I would seek his guidance, even when I was way out in Hawaii.

It's great to have someone you trust that you can pulse in on and get their viewpoint. That's really what I found most indispensable. And so, he was a terrific mentor. Helped me a lot. He was a reason for some of my success going forward. Clearly, mentoring is a critical job element for all CG officers, and essential for the professional development for those that work for them.

JD: What was it like leaving the Coast Guard, and ending your four years as a professor and leaving the Coast Guard Academy for a new assignment?

TC: We left New London with mixed feelings. There was substantial job satisfaction. It was a terrific place for my family to live. It was a nice fit. As I said, my wife's parents lived there. They lived four blocks from our house. Built-in baby sitters. We were about two blocks from some of the beaches in New London. We had bought this old house that was built around 1924. It was a fixer upper, but got it fixed up. We sold it for a reasonable profit, but it was hard to give up its perks. In its deed, the property had rights to a private beach two blocks away so I didn't have to pay an annual fee. During the summer, I would be going one way to the Academy to teach my courses, and my wife would be going the other way down to the beach with the baby in a stroller and the other one by the hand. So, it was a really nice, comfortable setup for them.

But, we saw going to Headquarters as an opportunity, and so off we went. Now, there was sticker shock in terms of housing costs in DC. Selling a house in New London and then buying something in Washington, DC was a challenge at my pay scale. Yes. There was a little bit of sticker shock there, but we got through that alright.

JD: One last question about New London. I want to give equal time to your second daughter. You became a father for the second time in New London?

TC: Yes, my second daughter, Kate, was born there, in New London City Hospital. That was the birth I did witness in the delivery room. What an experience that is! You walk away awe struck with the entire birthing process. I can remember being in the green garb and all of that, and I was at the head of the table my wife was on, and the doctor asked me, at an important juncture, to raise the table. Well, I hit the table pedal the wrong way, and lowered the table! The doctor said, "Get him out of here! Get him out of here!," since he was right in the middle of critical moments. We laugh about that 'til this day. But it was amazing to be there. And it was a fast delivery. Kate is now very much a grown woman and works for SAP, has two children—a five-year-old girl and two-and-a-half-year-old boy. They live about a mile-and-a-half from us in Charlotte, so that's really a treat. Her New London arrival in January of 1975 was a special moment for Nancy and me.

JD: New London has been very good to you.

TC: Yes. I spent a lot of time in New London. I was there as a cadet for four years; I was there on the faculty for four years; and, later on, I was just down the coast as Group Commander/Captain of the Port Group Long Island Sound. All great places to work and raise a family.

JD: And, you were a frequent visitor as Commandant, I'm sure.

TC: Absolutely.

JD: Is there anything else you would like to add about being a professor at the Coast Guard Academy, before we move on?

TC: Again, it was an important building block in your career experience that kind of shaped who you are and how you think and what you do. And, again, it's not only the academic side, but the professional side as well. I was involved in training officers on cadet cruises going to Denmark and Germany. One summer, I was the transportation officer and that was my duty for the whole summer program. I didn't realize how much went into arranging the transportation for the entire student body. They were going in different directions, in different ways, at different times, including going over to Rota, Spain, where we swapped out cadets on a cadet cruise. Halfway through the long cruise, we would swap out cadets—saw half of them leave and another half arrive. We went over there and orchestrated all of that, and had to work with the navy base in Rota, Spain, who were of great assistance. Had to charter a C-141 Starlifter flying out of Bradley

Air National Guard Base in East Granby, Connecticut. I mean, a lot of interesting fun stuff that one would never get to do otherwise—so, a great experience from many points of view.

JD: We chatted about this off-record last time. This is as good a time to bring it up as any. Can you tell me about the living conditions onboard the *Eagle,* when you were a cadet?

TC: Yes. It was very basic. A step above what the German seafarers had. As an underclassman, your berthing was via strung hammock in a gang setting on the mess deck—no conditioned spaces—original engines and related systems, the food was okay. The problem with the hammock setup was you had to string them and then you had to take them down each night, each watch period. Then you put them in hammock bins, and your blankets and stuff were in there. If you had to go on the mid-watch, you ended up doing that twice a night. If you had the mid-watch, you have to somehow get in there, with everyone sleeping, and get your hammock. String and unstring. It was a disaster all the time. As underclassmen, you performed all the menial tasks aboard ship. The engine was a straight block diesel German engine—open ports—and you had watch positions. The first oiler actually had these oil cans to constantly put oil in ports. Bottom line: the engines were old and tired, and took a lot of human TLC.

Having said all this, the *Eagle* was a great experience for a cadet. And, obviously since then, habitability and the equipment have vastly improved. The *Eagle* was and is a great platform to train on—I mean, in terms of learning seamanship. You know, the impact of the sea on a vessel, wind, sea. There's nothing better. And teaching teamwork. Again, most things aboard—you can't do anything by yourself. You can't launch a boat; you can't set sails by yourself. Most things are all-hands, evolutions—and you've got to have teamwork. So, coordination, teamwork, leadership. It's a great platform. And great public affairs platform, for the Coast Guard, as well.

JD: Has the Coast Guard Academy changed much in the four years that you were gone?

TC: Between my cadet experience and my instructor experience, the Academy had not changed substantially. Barracks life had not changed much; the academic program was much more expansive and of higher quality. And today, the Academy is vastly different—and all for the better. Continuous improvement is a good thing. One of the greatest and best changes has been the inclusion of females into the cadet corps. Another is the co-location of OCS with the Academy. And of course, there have been numerous facility upgrades over time.

JD: What guidance did you receive from the superintendent, higher-ups in the Coast Guard, regarding integration?

TC: I don't recall specific high-level guidance in that regard.

JD: Can you talk about how you got your next assignment in the Office of Research & Development?

TC: Well, I didn't even know we had one when I was at the Coast Guard Academy. I knew I was probably going to a staff assignment and not a command. That was confirmed by my detailer. He indicated I was likely going to a staff assignment at Coast Guard Headquarters, and that as an LCDR, I needed an HQ assignment for my career progression. He noted that the one place that he had a hole to fill was the planning and programming position in R&D. He described the job itself and its advantages. I signed on. It turns out that this transition was very important in my career in that it was one of those things that was a building block that ultimately led to a whole array of other options. The one thing that concerned me was how I was going to live in Washington, DC, with its high cost of living. We ended up in a townhouse, which adequately met our needs.

JD: Do you remember where your townhouse was located?

TC: Yes. It was off of Burke and Zion Drive, in Fairfax. It was a good, little neighborhood. There were a couple of other coasties—lieutenant-type—that lived there in the neighborhood. We ended up having a great carpool. We solved all of the Coast Guard's problems everyday, going back and forth to work. I learned as much there as I did working on the job. So, it worked out just fine.

JD: I think this is a great place to stop, if that's okay with you.

TC: Okay. Let's do it.

End audio file Collins2.2.Dolbow.USNI.2.4.16

Interviewer: Jim Dolbow (JD)

Interviewee: Admiral Thomas Collins, USCG Ret. (TC)

Begin audio file Collins3.1.Dolbow.USNI.2.10.16

JD: This is Jim Dolbow in Arlington, Virginia. It's February 10th, 2016 and this is the third session with Admiral Tom Collins. Admiral, can you tell us a little bit about your assignment in the Office of R&D, at the Coast Guard Headquarters, and your responsibilities?

TC: Sure. It was 1976 and I had just completed a four-year assignment at the United States Coast Guard Academy, and was assigned to my first staff job in Coast Guard Headquarters. It was an interesting time. The Coast Guard's leadership laydown included Admiral Owen W. Siler as Commandant for the first couple of years, and then Admiral John B. Hayes. The Vice Commandant was Ellis Perry, followed by Bob Scarborough—who had a reputation of being very gruff and stern, but actually, he was very personable and very competent. I had recurring dealings with him when I was Vice Commandant and Commandant. He was very active in the retired officers' association and attended many Washington, DC Coast Guard events. He was Vice Commandant the last two years of my R&D assignment. The Chiefs of Staff during that four-year period were Bob Scarborough, then Jim Gracey, who was followed by Jim Stewart.

Jack Costello was the chief of the Programs Division. I mention him because a great deal of the output of HQ's programs staff all filtered through him. So, he was a key actor for the Chief of Staff and all of HQ. While assigned to the Office of R&D, I worked for two flag officers in their capacity as Office Chief. The first was Rear Admiral Abe Siemens. The second was Rear Admiral Al Manning.

JD: Did you get to spend a lot of time with either the Vice Commandant or the Commandant?

TC: No, because I was so many levels below at that time. I did have an opportunity to engage with both Jack Costello, as the Programs Division chief, and the Chief of Staff, as we presented and responded to issues associated with our R&D appropriations and associated policy issues.

JD: Why do you think you were chosen for this assignment?

TC: I think one reason was that I was serving as a lieutenant commander without a staff assignment yet. The assignment detailers rightfully said this was the time for me to experience Headquarters. There are a number of planning, programming, and budgeting staffs at HQ. Given the importance of those staffs, the detailers tried to put mid-level officers in those planning and programming jobs that had a fairly solid track record. So, you found a pretty good quality of folks in that network at Headquarters, and the particular opening that was available at that time was Research & Development, so I was plugged in there. I didn't know quite what I was getting into, so it was baptism under fire.

JD: What was it like reporting to the Coast Guard Headquarters for the first time?

TC: A very different experience. I hadn't been in a big bureaucratic unit before, and that's what Headquarters was and still remains. But, it was clearly an excellent opportunity for me. Looking back on it, it put me in the planning and programming budgeting area, which was a great opportunity to learn how the Coast Guard works.

JD: Looking back at it now, if somebody would have told you back then, that one day you would be coming back to Headquarters as the Vice Commandant, and later on as Commandant, what would you have told them?

TC: I probably wouldn't believe them. It's such a lengthy road to travel from that particular point, and a lot of things have to fit in—a little luck, maybe; being at the right place, at the right time; and finally, and most perhaps most importantly, being associated with the right kind of people. All of those things figure into the equation.

JD: What was an average day like for you in Headquarters?

TC: As staff deputy, I was consumed with a wide range of policy, budget, and program matters. And it was more than just a budget. It involves the requirements of the program—how you identify/detail them; how you evaluate them; how you develop support for them; how you resource them. The chief of the R&D planning and programming staff was Captain Bob Platt. He was an interesting guy. He was a telecommunications-type specialist by trade. Also on the staff was a lieutenant-finance type, a couple of the civilian staff members, and an IT person. Our day-to-day job was to understand, assess, and develop the R&D appropriation. R&D was the one planning/programming staff below the Chief of Staff-level in Headquarters, that had responsibility for an entire appropriation: the RDT&E [Research, Development, Test, and Evaluation] appropriation. As I recall, the appropriation was between $20-$24 million a year at that time.

JD: Can you talk about the budget process? Like, as soon as you got done with one budget, did you have to start working on the next one?

TC: Yes. Of course, it involves a number of overlapping cycles. When I came into that office, I was dismayed a little bit, in that a good deal of the associated processes hadn't been standardized. For example, *How do you identify a RDT&E program requirement? How do you analyze a requirement? How do you report on a requirement? How do you include it in the budget, etc.? Then, how, on the execution end, is it being executed and monitored? Are the project staffs spending the money as they should, and on time?*

Everyone worries about timely obligations. So, one of my major tasks right off the bat was to try to put more rigor and standardization in how things were identified and how they were justified; how they were reported on. An integrated system was needed. We developed the Research Development Information System (RDIS) to help integrate document information relative to all program and project initiatives for budget formulation, justification, reporting, evaluation, and quarterly reviews. That information system not only provided information to the Chief of Staff's Office, but served the front office in R&D and the R&D project folks in their day-to-day efforts. The other thing about the Office of Research & Development was it was very valuable for me in my professional development. As an HQ support office, it serviced all of the programs at Headquarters who identified a requirement for a R&D project, test, or a study. Accordingly, you had to have a thorough understanding of all of the programs of the Coast Guard. So, it was very educational. When we got through, I really had a deep appreciation of all of the various CG missions and programs.

JD: Can you talk about how you prepared your RDT&E appropriation for submission to the Chief of Staff, DOT, OMB, Congress?

TC: It would start with a defined planning and programming process at Headquarters. The Chief of Programs Evaluation Division, the Chief Programs Division, and the Chief of the Budget Division were the three major Chief of Staff divisions that had governance over that whole process. It would start with a planning horizon that was generated by the plans and evaluation division of the Chief of Staff. They would develop that on input from all of the programs. There was a document called the Long-Range View and there was a follow-up document called the Determinations, where the Chief of Staff would be making policy/programmatic determinations on the various CG programs. They were akin to planning factors to guide budget development. The various HQ program offices would then develop documents referred to as Resource Change Proposals (RCPs). Admiral Jim Gracey was really the godfather of the RCP process, which defined the various program resource requirements and quantified them along with alternatives and impacts. In the Office of R&D, we ensured that the RDT&E RCPs were done in conjunction with the operational program requirement owner. Then, the Chief of Staff would whittle down all the RCPs to the precious few and, ultimately, arrive at a budget that supported the highest priorities of the CG.

JD: What was easier? Preparing the appropriation requests or defending it?

TC: Both presented challenges. Once we had a standardized RDT&E planning and programming process the process became very manageable, especially within the CG. Defending it was a little more difficult outside of the Coast Guard. You had to slug through the budget food chain. First, you have to be successful within the CG and there was a lot of whittling down there. Then, if you were successful at that stop, you've got to defend it at the Department of Transportation, who had a whole host of different priorities. After the DOT, your budget went to OMB. You had Coast Guard budget review hearings within the Coast Guard; you had hearings within the DOT; hearings at the OMB; and ultimately, hearings in Congress. At every level, you have to re-defend your budget request. Of course, at each step, things get cut and changed, and so forth. So, it's an interesting process. There is certainly a great deal of scrutiny.

The other thing about the Coast Guard budget food chain is that the Coast Guard is a very capital-intensive organization, relative to other agencies in the non-DOD part of the government. In our budget food chain, the non-DOD side of the OMB and Congress, was not as comfortable or familiar with the capital-intensive side of the budget (i.e., building big dollar ships, planes, etc.). In a way, the CG was an odd man out, in that regard. We were not subject to DOD experienced reviewers in the OMB. We had separate reviewers. That, along with the complexities of the overall federal budget process, made it challenging.

JD: Speaking of the food chain, was there one aspect of the food chain that was easier to deal with than the other?

TC: Well, clearly, if you had a very supportive secretary or departmental staff, that really helped. It moved things through because then you could seek their support to intervene if the OMB wasn't satisfied with something, wanted to defer something, or to kill something. And most departmental front offices have been supportive—it's just some had been more supportive than others. Each secretary of transportation faced a huge demand for resources across all the DOT administrations. They had so many competing priorities other than Coast Guard requirements and demands, i.e., building highways or bridges, or regulating airplanes and air space. The CG had difficulty. at times. in competing with the next mile of new highways when it came to the budget.

JD: One of your duties in the office was maintaining the office IT system. What kind of system was it?

TC: Initially, we didn't have a database that could easily integrate information across the appropriations—not only for budget formulation, but for financial reporting associated with the execution of RDT&E projects. So, I was involved in defining all of those information database requirements that would help both planning, programming, and project staffs run and manage their programs.

JD: This is a big picture question. Why does the Coast Guard have a RDT&E program?

TC: Interesting question. Clearly, it's not massive. There was very little research done. There was no basic research done. We just didn't have the scale to do that. If necessary, we could tag onto a Navy lab project. Basically, our R&D supported the technical needs of CG operational and regulatory programs: search-and-rescue, Commercial Vessel Safety, Recreational Boating, Port Security, and so forth, through the conduct of studies, tests, modeling, operations research, etc. Much of the work were studies to support new regulations. Other projects tested promising new equipment or techniques. Most were not conducted organically; they were contracted out. The project staffs wrote up the project requirements in response to program manager requests, and awarded and oversaw contracts to the private sector. There were really three major avenues to conduct project work: that done by contract, that done in-house at our R&D Center in Groton (now New London), and that done at other government labs. It all depended on what the issue was and what their technical skills and capabilities were at the time.

JD: When you were later Commandant, were there things that you worked on in this office that was helpful out in the field and you thought to yourself, *I'm glad I worked on that project*?

TC: There was certainly some that stood out. A great deal of it was really small job shop contracts. The contracted work to study and support the regulatory responsibilities for commercial vessel safety and recreational boating safety was extensive and had a very positive impact on the legitimacy of the CG regulatory initiatives. One of the things that I can remember the most, that had—and continues to have—the biggest impact is oil fingerprinting. One of the CG operational programs that we supported was marine environmental protection. Preventing spills and holding those who spilled accountable is a key responsibility of the CG. For example, there might be a mystery oil spill in the Thames River: *Who was the spiller? How do we identify and hold the guilty party accountable financially and legally for the spill?* This has been one of the R&D Center's real specialties. They had a talented staff at the center that developed a technique of matching oil and identifying where it came from using gas chromatography technology. You could get a sample of the spill, get a sample from a potential spiller, and match it. It proved very successful in court when going after someone for inappropriate handling of cargo, etc.

The other specialty at the R&D Center involved their efforts to continually develop and refine CG search-and-rescue techniques. There are certain technical areas that the CG has a basic and continuing need to be expert in. The technical side of search-and-rescue is one of those areas, as well as is the area of pollution response and monitoring.

JD: Did you work much with the Navy's Office of Naval Research?

TC: Some. I don't recall specific projects, but there was a relationship there. Again, we could go to them if there was a specific niche thing we were looking for, and they provided that capability.

JD: Can you talk about the Coast Guard's Research & Development Center in New London? And were you able to visit there often?

TC: Yes. I mentioned that was one of our sources to act as project manager for a given project. It was at Avery Point in Groton, located on the opposite side of where the Coast Guard Academy is located, down right on the water at the mouth of the Thames, on the Groton side. It was there for years, but has since located to the New London side.

In any event, I don't recall the number of people or the amount of their budget. It was approximately a quarter to one-third of the overall R&D appropriation that was supported at the center. I visited it several times, mostly talking to their budgeting and program people. The first couple of visits were just to get a greater understanding of what projects were up there and what they do, which I took advantage of. It was a talented group.

JD: This was your first assignment in Washington, DC. What was it like living in the national capitol?

TC: It was different than New London, Connecticut, I can tell you that. I had a forty-five to sixty-minute commute to DC—on good days—as compared to the ten-minute commute to work in New London. And I know there was a little bit of sticker shock trying to find a home that I could afford. I had previously bought and sold a home in New London and now I was faced with hunting down a new place to live. I had two young children, Christine, age 6, and Kate, age 1, at that time. So, it was a little bit of a challenge, but we ended up alright. We landed on our feet. Found a new townhouse in the Fairfax/Burke area at an acceptable price and good location. It worked out fine. I give my family great credit in being both supportive and flexible.

JD: Did you and your family take advantage of the cultural opportunities in DC?

TC: Yes. We took in the downtown sites, plays, concerts, etc. And there was a lot of things to see around the neighborhood. Fairfax County had a great deal of public services that you can use, and good park systems. Right behind our townhouse was a fairly good-size lake. There were hiking paths and all of those things. We had acquired a golden retriever that was part of the family, so he liked the lake. So, we did that.

I can remember taking advantage of the Fairfax County offerings, in terms of courses and whatever they offered for the public. One was training your dog. And, I will tell you, it was a lot of fun. I went off with the dog once a week for five weeks and went to these courses. I remember driving back laughing from those courses. It was so funny seeing various people and various types of dogs and how they latched up. It was funny.

A lot of people slam Washington, DC. I think it's a very decent, even exciting, area once you get past the traffic. The traffic, of course, has gotten exponentially worse since then. That's always a challenge. We had a solution for that too, because I was in a six-person carpool of all lieutenant/lieutenant commander-types. We had great interchanges. We solved all the Coast Guard's and world's problems, going back and forth on our commutes to and from Coast Guard Headquarters. That made the commute time go by quickly. And Headquarters—it's not bad for the family. There were and are good school systems in most areas.

JD: Your four years is coming to a close at Headquarters. Is there anything else about this assignment you would like to add?

TC: No. Just that it was fortuitous for me. It may not necessarily the preeminent office, at Headquarters, but in terms of learning the various Coast Guard programs, it enabled me to get in depth into every Coast Guard program. So, it was a great learning experience, number one. Number two, I got to know how Washington at-large works. I didn't have a front-row seat, but maybe a third-row seat. I got to see a lot of how things work, both inside and outside the Coast Guard. So, that was incredibly helpful.

The other thing is, it got me into planning, programming, and budgeting. And whether I realized it or not, I was at the beginning of a sub-specialty in that area. And I think it was that sub-specialty that got me to where I eventually got. So, good things happened with that assignment. The detailers did another good thing for me.

JD: One last question about R&D. In this era of tight budgets, it's really easy to cut R&D because that's for things out in the future. Any cautionary advice?

TC: You have to have your arguments spiffy and together, and quantified as much as you can. You must clearly articulate to those that govern the budgets what the benefits are that will accrue to the Coast Guard, to the government, and to the public by doing a given project or projects, and have your arguments together about the impact of not doing it. Those two things are terribly, terribly important.

JD: How did you get your next assignment as the Deputy Group Commander in St. Petersburg, Florida?

TC: Again, you are at the mercy of our talented detailers in the Office of Personnel. I did accumulate a pretty good record at HQ and the Academy. It had been some time since I had been in my Commanding Officer assignment—and it was not an upper-echelon field-type command. I was due for a field command—CO or Deputy. Deputy Group Commander St. Petersburg was open. It happened to be a dual-hatted assignment. You were Deputy Group Commander and Commanding Officer of Station St. Petersburg. I checked two boxes with that one, so I actively campaigned for it. Apparently, I convinced the officer assignments branch that I was a good fit for the job.

JD: Was it easy for you and your family to leave DC?

TC: My family was a bit apprehensive, at first. I've got a New England wife and I'm a New Englander, and it was further away from parents on both sides. That's always important, I think. How do you maintain the family network from further away? All that anxiety disappeared within the first month, when we saw the friendliness of the people down there, and my kids and wife saw the sunshine, and beaches, and things like that. So, they quickly fell in love with the St. Petersburg area.

JD: When was your assignment in St. Petersburg in relation to the Cuban boatlift?

TC: By the time I got to St. Petersburg, the vast preponderance of Mariel boatlift had already taken place I think. I recall one statistic when I got there: about 90-95% of the exodus had already transpired before I arrived in July. So, most of the heavy stuff was in April. We were primarily the mop up detail by the time I got there. Of course, the one major command that was in the middle of it—and it always is in the middle of a lot of Florida issues—is Key West.

Primarily, the rest of the units in the 7th Coast Guard District would mobilize from their subordinate units in the district and be deployed down to Key West to augment them for high-paced operations.

At the time, the leadership slate in the Coast Guard, included Admiral Haye, still Commandant. Admiral Jim Gracey became Commandant in 1982. The District 7 commanders during my tour were Rear Admirals Donald "Deese" Thompson and Bill Kime. My group commanders were both wonderful. I was very fortunate. Captain Ed Gilbert was the First Group Commander there and then he was relieved by Bob Nichols. Nichols was a 1977 Coast Guard Jarvis Award-winner based on his service in Alaska. He was a marine safety-type guy. They were both terrific leaders and I really was fortunate to have them as group commanders.

JD: Can you tell us about Group St. Petersburg's area-of-responsibility (AOR)?

TC: Yes. It was God's country. A beautiful part of the world. On the west coast of Florida, the AOR ran in the south from Cape Romano, Marco Island, along the west coast, past Tampa and Clearwater, north to Yankeetown and Inglis, Florida. It was a pretty good-sized group.

JD: You mentioned the names of the two commanding officers. Can you talk about their leadership styles?

TC: They gave you a long leash. They really gave you a long leash. I mean, they let you sink-or-swim-type of thing, but good guidance, good oversight, attentive to detail. But, let you do your thing. They were very talented in terms of their professional knowledge. Ed Gilbert was particularly bright and articulate. Also with a good, dry sense of humor. They were both very good COs.

JD: Can you talk about some of the units that were assigned to Group St. Petersburg?

TC: Coast Guard Station Yankeetown was a small station on the Withlacoochee River, way up north. Again, it was desolate. The station facility was a houseboat with several small boats assigned. The next one down was in Clearwater Beach, that was also a houseboat when I first arrived. So, houseboat, houseboat, then Station St. Petersburg, then Station Cortez down in Bradenton, that's south of Tampa Bay. It was an old rickety house. Then, our next station was in beautiful Venice Beach. Then, further down was our next station, Ft. Myers Beach. That was a new facility. It had just been built when I arrived. At the time, that was the only new station. There was a lot of tired facilities throughout Group St. Pete. So, one of my goals was to plan for a facility turnaround. We also had 82-foot patrol boats, one inland buoy tender, two construction tenders, and a buoy tender. The focus of Group St. Petersburg was search-and-rescue (SAR) and aids-to-navigation (ATON), with maritime law enforcement a close third. We did all of the CG operational missions, but SAR and ATON were the two heavy, heavy missions there on the west coast of Florida.

JD: How did you divide your responsibilities between a commanding officer and yourself?

TC: Well, you know, top level set the overall direction, and I did, but I was a halfway between a CO and an XO. So, I had a little CO-type focus and XO-type focus. But as the deputy group commander, I was typically heavy into the backroom functions of a command—heavy into the development of budgets and finances, personnel administration, and facility management. I had a capable lieutenant station XO Peggy Riley, and an eager admin officer that was an ensign, just out of Officer Candidate School (OCS). He was very good—Dean Lee, who later became a vice admiral. We had several experienced warrant officers. A warrant officer ran the engineering department, a warrant officer did the public works, another was at the finance/accounting/procurement shop. But, again, my role involved typical XO stuff: managing your inbox and heavy into overseeing the day-to-day management of the command. And all personnel issues/problems—disciplinary or otherwise—got deposited at your doorstop. You are the "buck stops here," in terms of personnel and budget/finance issues.

Also, as an XO, I was into safety and readiness. I saw that as a primo responsibility. All of the units in the group had district inspections. Over the course of a year or so, an inspection team would come from the district office in Miami and inspect all of the units so I was in the middle of ensuring we were all prepared for those kinds of things. We accumulated an outstanding inspection record in terms of safety and operational readiness. As I recall, we had eighteen separate district inspections of group units, and all eighteen had evaluations of excellent or outstanding.

JD: What went into preparing for a district inspection?

TC: Oh, they would give you a pre-inspection check-off list. You would have to go through those, but there are always wild cards with those inspection teams in our play. There is an administrative portion, i.e. personnel and finance/procurement administration. There were also extensive operational drills. The material condition of your boats and facilities would also be examined.

JD: How did you divide your time between being the deputy group commander and commanding officer of the station?

TC: It was sort of an integrated approach to a lot of responsibilities of both jobs. One role bled into the other.

JD: Did you have any operational duties as a deputy group commander?

TC: A lot of it involved oversight for material conditions and operational readiness, and training and safety. I didn't always leave that to others. I would personally make the visit. I had a game plan to visit each unit so many times in a given year. For example, I wanted to make sure I rode the buoy tenders. I made it a point to take one of the tenders down the inland waterway and observe the repair of aids along the waterway. I tried not to be locked to my desk in St. Petersburg. And, of course, you got a brief every morning. The group commander and I met with the ops guy and the admin guy, and we would go over what happened last night, what have we got going today. That would be a daily routine. I would also provide longer term planning guidance regarding the deployment of personnel and operational assets to our various missions.

JD: Did you have any hurricanes that you had to deal with during your time?

TC: Fortunately, not. Not that there weren't hurricanes in the Caribbean. They just never hit the west coast of Florida. Most went around Cuba and up the middle of the Caribbean up toward Texas. We did get a couple of tropical storms that were pretty big. We did a lot of hurricane contingency plans, both within the Coast Guard and in the community with emergency disaster preparedness civil staffs. We were all afraid of a hurricane hitting the right way and coming ashore with a wind coming in directly from the west, into Pinellas County in Tampa Bay. There would be huge flooding there because it would be like pouring water into a bowl. We did have one tropical storm that wasn't a hurricane, but acted, in many ways, like a hurricane. It flooded up the Tampa Bay. It clearly filled up my neighborhood. I couldn't get home. I had to park my car about four or five blocks away and take my uniform shoes and socks off, roll up my pant legs, and wade through the water. I did get home. There was about two to three feet of water on many of the roadways. But, thankfully, we never got a direct hit by a hurricane, which was a good thing.

JD: A hurricane contingency plan came in handy years later when you were Commandant and Florida was like a bullseye for hurricanes.

TC: Yes, it certainly was. There were some basic principles of how we approached hurricanes that have stuck with me. The basic formula is to move out of the path of a hurricane as many Coast Guard assets as you can. Protect them. Preserve them so you can be effective in the immediate aftermath of the storm. As soon as it passes in, you move in on the backside of the storm to assist/rescue/aid the public. That's typically what happens. You can't do much at the height of a hurricane except lose everything. We train to the plan. We resource to the plan. We exercise the plan in a very de-centralized way. We delegate operational authority to the lowest level that we can. Time and the perspectives of local command are so important in these circumstances. So, we don't have a bureaucratically-bound operational model. And joint planning with local civil emergency preparedness officials is essential.

JD: Can you talk about the facilities at Group St. Petersburg?

TC: The base used to be Coast Guard Air Station St. Petersburg, for seaplanes, but it couldn't handle C-130s when they were introduced, so all of the aircraft were relocated to a new air station, Coast Guard Air Station Clearwater, at Clearwater airport, long before I got there.

My overall facility goal was to leave St. Pete facilities and overall group facilities better than how I found them. We worked out of an old hangar. The admin/ops building at the group was an old World War II classic flat-roofed wooden Army building. The exchange ran out of a similar building. The barracks were old stucco, tiled roof, Mediterranean-looking buildings, but were inefficiently laid out and in a state of disrepair. The club and the pool house were all in a state of disrepair. Station Yankeetown was a boathouse. Clearwater was a boathouse. So, I spent a good deal of time planning on how to improve these facilities, and how to convince the district to budget for them. As a result, a new group ops building went in. It was built just after I left, but I did most of the planning/design, and presenting the case to the district. By the time I left, the following projects were either completed or they were started or approved for repair/construction: a permanent station in Clearwater, a permanent station in Yankeetown, a permanent station at Cortez, a new admin building in Group St. Petersburg, renovated barracks, renovated galley, renovated club, a pool, a new maintenance-assist team support building (MAT) for Medium Endurance Cutters that were moored at the station, and a new exchange. That's a meaty list and I had my fingerprints on all of those projects. So, I felt good when I left that St. Pete was in a lot better place in terms of facilities than when I had arrived.

The MAT building construction is an interesting case of "where there is a will there is a way." The anti-drug law enforcement buildup in the southeast United States at that time brought additional resources to St Pete. In support of that campaign, two 210-foot Medium Endurance Cutters were homeported in St. Pete shortly after I arrived. They had a shore side MAT but no facility, and they needed one to ensure the ship's operational readiness. However, there was an Army Reserve building on that south side of the harbor and on our property. They had built a new maintenance building to support their landing craft. It hadn't even been occupied, so I researched it a little bit. I found out that they didn't have a long-term lease with us. It was a short-term lease for pier space and was about to expire. The procurement rules say that you can't build capital improvements on a short-term lease. So, I gave the civil engineers at Ft. Stewart, Georgia a call, noting that they had basically built it illegally because we were not prepared to extend their lease since we had a newly arrived CG ship to support there. I offered to take over the new Army-built maintenance building and use it for a maintenance teams for the 210s, and then find a place in St. Pete's beach to moor their landing craft. I had already talked to the city and offered to build them—with our construction tender—a dock, dolphins, pilings, at St. Pete Beach for their landing craft and get them out of a pickle. I noted that I was also meeting a presidential mandate to support the drug effort with the arrival of additional CG assets to the area, and needed our moorings on the south side of the harbor.

That was an offer they couldn't refuse. So, the deal offered us an opportunity to take over a brand-new maintenance building for the 210s, at a very reduced cost over what it would have cost to build it in-house. The arrangement wasn't all that negative for the Army Reserve because they got a brand new facility out at the beach. So, they were happy. We were happy.

JD: How did you get the funding for all of the other buildings and improvements that you mentioned a few minutes ago?

TC: Some had to go in the Acquisition, Construction, and Improvement (AC&I) appropriation and get congressional approval. That's usually a two- to three-year project. They can also get some reprogramming of the capital account—Acquisition, Construction, and Improvements—support facility improvements. If, in fact, it's justified and you can get it approved, you can reprogram. Or, you can use, under certain conditions, dollars from the operational appropriation's Allotment Fund Control Codes (AFC). AFC-30 was the operating and maintenance account; AFC-43 was civil engineering money and they could do civil engineering projects up to a certain threshold, beyond which they had to go for capital money.

So, some of the improvements were supported by the operational appropriations, some by the AC&I appropriation. We also did some of the projects by self-help. The CG exchange, for example, and portions of the barracks. The exchange was an important facility since it provided support to our personnel, both active duty and retirees.

JD: How long did that take for the exchange?

TC: I think it took us a months-worth of weekends. Long weekends. But, you know, we had a big truck for all the debris. It reminds me of some of these shows on TV now. It's demolition day, and you go in there, and you bust down walls, and you do all of that. That's what we did. I think it brought people together. You could see you are doing something good and some good results at the end of the day. I think it motivated and energized people.

JD: What was the reaction of the retirees with the new exchange?

TC: They loved it. It was the closest base, other than going all the way over to MacDill AFB in Tampa. So, it was attractive, and all of those exchange profits go into non-appropriated funds for MWR purposes to do good things. So, it was a win-win.

JD: Were you surprised that you had such skilled craftsmen?

TC: I wasn't surprised. We had so many skilled people. Not only were they skilled, but dedicated and hardworking. If you want carpentry, if you want electrical work, you got it. There was a lot of talent and a lot of people that were very results-oriented. So, it was fun. It was a fun assignment from all of those perspectives.

But, Coast Guard personnel are always in the middle of things, bringing their skills to bear. Take for example, the area of disaster planning—disaster planning for airports and for downed aircraft. We worked with the St. Pete, Clearwater, and Tampa airports. We developed contingency plans because any catastrophe was probably going to be a water-type catastrophe, given how those airports are situated. So, we worked very, very closely with airport authorities, bringing our maritime expertise to bear, to try to make sure that we were prepared to deal with that. Knock on wood, there was no aircraft emergency, but we felt good that we were prepared if there was an emergency.

JD: You mentioned working with the airports and were there any other examples of inner-agency cooperation, like with the FBI or local police?

TC: There was and particularly with the Florida Marine Patrol. The Florida Marine Patrol was the Florida state police on the water. So, there was frequent interaction on a patrolling event or some other issue. If we had a drunk boater, you frequently prosecuted that case in conjunction with local authorities because you would apprehend the individual or individuals, and local authorities would help would administer the breathalyzers and make the arrest, as necessary. So, all of those types of things went on, and they go on in almost every CG group (now reorganized into Sectors).

JD: On October 14, 1982, President Reagan declared illicit drugs to be a threat to US national security. Can you talk about the impact this had at the group level?

TC: Well, having the 210-foot Medium Endurance Cutters assigned to Station St. Petersburg was the biggest impact from a support perspective. How do you support these ships properly in terms of both people and the platform? The other impact was that we would send boats and people down to Miami and Key West. Some went to Miami, but most went to Key West, and so we sort of had a rotating scheme going on where perspective patrol boats from the stations would be deployed down there supporting that operation.

JD: Did your assignment here help you later on in your career when you were Commandant and was dual-hatted as US Interdiction Coordinator?

TC: Yes. Every subsequent assignment builds on the preceding: getting people motivated, dealing with our other agencies. Those all come in and they build on one another.

The biggest case down there happened in the preceding month before my arrival, and that was the *Blackthorn-Capricorn* collision. USCGC *Blackthorn* [WLB-391] was coming out of a yard period in Tampa and going to its homeport in Galveston, TX, when it collided with the tanker *Capricorn* on the night of January 28, 1980. We tragically lost 23 sailors that night. I was just receiving my orders to St. Pete at the same time as the Blackthorn sank. Captain Ed Gilbert did a masterful job in response to this tragedy. In fact, he subsequently did a lot of speaking and writing about crisis management: *How do you respond and prepare to respond for disasters of this type, particularly in terms of managing people and talent? How do you get people at the right place at the right time?* But, like I said, this collision happened before I arrived in St. Petersburg.

In fact, the *Blackthorn*'s XO, Dave Crawford, was later assigned as admin officer at Air Station Clearwater, so he was in the area. Then, John Ryan, who was the OOD during the time of the collision, got reassigned to the group in St. Petersburg. He was the Exchange Officer, so there were a lot of lingering *Blackthorn* issues going on. Plus, the *Blackthorn* herself was raised and brought back to a shipyard in Tampa. Then, there was an investigation going on. I think that took over a year. Then, we worked with the Chief Petty Officers Association down there to orchestrate the preliminary beginnings of the *Blackthorn* Memorial.

JD: I've been there several times. Every time I'm in Tampa, I always stop at the USCGC *Blackthorn* Memorial at the base of the Sky Bridge, along the bay off of Interstate 275.

TC: Yes, there's an annual ceremony now. I went there several times as either the Vice Commandant or Commandant. I can't remember which one, but I participated in that. So, the

Blackthorn piqued my interest on crisis management, and I picked the brains of Ed Gilbert a lot on that. But, he did—I thought—a very, very credible job.

JD: While you were down there, did you have any memorable drug busts?

TC: We had small ones, but nothing major. The biggest drug event there was some drug use and dealing within the base. Alleged reports were that it was in the station boat crew and my first reaction was, *That's totally unacceptable.* I've got to get to the heart of this. So, I brought in a female Coast Guard reservist that, in her full-time job, was assigned to the narcotics unit in either the Jacksonville or Atlanta police departments. I can't remember which. I said, "I would like you to come on active duty with the boat crew and just be my eyes and ears. Tell me what is going on," because at that point it was just alleged.

Well, she came in and she worked harder than three men. She gained the trust and confidence of everyone in the boat crew and she got the facts; *nothing but the facts ma'am.* And, we identified two rotten apples in the boat crew. So, we ended up with a special court martial that was held right on the base. None of the base personnel knew that she was doing this. But when she showed up in high heels and a business suit to testify at the special court martial, all of their jaws dropped. We had put it together well and rooted out the problem. You had to remove that cancer and we did.

JD: You talked about this one particular reservist. Anything else about the role of reservists at Group St. Petersburg?

TC: They were very talented, hard-working folks. Worked hard to get qualified on weekends. Participated in big events like Gasparilla, which was an all-hands affair. Every boat, every patrol boat, everyone trying to keep sanity and safety in this, but not put a damper on the occasion in terms of participants. So, they were instrumental along with the Auxiliarists. Every active duty unit had a corresponding reserve unit, so there would be reserve unit Yankeetown. Reserve Unit Clearwater, etc. So, they would integrate and train with their active duty counterparts. It worked very well. The auxiliarists had a similar thing. I think we had about 1500 auxiliarists on the west coast of Florida. They do everything. They had their own aircraft. There's an operational demand, augmentation dimension. There's logistic support dimension. There's an admin dimension, and some would work in the admin shop. So, very supportive, and all up and down the west coast. Two of the auxiliary flotillas, Naples and Sarasota, owned their own facilities. They get involved because number one, they want to do good. They have the time—typically successful people in life, now retired—and they want to be involved. Nut then there is a social dimension to it, too. So, both the Reserves and the Coast Guard Auxillary are very productive components. They did a lot of great work for us.

JD: Was this your first exposure to both the reservists and auxiliarists?

TC: Yes, it t was my first substantive exposure to the Coast Guard Reserve and Auxiliary. Up to that point in my career, my other operational units, such as the *Vigilant,* were those where you don't really get much interchange with auxiliarists. On the *Cape Morgan*, likewise. So, it's really at the group/MSO level—those units that are directly touching the community, and engaging with the community all the time. That's why the group/station/MSO is where the rubber meets the road in terms of engagement with the maritime public, to a great extent. And, that's where the Auxiliary and the Reserves come into play.

JD: Can we get your thoughts on the organizational structure of the Coast Guard at this time in your career, and the disconnects you saw that you would ultimately end up fixing later on in your career?

TCA: I thought very early on in my career that it was confusing for the customers. You are right, I was aggressive on this later in my career, and we will talk about that later. I tried to look at it from a customer's perspective with the customer being the American public. It's like, *Who's on first? What's on second?* I mean, *Who is in charge here in Tampa Bay? I've got an MSO Captain over here. I've got a Group Commander over here. Who is the man in town?*

Also, it was inefficient because we needed the MSO sometimes, and their technical skills, and authorities on the water. A lot of times, they needed our boats to do their thing, and it was like a *Mother, may I?* all of the time—very inefficient. And, the group had certain priorities that were very different then the priorities of the MSO. So, "Well, you can't have our boat now because of blah, blah, blah." "Wait a minute, I've got to do…" "Well that's not my priority." So, I just thought there were overlapping inefficiencies. *Why do we have an admin shop, personnel shop, and all of that at the group and similar shops in the MSO?* I said, "This is crazy. How can you get standard approach to training, etc., group-to-group and port-to-port?" I said, "Something needs to be fixed here." I saw the need for a systems approach to our operational field structure. So, later I was in a position to work on that.

That was a good question because those early field assignments planted the seed for me regarding certain issues. I think of CG ships, planes, boat, and field shore ops as the tip of the spear. I call it our service delivery point. We need to get that point right. We can organize and reorganize at Headquarters, etc., but the most important thing to get right is, *Will you deliver your services?* Unfortunately, that wasn't the focus of a lot of people, but ultimately it became the focus.

JD: Moving to search-and-rescue, each SAR case represents the life of someone's family member on the line. Can you talk about the difficult decision that is involved when it becomes necessary to call off a search?

TC: It's always hard. Especially when the search hasn't produced satisfactory results from the perspective of the family of the loved one. You haven't recovered the body or whatever, or even found them. And, you've exhausted your resources and any probability of finding anything. I think the most important thing to do is be professional about it. You have to avoid surprises: update family members, friends, and so forth, as frequently as you can. Assign one senior person to do this daily. You are responsible to coordinate with the family, and then as the commanding officer, interject yourself and make yourself available so you answer every question that they have, e.g., "This is what we did today. We've got this many ship days on scene, so many hours, so many aircraft hours, so many people involved. This is the area that we've covered, etc."

So, communicate, communicate. When in doubt, communicate some more so you take the mystery out of it, so they are informed on what you've done. We exhaust every possibility before we say we are stopping the rescue phase and going into the recovery phase.

JD: Did you receive training on how to deal with families or was this all on the job?

TC: Most of it is common sense. Baptism under fire, Jim—in watching how others do it, and how they do it good and how they do it bad. Know what represents the good model and doesn't.

Later in this interview process, we can talk about the biggest one I was involved in, and that was the Air Alaska plane that went down off Santa Barbara, when I was Area Commander and District Commander out on the west coast. That was a big one, but a lot of good lessons and examples on how to do it.

JD: Can you tell us about an average day as a deputy group commander and CO?

TC: Well, you come in early in the morning, and you've got to be there before the group commander. I mean, that's the one thing. You arrive before him and you leave after him. That was always a good thing to do. That's partly in jest, but, I mean, it's not a bad rule to follow. But, typically, if we were both available or, if not, one of us would always take an ops brief every morning. The ops lieutenant would come over, and the station exec and the leadership team would come over and get briefed.

Of course, I managed my inbox and you do that as an XO. You are overseeing budgets, dealing with personnel issues, dealing with community elements, etc. I could never get away from budget development. Once I got into it, I would have my fingers all over that, all of the time. So, I was heavily involved in budget development/execution, expenditures, and procurement issues. Again, at least twice a week I would meet with those division chiefs and go over the course of the business that week, to ensure we were on the same page and whether they needed any help. No surprises. Surprises are bad. So, good communications and interactions with the staff.

Then, I would have unit visits that I would do periodically. I was always doing visits a couple of times a week—inspections of Group St. Pete. I wanted it immaculate. I felt that we represented the face of the Coast Guard to the public and everyone else coming in here. So the place had to look good. But, it was a busy week and the weeks went by like that. There was always something going on. If there was a personnel problem, it was deposited at your doorstep. If there was some kind of procurement issue, it was deposited at your doorstep. So, a lot of things. It was just unpredictable sometimes, but, it was great. It was a great organization and great fun.

JD: Were there times where you became acting Group Commander?

TC: Yes, when the CO was on leave or business travel. I would fill in and it worked well. Even when he was away, if there was a big issue that developed that he needed to be cognizant of, I would always know where he was on leave. There was a very good working relationship between the two bosses that I had there and myself. And again, as I said earlier, I was very, very fortunate to have had such talented, understanding guys that would give you a long leash and let you do your thing. Don't screw up—they would hold you accountable, but, you got a long leash and that made the tour very enjoyable.

JD: If the phone rang late at night, I'm guessing it was bad news?

TC: It usually was some kind of operational issue that was going on. Fortunately, we had no significant casualties people-wise. We had a casualty, maybe, when someone went on leave and they were driving a motorcycle, and fell off and broke their arm, or something. But, in terms of an operational issue casualty, I don't recall and that's great because sometimes that happens, and sometimes it happens because everyone is trying to do the right thing and there are just bad circumstances. But, we've lost helicopters and crews in the Coast Guard over time, and most of the time that's not because people are doing the wrong thing. Sometimes, you can always find something that you can tweak and do a little better, and you learn from a casualty. There is always an investigation and you learn from what are the contributing factors and how can you eliminate them in the future. But, sometime we just operate in very high-risk environments and stuff happens.

JD: Did you have to spend much time on the ops center watch floor?

TC: Not really. I would go in there periodically if there was a hot case on going. I would go in there and get an update from the watch. The group commander and the deputy group commander offices were separated from the ops building. They were in a separate building on a different part of the base. But it was a short walk if we needed to be there.

JD: Did you ever go back to visit the facilities later on?

TC: I have. Absolutely. I forget in what capacity, maybe it was Vice Commandant. There were additional facility improvements—an improved hangar. Renovations included new hangar doors, updated barracks, and the galley. So, it brought back fond memories. We even had the wardroom. There was a wardroom there, as part of the barracks complex. Earlier in its life, the base was an air station and they had a bigger officer component than a group component. So, there was a wardroom there and this wardroom had a World War II era project which decorated the bulkheads on all four sides with a Coast Guard painting: a mural of Coast Guard air operations in Alaska. It was a beautiful oil painting with Eskimos and all kinds of things. Over time, it was not kept up and, when people had painted the ceilings, trim paint had spattered on this canvas mural, and in several places a light switch had been cut into it. I felt that the mural had to be preserved and, while I was assigned there, we did preserve it through the use of non-appropriated funds. On my subsequent visit, later in my career, I was pleased to see the mural still there and it looked great.

JD: In the event that you had any spare time, what did you like to do?

TC: I took my kids to the beach, which they loved. For example, there were numerous sand dollars at St. Pete Beach, which they would dive for. They loved to take them home and let them bleach out in the sun. They would have sand dollars all over the house.

Activities were also available through the St. Petersburg Yacht Club. The group commander and the deputy group commander were complimentary members of the St. Petersburg Yacht Club, a very famous old yacht club. Great facilities. We got invited to all of their events. Unfortunately for the current St. Pete CG officers, you can't realize that type of benefit anymore. There has been an adjustment in ethics rules over time, to eliminate any possibility of any conflict of interest. But, at that time, there was no prohibition against it. My kids took sailing lessons there.

The little school that they went to was a parochial school named St. Raphael and it was a ten-minute bike ride away. They could get on their bikes and ride to school up in northeast St. Pete. It was a great place to raise a family. It really was a terrific place. A lot of things to do. Great weather. Summer storms were every afternoon, at about 16:00. You knew when you were going to get some serious rain and thunder. It's the lightning and thunder capital of the world. But, nevertheless, it's a great place to live.

JD: Would you say this was a rewarding assignment for you?

TC: Oh, absolutely. Many challenges and opportunities to master and to gain a sense of accomplishment. Someone was looking out for me over my career because I can't think of a bad duty assignment that I've had. Every Coast Guard assignment I've had, I've enjoyed. I mean, people might have certain impressions of what a given job is and isn't, or how it's going to contribute to you and your success in the Coast Guard. I didn't pay a lot of attention to that. I just dove into the job that I had and tried to leave my fingerprints on things in a positive way and do the best I could.

JD: Your three years is coming up and your next assignment is back at Headquarters. Was that something that you had asked for, or were you selected?

TC: Well, again, you know when you finish one operational assignment, the likelihood is you are going to go to a non-operational one, and you are going to go to a staff job. And I always thought *Well, let me go to one that can have some meaningful impact on me and my service*. My resume included planning, programming, and budgeting, so a staff assignment in that specialty was likely.

This is now 1983 and I was transferred from St. Pete to Washington to be a program reviewer in the Programs Division of the Chief of Staff CPA. The assignment was a four-year one. I knew all about CPA from my earlier experience in the RDT&E planning and programming staff. In fact, I had had frequent interaction with CPA members and several were still there. Most of the analysts were military, but the staff frequently had one or two civilian employees. So, in many ways, it was familiar territory.

I knew Headquarters. I knew what planning and programming was all about and experienced it. Now I had a chance to be the next echelon up. So, I thought if I had to go to a staff job, CPA was a very good fit. And so, I was fine with it. I felt fortunate. The Programs Division in Washington, DC is funnel for most of the important CG issues working there. If there is a program issue, policy issue, or a resource issue, it all goes through there. And, so you are at the heart of all policy and program issues that happen in the Coast Guard. There's not a better place to be, if you want to be engaged with serious, meaningful types of events. So, I put that on my wish sheet. That's where I wanted to go. I thought it was a good fit for me personally given my experience. Obviously, the detailers agreed and they sent me there.

So, I was there from 1983 to 1987. I was initially a lieutenant commander-type, and then a commander in that staff. The leadership laydown the first two years I was there: Admiral Jim

Gracey was the Commandant, followed by Admiral Paul Yost. The Vice Commandant was Vice Admiral Benedict L. Stabile, followed by Vice Admiral Jim Irwin. The Chief of Staff was Paul Yost first, and then he became Commandant from that job. Several commandants were made from the Chief of Staff job. Rear Admiral Deese Thompson, who was the 7th District Commander for some of the time I served as the St. Pete XO, was also the Chief of Staff during a portion of my CPA assignment. Rear Admiral Clyde Lusk was also Chief of Staff during my tour. The head of CPA was Captain Steve Duca, an aviator-type and a genuine character. Smart as a whip. He had a bark, but the bark was much worse than his bite. He was really a very capable, supportive leader of the staff. He was really strongly supported by his program reviewers. The deputy of the staff was Captain Dick Herr. He became a very close friend and was a very supportive mentor during the rest of my career. Captain Fred Hamilton relieved Dick partway through my assignment. So, that was sort of the personnel laydown, in terms of who I worked for during that time.

And, our family moved right back into the house that we had purchased when I moved from the Academy to R&D. We rented the house out when we left for St, Pete, and came back and occupied that house again. So, it was a pretty easy transition from all sides.

JD: In this assignment, you were one of eight program reviewers. Can you talk about what that entailed?

TC: Yes. You were usually assigned specific programs that you are cognizant over. For example, I was the AC&I Coordinator. So, I reviewed and assessed issues associated with it, developed capital investment plans, developed the associated budget and articulated it, defended it., and scrutinized it every which way to Sunday. And, I was the spokesperson for that account within the staff and outside the staff. I was also the program reviewer for the Office of Engineering. So, all engineering programs for the Chief of Staff, I had tabs on. That included naval engineering, aeronautical engineering, and civil engineering. So, my challenge was to know more than what the program knows about that program. So, I was in day-to-day communication with those folks. It was not only just the budget part, it's the program execution part and personnel part, organization part—all dimensions of that program. So, every reviewer in the Programs Division had a tasking like that, for a specific CG program area.

JD: How did you learn more about these programs than the programs?

TC: You do a lot of studying, and research, and talking. And you go out and walk the corridors, and you develop contacts and ties and credibility with the staffs involved. You attempt to gain their trust and confidence, and you help them move their program issues along, as much as you scrutinize them. So, if you are seen as a governing entity, but also a partner at the same time, that's success. If you don't, you are not going to get very far. And I'm not saying reviewers were more technically competent than the program staffs, but they came to know the program and its requirements exceedingly well.

JD: As one of the reviewers, can you talk about putting everything together for the budget? Has the process changed much?

TC: The planning, programing, and budgeting process has had common components over time. It includes planning factors, coming out with a long-range view, and the determination process under the plans and evaluations division of the Chief of Staff. As CPA reviewers, we'd have input into those documents. Resource change proposals (RCPs) were the documents that really got us involved as program reviewers because that's when the various program requirements were quantified and justified. Then we helped put together and formulate the budget for a given year. Then you submit a budget to the department, or the first-level of the budget food chain and they would have a whole list of questions, followed by a budget hearing. You would be fielding those questions. OMB was next. There would be hearings with questions. The same thing with Congress. So, you would be the clearinghouse for HQ on these matters. And congressional hearing support was a major, major work effort by the staff.

JD: Can you talk about what the process of preparing for a congressional hearing was like?

TC: Yes. It was a lot of paper. We developed hearing books. There would be a preliminary meeting, we would arrange between CG program managers, and with the Chief of Staff and CPA division chief. And the Commandant would frequently have a list of issues that would have to be developed, and included in the Commandants hearing book or the Chief of Staff's hearing book. It would be based upon our knowledge of the program. It would be our knowledge of what has transpired over the last year, in terms of incoming questions. It would also reflect CPA reviewer dialogue with Congressional staffers. The Commandant would go home and he would devour his hearing books to prepare for the hearings. Additional meetings between the Commandant and program managers might take place to answer questions he would have.

There would be a separate hearing for each of the House and Senate Authorization and Appropriation Committees. There is a different focus for each, and a different set of questions. So, all of those had to be run to ground and developed, and the objective was to have the best information we could for those that are considering our budget. Congressional staffers had a tough job too, and we had to make our principle as well-informed as possible on the issues that were in front of them.

JD: Can you talk about some of the programs you had to review?

TC: Yes. As AC&I Coordinator, I was involved with all CG programs and associated capital projects. There were numerous capital projects that supported the CG's ship and aircraft systems/subsystems, boats, C4ISR [Command, Control, Communications, Computers, Intelligence, Surveillance and Reconnaissance], and facility requirements. It also included all major aids-to-navigation, lighthouses, and electronics. So, hundreds of projects, worth billions of dollars, in those four years. They included the USCGC *Healy* [WAGB-20], the 378-foot high-endurance Fleet Renovation and Modernization (FRAM) project, the tail end of the acquisition of a 270-foot Medium Endurance Cutter, the 210-foot Mid-Life Maintenance Availability, just to mention a few.

JD: They are still both around today.

TC: Absolutely. We also programmed the WTGB-104 acquisition, and HH-60 and HH-65 acquisitions. I was in there from the get-go. That was to replace the H-3 and the H-52 helicopters.

JD: My dad used to fly the H-3, but for the Navy.

TC: I'll be darned. Well, the aircraft acquisitions were a major deal. The HH-65 was a major complication because it was a French helicopter made by Aérospatiale. We wanted to put in the turbo engine, which was designed for and mated optimally with the airframe. We got forced by

Congress to put in a Honeywell engine, which troubled us from a readiness perspective for years and years. I've got another story with that one because I was involved in trying to fix that program later, in a subsequent tour. The major sensors projects for our CG aircraft were multi-million-dollar acquisitions. The Electronics Technician School and the Unaccompanied Housing Projects at Petaluma that were also successful in our AC&I budget—brand new, multi-million-dollar facilities. The health clinic and admin building in Kodiak were also substantial facility construction projects. Numerous search-and-rescue stations rebuilds, family housing proposals, lighthouse modernization projects, modernizing and automating all of the lighthouses were successful. It is a huge list and, as a reviewer, you had to be intimately involved with all aspects of the process.

JD: Did you have a favorite program out of all of them?

TC: I think I liked the sensor projects. They were really interesting. By the way, the toughest sell in getting budget support was for our shore facilities. What happens is the priority becomes—and, rightfully so—cutters, planes, and ships and boats. The challenge on the shore side is that we have a considerable shore side capital plant worth billions. We were fortunate to attain an AC&I appropriation anywhere between $250 and $310 million a year. And, at that level, it was grossly inadequate relative to the value of our capital plant. I did put a model together that looked at the total value of our capital plant versus it's expected planned service life. To maintain this overall capital plant, at this kind of level, you need this much money per year if you are going to keep it around and replace it when it comes due. My calculations and my argument said we needed $600 to $700 million a year at that point in time, at least to maintain the current value of our capital plant given the cumulative planned service lives. We were getting $300 million. So, all of these projects were precious because only the crème-de-la-crème of our needs got serviced.

JD: Were there any programs that gave you a fit, like you just cringed because you had to deal with this one because it was like a problem child?

TC: No. I don't remember any problem child programs. Some of them were more effective and efficient than others. Our best managed project tended to be those in the aviation community. The aviation operational folks and the aeronautical engineers worked effectively together on things. They were very talented, very convincing. Vice Admiral Terry Cross, some years later, was my Vice Commandant. In the mid-eighties, he was involved with the aviation division and its appropriation requirements. Good stuff always came from him. The aviation division helped with hearing books and questions, and they were always done well. Captain Ed Barrett was also an excellent aviation professional—later became a Rear Admiral. He was the aeronautical division chief, and was heavily involved in projects associated with aircraft and aircraft systems. Great guy to work with and had a wonderful personality. So, they were all good, but the aviators were particularly good, I thought.

JD: How did you keep track of all of the programs? Was there a book that spelled everything out, like the different sensors?

TC: All of the CGs budget documents—the determinations, the resource change proposals, etc. Hats off to Admiral Gracey for developing this stuff—they were critical in staying on top of programs and projects. The execution side of a program—especially multi-year ones—once funded, were also closely monitored by the Chief of Staff divisions.

JD: The first time that you were in DC, at Headquarters, and dealing with the Department of Transportation was during the Carter administration. There was change, and this time it is with the Reagan administration. Was there a change in the perception of the Coast Guard at DOT?

TC: It kind of ebbed and flowed. There is turnover in the Department of Transportation when there is a change in the White House because all of the political appointee positions that change out. The Coast Guard, in contrast, does not have one political appointee. It has civilian personnel, but not one political appointee in the entire Coast Guard. I saw that as a good thing quite frankly. But, obviously, there are reasons for having that kind of presence, but not necessarily in our organization.

What was the new team at DOT during the time you refer to? During the bulk of that time, I was in CPA as a reviewer from 1983 to 1987, it was Elizabeth Dole, and she was a pretty strong advocate. Andrew Card was also part of the Department of Transportation. He later came back as White House Chief of Staff under President George W. Bush. Card was a Massachusetts guy, by the way, and he came from a town a couple of towns away from the town I grew up in. That was always a great icebreaker when I ran into him later, during my term as Vice Commandant and Commandant. He was a very capable leader and was very supportive—he thought highly of the USCG, both when he was with DOT and later in the White House. But overall, DOT support, including staff support, ebbed and flowed, given the overall resource demands, priorities, and associated budget competition within DOT. Clearly, the Coast Guard is not the only demand that a secretary has on their plate. The other agencies in DOT are important agencies. The FAA is an important agency, and is critical to the United States of America and aviation safety. Then there are the highways. Everyone wants a highway. Everyone wants a new road. So, you've got these pressures that pop up, so there's a balancing act. And the CG had to compete in that environment.

JD: Talking about pressure, I was reviewing Admiral Jim Gracey's oral history that was conducted by the Naval Institute, to prepare for this session, and he talked about how he spent most of his time as Commandant fighting off proposals to privatize certain missions of the Coast Guard and while the DOD was receiving huge funding increases, and the Coast Guard was DOT, which was non-defense, was being cut. Can you talk about that?

TC: I talked a little about that phenomenon previously where the DOD has an armed forces-related budget food chain or budget reviewers that are familiar with the ins and outs of the armed service programs and capital budgeting. And then there was the non-national security budget review process that the CG was subject to, even though we are an armed force of the US. So, I always thought that there was an additional education to do every time our budget went forward.

The issue of contracting out government functions popped up frequently, even though we are an armed service. It was OMB Circular A-76, which provided the OMB impetus, which was if a function met certain criteria, then it was subject to a A-76 review for contracting it out. You had to do a series of studies and they gave every agency a threshold. You had to do a detailed study to justify not contracting out a targeted function. It happened at its height when Admiral Gracey was Chief of Staff and Commandant.

One of the big A-76 targets was our aids-to-navigation function—all the buoy tenders. OMB's going-in position was, "Why is the government doing this? Why are we doing navigational aids in navigable waters of the United States of America? We should have the private sector do this.

This is something that we can contract out." The fact that our buoy tenders are multi-mission assets doing multiple missions ultimately prevented them from being contracted out. It has been one of our major defenses in defending our programs and preserving our assets.

We are multi-mission. We are maritime. And we are military. Those three things. The three "Ms" as I call them. They are powerful. There are powerful ways to appropriately justify our mission. It's a powerful argument and, by the way, look what efficiency the American public is getting. That philosophy goes for our people as well. Most are multi-mission-trained and experienced. In a nutshell, you get a two-for, three-for, and a four-for from Coast Guard assets and people. The taxpayers are getting a huge bang for the buck. And, that's something that we articulated over and over again. Sometimes it fell on deaf ears, but certainly it's true, and I think it's absolutely true to this day.

JD: Admiral Gracey talked a lot about the J. Peter Grace Commission.

TC: There was the Balanced Budget and Emergency Deficit Control Act of 1985. That was Gramm-Rudman-Hollings Balanced Budget Act and that carved out $230 million out of our operational expense account, which was a lot of money for us. *How are we going to accommodate that?*

JD: How did you?

TC: Doing planning for the Gramm-Rudman-Hollings was another collateral job I had as a program reviewer. I coordinated the programs that we could whittle down while minimizing impact to missions. I was one of the architects of the reduction approach to that. We tried to do things that made sense—things that wouldn't seriously impact our operational readiness and overall service to the public. I forced the programmers to identify those things on the bottom end of the ladder; get rid of things that were old and aging and tired anyway, etc.

The biggest, hardest battles were attempts at closing outdated small boat stations or air stations. There was always a constituency issue with selected members of Congress. We got rid of some via budget reductions, but it was hard, and the victories were few and far between.

The other big related collateral duty was the Gilbert study. If you remember, I talked earlier about Ed Gilbert. He was my boss in St. Petersburg. The Gilbert study was another attempt in the face of budget reductions to get more efficient and attend to budget reduction mandates without seriously cutting services. It was an effort to reorganize, reduce headcount, and get a little more efficient. My task was to develop a concept paper for the Commandant's approval that would articulate what reorganization we should focus on in this budget cutting environment of the 1980s. The concept paper identified several options including an outline addressing how to execute each. It specified a flag-led study team, and what type of members it should have. The concept paper was submitted to the Commandant for his approval to commence the study. He approved, for further study, the recommendation to consolidate support services from various CG districts into two maintenance logistics commands, east and west coast. I was also responsible, along with several other CPA reviewers, in reviewing and commenting on the work of the study group. The study, when completed, essentially recommended the concept that was outlined in the concept paper. The Commandant and the Chief of Staff ultimately approved everything I had put forward in the concept paper, except reorganizing operational field commands into sectors. My assessment was that they thought tackling field commands, along with support services, was too big of a bite.

There were in fact two flag study groups that were launched, based upon my concept paper including one near the tail end of my CPA assignment. The second study involved a reorganization of Coast Guard Headquarters, again to get more efficient and reduce headcount. Looking back, I can say I that I was involved in almost every major reorganization the Coast Guard undertook during my active duty service time.

JD: What rank were you when you were writing these concept papers?

TC: I had just made Commander.

JD: You had to feel really good about yourself just because your papers are being approved by the Commandant.

TC: Yes. But I had a great deal of help, especially from my fellow CPA reviewer, Commander Fred Hamilton—Captain Hamilton when he retired. He was the deputy in CPA. He offered great ideas and did the major blocking for me, to put it into football terms, and so, he was incredibly helpful in making the study process work. Fascinating times and, when you look back, you had a chance to really fundamentally alter how we conducted our business. I think the support function improved, bottom line. Of course, there have been additional changes to the whole support layout since I retired. There's been another iteration of this that's even further centralized and focused for support. But, our efforts were the building blocks that allowed that to happen.

JD: What was the layout of the concept paper?

TC: It was essentially a position paper and it laid out the issues and the current inefficiencies. It identified potential savings and opportunities. There were a number of moving parts to all of this. One detailed the option of getting off of Governor's Island and moving to Portsmouth, and then working that whole issue on how are we going to get to Portsmouth—steps involved, costs, timeline, etc. You've got to understand that it was done at a time when we are having all of these external pressures to take our budget away. So, failing in this effort was not an option. We don't want to lose ships, boats, planes and our capacity to do the King's business. We don't want to lose that. *So, how can we do other things that will avoid that?* In the end, we were successful in preserving most of our operational capacity. We laid off some assets, but the bulk of it, we were successful in keeping.

JD: Were there any things that you recommended that, years later on, you said to yourself, *I wish I didn't recommend that. I could really use that capability today?*

TC: No. And I'm saying it wasn't perfect, but all of the changes were in the right quadrant. And those things that we closed were meritorious. They should have been closed and the ones we couldn't close were because we just couldn't develop enough momentum in the face of the political opposition to closing.

This is no hit on Congressmen or Senators who were protecting the interests of their constituents and their districts' resources. That's what they are paid to do. I don't have any problem with that. But, from an operational perspective, that wasn't the highest priority for us to keep funding, especially when we had to tie up ships and aircraft because we didn't have the budget for fuel.

So, we were trying to do things right even though we didn't have any BRAC mechanism to help push a number of budget reductions through.

JD: What were your priorities when you tasked to chop out the $200 million?

TC: The priorities were to preserve our essential operational capacity and capabilities: boats, ships, and planes. We were challenged in keeping the assets alive, given the size of our budgets. Additional national deficit driven cuts added to the problem. Our appropriations were not sufficient to maintain the capital plant that we owned, whether it was shore facilities or whether it was a boat, ship, or plane. If you don't get that funding, you're in the consumption mode. You are consuming your capital plant. We were running ships old enough to collect social security. That's how old some of our ships were when we tied them up. They were sixty, sixty-five-year-old ship like USCGC *Acushnet* [WMEC-167].

JD: *Acushnet* first saw service in World War II.

TC: Yes. That cutter and its crews provided long and outstanding service to the public, but at a point, older assets stop being reliable and cost effective, and technologically obsolete. So, we were consuming our capital plant and we were in a tough situation. We had all of these external things to shrink government and get more efficient like the Hammer Award and Gramm-Rudman-Hollings. All of those things which, on the face of it, were meritorious things, but it hit us—our service—very, very hard. So, the question is: *How do you manage that? How do you attend to the mandates of Congress and the White House and still maintain the peak capabilities of the United States Coast Guard?* That was the focus.

JD: Did you get to work with Admiral Gracey much?

TC: I did interact with him periodically, and, of course, also with Admiral Yost. I mostly dealt with the Chief of Staff and, obviously, CPA. If I can remember, the Chief of CPA sequence right: it was Steve Duca, Kent Williams, and Jack Trainer. And, of course, Kent Williams went on to be Chief of Staff. Kent was a very outgoing, dynamic, capable, and effervescent type of guy.

JD: Admiral Gracey had served in CPA earlier in his career.

TC: He is considered the godfather of CPA. We bow down to him. Look at the graduates of CPA: Dick Herr, later Chief of Staff and Vice Commandant; Dave Pekoske, later a Vice Admiral; Thad Allen, later Chief of Staff, Area Commander, and Commandant; and, numerous other flags—Jeff Garrett, Roy Casto, Gary Blore, etc. Admiral Gracey started the foundation for CPA, as it is known today—the culture, the processes, etc. The CG owes him a great deal.

There was a famous picture of seagulls. It was from the *New Yorker* magazine, and was a picture of seagulls just sitting on a rooftop. You just see the peak of the roof, and they are all are sitting on it, and all of the seagulls are looking and pointed one way—beaks headed one way, except this one gull looking the other way. Admiral Gracey perpetuated that image. What he wanted CPA reviewers to be like: to think different think against the crowd, when appropriate; don't think conventionally; think outside the box, to get things done. A symbol.

CPA is tight group that works hard. We worked long hours, but had a great feeling of accomplishment. When people left CPA, they would get out the seagull picture to serve as a *You've done good here* memento. Gracey—not only was he CPA, but he was later Chief of Staff. So, he continued to reinforce all of the processes he introduced. So, they became very embedded. It would be interesting to go back now, and just kind of sit in the room and see if the same types of things still persist. I'm sure a lot of those still persist, as I'm sure there are some changes—as there should be. But, procedurally, I'm sure a lot of those things persist.

JD: We are coming up on the end of your tour in this. Is there anything else you would like to add about your Headquarters assignment before we go on?

TC: Not really—just that it was a whirlwind. It was challenging and very rewarding all at the same time. And it made me a better officer. My next job was going to Group Long Island Sound (GLIS) from 1987 to 1990. CPA was very rewarding, but getting back into CG operations was my goal. So, we were thrilled about my upcoming assignment. My wife was a local lovely from New London, Connecticut. I met her and married her in New London. I met her when I was going to the Coast Guard Academy. I went to Wesleyan University post-graduate school. I taught at the Coast Guard Academy for four years in New London. I got another degree. So, I had been in Connecticut a number of times, but I hadn't been there in an operational capacity. The other thing that was very, very attractive to me was that it had a Captain of the Port function along with group ops; and there's a trend here. GLIS would get me not only into SAR and law enforcement and aids-to-navigation missions, but would get me into marine environmental protection, port safety, and security. Maritime Defense Zone Concept was coming of age at that time. I was Maritime Defense Zone Commander, in addition to Group Commander. It offered the concept of more integrated operations—something very attractive to me. It may not be the biggest command, but it was diverse, most interesting, and very busy. It is a busy AOR. So, I felt very, very fortunate to move on to Long Island Sound.

JD: Was your family ready to leave DC for Long Island?

TC: Yes. Absolutely. One of the challenges was finding a place to live up there. It was at the height of the housing market. It was in 1987, and the housing market in Connecticut was peaking. I have a great propensity to buy high and sell low, and it's not a function of competency or lack of it—it's a function of what housing options existed at the time. And, in 1987, it was a challenging market—you have no control over market circumstances.

Unfortunately, in a number of these assignment relocations, I ended up losing money on houses. For this assignment to Connecticut, I had to go up three or four times, and every time I went, I was in a bidding war on a house. I finally nailed down a house in Westbrook, Connecticut, which is about 35- to 40-minutes east of New Haven, the HQ for GLIS. It was a nice, brand new Cape Cod-style house on a four-acre piece of land in the woods of Westbrook. I loved it and I bought high there. The next year the housing market collapsed. When I sold three years later, I sold at a little bit of a loss. But, it was a great experience and everyone wanted to go to Connecticut. It was close to New London, and wasn't too far from my family in Massachusetts. So, from a family perspective, it worked out very, very well and from a professional perspective, it worked out very well.

JD: Was it a problem being surrounded by Yankees fans?

TC: It's amazing. There is a line there, somewhere—it kind of goes through New Haven or maybe it's the Connecticut River. People to the east of that in Connecticut are mostly Red Sox fans. So, there were ample Red Sox fans. But, you're right. There are also a great many Yankees fans. But, you could watch that rivalry firsthand, which was a good thing.

JD: Do you remember who you relieved as Commander of Group Long Island Sound?

TC: Yes. Dave Lyons.

JD: Can you talk about the transition?

TC: Dave Lyons graduated one class ahead of me at the Coast Guard Academy—the class of 1967. Three years later, I was relieved by a classmate of mine—Bruce Dickey. It is interesting to note that this was a well sought-after job. Everyone had the same view of it as I did because, subsequently, there were two other very successful officers that occupied the same job I had. One was Thad Allen (future Commandant)—he was also Group Commander Long Island Sound—and Dave Pekoske (future Vice Commandant) was another one. So, some interesting folks that went through there.

JD: Very interesting. Did you have a change of command ceremony?

TC: We did—it was a little more elaborate than what I recall I had for *Cape Morgan*, for which I stood on the fan tail of the WPB. It was on the edge of New Haven Harbor. The base stood on the east side of the harbor in a fairly modern facility. The ceremony was well attended. A large section of community maritime interests attended, many relating to the command's Captain of the Port function.

JD: Can you tell me about Group Long Island Sound's area-of-responsibility?

TC: Yes. When the 3rd and 1st Districts merged as part of budget cutting reorganization efforts, GLIS absorbed some of the old 3rd District territory, namely the sound shore of Long Island. We took over Captain of the Port responsibility for the south shore of Long Island. So, basically, we had all of Long Island from the Captain of the Port perspective. So, it went from Rockaway all the way to Montauk, almost to Block Island. It went from the Connecticut-Rhode Island border, and extended between Long Island and Connecticut, and drew south. That's where we went on the east side—almost to Block Island, and then all the way down—for Captain of the Port purposes. Then, for group operations purposes, we had all of the Long Island Sound, from roughly the Merchant Marine Academy, down on the north side of Long Island near the city, all the way up to Fishers Island Sound, part of Block Island Sound, and all of Long Island Sound.

The AOR was interesting. It was a major highway for barge traffic, tanker traffic, tank barge. All of the oil refined out of New York, port Arthur Kill and all of that, would come up through Hell's Gate, up into the sound, all destined for New England. A good bulk of New England oil supplies came from oil barges—tank barges out of New York. It was just a nonstop highway. It was also one of the busiest recreational boating areas on the east coast. We had regatta, after regatta, after regatta, after regatta in Long Island Sound. So, you were de-conflicting that traffic all the time—regulating, prescribing, and permitting various sailing regattas. It was an area of numerous yacht clubs. Prestigious yacht clubs like Stanford, and all of the others. It's Great Gatsby country—the ascots, blue blazers, caps, and all of that kind of thing. Anyway, it was a very interesting AOR.

JD: Can you talk about some of the units that were assigned to Group Long Island?

TC: Yes. In terms of number of units, it was smaller than the group in St. Petersburg that I had been assigned to. It included Station Eaton's Neck, a small boat station located on the northern tip of Eaton's Neck on Long Island—Great Gatsby country. By the way, Eaton's Neck was the site of one of the very first expenditures by our new nation in 1789. One of the first, if not the first, acts-appropriated money for building lighthouses in New England and New York. And Eaton's Neck was one of the first sites. So, there is a lighthouse there at Eaton's Neck. It should note that there are 23 lighthouses in Group Long Island's AOR. A lot of them are water-borne lights, only accessible by boat or buoy tender. A bit of historical trivia—the Race Rock lighthouse at the entrance to Long Island Sound Race took seven years to build, after the Civil War, from 1871 to 1878. Nine people lost their lives building that because of the conditions they were building it in. It is very treacherous water there.

There's a station and port security detachment in Port Jefferson on the north side of Long Island; there is a station at New London; a station at New Haven; there is an SAR detachment at Fishers Island; and there was an 82-foot patrol boat in New London. There was also a small icebreaking harbor tug, USCGC *Bollard* [WYTL-656140].

JD: Can you talk about the responsibilities of a Maritime Defense Zone (MDZ) Commander?

TC: Well, it was all about security, organization, and contingency plans for port and coastal defense. MDZ addressed various security conditions, e.g., *How do you mobilize? Who does what? What are the authorities? How do you protect certain areas or facilities? How do you put security zones in place? Where are the vulnerabilities and risk, etc.?* The MDZ function fits nicely with the Captain of the Port function and associated authorities. In addition to LIS MDZ Commander, I was the Captain of the Port of New Haven and New London. With those authorities, a permanent security zone was established to protect Submarine Group 2 at the submarine base in Groton, Connecticut. General Dynamics was also an area periodically subject to security zones. In fact, there are numerous facilities on the Thames River that had security implications. The GLIS MDZ Commander shared the AR security responsibility with the Chief of Staff of Submarine Group 2. Together, we developed contingency plans and coordinated them.

JD: What were some of the contingencies that you planned for?

TC: Most were focused on New London and Submarine Group 2 security. Also, LIS Nuclear power plant protection. We identified the high national security interest areas and then we created appropriate security arrangements. In many cases, it is a federal, state, and local shared responsibility, but all incorporated into multi-agency contingency plans for security.

JD: Can you talk about what was involved in escorting a submarine?

TC: We would detail the prescribed resources that would support it. It was usually a WPB and a number of small boats. The coordinator of the operation would be on the WPB, and they would be escorted by boats coming in, when need be—when the threat existed.

One time that we did invoke a security zone and elements of our security plan, was for the September 9, 1989 commissioning of USS *Pennsylvania* [SSBN-735] at the Naval Underwater Sound Lab/Warfare Center and CG Station New London. Greenpeace and other protestors were out in force. They had their own boats, and they were intruding on the zone by doing kamikaze-type runs. We had the FBI and Naval Criminal Investigative Service (NCIS) positioned at the New London station. We had observers on the station roof. We had patrol boats and small boats deployed to control the security zone. I was there on the patrol boat, coordinating things, and it was interesting. We had Greenpeace inflatable boats doing kamikaze runs into the security zone. They launched about four boats, all at the same time, during these Kamikaze runs. Several were apprehended and its members arrested. Now, this operation just involved a protest. But, it's one example of invoking the security zone construct.

JD: It sounds like your group covered a lot of the Coast Guard missions. What were the biggest ones in terms of resources?

TC: Captain of the Port was a big one. There were an amazing number of tanker vessels coming into New Haven that would supply Vermont, New Hampshire, and upper Connecticut with a lot of fuel from a fuel farm on the Branford-New Haven line. So, there was a lot of tanker traffic coming in and we were overseeing the safe movement of that tank traffic in and out while coordinating with the pilot's associations.

There was also a lot of Marine Environmental Protection (MEP) business. There were waterways spills. Mystery spills that we had to track down, and go to our R&D center; get oil fingerprinting; pinpoint the culprit, and be prepared to take over the responsibility for spill response, if we couldn't identify the spiller. So, MEP, security and port security, port ops, safe tanker traffic, both barge and tanker vessels, were missions that were time and resource intensive.

In addition, there was plenty of SAR because there is a high density of recreational boats in LIS. The group was also big on ATON—we had twenty-three lighthouses to maintain. Our aids-to-navigation team on Long Island Sound is one of the biggest ones in the Coast Guard because of the number of floating and fixed navigational aids in the AOR.

Clearly, it was a busy group with a number of different missions. Our 82-footer conducted fisheries patrols off of Cape Cod. The 82-footer deployed outside-of-the-group AOR to do that work. The only function that we didn't have was an officer in charge of marine inspections, documentation, and licensing (OCMI). OCMI New York provided that function and covered an AOR all the way to the Connecticut-Rhode Island border, overlapping our COTP and group responsibilities. The existence of this overlapping functionality was just another experience that convinced me that we needed to change the group/MSO structure throughout the CG. But, at least in LIS, I had two-thirds of the equation: Captain of the Port and Group Commander.

JD: Can you talk about the unique responsibilities of Captain of the Port (COTP)? You are almost like a god.

TC: The authorities embedded in the COTP are extensive and codified in statute. They cover authorities over facilities, ships, maritime personnel, and the waterways. Before I even got to GLIS, I felt that I should brush up on the vast amount of COTP authorities and regulations that are in the Code of Federal Regulations (CFR). So, I prepped up on that as much as I could and then just lived it when I got there, and when certain things came up. One of the biggest cases that I recall from GLIS was a Captain of the Port case and a SAR case combined. The incident further cemented the idea that an integrated field command was the way to go, to have time to start sorting through the deck when there is a crisis.

The incident occurred on August 31, 1988. It involved an explosion in a cargo tank onboard the Maltese tank vessel *Fiona*, moored about two miles offshore, near the Long Island Lighting Company (LILCO), while preparing to discharge fuel oil. LILCO had an offshore docking arrangement: little pier structure than a pipeline that went ashore, and the tank vessels would come in and moor there for oil transfer. Before the *Fiona* could unloaded its cargo, they had to have it surveyed. They measured/sampled tank content, they gauged the tanks. They had a commercial contracted inspector doing that. When he did that at about 22:15, he set off a spark and an explosion occurred in the cargo tank, blowing the three-quarter-inch steel hatch cover up over the side, killing one. The explosion caused broken windows half a mile ashore. So, it soon became a SAR case because we were looking for any injured, and/or to recover bodies. But, it also turned into a Captain of the Port issue because when needed to understand the reason for the explosion; any ongoing threat with the cargo; and the disposition of the vessel, crew, and facilities ashore. We brought in a chemist to do further testing and found out that a number of the tanks were only half full or three quarters full, and that the atmosphere in the tanks were in an explosive detonation range. Also, some of the void spaces—tankers have void spaces on either side of their tanks—were in the detonation range.

So, the ship remained in a hazardous condition. And to complicate matters, the Long Island Lighting Company wanted *Fiona* away from their dock, requesting a Captain of the Port order to move the vessel immediately. In response, I did order it off and I put it in anchorage, a short distance away. Ultimately, we had the vessel and contractors inert the *Fiona*'s tanks to eliminate the explosive risks. It was No. 6 fuel oil. No. 6 is that heavy, heavy oil that power plants burn. But No. 6 doesn't explode, supposedly. So, the vessel had not gone through an inert procedure with their tanks before beginning then gauging process. The problem was created by having less-than-full tanks over an extended oceanic voyage and a previous cargo of highly volatile naphtha concentrate. It was an older ship that had developed hairline cracks in some of the tanks, with seepage into void spaces, and the tank had developed an explosive atmosphere.

Ultimately, we had the ship inert its tanks away for the dock facilities and to get re-inspected. To complicate matters, the Lighting Company refused the cargo, saying it was contaminated. But they finally accepted it at $.50 on the dollar. Nothing really wrong with the cargo—it was the air around the cargo. This played out over seven or eight days. Then, the state of New York's legislative authorities were all up in arms about it and they had field hearings, for which I attended and provided testimony. As a result of the incident, the legislature wanted to make Long Island Sound a tanker-free zone. I testified to the overall safety issues involved and to the economic consequences of their tanker-free zone proposal. It was a very interesting process. In the end, they let reason prevail and didn't make LIS a tanker-free zone.

I note this case because it is illustrative of the range of COTP involvement in these types of matters, and the authorities and influence a COTP has.

JD: Was this the first time you ever had to testify before anybody?

TC: Yes. First legislative-type of hearing. I had been to others while in HQ, as staff support, but did not testify.

JD: Who was the district commander?

TC: Rear Admiral Richard Rybacki was District Commander. Admiral Paul Yost was still Commandant. Clyde Lusk was the Chief of Staff at Headquarters. Secretary of Transportation (SECDOT) was James H. Burnley IV and Samuel K. Skinner, in that order. Then Captain and later Rear Admiral Bob North was at Group/COTP New York. Bob was a great marine safety guy. The CG always put a marine safety guy in New York, just because there is so much marine safety business there. Fred Hamilton, former Deputy CPA and good friend, was at Group Cape

Cod. So, I had well-known entities on either side. We got together a great deal and ensured coordinated ops between our respective commands. We would have periodic CO conferences with the District Commander and all of the COs in the 1st District would go to Boston. I advocated, on a recurring basis, the need to merge field commands—to go to a Sectors concept, combining group ops, COTP, and OCMI functions. Ultimately, Admiral Rybacki commissioned a study group to examine the issue, which included the chief of ops in the district, Captain of the Port New York, Bob North; Gary Blore, another ex-CPA reviewer; myself; and several others. We met for two or three weeks before Christmas, at OTIS Air National Guard Base on Cape Cod. When we finished, our recommendation was to create activities (now known as sectors) throughout the 1st District, along with all the details on how to do that. Rear Admiral Marshall E. Gilbert, who was a close friend of Rybacki, also supported it. When the proposal was submitted to Vice Admiral Howard B. Thorsen, Atlantic Area Commander headquartered in New York City at the time, he disapproved it. From my perspective, our recommendation was spot on. Nevertheless, it was my second failed attempt to integrate field operations. But, you've got to be patient. Like fine wine, it takes time. When you are going against the grain a little bit, it takes time.

JD: Did you save these studies for future use when you would be in a position to implement them?

TC: I did. It served as good reference material.

JD: You were obviously a change agent throughout your career. What advice would you have for officers today that have ideas, and are putting together concept papers, that might have to run it up the flagpole and get shot down—like in your case, at least two times?

TC: Be persistent. Make sure you have your act together, do your homework, make the best case you can, and prepare the battlefield. Quantify, quantify, quantify. And the process is almost as important, maybe more, as the message. So, you've got to ensure that the review and the approval process is at least equitable, fair, and open-minded. Build alliances. Build supporters—over here, over there—as much as you can, so you are not looked at as a crazy, lone stranger with crazy ideas. Not that we were like that in the first couple of cases, but it was just a tough concept to sell because it was such massive a change. You got to keep in mind how longstanding the tradition and culture is regarding certain parts of an organization, especially with the CG and its long-standing culture, values, and histories. So, you have all of that inertia against it.

JD: You mentioned that in the last year of your tour at Group Long Island that you were promoted to the rank of Captain. At what point did you think about flag rank? Did you think *I might want to try and become an admiral?*

TC: I think I can truthfully say, I was never obsessed with that. You think about it. You also think about the possibilities, at some point, of doing something outside the CG. A lot of things cross your mind. But, I was never obsessed with it, I don't think. Let other people judge, but I don't think I was. You know, my approach was, *Have fun with what you are doing, do the best job you can, enjoy a lot of satisfaction about that, and let the chips fall where they may.* And, if I'm competitive within the advancement process, whether for captain or for flag, so be it.

JD: You mentioned when you were down in St. Petersburg, that your Group Commander gave you a long leash. Did you give your XO at Group Long Island a long leash?

TC: Well, you need to ask him. How you view that is what glasses you've got on, or where you sit. I think I did. Joe Coccia was my XO tat Long Island Sound.

JD: Can you talk about the annual Sailfest event?

TC: It hadn't been in existence that long when I was up there, maybe eight or nine years. It focused on Thames River and it was a New London thing. Most of it was ashore and the merchants in the town were very supportive because they had entertainment, and booths, and parades ashore. There were a lot of incentives for boaters to come in, park their boat, and go ashore. There were some sailboat races and things like that.

JD: Okay. How did you divide the responsibilities when you were Deputy? Was it the same?

TC: Well not unlike what I did when I was on the other end of the desk in St. Petersburg. It was similar at Long Island Sound. Again, the only new twist was the Captain of the Port responsibilities. The management of the inbox and the administrative details of the group was left to the XO.

JD: How did you manage your inbox? Before email, that is.

TC: I wanted it staffed before it got to me. I believe in completed staff work. So, if something incomplete came to me, I said, "You're asking me to do the staff work?" That's not how it works. I said, "You need to do a complete examination of this issue and come forward to me with a conclusion or recommendation. Where's your recommendation?" So, it was a learning experience for some of the staff, but that's what I expected. I didn't expect to do the staff work for that person. But, I will make the final decision. I will be glad to do that but I want a substantive input on a decision that will be an informed decision, not guess work. I'm going to ask you questions. I'm going to ask your opinion. I want it. I need it. You are the expert in the area and I may ask other parts of the staff, as well. So, after six months or so, everyone got the routine down.

JD: Can you talk about the role of reservists and auxiliarists in Group Long Island?

TC: They were very active—really active everywhere I've been. We had reservists augment our port security detachment in Port Jefferson on Long Island. The reason that we had one was, there were a lot of tank ships that went into Port Jefferson. People would be surprised how many tank vessels are in the Long Island Sound. Huge. The reservists, many firemen or policemen during their full-time job, were very active in the augmentation of CG missions.

I would have to stress that the auxiliarists were very active too. I was impressed with the amount of administrative support that they gave. I always had an auxiliarist in the group office doing meaningful stuff, so the active duty didn't have to do it. They also supported with both personal aircraft and boats. There was one difference between the Long Island Sound and St. Petersburg, and it was the sailing regatta after sailing regatta, and other boating events in LIS that needed permits and on-the-water oversight. They had to apply for permits for these events. They had to be reviewed, and then they had to be staffed. Operationally, the boats had to be put into position to enforce the regulations of the permit. You could set the terms of engagement in your permit. It was particularly important for fireworks events. There were many water-borne fireworks launched from a barge, along the Connecticut coastline. The manpower of the Auxiliary was indispensable to our success in controlling these events, because it was one after another after another after another, all of July. So, trying to orchestrate that was challenging, high-paced ops.

JD: Did you feel, as a Group Commander, that you were on duty 24/7?

TC: Yes, you always had to be available for a call and all of these things seem to happen at inopportune times. You had to be available 24/7. I made myself reachable one way or another, no matter where I was.

JD: Did cell phones come along then or was it a little bit later?

TC: It was still those old Motorola things—the big things with the antennas sticking out of the top. I usually had a beeper. Or, if I was out at a certain place and couldn't be notified, there was a place that I would notify the ops center of my contact info.

JD: Is there anything else you would like to add about your time as Group Commander?

TC: It was a great assignment because it was so diverse in terms of its missions, and it got me into every aspect of the community. Just as an example, there was a New Haven pollution co-op comprised of the terminal owners, the pilot's association, and the owners of the tank vessels, coming in and out of the port. This pollution co-op said, "Okay, if we have a spill, this is how we are going to cooperate together to deal with it. We are going to define the process to share pollution response equipment. Who does what to whom? How do we relate to the Coast Guard?" All of that was for effective pollution prevention and response, all built into a multi-agency co-op. It was good spirited, very cooperative, and the right thing to do by industry. It also got me into the maritime community throughout the AOR.

The same thing with the yacht clubs that are all up and down Long Island Sound in the New York and Connecticut shorelines. They would typically close the yacht club at the end of the boating season in winter. Basically, they would decommission the yacht club and then they would recommission that yacht club the following spring. I would get invited. I couldn't go to all of the opening ceremonies, but I did attend a few of them. It is a great way to build relationships into those yacht clubs and good avenues of communication during the boating season.

JD: Did being Captain of the Port come in handy years later, like on 9/11?

TC: The experience was very valuable because so much of the post-9/11 world is about port security. I became exceedingly familiar with all of the statutes and regulations associated with port security and Captain of the Port. I gained experience in dealing with how you bring people together to do contingency planning, because you just can't throw something over the transom and say, "Here's the plan. Everyone, abide by it." It doesn't work that way. I mean you've got to have eager participation by all of the major owners of the issue to contribute to the solution. Then they buy-in and they will cooperate when something really happens.

JD: What advice would you have for officers that have been named Sector Commander, and how to prepare to be Captain of the Port?

TC: I would make sure that you have competence built into your staff. You are not going to have everyone that knows everything, but make sure that the competence areas are there. One of the concerns in going to sectors was whether we were going to water down the technical focus and experience of the marine safety function, in particular. So, you've got to ensure that you attend to that issue. And you must embrace the operational concepts that ensure an integrated systems approach to CG business and its missions.

JD: You had been selected to attend the Industrial College of the Armed Forces (ICAF) while at Group Long Island. Can you explain your decision on why you declined the offer?

TC: The reason I declined was it would short-tour me as Commander of Group Long Island Sound. I would have only had two years at Long Island Sound, not three. I was having fun there. It was meaningful employment. I didn't want to leave a command assignment to short-tour myself to a classroom. I also knew with absolute certainty that 99% of the people that go to ICAF end up in Headquarters following ICAF. I've already done that Headquarters stuff. I had been there a number of times. And very importantly, I did not want to uproot my family more than I had already done. So, I declined it.

JD: Can you tell us about your next assignment? I know it was a tough duty.

TC: I had orders to the 14th District out in Hawaii. I was going to be the head of their administrative division, a captain's billet. I must say, I had some Maalox moments because I had a tough time selling my house in Connecticut. The market was bad. I had mentioned earlier I bought high and now I was about to sell low. No one even looked at it. I had three or four real estate agents. I had it on the market for over five months. Not a nibble. I couldn't sell it and I couldn't rent it. It was a nice house, by the way. At the midnight hour, I had a transaction that allowed someone to come in with a lease, with the option to buy, and they ended up buying it. I was lucky, especially since I was looking at the possibility of being a geographical bachelor out in Hawaii, and that's a long way to be a geographical bachelor. So, by the hair of my chinny-chin-chin, I avoided that.

We sold the house and drove across country. It was an interesting trip across the country. My car was shipped out of Oakland, California, and it arrived a week or so later, and then I flew out to Hawaii. I lived in government quarters at a place called Wailupe. It is on Kalanianaole Highway, on the other side of Diamond Head. Nice quarters. They are all old Hawaiian-type homes. They had been a part of a Navy communications station in World War II. The Coast Guard had taken over the buildings years ago, and made them into homes.

Chief of Staff was out there. One of the 378 COs was there. Chief of Ops was out there. There were several 0-6 quarters out there, and the admin guy lived in one of them. It was a duplex. They had a swimming pool there and a tennis court. So, it was a nice environment for my family. In the District A job, I relieved Captain Bodner. He had been in the aviation part of the Coast Guard and finished up his career in D-14 admin.

I went there with the goal to be an activist. I asked myself, *What rocks can I kick over? What kind of thing should I do to add value? How can I leave this place better than when I got here?* I always ask that question of myself. Guess what I attacked first. Finance and budgeting processes. *How do we identify our requirements? How do we budget? How do we convince PACAREA about what we needed?* I sought to standardize the budgeting process throughout the district staffs and in subordinate units. Housing administration was also on my agenda. Housing was critical in the islands given its high cost. We had 245 units of CG housing to sustain and manage. It is tough to manage 245 units with the staff that I had. I ended up approving the building of some additional units while cutting back on the outdated. We also turned the housing management over to the US Army, which saved us in maintenance and management costs. We still had dedicated housing, but the US Army ran it along with their other thousands of units. This initiative was good for the CG, and especially good for our personnel.

We also engineered improvements in our finance-related staffs and processes. In keeping with the centralization of CG support functions, to save money the accounting offices in all districts were being done away with. It was a double-edged sword in Hawaii since D-14 had, perhaps, the best accounting office in the CG. I happened to have, out there in Hawaii, I had the best accounting in the Coast Guard. The reason being—I'm not trying to stereotype ethnically—but, the district had a number of Japanese who were extraordinary CG employees and accountants/finance types. They were so loyal. They were hardworking. They were great accountants. They were awesome accountants. So, we had the best one in the Coast Guard, now I'm doing away with it. So, I had to figure out how to not lose these employees. So, I worked hard to transition them into other jobs as best I could—make it an easy transition for them. I felt good about that.

I also had a collateral duty in the area of Total Quality Management, an initiative just starting throughout the CG. I was tapped by Admiral Donnell, who was the District Commander, to be the TQM Coordinator for the district. I was busily employed, identifying process improvement opportunities, creating quality actions teams, educating people about the initiative, and training total quality management facilitators. So, the tour was not a boring, do-nothing job.

JD: Did you and your family take part in the cultural activities?

TC: Oh, yes. We traveled among all the islands and saw all the incredible natural wonders of the place. The water sports are out of sight, And we learned and experienced the *Aloha* spirit of Hawaii. My younger daughter was still with us at that point, and we enrolled her in a private school, 'Iolani—a very good school. At first, she did have a little culture shock because she was now a minority. She had never experienced that type of environment—she was Caucasian and most of the other students were Chinese and Japanese, mostly Japanese. And they were unbelievably talented students. So, it was a different atmosphere for her. I will have to say, by the time the tour was done, I was very proud of her. She knew she was an odd man out, so she had to find out how to fit in quickly. I think she did very well and she did pretty good in school. And, she was a better person for the experience because she had an opportunity to walk in someone else's shoes for a while. And the telling thing was, when she left, all of the Asian kids had a big party for her. They came to the airport as we were going. *Aloha*. They gave her a special head lei and other gifts. The tears were flowing—lots of hugging. I said, to myself "Wow, she really mastered this challenge." And, she has turned into a very strong, independent, grown woman, maybe because of all of those experiences as a CG dependent. So, it was an interesting tour. My first exposure to Hawaii. I loved it and I found myself working hard and playing hard. There is a huge armed forces presence there, and there are close ties with the other services on a lot of issues and activities.

JD: Did you work closely with the Navy? And did you meet people in the Navy that you would work with later on in your career?

TC: Yes, very much so. I built some ties there, and familiarity with the other services and their organization, and so forth. So, when I came back later in my career as a district commander, it was like old home week. I'm repeating myself but, one experience builds on another and builds on another. Hats off to the Coast Guard detailers. They understand all of this stuff. I mean they try to put the right block in the right hole, and consider your experience, and try to give you meaningful assignments. The other thing that was interesting is that some people said, "Well, admin, that's interesting, but what are you going to go here for?" Well, I went back to CPA as the Division Chief after the D-14 admin assignment. CPA is one of the most impacting captain's jobs in the United States Coast Guard. So, that admin job didn't hurt me. My decline of ICAF didn't hurt me.

So, my message to others is that one's assignment progression is not a cookie cutter thing. You can make meaningful contributions in almost any assignment, and further your career at the same time. In fact, D-14 admin was an interesting assignment. I had good people working for me. My staff supported all—and got intimately involved in all—district programs. We supported their budgets, procurements, training, housing, and so on. It was a great tour.

JD: This is a good time to wrap up things because we are coming up on our deadline.

TC: Okay. Well, good. And then, the next issue is back to dear old, dear old Washington, DC.

That was a familiar route—back to planning, programming, and budgeting. It was back to CPA. You can see why the Programs Division of the Chief of Staff office figured so materially in my career, and for other CG leaders it figured materially, as well. I mean, Gracey for example—It was a big part of his career. You know when I came back to be Division Chief in the Programs Division—guess who was my deputy? Thad Allen. Then, when I became Vice Commandant and Commandant, guess who was the Chief of Staff? Thad Allen. So, you know, a little incestuous, but not really. You know, at those levels, it's all about your experience and performance. *What is your accumulated knowledge? What's the best fit for the organization?* And that's what unfolded in terms of assignments into critical CG jobs. That's the great thing about the Coast Guard. I mean, you just move up from the bottom through the organization, accumulating a network of expertise and friends—comrades—that understand the business, and work hard for the good of the service and the American public they serve. That's been my experience.

JD: Is there anything else you want to cover? Anything you forgot to mention?

TC: No. I think we got the general outline of it and we will continue on. The story goes on with the next assignment as Programs Division chief, and then that's where I made flag officer after two years there; then onto the Office of Acquisition. I was there for two years. Then, as punishment, the CG sent me out to be District Commander in Hawaii, which was an interesting, interesting job. It's more than drinking Mai Tais, I mean, it's meaningful employment out there, with some real meaty Coast Guard business activity. And then, on the west coast as PACAREA Commander, followed by Headquarters as Vice Commandant and Commandant. So, that's the list, the remaining assignments—and there were significant things that happened during that timeframe, and there were a lot of people that assisted me, and saved my bacon, and helped moved things along down the road. Thad Allen was absolutely one of those, as my deputy in CPA, then my Chief of Staff. We worked closely together and worked to advance the interest of the service and the public. So, I look forward to talking about those things in the next session.

JD: Yes. Well, thank you for your hospitality. Let the record show, the Admiral is a marathon interviewee. I think he had two sips of water the whole time. I've finished a bottle.

TC: Okay. Thanks, Jim. I appreciate it.

End audio file Collins3.2.Dolbow.USNI.2.10.16

Interviewer: Jim Dolbow (JD)

Interviewee: Admiral Thomas Collins, USCG Ret. (TC)

Begin audio file Collins4.1.Dolbow.USNI.2.23.16

JD: It's February 23rd and I am here in Alexandria, Virginia, with Admiral Collins for the fourth round of interviews. Admiral, can you tell us about what it was like coming back to the Programs Division?

TC: Well, when I arrived at HQ this third time, I had ten years under my belt in planning, programming, and budgeting assignments so it wasn't new territory. While that made it comfortable, I had mixed feelings because it was a great tour in Hawaii for me and my family. As administrative division chief, in Hawaii, I had been involved in meaty issues important to the district, and had made some progress that I feel really good about. And I left good colleagues and friends behind. We made great strides in improving the housing situation for the entire district with our comprehensive multi-year housing strategy. We ended up transitioning all our housing to the Army for maintenance and management purposes. It relieved us of that burden. We actually made money on the transaction.

We led major Total Quality Management (TQM) initiatives in the district. I was the TQM facilitator for the district commander, and I really changed the culture of the district to focus on process improvement, balanced scorecards, and all of those quality practices. I also felt good about the fact that we instilled a more rigorous planning and programming and budgeting regime there in the district. By the time I left, there was regime in place and there were analytics and metrics, better internal controls, and a senior resource management board in the district that made priorities and allocated resources to the highest priority need. Plus, the district staff were wonderful people to work with. I had great folks that worked for me—a loyal and capable civilian staff: Susan Matsudo, Brian Tanaka, and Maxine Lum, among many others. My deputy, Lieutenant Kathleen Donohoe—very talented lady—kept me out of trouble.

I lived in government quarters for senior officers, off Kalanianaole Highway, east of Diamond Head. There was a swimming pool and a tennis court available for the housing occupants. It was a great environment for my family. They we anxious about leaving as well. But, I knew I was destined for another staff job. And there was no better one—the way I looked at it—than the Programs Division in the Office of the Chief of Staff. I had spent four years there, as a program reviewer and coordinator of the Acquisition, Construction, and Improvements (AC&I) appropriation. I knew what I was getting into. I also knew this timeframe was a key time, programmatically and budget-wise, within the Coast Guard.

JD: Can you talk about this time in Coast Guard budget history?

TC: Yes. It was a challenging time for the service. In a previous interview session, we talked about my first tour there, in CPA. The 1980s were the time of Gramm-Rudman-Hollings, and budget reductions and financial/programmatic slicing and dicing. The 1990s was more of the same. Those decades—the 1980s and the 1990s—were decremental decades from a budget perspective. They posed a host of budget constraints. The public has high regard and high expectations of the USCG. In the face of budget constraints, our challenge was to ensure the key missions of the Coast Guard could still be conducted safely and effectively for the American public. That was the challenge, and I was there in both the 1980s and now the 1990s, dealing with these issues.

If you look at a budget information sheet for that timeframe, it basically shows flat budgets from 1992 to 1996. As you know, costs don't stay flat with flat budgets, especially for a capital-intensive organization. And assets get older and older, and cost more to maintain and keep operationally ready. So, you are dealing with rising costs/flat budgets, while you are trying to bring new assets in that have a different life-cycle/cost profile—it was a heavy lift to balance those issues. These conditions led to what was referred to as our streamlining effort—examining and restructuring the Coast Guard's infrastructure to attain efficiencies, but avoiding cutting the "meat and bone" of the organization (aircraft, boats, ships, and the people that run them and maintain them). We wanted to keep our operational capabilities—both capacity and capability in operations—so, we looked at all of the support and overhead command structures.

So, I was on my way to a key HQ O-6 job, in an era of substantial resource constraints, and right at the center of personal resource changes, budget changes, resource reallocation, reorganization initiatives, etc. But in fact, it was exciting to go back to HQ in that kind of job, at that time in the history of the Coast Guard, because there was a lot at stake.

I had owned a townhouse on earlier assignments in Fairfax, and I had sold that when I left. So now, I was faced with the adventure of finding a new home in a not so cheap housing market. We scurried around and ended up buying a brand new home out along the Fairfax County Parkway, in Chantilly. We bought a four-bedroom colonial in a nice neighborhood. My youngest daughter was about to be a senior in high school—her third high school given all our transfers. She left Iolani School in Honolulu after concluding her junior year, and moved all the way to the east coast, to Oakton High School in Vienna, Virginia. But, I have to give her credit, she handled it well. So, everything worked out on the home front. On the job front, my aim was to hit the decks running. I was very much aware of the kind of things that the Coast Guard was faced with.

JD: Can you talk about the streamlining initiatives you had to undertake?

TC: Yes. It involved a close look at support infrastructure and our command structures—districts, areas, HQ—to make reductions in order to make budget targets, while preserving operational capacity and capabilities. We looked at infrastructure. We looked at staffs. So, off the top, Headquarters staff levels were in the running for cuts, as were district staffs. We established a multi-year budget strategy since downward resource adjustments would likely be with us for a number of years. Such an approach enabled us to look at this from a system perspective and not just look at it in increments. We looked at a five-year envelope and planned sequenced cuts that would, on net, do us the least amount of harm. We required all of the CG program staffs to program and formulate the budget requirements that way. The flag corps met as a team to review the strategy and provide necessary guidance. It was an effort to develop a broad systematic game plan over five years, which would allow us to do things in a very system-like way.

Admiral Kime bought into that, and so did Vice Commandant Bob Nelson. Admiral Kramek was the Chief of Staff and Dick Herr, who had been Deputy Division Chief in CPA when I was there, was the resource director. It was a good mash-up of leadership folks that we had—with trust and confidence in each other. The multi-year budget strategy was a good approach, and the senior leadership bought into it because it made a lot of sense. The strategy looked at the districts—reducing staffing levels in districts, and consolidating district support functions to the Maintenance and Logistics Commands (MLCs) that had been set up in the 1980s, as a response to budget austerity during that period. What we did with MLCs in the eighties allowed us to take further steps with the support structure in the nineties. We reduced district staff anywhere from 10% to 12%. We also merged the 8th District and the 2nd District. The 2nd District used to be headquartered in St. Louis, MO, with a focus on inland rivers. The rationale for the merger was to create a combined district, HQ'ed in New Orleans, that would have oversight over the entire inner central river system and its major destination ports, especially New Orleans. The merger allowed staff reductions given the synergies we realized.

We also moved off Governor's Island. The CPA study that was done detailed the specific savings and cost avoidance that would accrue. The approach we took was, anything that didn't have to be in New York operationally, was going to move. So, we moved everything that didn't have to be in New York—i.e., local operational services—to previously BRACed [Base Realignment and Closure] old Navy facilities on Staten Island. We moved the Atlantic Area staff to Portsmouth, Virginia—a low-cost area—and move major cutters to less expensive ports. All of that made sense, budget-wise. Another thing that was done was to merge the 5th District with the Atlantic Area staff—they were co-located in the same geographical area. We did the same thing on the West Coast, merging the D-11 and Pacific Area staffs in Alameda. So, the Area Commanders on both coasts were double-hatted. There used to be a District 12 in San Francisco—we did away with those overlaps. Streamlining reduced headcount as well as provided for facility economies. All of these things, and more, were included in our multi-year budget strategy.

But it got to the point by the mid-nineties where there were not many efficiency alternatives left, you know. When you get to the 1995 and 1996 budgets, the CG had to get into muscle to make the budget work.

You know, Jim, we frequently lived off of supplemental appropriations bills passed by the Congress especially in the late-eighties and early-nineties. The reason we were able to keep the doors open, and the ships going, and fuel in the ships, was thanks to several senior senators that were great supporters of the United States Coast Guard. They provided us with supplemental appropriation bills from the DOD that allowed us to maintain business operationally. 1992 was my first year back in the Programs Division as Division Chief, and Andy Card was the Secretary of Transportation, and then Secretary Federico Peña came in the balance of the time during my tour. And, of course, it's not that they didn't support us—it's just that every DOT agency was in the same boat. There was a decremental budget environment across government, and things were getting cut. But, I wouldn't want to be in any other staff job in the United States Coast Guard between 1992 and 1994. It's like, *Coach, put me in.* You know, the game is on the line. I want to be there: program the resources to the highest need, so we can serve the United States and the people of the United States. That's what we worked hard doing. It was a great opportunity. And the coast Guard was fortunate to have talented leaders at the helm—Kent Williams, Dick Herr, Bill Kime, Bob Nelson, Bob Kramek, among many others.

Yes, it was streamlining time but, as stressed by Admiral Kramek, streamlining with no reduction in essential services. That's what his mandate was. One of the toughest things, was trying to close down search-and-rescue stations as part of the streamlining effort. We did districts and we did areas and that was not exceedingly difficult to get through politically because that wasn't where the service delivery was. That wasn't the visible part to the customer in a congressman's constituency. SAR stations are. It's not the Coast Guard's SAR station. It's not the federal government's SAR station. It's the local public's station—that's how they view it, which is a nice way to view it. I mean, in many ways and at most times. But, from a budget perspective and trying to cut them, it was almost mission impossible. Several stations were restructured into seasonal stations thereby yielding some level of savings.

At one point, we had a number of stations included in our budget that made it through the administration to Congress. The total budget reduction associated with the proposed station closures totaled something like $6.5 million. But congressional action on the budget required that we keep the stations open, but they took the $6.5 million as a reduction anyway. I note this incident to illustrate what kind of budget environment we found ourselves in during the nineties.

Incidentally, we had talented people in CPA to work these budget challenges: Thad Allen, my Deputy, later Chief of Staff and Commandant, and Dave Pekoske, a key reviewer who eventually became up Vice Commandant.

JD: Can you talk a little bit more about how the men and women in the Coast Guard delivered? What did that require of them?

TC: There were new lines of command that they had to adjust to, and the execution side of budget reductions can be messy. There were promotion gates that were elongated, and perturbations in the human resources management-end of the business, to get down to the reduced personnel levels reflected in the budget. Because you make a budget reduction such as making a SAR station seasonal, you don't realize the savings on day one. And you close facility or reduce a staff, but you have what we referred to as exit cost. It costs you to reduce. You may have to give civilians severance pay; you may have costs to get people out the door; you may have costs to mothball facilities. So, all of those things have to be dealt with as you reduce, and you often don't realize recurring savings until the out years. We were managing austerity, you know, and everyone experienced it from the field level upward. There were some cut backs in money for spare parts and maintenance funds, which had a potential readiness impact on our units; and CG men and women worked longer and harder to maintain our readiness posture. So, all of those things added up and made life more difficult, not easier, for the CG men and women on the frontlines.

JD: Can you talk about what went into selecting which SAR stations to close?

TC: We had metrics and performance standards for all of our activities and one was our response standard—how fast and how far must you respond and get on scene. We measured all of the stations against those standards. And, where we were in excess of the standard, we would carefully assess whether we could reduce or eliminate that facility. Especially where there was an ability to operationally cover that area with adjacent stations, or with a new capability where response performance standards could be met.

In the face of budget constraints, the Coast Guard continued to deliver essential services—delivering incredible bang for the buck for the American taxpayer. If you added up the value of lives saved, the value of property assistance, etc.—by all of these measures, it's like four-, five-, six-to-one return to the American taxpayer. And that is why—and I know Admiral Kime pushed this point to external audiences, Kramek pushed this point, Jim Loy and I pushed—the United States Coast Guard shouldn't be subject to across the board cuts. Governmental programs are not equal in terms of the value they bring to the nation—they shouldn't be treated as equal in the budget process. Rather the CG and other governmental agencies should be measured on the performance and value to the public and their budget adjusted accordingly. Unfortunately, across the board cuts are often unavoidable given the timing and political complexities involved.

JD: Did you ever think what you would be doing if you didn't have to worry about these declining budgets and going through these budget drills? Like, what could you have been doing instead?

TC: Well, I suspect we will get to that a little later in the interview because, you know, that's what happened as a result of 9/11. It took 9/11 to change the budget dynamic. We had two decades of austerity—the 1980s and the 1990s in the United States Coast Guard. We were struggling to eke it out—counting every penny and every nickel to keep the organization ticking, and to provide essential maritime services to the American public. Adequate funding during that timeframe would have allowed us to get ahead of the power curve, in terms of caring for and replacing aging and obsolete ships, boats, and aircraft. Instead, we fell far behind with serious readiness consequences.

It changed in the aftermath of 9/11. As tragic and awful and horrendous as 9/11 was, one thing it did was turn people around, in and out of government, on how they viewed the United States Coast Guard. They valued the United States Coast Guard, and recognized the nation's need for the kind of authorities and capabilities we bring to the fight. People think about us a search-and-rescue agency, and that's a nice thing because we are good at it. But, there is an extensive range of other things that we do, other authorities that we have, that bring great value to this nation. We're a military service and a law enforcement organization at the same time. What other agency in the United States of America has those two very powerful authorities? None. People started to recognize that in the wake of the tragedy of 9/11. And, our budgets went up. I mean, we were at $3.5 billion-levels in 1996, 1997, 1998, but we were at $9 billion when I retired in 2006. Now it's up over $10 billion—almost a three-fold increase. In my view, it was really overdue.

The day before 9/11, because of budget constraints, we had cutters tied up to the dock in the west coast and other places because we didn't have the money to buy the fuel for them. That's how bad our budgets got. We were putting planes in the desert and mothballing them because we didn't have the money to maintain them and fuel them. That's the state that we were in. But we were getting by, in large part thanks to strong advocates like Senator Daniel Inouye and Senator Ted Stevens—key figures on the Senate Appropriations and Appropriations Subcommittee on Defense. They provided the US Coast Guard in the range of $200-$400 million a year to meet critical budget requirements.

JD: So, looking back and looking forward at the same time—looking back at your days in the Programs Division—would you say you did very well setting the Coast Guard up for post-9/11 because you cut the right things and didn't cut the wrong things?

TC: I think so. Most of the reductions were focused in the right areas. The other thing, streamlining brought a greater command focus on resource-related issues and an integrated approach toward business, both on the support side and the operational side. So, we flattened the organization a bit. As an organization, we took a more systems view—an integrated view—of our world of work. We became a more efficient and process-oriented organization. And many of the organizational and process changes made in the eighties and nineties provided a great foundation for the adjustments made post-9/11.

JD: I want to talk about Governor's Island. How much resistance did you meet from the New York congressional delegation?

TC: We didn't meet a great deal of resistance. Obviously, we had to work it out and we had to explain what we were doing, why we were doing it, and the alternatives. Explaining that, if we had to make budget reductions, we could cut ships, and planes, and boats—or we could look at our organization and infrastructure. And, it was very difficult for congressional staffers to really argue against that latter approach. To the credit of folks on the Hill, when they saw that, they didn't want to have to cut operational assets or capability. And we did leave selected resources in New York—those that provided local services. But the Atlantic Area staff could be anywhere on the east coast. It didn't have to be in New York. It was cheaper—much cheaper—to be in Portsmouth, Virginia. When it was all said and done, with Governor's Island and all other streamlining efforts, we cut upwards to $400 million and a significant number of personnel. If I recall correctly, it was around a 12% reduction across the Coast Guard. It was approximately 3,200 military folks and 800 civilians.

JD: What was an average day like for you as Chief of the Programs Division?

TC: It was always busy. Of course, much of my or our efforts were focused on tending to major initiatives, like overseeing and moving ahead on the various streamlining strategies; creating a multi-year budget structure and process; and refining/enhancing our capital investment plans to deal with increasingly obsolete and maintenance-intensive ships, boats, and planes. But we also dealt with all the day-to-day resource and programming issues, tending to the mechanics of the various budget cycles, review and disposition of personnel reprogramming requests, monitoring program matters, preparing Q&As and hearing books for the hearing process—internal, DOT, OMB, or congressional—reviewing and acting on various policy issues, attending briefings and meetings with senior CG staff throughout HQ, etc. All resource matters—dollars, personnel, assets—requiring the Commandant's or Chief of Staff's attention and/or approval were staffed through CPA.

We were also the coordinating point for communications, meetings, and briefings for departmental, OMB, and congressional staffs, and much of this engagement fell to me as the office chief. So, all of those things were in motion and, as Chief of CPA, I had to ensure the various issues were being worked on by the right staff member, assign priorities for all the office efforts, and ensure timelines were being met. The first thing each morning, I met with all the staff's program reviewers—the meeting was referred to as the round room meeting—to go over current priorities, works-in-progress and, most importantly, share views on policy/programmatic issues and approaches to various matters before us. It was a very important and time-tested approach to CPA's world of work. Round room was a CPA institution.

I was also at the call of the Resource Director, Chief of Staff, and the Commandant. Occasionally, they would seek my input or clarification on a program or resource issue before them, or want clarification on a matter that they had to discuss with the Secretary, White House, or Congress. So, I had frequent interaction with very senior CG leadership.

JD: How large of a staff did you have?

TC: Oh, in term of program reviewers? About eight to ten people. We were organized into two branches. One was CPA-1 which included all the program reviewers and analysts. There was an

Operating Expense Appropriation Coordinator as well as an AC&I Coordinator and those two tended to be the more senior reviewers. There were also one or two civilian reviewers, who provided staff continuity. Joe Liotta was one of the civilian staffers, and he was also a carpool mate, occasionally, during my CPA tours. The second branch, CPA-2, was a staff of about four people and had a personnel accounting function. It kept track of all service-wide personnel changes in terms of what units have how many people, what grade, what specialty, etc. All of that was done within CPA-2, where they also administered an information system that helped tracked service wide personnel status and resource adjustments.

JD: Can you talk about those streamlining efforts and the impact on the Coast Guard Reserve during this time?

TC: Reserve units are, in large measure, structured around the counterpart active duty units they augment. For example, in a previous tour at Group Long Island Sound, I had Station New Haven and a Station New Haven Reserve unit. If budget or resource adjustments were being made to Station New Haven in terms of personnel strength, mission profile, etc., similar adjustments would be made to the supporting Reserve unit. Another example: if you reduce Area staff, and move it to Virginia, the Reserve structure there has got to change, and that's basically what happened across the streamlining efforts. It mirrored all of the transactions that we took with the active duty force—the level and location of Reserve augmentation was impacted.

JD: I guess you were very appreciative that you had been in the Programs Division earlier in your career. Did you ever think what would have happened if you hadn't been thrown into this?

TC: It would have been exceedingly difficult because, as in any job, you build up experience and knowhow—a feel for the job that is tough to manufacture overnight. I think our folks in Office of Personnel do—and continue to do—a great job in trying to match the experience of an individual with the requirements of the job, especially when you get to a unit or staff, such as CPA, which has such significant impact on the service. My pervious assignments in the Office of Resource & Development, and my first assignment in CPA as a reviewer, provided a solid path to the Chief Programs Division assignment.

JD: You mentioned Admiral Gracey held your job as Chief of the Program Division at an earlier point in time. He was also one of your predecessors as Commandant. He mentioned in his oral history that was conducted by the Naval Institute years ago, that the function of the Office was to look at the programs that the Coast Guard was going to pursue—the *What is it?* aspect of what's going to be in the budget. Look at priorities—where we need to put our money. Was he right on the money?

TC: Well, that's clearly about resource management, allocation, formulation, defense, and all that—so he hit the nail on the head. Resource allocation, building the content of the budget based on sound analysis and assessment of service, wide programmatic priorities—all of that was clearly a primary role for CPA. That was a priority job. But, I think even broader than that—because it involved analyzing programs, policies, and authorities while redefining, expanding, reducing, changing, and, most importantly, including human resource allocation.

People are an incredibly important resource and CPA was at the heart of all of "people as resource" matters. So, policy, programs, money, people, and organizational structure—all of those matters went through CPA. So, yes, he's right and much more.

JD: Was it frustrating that, to DOD, a $400 million cut was decimal dust compared to cutting into almost the bone marrow for the Coast Guard. Do you wish you could have gotten like a billion from them for relief, and just save all of these headaches?

TC: In terms of budget or resources, DOD was clearly on another level, as compared to the CG. They have more depth on the bench, and more sophisticated processes. For example, they had cover provided by BRAC legislation that gave flexibility for making cuts because it was all up or all down. You couldn't nitpick. So, they had a great advantage in getting some of their reductions through that they had to get through. It's like apples and oranges trying to compare us to them just because of the sheer scale of it. You know, $400 million to them and then $400 million to us are two different things—it's much more impacting to the USCG. As a point of comparison, our annual entire capital budget through the 1990s was in the low-$300 millions. In 1993, $311 million; in 1994, $320 million; in 1995, $361 million; in 1996, we needed at least 50% more to keep our capital plant alive and well, never mind introducing new replacement capital systems.

Given the size of our capital plant and the expected service life of component parts, our capital funding needs far exceeded those levels appropriated in the '90s. During that period, we were consuming our capital plant, and it was eroding and dying without replacement. If you look at all of the CG shore facilities—we've got units and small boat stations all over the country. And, in terms of the number of our ships—over 220 ships—boats, and aircraft, you will find that the USCG is bigger than most of the world's navies. So we have size, but in the '80s and '90s, we didn't have the budget to sustain and keep all of that capital plant alive, and all that piled up on us as we moved into the twenty-first century. So, the entire 1980s and 1990s was a challenging time and my hats off to the CG's senior leadership and Commandants during that time that we were fighting and scraping to keep the organization headed in the right direction, and, most importantly, to preserve essential services. My hats off to them.

JD: What advice do you have if, heaven forbid, the Coast Guard ever has to do more streamlining? What advice would you give to your successors, be it another Commandant or in the Programs Division?

TC: You know, have a methodology—a clearly articulated and integrated strategy. Have standards. Don't do it by the seat of your pants. Be strategic and process-focused—good TQM practices help here at the same time. It's how you think about your world of work. Ask the right questions: *How do you make your structure, processes, and assets more efficient?, How can you best control costs?,* etc. You need metrics along with solid analysis. You need to make it an all-hands affair, all CG leadership needs to be intimately involved. You also need to proceed in great consultation with the rest of the government budget food chain, and you must get your Secretary on your side to approve the direction you taking. In the end, it takes informed and measured approach to this stuff. Preparing the battlefield for your initiatives is critical.

JD: It was during this time that there was a transition from the Clinton to the Bush administration. What did your office have to do to prepare for the transition teams for the incoming administration?

TC: I had been reassigned in 1994, before the advent of the G.W. Bush administration in 2001. G.H.W. Bush was in office until 1993, followed by President Clinton. But in any event, transitions do involve additional prep and staff work, but not an overwhelming amount.

Providing background information on the service and its current issues is the primary tasking. In terms of budget oversight, there is some level of continuity within OMB. There is a professional staff, so those people stay. There is a certain level of continuity within the department. When you get a churn in the political appointee positions, you may get a different focus—a different emphasis. But the relationships established with the professional government staffers—both executive and congressional—are important. It's those permanent relationships that help you transition from administration to administration. Overall, the transition was not a monumental thing. We were still in a decremental budget environment—that didn't change, so here we go again.

JD: Would you say the Coast Guard was plagued by "the curse of can-do" at this time?

TC: Well, it may be. That's an interesting point. We kept delivering on our essential services. We met our SAR standards. We still responded to oil spills. We still inspected ships, etc. But, as I have said, our approach was to reduce overhead, support structure, and preserve operational capability. But you can do that in the short term but eventually it will catch up to you in terms of reduced maintenance, spare parts, etc., and eventually a serious drop in mission readiness will result. That's what was happening to the CG by the end of the '90s.

The operational readiness problem happens when you don't have enough money to recapitalize yourself, or you don't have enough money to buy the necessary spare parts, or you don't have enough money in your Allotment Fund Code 45 [ship maintenance]. If you don't have enough money there to maintain your ships, then a serious readiness problem can occur.

I'm a readiness fanatic. We are a readiness organization. We are a response organization more than anything else. That's what we are. That's in our genes. That's what we do. And, when you start losing the readiness posture through decreasing maintenance budgets, it starts going downhill because, in addition, you don't have the budget to recapitalize: lack of fuel, lack of spare parts. I recall a speech that Admiral Loy gave one time about a C-130. He was talking about a particular offshore SAR case. We could have done this case a lot better, but we had a hangar queen. We had a C-130 hangar queen in Air Station Sacramento and we didn't have enough spare parts to fix it as fast as we could, and we didn't have a backup. Always the standard thing is to have a backup. Especially on a C-130 on long deployment, there is a backup

C-130. We didn't have a backup C-130. Not because we didn't want to have one. We couldn't afford to have one and that's a readiness problem.

Decreasing readiness posture as a first responder organization—that's not a place I want to be in. That's not in the national interest. Both Admirals Bob Kramek and Jim Loy articulated our readiness dilemma exceedingly well during their time as Commandant. But, you know, we were part and parcel of a larger mosaic in the federal government regarding budgets. You are one moving part. You get carried along in the stream. Even to the point of having across the board cuts—a terrible budget approach where you get caught up with everybody else—that's not budgeting by merit or programming by merit. I always had a problem with that. Whenever we got into those across the board cuts scenarios, I got nervous. We would get cut with the same axe as everyone, despite the value we provided to the public.

JD: This is jumping ahead, but I'm guessing you were glad that you were retired when sequestration became the law of the land in 2011.

TC: Yeah. I mean, it's just another challenge when you are in this world of budgeting and formulation of resources and trying to match it to requirements and meet all of your missions. If it wasn't sequestration, it would be something else—some other challenge. The challenge of post-9/11, for example, wasn't necessarily budget austerity, but it was how to grow smart. You can streamline stupidly or you can downsize stupidly, but you can also grow stupidly. You can do a lot of harm to your organization if you are not growing in the right way. So, it's not just easy street on the growth part. *How do you grow well? How do you grow efficiently? How do you maintain the core values and culture of your organization, which has developed since 1790 and has served the American public exceedingly well? How do you ensure you don't damage that kind of culture?* People value our culture. You can talk to Tom Ridge and ask him if he valued what we stood fo—or to Norm Mineta or Andy Card—and ask what value we bring to the table, from a cultural, ethical, and selfless service perspective. *How do you grow and not damage that? How do you grow wisely?* So, there's challenges in all different types of settings. And, again, if it isn't sequestration, there's some other challenges that are going to be thrown your way.

JD: I want to go back to one more question about the efficiency initiatives. Did you seek input from across the Coast Guard from the bottom up on things on how to improve and save even five or ten thousand dollars?

TC: We had embraced process improvement and quality management. *How do you do things smarter? How do you do things more efficiently?* And, we had them from the lowest level up. There were process teams throughout the CG. We looked every which way we did things. Same thing with acquisitions. We radically altered some of the processes within Acquisition and there was still room to do more when I left there. It's that "continuous improvement" imperative of quality management; it's never over. There's always a way. There's different challenges, different environments, and different ways to do business, and the taxpayer should be pleased that the Coast Guard is right in the middle of that kind of process improvement. Later, in my assignment as Vice Commandant, I oversaw wide quality management initiatives.

JD: When you were Chief of the Programs Division, did you travel much, or were you pretty much stuck in Headquarters?

TC: I didn't do a lot of traveling. My job was mostly an "inside the beltway" job, to a large extent.

JD: How did this job help you later on, as Commandant?

TC: Oh, the experience was indispensable. I would have to say, I gained greater knowledge of our authorities and our missions; and how resources were matched to our limitations and our constraints. I got to really know CG business. And, very importantly, I had an up-close and personal look of how Washington, and the government, and the interagency process works. All of the Commandants have had similar experiences. Now, they've had different styles and different personalities, but they all had a very extensive résumé and understood our business. The CG has a very thorough process to vet and assess our senior leaders and you don't get there unless you have gone through the ringer a bit.

JD: Can you talk a little bit about Admiral Kime's style and personality?

TC: He was a brilliant guy. Unfortunately, he's passed on now. He was District 7 operations division chief in Miami while I was assigned to Group St. Petersburg. Bill was exceedingly smart and didn't suffer fools very well. He held people accountable, and he was perhaps the most professional and accomplished maritime safety professional ever in our service. One of the real thrills when I left CPA was to have him personally present me, in his office, with the Legion of Merit which wasn't that easy to come by from Admiral Kime. So, that meant a lot.

Again, I thought he was a brilliant guy. I thought he did a wonderful job. He was incredibly brilliant on marine safety and environmental matters. He made so many incredible advances within that community and was a very respected international maritime safety leader as he headed numerous US delegations to the International Maritime Organization in London.

Kramek was a very personable guy. Very outgoing, extroverted type of guy. A people person. A good communicator. Very talented in the technical world of naval engineering. He was a ship driver and a naval engineer, and had a lot of confidence. He brought that to bear in his job.

JD: Did you have as much interaction with Admiral Kramek, as you did with Admiral Kime, on issues?

TC: I had a great deal because he was the Chief of Staff when I was Programs Division chief. I dealt with him nearly every day. I made flag in a Commandant transition year because Admiral Kime was retiring and the new guy, Kramek, had been selected, and he was putting together his team. I happened to be part of that team as a new flag pick. Typically, a new Commandant, coming in and not yet in the seat, will gather his new team together in the spring, and he will develop his game plan for his coming assignment as Commandant.

JD: Can you talk about the time you found out that you were promoted to flag rank?

TC: I found out at work and I called home to my wife Nancy. I just gave her some hint that there were some interesting things going on at Headquarters, and that I needed to talk to her about them when I get home. So, I didn't tell her right away. Oh, by the way, she's not a dumb lady. She had a bottle of champagne waiting when I got home that night. But, it was a humbling thing to be picked for flag. There are so many variables. It's no sure thing. There is a lot of talented people that are deserving, so being selected was humbling. Like I've said, I never started out on day one saying, "Oh yeah, this is my goal, and, if I don't make it, then it is a failure." That's not the way I looked at things. But, it came to pass and I was obviously thrilled to have been selected for flag rank.

JD: What happened next after you got the promotion? How long is it before you get to pin on your first star?

TC: Well, actually, I'm trying to think back. I can't remember the timeframe quite frankly.

JD: Well, you still have a few more incoming phone calls the rest of your career.

TC: I did.

JD: How long of a transition was it between the programs office and pinning on your first star?

TC: I finished up that in May or June, and then went up to the Office of Acquisition (G-A), which I thought was a really good fit. So, this is finishing up from '92 to '94 in the Programs Division, making flag, and then transitioning to the Office of Acquisition. It seems every new flag wants to have an operational command in one of the districts out there, but of course, not all new flags got operational commands and some may be disappointed in that. I thought the G-A was a great fit for me. I had some level of confidence that ultimately I would get an operational command. I would rather cut my teeth on a staff assignment and it was familiar territory. Why do I say that? Because all of the capital programs that I had fought so hard for—for over eight years, between two assignments at Headquarters—were finally getting some funding. They are going to have a contract, and they are going to get an award, and they are going to get built. And, I was part of that. I knew all those programs, intimatel—all of those capital initiatives which represented the future of our service. It also allowed my family to stay put and avoid yet another move. So, the assignment was attractive from a number of perspectives.

JD: If you hadn't been selected for flag, were you going to stay another year at CPA?

TC: That would have been at the pleasure of the Commandant and the Chief of Staff. The Commandant doesn't necessarily get involved in all O-6 jobs. The Commandant is the flag detailer. He and the Vice Commandant make up that slate. That's not done in the Office of Personnel. That's done by the Commandant and the Vice Commandant. That's their slate. He built that team. So, he doesn't typically get involved, except for select O-6s positions—except for assignments like CPA.

JD: What was your promotion ceremony like?

TC: It was in room 2415 which was a big interior room on the second floor where most of these things happened. I vaguely remember it. I think there was the shoulder board thing where they put the shoulder boards on you, and there are some nice words spoken, and so forth. But, that's all I remember of that.

JD: Did you attend the capstone course for new flag and general officers?

TC: I did, but it wasn't right away. It was the next year because the Coast Guard can only send so many. Usually like one or two max. And there is a queue because, of course, it is primarily a show for new DOD flags or general officers. Capstone is about jointness. How to you get joint—capstone exposes you to all of the joint commands, National Security Council folks, and State Department; and typically, the leader of those enterprises. It's a great six weeks in length. I recall you spend two weeks in DC, two weeks travelling around the country visiting military installations and the combatant commands, and then you go overseas for two weeks. They usually split the class up into three components. One goes to Asia; one goes to South America; one goes to Europe. I went to Europe, hallelujah. It was really interesting. It was a great way to understand the DOD a bit more, and the entire National Security apparatus.

JD: Did it help you when you became Vice Commandant, and later on Commandant?

TC: It helped me in Hawaii. It helped me in all of my subsequent jobs because I had extensive interplay with DOD leadership in D-14, as PACAREA Commander, as Vice Commandant and as Commandant.

JD: Is there anything else you would like to add about your time as Chief of the programs office?

TC: It was a whirlwind two years. I think my family was comfortable living in the DC area, especially for my kids. They almost consider DC their home because we've been in and out of the DC area so many times. My daughter graduated successfully from Oakton High School, and she went to Elon College down in North Carolina. My older daughter, Christine, worked in the

DC area. So, CPA and DC was a good fit, and the G-A assignment gave me some stability, family-wise. We had bought a new home and now I didn't have to leave it after two years because I was still at Headquarters with the Office of Acquisition job. So, that was nice to be in one place with a new home for four years. You hate to buy a house and then move. All of those transitions are not always easy. Sometimes you sell low, buy high, depending on the timing of markets that you have no control over. So, you would like a little bit of equity growth. I saw the assignment as making sense for my family while making sense for me. I had a very supportive spouse, as usual. So, we signed up enthusiastically for the new job.

JD: Can you talk about the morale of the Coast Guard, with all of this streamlining going on?

TC: Look, I think our Coast Guard men and women are just absolutely superb in all circumstances. They just excel. When it's the most challenging, that's when they want to be involved. I have always witnessed a can-do spirit among CG men and women. The ups and downs of the budget cycle does not change that spirit. Throughout streamlining, reenlistment rates did not dip significantly. In my experience, active CG operations and support of those operations is the key ingredient to good morale. And streamlining did not stop the service from doing what it does best—serving the public selflessly. I think that's what draws people into our service—engaging in meaningful employment.

JD: I want to move on to your job as Chief of Acquisitions. I just want to set the stage. Who was the Commandant when you were Chief of Acquisitions?

TC: Admiral Kramek had just become Commandant. Gene Henn was Vice Commandant from '94 to '96, and then Admiral Herr became Vice Commandant from '96 to '98. Kent Williams was the Chief of Staff. Rodney Slater was Secretary of Transportation at the tail end of my time as Chief of Acquisition.

It was a good team and, like I said, there was a lot going on within acquisition and I felt comfortable going there. I had been working acquisition issues from the resource side for a number of years. There was a lot at stake. A lot of our systems and major platforms were nearing the end of their service life. They were technically obsolete in many cases. They didn't have all of the capabilities of modern-day platforms or systems. Plus, they were more expensive to maintain as they got older.

And there was great interest throughout government to improve the way the federal government acquires things. When you get to big systems acquisitions, it's a very elaborate process—very cumbersome. My objective going in was, *How do we buy things more effectively? How do we drive down the life-cycle costs?* Acquisition costs are important but they are dwarfed by life-cycle costs. When we buy something, we should be focused on the life-cycle cost. We should be buying things with life-cycle costs in mind. We should be designing with life-cycle costs in mind. We should be buying commercial off-the-shelf as much as we possibly can—commercial off-the-shelf, with competition and life-cycle costs in mind.

We also need to be better at integrated logistics support because we clearly can manage our inventory more efficiently. Performance-based acquisition was also an emphasis that had the potential to pay off in a big way—and they ultimately did witness a number of big systems acquisitions during that timeframe, especially our coastal and seagoing buoy tender acquisitions. Both were performance-based contracts. Clearly, there were a number of improvement opportunities within the acquisition world. There was an opportunity to be innovative with procurement practices, and to change the culture of acquisitions in our service. There were over twelve major systems under contract in my two-year tour—worth over three billion dollars—including contracts for boats, aircraft systems, ships, and IT systems. For example, the new coastal patrol boat was bought via a parent craft concept/performance-based approach, which greatly improved our patrol boat platform with stern launch capability and habitability improvements.

JD: Can you talk about some of the new acquisition programs, like Vessel Traffic Service (VTS) and other IT efforts?

TC: VTS is our eyes and ears for our ports. The systems acquisition project known as VTS-2000 was very successful in modernizing the command, and control, and sensor packages for seventeen VTS ports. Prior to 9/11, VTS was always thought of as a safety of navigation issue—*How do you control vessels in a congested port so there are no collisions, accidents, and pollution?* But after 9/11, you had to overlay security to it. So, VTS becomes, in many ways, your eyes and ears for all port issues—to help you acquire situational awareness to understand risk and vulnerabilities; to help you have maritime domain awareness for what's going on in your port.

So, it's was a very, very important system. And the acquisition was a largely Commercial Off-the-Shelf (COTS), performance-based contract. We also did a systems acquisition to consolidate and support most of our IT systems at the USCG Operations Systems Center in Martinsburg, West Virginia. We also completed a successful Marine Information for Safety and Law Enforcement (MISLE) database systems project for the marine safety program.

JD: Can you talk about the problems you encountered with the 49-foot Buoy Utility Stern Loading Boat (BUSL) and the Fleet Logistics System?

TC: The BUSL was a small buoy boat that had a little A-frame on the back that could haul up buoys of a certain limited size. Not like the big tenders. It was outdated and needed to be replaced. There was a company in Seattle that had won the contract before I got to G-A. It was one of the only substantial contracts that we had problems with. The contract was going south. It was running up double the costs and wasn't meeting schedule or technical requirements. So, we terminated it. Then, the company filed a claim against the US Government for the money they thought was due to them. At that point in the contract, they had almost completed just one boat—$4.7 million was their claim. In the course of the legal back and forth on the issues, they wouldn't give us the boat. Working with our talented procurement lawyers, the Justice Department, US Marshals, et. al, we ended up arresting the boat. Yes, I found that you can really arrest a thing. Ultimately, we got our boat, was successful defending against the company's claim—we paid about $1 million versus $3.7 million, and started a new and successful BUSL construction effort, this time at the CG Yard in Curtis Bay, Maryland.

The Fleet Logistics System (FLS) was also very problematic. We were trying to develop an integrated logistics support system for ships. The effort was an important one, since logistics is an important, and very expensive, part of the life of a ship. We were driving for lower lifecycle costs for ship support. We had a very good aviation logistics system that had been groomed, shaped, and tweaked for years—not so on the ship side. The project that was underway to address the issue had taken an outdated, all design-in-house approach, and wasn't producing what was needed. We terminated the current effort and used the aviation logistic system as a model supported by a performance-based contract. We ultimately saved over $75 to $80 million dollars by going a new way with this acquisition.

The BUSL and FLS acquisitions turned out to be the only troubled ones, but we were able to successfully turn them around. And all of the other major system contracts were very successful—using innovative acquisition approaches and meeting all cost, schedule, and performance requirements. It was a satisfying experience because we were tweaking the process all the time. In fact, we rewrote the Coast Guard Major Systems Acquisitions Manual. We worked the transportation department to streamline some of their bureaucracy. And, I think we did it very, very successfully. We achieved a focus on life-cycle costs on commercial off-the-shelf procurements, and a focus on performance-based specifications—all which drive costs down and reliability up.

And the foundation for the Deepwater Major System Acquisition—replacement of our largest seagoing cutters, their boats, patrol boat, sand aircraft—was laid while I was in G-A. The CG had to jump through many hoops to get that effort going, including to an interagency task force on Coast Guard roles and missions required by OMB. Deputy Secretary of Transportation Mort Downey headed this interagency commission. OMB required us to review and validate every Coast Guard mission before we could proceed with Deepwater—a very unique pre-acquisition requirement placed on the CG, which significantly delayed the start of the acquisition itself. Ultimately, CG missions were revalidated through the interagency study. The Interagency Task Force on US Coast Guard Roles and Missions issued their report in December 1999.

JD: I was on Capitol Hill when they released it, and the Coast Guard people I knew breathed a huge sigh of relief because it could have gone the other way and said, "You don't meet these requirements."

TC: We owe a heavy debt of gratitude to Mort Downey. Number one, a terrific guy. He really appreciated our service and he worked hard. I mean, it wasn't padding the deck, or rigging the books, or whatever, but he did a very thorough job of convincing and engaging with the other agency heads and leaders participating on this task force. We assigned a few Coast Guard officers to the effort, to facilitate the flow of information in a liaison role.

I lived and breathed all of this stuff for so many years. The projects we dealt with from 1994 to 1996 were all very successful projects. I can objectively say to American taxpayers that these projects were very efficient acquisitions and they got a lot of bang for the buck. For example, there were efficient, highly capable subsystems that were being built into the seagoing buoy tender. It's an awesome platform. It's half icebreaker. It has a dynamic positioning system in it that is computer controlled. You dial in the latitude and longitude you want and it keeps you in position within fairly close dimensions in up to 30-knot winds and 8-foot seas. It's great for positioning buoys that have to be precisely positioned, especially those situations of adverse weather and dangerous shoals. And you can do the whole thing with less people. Marinette Marine, the designer and builder, cherry-picked the best aids-to-navigation ship features from around the world and incorporated them into the design. And, most importantly, the project was completed below government estimate, and done within schedule while exceeding all performance requirements. A very successful acquisition, in my view.

JD: You talk about the acquisition initiatives that you undertook like COTS [Commercial Off-the-Shelf] and life-cycle costs. Where did those ideas come up? Were you reading a textbook or just a change agent?

TC: Well, I did have a solid TQM background, focusing on process and efficiency, and how you wring costs out of a system. I would read everything that I could get my hands on relative to capital acquisitions in DOD. Most importantly, I had been involved in the review of all previous acquisitions as a program reviewer and as the AC&I Coordinator in CPA. In addition, I was the program reviewer for the Office of Engineering. So, I was reviewing and programming every system that was bought out of the Office of Engineering, even non-major type procurements—not only to fund them up front but to monitor their execution, especially the multi-year projects.

As the CPA reviewer trying to shoehorn the highest priority projects into the budget, I was concerned with the life-cycle costs associated with major systems. The maintenance tail associated and inventory with major acquisitions are really significant. *How do we reduce this maintenance tail?* So, emphasizing greater acquisition effectiveness and efficiency was the natural outgrowth of those previous review responsibilities—observing good acquisition approaches and not-so-good ones. I also had a super staff of knowledgeable project managers, legal procurement specialists and contracting officers who took the lead on many of our improvement initiatives. Our acquisition team was recognized by Dr. Steve Kelman, Administrator of the Office of Federal Procurement Policy in the Office of Management and Budget, for our approach with performance specifications. I also was awarded a Hammer Award by Vice President Al Gore.

JD: The Hammer Award probably looked good on your fitness report.

TC: Well, it thickened the package. I spoke at a luncheon meeting hosted by the Office of Federal Procurement Policy about our experience with the buoy tender projects. They were overjoyed because both DOD and the CG were advancing innovative acquisition concepts—*How do we get more and better performance specs? How do we emphasize COTS? How do we get things better, cheaper, and smarter?* They had a good example to use with the CG's coastal and sea-going buoy acquisitions. The assignment as Chief of the Office of Acquisition was a great opportunity for me as a new flag officer to take the ball and run with these things. And I was fortunate to have a staff of talented men and women who often led the way. It was right in the middle of streamlining and the office was delivering more efficient systems.

The office was also involved with improving processes for over $500 million in non-major systems procurements that were underway across the CG. Some of the under the radar, smaller procurements needed attention from a process perspective. One of the first quality actions teams that was put together to looked at the non-major systems and the process by which we do them—how we monitor, how we run them, how we manage them, how it gets reported on, etc. These smaller procurements often didn't get all of the visibility that they should have, but there were some really significant improvements done there.

JD: Can you talk about that?

TC: Yes. Mostly, it involved refining requirements definition, improving and standardizing the source selection process and what contract vehicles were used, and what were the decision points associated with the procurement—what controls were in place. The smaller procurements weren't going to be as laborious as the majors, but they should have distinct no-go/go points where you have to have everything done right and everything is in order. And, that's what we incorporated into the rewritten Coast Guard Systems Acquisitions Manual (SAM). We incorporated into the SAM guidance and governance requirements for the non-majors.

Overall, G-A was a great experience—the buoy tenders were perhaps the most successful and interesting project for me. I enjoyed going up to Marinette, Wisconsin, the shipyard building the vessels, because everything was done right by shipyard management/engineers—very talented shipyard workers in all the skilled trades, and the CG Project Resident Office (PRO) that was located there to oversee the construction. The ship launchings were terrific. When finished, the vessels were side-launched making a huge splash in the river. A large gathering of the local public would sit up on the opposite bank of the river, picnic, and take in the big launch.

It was an experience, except going up there in the winter. That wasn't cool, I mean, that was really cold.

JD: And you are from New England.

TC: Jim, it was much colder than New England. It was downright freezing. I can recall flying into Green Bay on a regional type commercial jet, and then getting one of those small puddle jumper things out of Green Bay to fly up to Marinette with the wind howling. The head of the CG Project Resident Office up there would meet me at the small local airport with extreme cold weather gear in hand—extreme cold-weather gloves and hood, etc.—to put on.

Later, during a more pleasant period, weather-wise, I visited the shipyard in Marinette for the launching of the USCGC *Aspen* [WLB-208]. My wife is the *Aspen*'s sponsor and she had the opportunity to break the champagne on the hull. My wife and I were looking at memorabilia of the event the other night. It included a broken champagne bottle in a little wooden box that looks like a casket. It's engraved and all. My wife had a lot of fun with that, and was very honored to be the sponsor of USCGC *Aspen* [WLB-2080], which was later stationed in San Francisco, right down below the quarters on Yerba Buena Island, when I was assigned there as PACAREA Commander.

JD: Was there ever a time that you wished you had another assignment than this one?

TC: No, I had fun and it was a satisfying assignment. We were building new capability which the CG needed. For example, the 87-foot coastal patrol boat was such an improvement over the 82-foot it replaced, both in terms of operational features and improved habitability. G-A was a great job and I'm glad that Admiral Kramek had the confidence in me to make that assignment—to start me off as a flag officer in that way.

JD: In this job, did you have anything to do with the naming of the cutters?

TC: Not directly. For a new class of cutters, there is a special naming committee run within the Office of Operations and they have various representatives on it. Later as Commandant, I did make subtle suggestions to the operations staff about naming options. The national security cutter is named after notable people in Coast Guard history and, as Commandant, I strongly suggested that the first one be named *Bertholf,* after Commodore Ellsworth P. Bertholf, the first Coast Guard Commandant. He was the heart and soul of making the merger between the US Revenue Cutter Service and the US Life-Saving Service, to form the modern Coast Guard in 1915. Without Bertholf, we may have been moved to the Navy Department or been dismembered after World War I. He was an incredibly important figure in Coast Guard history. And no ship had ever been named after him. By the way, he was awarded a Congressional Gold Lifesaving Medal for his efforts to successfully rescue 275 American whalers at Point Barrow on the north slope of Alaska under very difficult conditions. Amazing guy, and we had to honor him.

I also suggested that the new seagoing buoy tender that was to be assigned to Hawaii had to have a Hawaiian name, consistent with the general requirement to name them after trees or shrubs. And the name should be CGC *Kukui*. That was just natural. I mean, number one, the kukui nut tree is the official state tree of Hawaii. Number two, there was a famous previous CG ship in the immediate post-WW II pacific theater named *Kukui*. It was a no-brainer.

JD: Can you talk about the feedback you received from Senator Daniel Inouye of Hawaii, about a new buoy tender being named *Kukui*?

TC: He thought that was the most marvelous name that we could ever come up with. USCGC *Kukui* [WLB-203] would be commissioned later when I was PACAREA Commander. The *Kukui*'s commissioning ceremony took place at our Coast Guard base at Sand Island. Senator

Inouye was a guest speaker. We had a Hawaiian blessing included in the ceremony. I remember at the reception the senator came up to me and said, "Tom, the Coast Guard really knows how to name their ships. The Navy needs to take a few lessons from you. It is a perfect name for this cutter." Of course, the senator was very pleased. He loved that ceremony! It's a magnificent ship in an extraordinary place, and it's giving great service to the people of Hawaii and the islands.

JD: You had twelve major systems. How did you prioritize them?

TC: Well, the ones that were the biggest in dollar terms, and in potential service impact, certainly got our attention. Those that had some innovative twists, or turns, or challenges to them, took a lot of attention. The BUSL took a bunch of time to work through the problems we had with it. If there is a protest, that took your attention. So, you know, the priorities came and went depending upon the issue that you had to deal with at the time. But, the major acquisitions and associated decision points were scrutinized all the way to the department level. CG HQ operational program managers who owned the requirement for a project had a major say regarding priorities, as they should. Of course, the priority of projects within the budget was at the hands of CPA and the Chief of Staff, with input from G-A and the sponsoring CG programs.

JD: Do you recall how large of a staff you had in acquisitions?

TC: It wasn't big enough. I forget the exact number we had. I know we had to cut it by 12-15% as part of Headquarters streamlining. So, at the very time we are ordering $3 billion worth of things, I'm cutting out staff. Oh, by the way, that's why we did some processes improvement work and have quality action teams to identify how we can do things with less staff. But, that was a challenge and I would submit that, ultimately, staff reductions did not serve us well as an organization. I know it was support infrastructure, but I considered it the meat and bones. I noted earlier, that the CG wanted to cut the fat in streamlining and not the muscle. I considered Major Systems Acquisition staff muscle because there were huge dollars at stake and cutting it didn't serve us well as we were about to move into the Deepwater acquisition. We had less staff and OMB and the Hill wanted to cut more as we were about to enter Deepwater. And, the problem with that is that it shaped the acquisition strategy we pursued for Deepwater because we didn't have enough people. There's two reasons why Deepwater was shaped the way it was, as an integrated system of systems, with two contractors as system integrator via a joint venture arrangement.

Number one, OMB insisted upon a comprehensive system-wide mission analysis. It was difficult to consider procuring Deepwater by component platforms and sub-systems. They wanted tradeoffs between component assets of the overall system. They wanted a system of systems analysis. They wouldn't approve just one piece. So, that's the number one issue that drove us in the system of systems direction.

Number two, when it came to actually running and implementing projects, we didn't have enough project management staff or expertise to contract Deepwater as a number of separate contracts—for individual ships, boats, aircraft types. The CG didn't have enough talented procurement people. Acquisition requires a highly professional competence.

So, professionalism was a problem and numbers were a problem. And, how does the CG pursue separate contracts in the conventional manner? When we are replacing three classes of ships, all of the aircraft—fixed-wing and rotary—and all of the other piece parts associated with these systems, like sensors, how do we do that with the staff we had? So, that forced us to go to a commercial systems integrator, to Northrop Grumman and Lockheed Martin, who eventually won the Deepwater contract. So, we had to go non-organic because of the lack of professional competence and head count to manage these projects. Did we want to do it that way? We would have preferred not. The system of systems with a contractor as the integrator, for this size procurement, was an innovative concept. And I can't slam OMB for demanding that we show how all of the component parts of the systems related to everything else. They wanted the most efficient overall performance of our operational assets—that's what they were asking for. So, we did extraordinary, innovative operations research analysis to show how all of the pieces intertwined—how, on net, the whole system produced the same operational outcomes at less cost. That was the one way we are going to get this improved in a decremental budget environment. If we can show that we can produce the same or greater operational outcome with less of this, and more of that, and less of this on net—it's going to be a less expensive system— that was the way to be successful in the budget environment we were in.

So, given the external and internal circumstances, the concept, I think, was still very valid. The problem was in the project management side, the governance side. We ultimately got a contract awarded [in 2002], and the overall system design was good. I should note that, upfront, in the systems design phase, we had three different companies—a consortium of companies providing designs of the system of systems—and the Lockheed Martin/Northrop Grumman design won. The design was fine, other than the approach to stretch out the 110-foot patrol boat to 123 feet. Later in construction, the design proved to be a bust—structural problems with the design that caused the program to be terminated at Hull #8. The overall system of systems design—i.e., the number and types of ships, boats, aircraft, and associated C4ISR—it was alright. It was in the project management/governance side that difficulties arose related to the systems integrator—hiring a systems integrator for that big of an effort, instead of doing that function in-house, proved a challenge. As I noted earlier, at an early juncture in the project, we did not have the numbers or talent to take that role on. The workings of the two organizational elements of the commercial joint venture taking on the systems integrator role, Lockheed Martin/Northrop Grumman, did not function as smoothly as anticipated.

And, so anyway, that's a quick introduction into the Deepwater Major Systems Acquisition. Most of that happened subsequent to my assignment in G-A, and we can get into it more later if you want.

JD: How did the name Deepwater come about?

TC: Well, essentially it was because we were building an offshore, deep-sea, long-range system of assets to replace major assets like the High Endurance Cutter, the Medium Endurance Cutter, long-range aircraft, helicopters, and the like—having the capability, sustainability, and endurance in all weather conditions at long-range. For example, you don't want anything small in the Bering Sea, given weather and sea conditions, and distance from support facilities. These were the long-range, deep water, non-coastal assets, so Deepwater appeared to be an appropriate title for the project.

JD: You and I know this, but for the purpose of history, so when decades from now, people are reviewing your transcript—why did the Coast Guard need to modernize its fleet of cutters, aircraft, and sensors at this time?

TC: Well, they were all arriving at block obsolescence at the same time—all at the end, or approaching the end, of their planned service lives. The replacement acquisitions for the CG's various capital assets—ships, boats, planes—kept getting put off and put off, due to an inability to fund them (i.e., don't replace it, repair it). Like the Fleet Renovation and Modernization (FRAM) program for the 378-foot High Endurance Cutters. FRAM was put in place to keep the 378s around longer. Same thing with icebreakers: "Keep them around. We don't have money to buy new ones." We were only getting $300 or so million a year in the AC&I appropriation. We needed at least $700 million to start to make a dent in ship and aircraft replacement requirements.

So, pretty soon, that all collapsed on itself. You can only extend them so long. It's just so inefficient in terms of life-cycle costs. It's costly to maintain and run these older ships and aircraft. Plus, they don't have the capability you need in today's world—you can do missions with less, more efficient, new, and more capable assets—like we did with the buoy tenders when thirty new ships replaced thirty-seven old ones.

We were faced with this block obsolescence of most of our essential capital assets. So, how do you replace them all at the same time? We could have had a much shorter buyout of the component parts of the Deepwater system or systems, but it had to be done with only "X" amount of money per year at a total cost of "Y" (given budget constraints imposed by OMB/Congress). So, that stretched it out to over twenty years, and longer as the project unfolded. I always said, you know, "Who in the corporate world would ever have had a recapitalization program that went twenty years? Who would ever, ever do that?" It didn't help in attaining an efficient project since it stretched out over twenty years. You are susceptible to technological, political, and budgetary changes—all of these moving targets over twenty years. The OMB mandate was to replace all our Deepwater ships, aircraft, and boats while maintaining the same or greater level of operational output as the legacy systems—but do that at lower operational costs of the systems.

So, we were looking at moving targets, and still we had to manage the legacy systems during the transition periods. Part of taking the 110-foot patrol boat and stretching that to a 123-foot patrol boat was to make it more capable and keep it around a bit longer. We couldn't afford to buy the new patrol boat scheduled for the system of systems because it did not fit within budget ceilings. We couldn't afford to have the ultimate patrol boat, the Fast Response Cutter, until later in the twenty-year period of the overall project. We had to have a gap filler with a legacy asset, hence, the 123-foot patrol boat project tied us over until we could afford the ultimate replacement. Did we want to do it that way? Not necessarily. But, it was budget-driven. So, we had to manage this system of systems—new, along with legacy systems—and sometimes the tradeoffs were not the most desirable.

Unfortunately, every dollar put to the maintenance and repair of existing old and tired ships, boats, or planes was a dollar not put in the asset replacement bucket. Plus, we were delayed in getting the advanced capabilities we needed. We had old platforms, we had ships—as I used to say—old enough to collect social security. Spare parts were difficult or impossible to obtain and the habitability conditions for CG men and women were substandard. So, it was frustrating in many ways. In a nutshell, there were a great deal of externalities that influenced the strategy and the structure of how we managed and conducted the Deepwater program.

Deepwater, especially the National Security Cutter (NSC), got beat up a bit on the Hill after 9/11. You know, the Deepwater contract was awarded on June 25th, 2002 (I remember that date well because June 25th also happens to be my birthday. So, getting this contract awarded was my birthday present to myself). The Deepwater program award in 2002 was based on pre-9/11 requirements. So, the performance specification that governed the National Security Cutter was a pre-9/11 performance specification, but it was pre-9/11 requirements. So, the Secretary and the President, rightfully, directed a reassessment of the mission requirements of the cutter, with 9/11-type threats in mind.

In effect, they directed the CG to redo the mission needs analysis which specifies the performance requirements that you need in the system. They wanted to know if any of the requirements had to change because of 9/11 and a realization that world security conditions and threats had changed. We did a new mission analysis and identified several significant things that were not included in the cutter's design given post-9/11 world conditions. It recognized that the cutter should have nuclear, biological, radiological detection and protection capabilities—the current design did not. The other thing was a Sensitive Compartmented Information Facility

(SCIF). The ship needed a SCIF to deal with all the highly classified information in this new environment. The Secretary and White House approved the new mission analysis with these and other changes. Of course, the contract had to be modified and, when an already awarded contract gets changed, costs go up. However, these contract changes were based on a mission analysis directed and approved by the White House and the Secretary. We made the contract changes; the changes drove costs up.

Then, there was another thing that happened. A hurricane went through the shipyard where the National Security Cutter was being built. It did significant damage to the shipyard. Getting the shipyard back in working order was borne partially by the customers who had work being done there—Navy and CG. So, there were two new price tags. One was due to new requirements based upon the post-9/11 world and the other was the hurricane. We presented all of this to the appropriations committees on the Hill and did not get a great reception, even though we were dealing with externalities that were not as a result of poor management or poor shipbuilding. We got beat up fairly well by the appropriations staff, particularly in the House, for cost growth.

Looking back, I think we got a bad rap on all of this, quite frankly. The design of the National Security Cutter was also criticized. The first cutter had several minor structurally weak areas, but could be corrected—and was. They were frequent design maturation issues associated with new ships. The overall design itself was, and is, an awesome design. In fact, it's the best, most capable, most crew-friendly ship the CG has ever built, going all the way back to 1790. Ask any CG NSC sailor and they will rave about that cutter. Deepwater and the NSC took a great deal of slugging through the Washington gauntlet—a torturous route, but at the end of the day, it was well worth the effort because they are wonderful platforms that are giving great service to the American people.

JD: You were responsible for a dozen major programs. Could there have been more programs if you were not so resource-constrained?

TC: Well, the major [ones] were getting done. But increased funding would have accelerated many of the multi-year projects, thereby driving down costs and getting better platforms and equipment in the hands of CG men and women. One thing that took a back seat while we were doing all of these capital investments were our major shore facilities. The amount of funds allocated to those projects dropped considerably. But, there were some shore capital investments still being done. For example, we put a good deal of money into Kodiak facilities.

Clearly, the most impacting thing we could have done with extra resources was to compress the timeline for the Deepwater program. There were so many advantages to compressing the Deepwater program—like removing cost, schedule, and performance risks. We could have substantially reduced acquisition costs and reduced the costs to maintain the legacy systems, since they would have been replaced sooner. A twenty- to twenty-five-year program is a huge risk in terms of cost, schedule, and performance. The ability to control those things is hard, and then you are making tradeoffs between the legacy systems and the systems that are going to replace them. We saw the program stretched out, and an increasing proportion of the Deepwater dollars going into the legacy systems to keep them alive. There were a lot of juggling acts to make everything fit. We were not dealing in a perfect world. And key to everything was to ensure that between our new and legacy systems, we maintained the necessary level of operational capacity and capability.

Oh, by the way, to get more specific regarding your earlier question about acquisition staff size, I have a few notes on that issue. They show: 360 people were in Coast Guard Acquisitions. The 360 included a procurement division, a major procurement division of the Coast Guard (which serviced more than CG HQ projects and major systems), a project management division, quality assurance division, and a planning staff. 255 were in Headquarters, and the rest were in the field, such as the resident project officers at shipyards. And I should note the staff did more than major systems acquisitions; they did a good deal of smaller procurements for the entire CG.

Of course, DOD has a huge acquisition empire that includes the Defense Acquisition University, and that's why, for certain things, we went to the Navy to build certain ships. One acquisition that we haven't talked about yet was the USCGC *Healy* [WAGB-20]. The *Healy*, an Arctic research vessel, was named after Captain Michael A. "Hell Roaring Mike" Healy, USRCS. The construction of the Healy was strongly supported by the distinguished, now deceased senator from Alaska, Senator Ted Stevens, whose wife was the sponsor. For that procurement, we went to the Naval Sea System Command over in Crystal City. We went to them and established a joint CG/Navy project office; one of the reasons being because all of the funds to build the *Healy* came from the Ship Construction Navy (SCN) account, and the Navy has the right acquisition talent for the procurement.

There was also another cooperative effort conducted between the Navy and the Coast Guard, and that pertained to the HH-60 helicopters. The Navy built the Seahawk; we were building the Jayhawk. We had a joint effort because the commonality of the parts in the two helicopters was between 70 to 75%. We were trying to do smart things given our limitations. So again, we took advantage of the scale and talent within the DOD. We have also used Naval Air Station Patuxent River to do studies for us. So, when we can partner and leverage their capabilities, we've done so.

JD: Given all of the challenges, how would you describe the morale of your office at this time?

TC: I thought it was really good. Everyone was involved. I didn't stand in the front office and issue edicts. I tried to ensure a team approach to things. An example—when we were arresting the BUSL, I had the lawyers in there; I had the contracts specialist; I had the project manager; I had the operational sponsor. We worked through the issues involved collaboratively, and I think everyone appreciated feeling that they were part of the solution and that they had a voice in it. Everyone had an opportunity to contribute, and I gave the project manager a lot of leeway to be innovative and work the issues. But objectively, you would have to ask someone else about the morale. I mean, it's tough for me to be totally objective. But, my assessment is that the people in G-A had a good feeling about what they were doing—there seemed to be excitement associated with acquiring the new systems for our service, and great enthusiasm for the innovative things we were pursuing.

JD: How did you handle that flow of information on all these acquisition programs so that you can carry out your duties?

TC: Well, when I first got there, the IT functions were a little fragmented across the office. Number one, we established a single, organized, unified structure for IT. Number two, we developed an acquisition management information system for the office that was common to all of the projects. So, in terms of how you would report out and how you would monitor, it was centralized in a standard format. That seemed to be a good improvement since everyone gave it a thumbs up.

JD: Did you go to daily flag plot briefings in this role?

TC: Yes, of course. In Headquarters, there are frequent gatherings in the morning with the Commandant and his flags—not every morning, because sometimes he was travelling. And several times a week, you would have a gathering of the flag officers, hot issues would be briefed to the Commandant, and that would often spurn some follow-up activity. And streamlining efforts were still going on, so there were flag meetings about streamlining and how are we going to do the multi-year budget strategy. There was a frequent give and take on the issues of the day between Coast Guard leadership all of the time.

JD: What was it like to be a one star at Coast Guard Headquarters?

TC: Every flag office had a front office supported by a secretary and sometimes an aide. There would also be a front office reception area, but it wasn't huge. The Commandant's front office was bigger than that, but it was nothing compared to the CNO's front office. Of course, the flag mess was clearly available to one stars. Lunches there provided a great venue for dialogue and info exchange among senior CG leadership. Most importantly, every HQ flag officer, including one stars, had the opportunity to be heard. No one was bashful in speaking up and their input was most welcomed most of the time.

All of my tours in Headquarters were in the same leased building at Buzzard Point. When I first got to Headquarters for the R&D job, the Commandant was up at the Department of Transportation building on 7th Street. But then, very shortly during my second tour, everyone had moved down into our own building. So, we had our own building, your own identity. But, we have been in a leased facility since 1790. Until very recently, the US Coast Guard had never been in its own government building. Now, we're in a new CG building not far from Bolling AFB. The new building was built and occupied during Admiral Bob Papp's tenure as Commandant. He accurately noted during building opening ceremonies that the Coast Guard had led a very nomadic existence relative to our Headquarters, because we moved from one leased Headquarters to another over our existence, and now finally, we had a stake in the ground. And, today the Douglas Munro Coast Guard Headquarters Building is a beautiful facility. I'm very impressed with the job done by the CG and GSA. The only downside is that the CG currently is the lone stranger over there—it was supposed to ultimately be a Department of Homeland Security campus, [but] budget limitations have slowed down that process. But the plan, I believe, to move DHS to the campus is still intact.

JD: You had a lot of accomplishments, given the many challenges during this time in the Office of Acquisitions, as Chief. What would you say would be the most significant accomplishment?

TC: Managing the cost, schedule, and performance of all the projects. All of the projects were done within cost, schedule, and performance dimensions. There's not many times you can say that because it is a challenge to keep it to cost and schedule, because things happen. I was also pleased that we were at the vanguard of performance-based specifications and going more to Commercial-Off-the-Shelf (COTS)—driving the life-cycle costs considerations upfront into the requirements and ensuring integrated logistics support was an upfront consideration of all of those. And fortunately, significant improvements in acquisition have continued at a fast clip especially during Admiral Thad Allen's tenure as Commandant.

JD: What would you say was your toughest decision that you had to make?

TC: Tough? I don't know. I think, clearly, the ones associated with Deepwater were the most challenging, and they continued to be in my later assignments as Vice Commandant and Commandant. That is the most complex project we ever, ever have tackled and, as we discussed earlier, there were numerous external constraints on it. Clearly, Deepwater (now separated into Deepwater component projects/contracts, with the CG as systems integrator) has been, and continues to be, the most important and challenging set of projects.

JD: We are coming up on the end of your tour as Chief of Acquisitions. Is there anything else you would like to add about this assignment?

TC: I think we covered great deal of ground. Oh, one other thing. I don't think I mentioned this. Almost every contract award experienced a protest experience from a competing contractor.

JD: Can you talk about the protest process and how it worked?

TC: Yeah. There is area host of reasons that a competing company can protest an award. They can even protest it before the award is made if they have, or think they have, justification. There are various avenues and access points to do a protest, including the court system. Much of the basis for protests typically surrounds the source selection process—how you've evaluated the proposals that have come in, especially if they perceive cracks or inconsistencies in that process. In other words, you told competing companies you were going to evaluate it one way but didn't follow that process or inconsistently followed it. Every one of those major acquisitions has a source evaluation plan—specific documents which outline how the proposals would be evaluated. So, one thing we paid great attention to was ensuring great source evaluation plans and procedures, and sticking to them during the source selection process. But there are all kinds of other reasons for protests. I should note that the CG won every protest during those two years.

JD: This is as good a point as any to stop for today. Thank you so much for your hospitality and for sharing so much wisdom with us. It's going to be a real treat for everyone to read your oral history.

TC: Well, I hope that I haven't done any revisionist history. To the best of my knowledge, all of these recollections are accurate. It was a lot of fun talking about them. Thanks.

Interviewer: Jim Dolbow (JD)
Interviewee: Admiral Thomas Collins, USCG Ret. (TC)

JD: It's February 24th, 2016. This is Jim Dolbow and this is our fifth session with Admiral Thomas Collins. How did your assignment as the Commander of Coast Guard District 14 in Hawaii come about?

TC: My District 14 (D-14) assignment covered the period from 1996 to 1998. I transitioned to that job from my position as Chief of the Office of Acquisition in HQ. As context, at the time of my assignment, Admiral Kramek was still the Commandant and Admiral Jim Loy succeeded Kramek in 1998. Apparently, Admiral Kramek felt D-14 was a good fit for me. An operational assignment as a flag officer was a logical follow onto my HQ assignment and D-14 was high on my preference list. I had been assigned to D-14 staff previously, and had experience with all facets of the CG in Hawaii. I also felt D-14 was important because it was, in a way, a testing ground for the Deepwater program as most cutter utilization was long-range in the 14th District.

I relieved Rear Admiral William C. Donnell as the Commander of the 14th District in the summer of 1996. My wife and I went out to Hawaii as empty nesters and were fortunate to live in the original, Hawaiian-type command quarters sitting right on Diamond Head Road, right on the edge of the Diamond Head crater precipice. It was a beautiful spot to live. My wife Nancy was thrilled with the assignment and the living arrangements.

Having been the budget and administrative guy just four years previously, I knew my new assignment would be a very different role for me in D-14, but I was very familiar with the lay of the land. Now, the focus for me would be operational, and readiness, and how we can serve the public like we are charged to do. My first priority was to schedule a leadership conference of all of the senior officers in the district—a two-day off-site at the CG base on Sand Island to articulate my command priorities and strategic direction, and gain their feedback. It was a productive two days.

JD: Who was the PACAREA Commander at the time?

TC: Vice Admiral Roger T. Rufe, Jr. A terrific guy with a wonderful leadership style and personality. Great leader and very savvy Coast Guard officer. Then, after my first year in command, Roger was relieved as PACAREA Commander by Vice Admiral Jim Card. And, of course, those bosses were thousands of miles away which added, in a way, an additional layer of independence given the distances involved.

JD: As District Commander, how often did you interact with the PACAREA Commander?

TC: Frequently. And our staffs had frequent staff-to-staff exchanges regarding cutter utilization. We were frequently trying to obtain sufficient High Endurance Cutter (HEC) hours to allocate across D-14's AOR. Most HEC's were on the west coast, except for the two that were home ported in Honolulu. Much of the HEC hours were committed to enforcing the maritime boundary line up in the Bering Sea (D-17 AOR) against Russian fishing vessel intrusions. My staff was positioning to justify the use of additional WHEC hours in the D-14 AOR. Strategic planning, resource allocation, and related issues were the source of recurring interchange between the staffs. And Vice Admiral Rufe had all of the PACAREA District Commanders meet together at least twice a year to go through specific area agendas and work items.

JD: Can you talk about the vast AOR you had in D-14, and its fisheries mission?

TC: It's huge. The area-of-responsibility spanned over 12.2 million square miles and included the Hawaiian Islands, Guam, American Samoa and activities in Saipan, Singapore and Japan - a region nearly three times the size of the continental United States.

Fisheries enforcement in our Exclusive Economic Zones (EEZ) (the area from 3 to 200 hundred miles off the shoreline) was of big interest to PACAREA and US Pacific Command (USPACOM). The Pacific is the home of several pelagic fish which can travel at fast speeds and are highly migratory. Two of the most prominent pelagic fish are the tuna and swordfish. Globally, both of them are huge food stocks and overfishing or illegal fishing are constant risks with foreign vessels intruding into our EEZ to deplete our fish stocks with illegal fishing methods such as the high-seas drift nets. Some of these nets were up to eleven-miles long and were very effective fish catching machines, but they were indiscriminant, catching everything in their path including like sea birds, turtles, and porpoises. Such techniques were banned by a UN convention and as a signatory the US/USCG was active in enforcing its provisions.

So, with vessels using illegal methods of fishing, vessels fishing in the wrong areas, and oversight of our domestic fishing, D-14 was involved in a vibrant fisheries mission.

JD: Previously, you have talked about decremental budgets. Can you talk about the impact of decremental budgets on you as a District Commander from 1996 to 1998?

TC: The 14th District was the largest in PACAREA in terms of AOR, and the smallest in resources with a staff of about 1,500. The average sortie time, in terms of distance and time, was triple anything else in the Coast Guard. Huge demands on resources and huge areas but not a lot of assets. So, my focus coming into the job was, *How do I make all of this work? How do we effectively meet our mission responsibilities given the expansive nature of the AOR and constrained resources?*

We were in an environment during both the 1980s and 1990s where we struggled with flat budgets and trying to deal with increasing costs of operating aging assets. Aging assets require higher maintenance, so maintenance costs grew steadily while budgets declined. The platform was getting old and we didn't have the funds to keep them going. And you ended up depleting the spare parts inventories because you were extending the time between shipyard availabilities. Overall, there was a negative impact on operational readiness—a huge issue for all operational commanders. All of that was problematic. Admiral Kramek certainly articulated this problem in Washington, frequently noting that the CG had streamlines, cut out all and any fat in the budget, and now the CG was cutting into muscle—the muscle being the ships and aircraft that are getting more and more tired. Readiness was at stake and, ultimately, the service to the public was at stake. Obviously, these were huge issues for Admiral Kramek. Subsequently, it was a huge issue for Jim Loy, [even] when he became Commandant in 1998. His big slogan was "Restore our Readiness"—restore our readiness and build for the future. Those were his two mandates. And build to the future meant recapitalization—replacing aging legacy assets that were at the end of their service lives.

Given budget challenges, it was a demanding time to be a district commander. Our challenge in D-14 was to use the assets we had—albeit with reduced budgets—as effectively as we could. Our challenge was to manage our scarce resources or aging resources, and put them at the right place, at the right time to maximize mission outcomes. The responsibility of every operational commander is how and where do you place assets to get the best bang for the buck for our customers, the American public. And, that's what we were challenged to do, and my focus was do it intelligently. Do it based on the facts, understanding the risks, and using threat-based analysis.

JD: Admiral Loy mentioned in his oral history that you had a lot of Navy contacts from your time in the Pacific. Can you talk about that?

TC: The number one business in Hawaii is tourism, right? Everyone knows that. But, the number two industry is the Department of Defense. All of the service chiefs in the Pacific were there—the Commander-in-Chief of the US Pacific Command (CINCPAC), as well as its service components like US Pacific Fleet (USPACFLT), Pacific Air Forces (PACAF), United States

Army Pacific (USARPAC), and Marine Corps Forces Pacific (MARFORPAC). All of the Pacific service component chiefs were all three or four stars while I was a one star. Nevertheless, I would have to say that I was most welcomed, despite the disparity in rank and scale of the Coast Guard presence in Hawaii. The three- and four-star service chiefs were a very inclusive community, including my participation in many events and activities, [both] business and social. For example, we would all visit together, a couple of times a year, with Hawaii Governor Ben Cayetano. Given the extensive services provided to Hawaii by the USCG, many of the governor's comments and questions were directed to me. Governor Cayetano was very interested in domestic fisheries, safety of navigation, and port development. His interest shown was not lost on the other component commanders present. All of these things were on his mind, so it was an interesting give-and-take.

The closest relationship we had was with CINCPAC Fleet. We had liaison people there. Admiral Archie R. Clemins was Commander of CINCPAC Fleet the whole time I was there. He was a brilliant leader. He thought differently and he was very intelligent. He was very much into IT/innovation and bringing all of the 7th Fleet and the 3rd Fleet to the pinnacle of "IT-ness," and the use of the internet and open architecture. He was well ahead of his time in thinking about different ways to do business and increase the effectiveness of the fleet. So, I dealt with him and his staff frequently, including with those issues associated with the Coast Guard's Maritime Defense Zone (MDZ) responsibilities.

JD: Can you talk about your collateral duty as Commander of the Maritime Defense Zone Pacific (MARDEZPAC)?

TC: The maritime defense zones perform port security, harbor defense, and coastal defense missions under DOD contingency plans. I was involved with the planning and exercising Naval Coastal Warfare (NCW). We worked closely with Navy Reserve units since they had a primary role to play in NCW. It was also a large role for the Coast Guard Reserve. There was a dependence on both Navy Reserves and CG Reserves in the district staff in Honolulu in addressing MDZ responsibilities, and then when I got to PACAREA in a subsequent assignment, using Reserves to help develop MDZ plans approved especially effective. Part of our approach was to recall Reserves to active duty and assign them as liaisons to the staff of CINCPAC Fleet.

It became a very close relationship, both from a maritime defense zone perspective and from an operational perspective, since we leveraged the capabilities of the Joint Intelligence Center Pacific (JICPAC) a great deal.

We made huge steps forward in the use of intelligence to queue, schedule, and deploy our assets like never before, in both PACAREA and D-14. That was one of the pieces of the puzzle to accommodate a very expansive AOR with limited assets. It's all about putting cutters, aircraft, etc., at the right place at the right time. And, that is dependent upon the leveraged partnerships that you have. The USCG, starting in the mid-nineties and extending to the present, has really become much more sophisticated, more adept than ever before in the wide use of intelligence, and developing our intelligence competence. And some of that progress started in Hawaii with our partnering with Joint Intelligence Center Pacific (JICPAC).

Another thing that helped us tremendously was Joint Interagency Task Force West (JIATF West)—another DOD Command. JIATF West was headquartered in Alameda, California at the time, but its focus was counter-drugs, just like JIATF East down in Key West, Florida. When I became PACAREA Commander, my next-door neighbor on Coast Guard Island was the commander of JIATF West, Rear Admiral David S. Belz. Dave was a Coast Guard aviator extraordinaire and a good flag officer. With a Coast Guard guy as head of JIATF West, we leveraged that relationship to queue and schedule long-range assets for counter-drugs. Huge progress, but all of that meant relationships with the Department of Defense—getting back to the original question here. It was critical to build those relationships.

There was also a social dimension to those relationships, by the way. When I got out to D-14, I felt it was important to celebrate our heritage and our culture, and do that through an annual Coast Guard Ball. So, we initiated an annual Coast Guard Ball. The first one was very well attended and was at the Royal Hawaiian Hotel in Waikiki, a pink, very classic, luxury hotel overlooking the water. A number of Navy folks were invited and attended. One of them was a high ranking civilian navy employee named Bill Ryzwick. He was the senior Navy civilian in the Pacific, and ran all of the ship maintenance programs and readiness programs for the Navy. Well, typically toward the end of that evening, you get up and you sing your service song, *"Semper Paratus."* We all stood up, including Bill, and he's belting out *"Semper Paratus."* It's a small world. Bill grew up in the housing projects in New London, Connecticut, and, as a youth, he worked in small stores at the Coast Guard Academy packing sea bags for the new cadets. He noted that he probably packed my sea bag. So, I had to go over and introduce myself. It turns out that we and our spouses became very good friends. Unfortunately, he developed cancer and recently passed on. A terrific guy. It's just those kinds of relationships you build. Bill was well thought of by Admiral Archie R. Clemins, Commander-in-Chief of the US Pacific Fleet. He often assigned Bill all kinds of out-of-specialty, often difficult projects because he knew Bill always got results. So, it's those kinds of relationships that you make and you build on, and it leads to other relationships within CINCPACFLT staff. So, I've got good memories, both from a social and business perspective relative to those staffs.

JD: Why do you think it took until the 1990s for DOD to recognize the unique capabilities that the Coast Guard brings?

TC: I think that there are peaks and valleys in any relationship. Over the years, there have been very close USCG-Navy partnerships. We have fought alongside the Navy in every conflict since the beginning of our nation. In World War II, we were moved within the Navy, we were a Navy-CG team player in the Korean War, Vietnam, and, more recently, in the Middle East. And, throughout these years, DOD has gained an increasing appreciation for our unique blend of authorities and capabilities (i.e., armed forces and law enforcement agencies at the same time), and certain niche capabilities we bring to any engagement. Clearly, 9/11 brought that into an even sharper focus.

JD: Can you talk about the units assigned to D-14?

TC: D-14 is far flung. We had a MSO group/Captain of the Port function in Apra Harbor, Guam, and a detachment of the Captain of the Port, Honolulu, in American Samoa. We also had presence in the town of Hilo on the Big Island. We had a patrol boat there. We also had a small boat station in Maui and a patrol boat in Kauai and in Guam. We also had USCGC *Basswood* [WLB-388] in Guam. *Basswood* was involved in one of the most interesting cases in the history of the 14th District which we can talk about later.

We had a staff in Japan called US Coast Guard Activities Far East (FEACT) that had a marine safety and inspection mission. We had a Marine Inspection Detachment (MIDET) in Singapore. On several occasions, I visited Singapore to support them and see what they were up to. Despite the huge distances, part of my responsibility as D-14 Commander was to go out and make sure I understood every moving part of the enterprise.

My Headquarters was located in the Prince Kuhio Federal Building on Ala Moana Boulevard. I had a corner office on the tenth floor. It was the best office in the building because it overlooked Honolulu Harbor and the runways at Honolulu International Airport. I had to keep the blinds closed because I would get distracted looking at the great scenery. Down below on the harbor was the Captain of the Port's office.

On the south side of Honolulu Harbor was the Coast Guard base on Sand Island. We had USCGC *Jarvis* (WHEC-725) and USCGC *Rush* (WHEC-723) homeported there. We also had USCGC *Sassafras* (WLB-401) as well as several 110' Patrol Boats tied up there as well. In addition to the ships I just mentioned, there was also Coast Guard Station Honolulu. All of the Coast Guard's small boats on Oahu were run out of there. During my assignment, we were successful in obtaining funding and building a new station complex and named it after Commander Ray Evans. Commander Evans was a shipmate and close friend of the CG's Medal of Honor recipient, of Douglas Munro. They were from the Seattle, WA area and went to high school together. They enlisted together and went to boot camp together. They deployed to the Pacific together. They were at Guadalcanal together with Monroe killed in the engagement but Evans surviving. Evans earned the Navy Cross for his actions with the landing craft supporting the Marine Battalion that had landed but needed to withdraw because they were under heavy fire.

After the war, Evans rose to rank of Commander in the Coast Guard. He was in the marine safety business and later served as Captain of the Port in Houston, TX. But, he had been retired since 1962 when we located him and paid his way out to the commissioning of the Raymond Joseph Evans, Jr. Boathouse. To the young CG boat crews, he was a really cool guy. The young kids on his boat crews were in awe of him because he was a kind, quiet, humble guy, but with great insight regarding his Pacific and CG experiences. They had a little reception for him with the boat crew during his visit. Their mouths were hanging open listening to his stories. It was a wonderful thing for a current day boat crew to listen to a true Coast Guard hero. Those little things are important so as to understand who you are as an organization, and what road those in the organization have travelled—the long blue line. So, I felt the boathouse naming/commissioning was a really good event for all concerned.

We also had a major USCG Air Station presence at NAS Barbers Point that soon became a facility management issue that I had to contend with. The 1993 Base Realignment and Closure Commission (BRAC) recommended the closure of NAS Barbers Point on the island of Oahu. This became a major problem for us. We were a tenant on the Navy base and received a great deal of support from them that we received at bargain basement prices or didn't pay for at all. We didn't have to contribute to runway maintenance; we didn't have to run the tower; we didn't have to run the fire services—all of these trappings of an airport. We didn't have to run them. We were very fortunate to receive strong support from Senator Inouye to gain similar support from Hawaii state's DOT when they took over the Barbers Point airport facilities.

So, this was the resource laydown with a little less than 1,500 people. It had been 2,000 before "district light." If I remember right, 47% of the entire search-and-rescue area of the United States of America was in D-14. It gives you an idea of what kind of area to resource mismatch we were dealing with.

To address mission versus resource issues, I got out on the Pacific Rim and I talked to our folks. I listened. Sometimes that's one of the greatest skills that a leader can have. Some don't practice it. They just talk and direct, but don't listen. It's a skill. Listening is a communications skill. One has to get out in the trenches and listen. Within every element of our service there is a good idea or two or there is a comment that one can learn from—to improve your organization, to make their jobs easier and more effective. I did a lot of that because I wanted to be the smartest in the district about district affairs. I wanted to know and I couldn't do that sitting on the tenth floor of the Prince Kuhio Federal Building in Honolulu. So, I got out and about. I talk to our people and I talked to our customers to find out. An example of the benefits of this management style is the property challenges with Sand Island Base. Local interests, both in the government and in the private sector, had eyes on our property for their use and were campaigning with state authorities to make it so. I dove into the details of the issue, talking to interests on all sides. I was able to gain a seat on the harbor ports commission as a member to help deliberate the issue. It was very effective in dealing with that issue and the land grab got off their agenda. So, those "out and about" engagements and partnerships are important.

JD: What did you do to get the Sand Island issue off the table?

TC: Sand Island was attractive to commercial interests issue because right on the periphery of the Coast Guard Base on was a container port. The owners of the container port wanted our property at Sand Island because they wanted to expand.

I clearly explained how valuable our presence on Sand Island was to the state of Hawaii and that we did not have any reasonable location alternative. The senior senator from Hawaii was also sympathetic to our cause. Senator Inouye was terrific to have in your corner. I noted earlier that he was a major force in ensuring the state's DOT provided the necessary airport services to us at Barbers Point when thy took it over from the USN.

JD: Earlier you mentioned leveraging partnerships, and you mentioned JIATF West. Can you talk about other partnerships that you were able to leverage?

TC: It was extensive because our line of business thrusts you into all types of relationships in every corner. If you line up our mission set, it gets you into so many different agencies in local and state government. Internationally, it gets you into not just one ministry [but] about eight because they have our mission spread across a bunch of ministries. All US marine safety, enforcement, environmental protection, etc., missions are consolidated into one agency: the USCG. We had extensive ties and partnered with state safety agencies, state transportation, state and local enforcement agencies, state environmental agencies, the National Guard for disaster planning and response, NMFS/Western Regional Fisheries Council, etc., etc. All such relationships facilitated both our missions and those of our partners, all in the public's interest.

JD: Can you talk about the closure of the Omega Station in Haiku, Hawaii that was decommissioned on September 30th, 1997?

TC: Omega radio navigation systems, including the one at Haiku, are part of a bygone era—a technology and nav system no longer providing essential services. It also interfered with a major transportation project by the state. The Omega station that was in Haiku Valley, not too far from the Marine Corps base in Kaneohe, was part of the system to be dismantled. It was located in a very remote u-shaped mountain valley with steep vertical sides. The Omega antennas spanned the valley from mountain ridge top to mountain ridge top. The state of Hawaii was building the new H-3 highway tunneled through the mountains and it came right out at Haiku Valley as an elevated highway. The antennas had to come down. There were a number of factors to consider: there was the cost involved; there was an engineering challenge in determining how to safely remove the massive antenna system; there were environmental considerations involved. I initially envisioned putting Coast Guard housing in there because we needed housing and it was a great place with great views. We backed off that initiative given the presence of an ancient burial ground located on one side of the valley.

Many of the tough issues involved in dismantling the station were resolved with the state, in part due to the partnering and the relationships developed between my staff and the state of Hawaii. There was also a strong imperative to get H-3 done. It was important to the island. This factor drove parties to the table to quickly remove obstacles. Part of the resolution included shifting title for parts of the property to the state, which included the "stairway to heaven," a very rustic stairway on one side of the valley which ran from the valley floor to the mountain ridge. [It had] beautiful views and [was] popular with the locals and tourists. In the end, we got everything done in time so as to not hold up the highway and the state of Hawaii paid for the dismantling. So, we were successful with Barbers Point, Sand Island, and now with Haiku Valley, in terms of a facility and land-management perspective. In all of these instances, it was partnerships that you create and trust and that allows you to move forward on these things.

JD: Did you have a partnership at all with the Federal Bureau of Investigation (FBI)?

TC: Yes. We did get to work with them when we had to deal with illegal Chinese migrants, which was one of the growing mission areas in the Pacific. And, it wasn't just contained to the Hawaiian Islands. It was down in Guatemala, and Mexico, and whatever. When I got to

PACAREA, there were three or four ships we interdicted with Chinese migrants off Central America.

JD: How about D-14's partnerships with the Hawaii National Guard?

TC: There was substantial engagement with them because they were involved in Maritime Defense Zones-type considerations—coastal defense, but most importantly, civil defense and disaster response. They were immersed in the civil defense planning efforts for the state. Their emergency operations center for civil defense was in Diamond Head crater. So, for all of the associated contingency plans, we worked with the Hawaii National Guard.

JD: How about D-14's partnership with the Honolulu Police Department (HPD)?

TC: Yes. We dealt with them a lot on issues like boating safety, harbor issues, and drunken boaters. The biggest reason we had a relationship with the HPD was so when we boarded a vessel and arrested someone, we have someone to hand the person off to. Simple as that. We would do the initial engagement with the perpetrator on the water, and then we would hand them off to local police.

JD: Can you talk about the Coast Guard's partnership with Joint Intelligence Center Pacific (JICPAC)?

TC: The need to establish strong a strong relationship with JICPAC was driven by our desire to develop improved intel driven operations--the ability to put assets at the right location at the right time to get mission results. This was critical to us given our limited assets and geographically huge AOR. We established a liaison billet person there to assist in these efforts. We leveraged everyone's capability to work together. We also wanted to ensure a strategic assessment of our AOR—that was one approach to solving the time-distance dilemma that I faced. The other thing was leveraging technology. Another thing was to think differently about your business—strategically, not incrementally. Take a strategic look at your AOR. Our intel relationships helped us do that.

JD: Can you talk about the strategic overview of D-14's AOR that you launched?

TC: It was called a Regional Strategic Assessment and it led to a document called Future View 2010. D-14 was the first Coast Guard District to do a strategic assessment of the future, independent of Coast Guard Headquarters. When we launched the strategic overview of our AOR, we asked ourselves, "What are the threats and risks? What are the probabilities, potential consequences, etc.?" We then rank ordered the top 100. After we ranked them, we developed contingency plans associated with the high priority ones. Our strategic assessment also informed us on what resources had to go during our next budget build. This strategic assessment was completed by the end of my first year as district commander. Our efforts were materially aided by a culture of TQM—process improvement, quality assurance, balance score cards, metrics that existed in D-14 due to the work we had done in my previous tour in D-14 as Admin Chief and District TQM Coordinator. Our efforts soon became the blueprint for all of PACAREA.

So, our strategic assessment made us a leader in the Coast Guard on strategic assessments and how to make sure you are allocating and utilizing your resources in an informed way and with the greatest impact. The nineties were sort of a high watermark in the Coast Guard for business plans and performance planning. Much was being done at Headquarters in DC and one of my goals was to ensure that we were planning effectively in D-14, and that we dove-tailed with the endeavors at Headquarters. In the final analysis, it was all about how to make D-14 more effective and productive.

Our strategic assessments also stressed the need to leverage technology where it would enhance operations, and we made great advances here regarding our fisheries law enforcement mission. We were responsible for overseeing permitted domestic fisheries EEZs [Exclusive Economic Zones]—i.e., the Hawaiian archipelago—and there were regulations and permits associated with those that only certain folks could fish at certain times. There were also extensive Exclusive Economic Zones throughout the western Pacific that were off limits to foreign fishing vessels, but were often penetrated illegally by foreign fishing vessel fleets from the Philippines, Taiwan, and mainland China. These big fleets were after swordfish and tuna, but mostly tuna. Our challenge was to enforce our resource rights and sovereignty in these areas as well as protect the domestic fishery within the Hawaiian Islands.

Airborne surveillance is the key in the Pacific because it's such a large area. Initially, most of our C-130 hours were going to surveil the domestic fisheries and we didn't have the capacity to monitor the vast EEZs. The use of technology made us more effective in addressing these challenges. Working with the Western Pacific Regional Fisheries Council and the National Marine Fisheries Service, we put a transponder on all vessels that were permitted to fish in domestic fisheries. In order to fish, the vessels had to have this black box and they had to be communicating via satellite to D-14's Operations Center.

There was very limited pushback from domestic fisherman about using this technology with their position being monitored in a Coast Guard Operations Center. If it was monitored anywhere else, they wouldn't have bought in. This position information is closely held by all fishermen. They don't want to broadcast where they are fishing from a competition perspective. So, we monitored the fishing fleets with a complete picture of every fishing vessel and what it was doing. There was a distinct signature on the positioning of the fishing fleets when fishing. It's called hauling back and they make a certain movement with their vessel to haul their catch. The transponder system, called Vessel Monitoring System (VMS), allowed us to ensure that fishing was being done by the authorized vessels in the right areas at the right times. [Without] their VMS system, their permit was pulled. If they were underway, they had to have one.

So, it was a partnership between the fishermen, the regional council, and the national marine fisheries using this technology. And it increased our fisheries law enforcement substantially since all of the C-130s maritime surveillance patrol hours that had been devoted to the Hawaiian Islands could now be used on foreign vessels threat intrusion in the EEZs. Based on our experience in D-14, the USCG would shortly expand use of similar technologies in other fishery locations. I give great credit to my D-14 staff in seizing the initiative here. I have to give credit to a creative staff that bought into strategic assessment, planning, and the use of technology. It was a culture change and they seized it. They ran with it, seeking to improve the process, to improve the way we were doing business, all in the customer's interest. Captain Mike Mierzwa was my Chief of Staff. Terrific guy. Captain Denny Sirois, later flag, was the ops chief. I also had great civilian staff. Looking back, I have to say, it was a great all around team effort.

JD: Do you feel that the progress you made and your partnership with JICPAC helped make the case years later, when you were Vice Commandant, for the Coast Guard to formally join the Intelligence Community (IC) on December 27th, 2001?

TC: It was one of the building blocks. People started to realize our intelligence needs and capabilities. But I would have to say, most intel growth came later. It was the impact of 9/11 that drove the greatest intel enhancements, growth, and community membership.

JD: Can you talk about the intelligence-driven and threat-based scheduling you pioneered at PACAREA?

TC: The objective was to get away from scheduling cutters and aircraft patrol blindly in the same patterns. We had scarce cutter resources that were getting scarcer because with an aging fleet comes lost cutter days due to maintenance. We wanted to position them the best way we could, based on mission analysis driven by intelligence and threat-based scheduling. That's what we wanted to do. We turned things around regarding how we utilized cutter and aircraft assets, resulting in incredibly productive outcomes in our fisheries and drug law enforcement missions. It was about new, fresh ideas to the way we do our business. That was my mindset in D-14, and also at PACAREA.

JD: Can you talk about high seas drift net case involving the *Cao Yu* 6025 in the western Pacific?

TC: The *Cao Yu* 6025 was a large seagoing fishing vessel. It happened to be an illegal joint venture between Taiwan and the People's Republic of China (PRC). It had a crew from both Taiwan and China. Who said they can't cooperate? Typically, there was a mainland crew and a Taiwanese master and engineer.

High seas drift net fishing had been banned by a UN Convention. We were a signatory and it was one of the Coast Guard's responsibilities to enforce it. We partnered with Canada and Japan to deal with this issue in the northern and western Pacific. We had cooperative approaches to this. C-130s flew maritime surveillance missions out of Kodiak because it was the closest to the fishing grounds. We had also assistance from JICPAC on sightings, so not only were we flying C-130s, but we had their surveillance assets and intel on ship positions in the Pacific. This greater maritime domain awareness assisted in our high seas drift net enforcement, locating vessels like the *Cao Yu* 6025.

We didn't have an abundance of High Endurance Cutter hours in D-14 because most were programmed to the D-17/Bering Sea to conduct boundary enforcement missions. Frequently we had to be creative—in this case, we frequently used D-14 buoy tenders. They are billed as multi-mission assets and we used them as such. They can do law enforcement in addition to their aids-to-navigation (ATON) mission. For example, I sent USCGC *Sassafras* [WLB-401] and USCGC *Basswood* [WLB-388] as well as 110-foot patrol boats on a 5,000-mile patrol to far flung EEZs. To ensure adequate communications over the great distances involved, we outfitted all of our 110-foot patrol boats with Inmarsat. A 180-foot buoy tender, the Basswood was the primary cutter asset used in the *Cao Yu* 6025 incident.

The *Cao Yu* 6025 was cited by a P-3 Orion, and then *Basswood* intercepted it and took pictures of it illegally fishing using high seas drift nets. The *Cao Yu* was ordered to stop but refused. After checking with the Chinese government, who said it was not one of their fishing boats, we classified it as a stateless vessel, thereby coming under US jurisdiction. Since it was stateless, you can board it. They refused to stop and to allow us to board and headed back on a course to China. We tracked them for over 2,000 miles with the *Basswood* in chase and then flew a C-130 for continued air coverage. The C-130 was based out of Kodiak, Alaska, but it staged/flew out of mainland Japan. This flight was a very first in post-war Japan because they didn't allow law enforcement flights out of Japan. Speaking of partnerships, we had to go through the State Department to get authority to fly our C-130 for recurring airborne coverage.

The *Cao Yu* 6025 wouldn't stop and tried to ram the *Basswood* several times. So, there clearly were hostile acts against us. In the meantime, USCGC *Chase* [WHEC-718], a High Endurance Cutter, was coming off of deployment in support of CINCPACFLT on the Pacific Rim. We coordinated with PACAREA and CINCPACFLT to get the *Chase* diverted to assist the *Basswood*. After my discussion with the *Chase* co, a coordinated *Chase-Basswood* op was planned, which involved the *Chase* coming over of the horizon at very early first light to intercept the *Cao Yu* while the *Basswood* was in a stern chase with the F/V. The two USCG ships coordinated a forced boarding with long guns and small boats from their respective ships coming alongside. Boarding team members scaled the sides of the ship and took over the bridge in an armed fashion. No one was injured and the F/V crew and master were so shocked that they did not resist. A pretty amazing set of circumstances. We seized the vessel and escorted it halfway back to China, where we were relieved by a Chinese fisheries agency law enforcement vessel.

The case was marked by very effective coordination with the People's Republic of China. That's another partnership we developed on fisheries—strong relationship. After we passed to them the seized vessel, they escorted it all the way back to port and impounded the vessel. They then took the fishing permits away from all of the fishermen and fined them millions of dollars, etc. So, a wonderful and unique case that shows the importance of pre-need relationships, and not being afraid to exercise your authorities.

The next morning, I attended a breakfast and Admiral Joe Prueher, Commander-in-Chief of the US Pacific Command (USPACOM), was in attendance. He had been briefed on our *Cao Yu* case the night before. At the break, he approached me and commented about our forced boarding and seizure of a Chinese vessel in the western Pacific. At first, he seemed very apprehensive about it. But he also seemed impressed as I explained our capabilities and authorities in such cases and how much coordination we had done through our government and through foreign governments. I stressed that all of the boxes were checked and that our people are trained to do this type of operation.

Again, it comes back to partnering and the unique use of resources. We used the resources at hand coupled with technology, partnering, and intel queuing to get the job done. The D-14 staff thought it was cool. This is what we signed up to do. There is nothing like getting results. It was just like when the CG developed the use of force of initiative with armed helicopters from cutters—one of Admiral Loy's big initiatives. We armed our helicopters—sniper rifle/machine gun combo developed with aid of the Marines—to go after the go-fast drug boats. Up to that point, we were often just spotting them, surveilling them, and watching them go because we had no end game. We just didn't have the speed to close the game. But, we did with the use of force from helos. The USCGC *Gallatin* [WHEC-721] on the east coast was one of the first cutters to be supported by a use-of-force helo coming back from patrols with successful busts of go-fasts that had just come back from a patrol utilizing armed helicopters. It was not long before *Gallatin* had the highest reenlistment rate of all the High Endurance Cutters in the Coast Guard. *Why?* It was the end game and there are results. That's why people join the service—to get those kinds of results. It was instant gratification with the effort you put in, and you are getting good operational results. Well, we also got great results in the western Pacific high seas drift net cases and it bolstered the ship crew's spirit as well as that of the district staff.

Who says we can't operate effectively in the far western Pacific with limited resources? Travel 2,000 miles with a buoy tender and seize someone? You know, we can! Who says we can't send a 110-footer on a 5,000-mile patrol? We can! But, if we do it, assess the safety and operational risks. Accommodate the risks where possible. If not, we don't do it. Overall, it was interesting—a very interesting experience for all involved.

JD: Can you talk about the relationship between the United States Coast Guard and Singapore?

TC: Singapore was and is a strong international partner for the US and the USCG in the areas of maritime security, safety, and environmental protection. They have a compatible value structure regarding public policy and standards in these areas. The same focus. Very results oriented, very efficient. And [they] tend to be very supportive of us in various maritime forums, especially the Pacific CG forum and the International Maritime Organization (IMO). [They] were often our best ally in pushing issues through, whether it was search-and-rescue or other issues on the agenda. We also had cooperative relations with Hong Kong, especially in the area of search-and-rescue with an annual international SAREX held there. Even after it was transferred back to the People's Republic of China in the late-nineties, the annual search-and-rescue exercise in Hong Kong continued.

JD: What were the SAR exercises in Hong Kong like?

TC: They were very productive regarding the enhancement of SAR competencies among the nations involved and in building trust and cooperation among the participants. At a minimum, we would provide a C-130 for the exercise. Typically, there was both a coastal SAR exercise and there would be an offshore search-and-rescue exercise. *And what was the purpose of it?* Again, it was to raise the competencies of all of the countries around the South China Sea. We were the controllers of the exercise, the United States Coast Guard. Why? Because we are considered the premiere search-and-rescue organization in the world. So, we set up the exercise. We were the controllers and managers of the exercise. And, in addition to a C-30, at least once, maybe twice, while I was district commander of the PACAREA, we contributed a High Endurance Cutter to the offshore exercise. Clearly, these were critical and scarce assets for Coast Guard missions that were diverted to the exercises, but we considered the Hong Kong SAREX essential to our international strategy and supportive of the regional risk assessment that we had done. We considered the effort a high payoff area. These international partnerships are terribly important to us. We need these search-and-rescue relationships in the vast areas of the Pacific. So, anything that we can do to raise the professionalism and the partnerships in a pre-need relationship environment, is a good thing. So, we did that every year.

We did have to send our air crews to receive simulator training, to get in and out of the former Hong Kong International Airport in Kowloon City. The pilots had to make a really low approach and then a 90-degree turn into the runway at the last minute. I remember flying in there and looking out the aircraft window, and looking into people's apartment windows. It was a white-knuckle trip. During that period, the Chinese were in the process of building a new airport at one of the outer islands in the Hong Kong area—one of the most spectacular engineering feats in the world. They built a big suspension bridge, the longest in the world, over to this island. They chopped off the top of this mountainous island and created a runway. The train takes you right into the airport. Pretty amazing. They kept a number of British experts from the Hong Kong Civil Aviation Bureau around because they knew their business and they needed to have this project successful and it was.

In a nutshell, engagement with both Singapore and Hong Kong was about partnering for our mutual benefit. It was about how to extend our reach; how to make scarce resources more effective; how to pool our resources to get results. The same approach as creating a ship rider program with China. We partnered with them. Chinese fisheries law enforcement officials rode our ships to enforce the UN resolutions against Chinese flag vessels who were in violation of our mutual high seas drift net laws. We didn't have CG officers that spoke Chinese, and [so we] needed the authorities of their government to go aboard their vessels and search and arrest as necessary. The ship rider program effectively facilitated the enforcement of the UN convention.

Another effective program was the Automated Mutual Assistance Vessel Rescue System (AMVER). Well over 50% of the total use of AMVER was from the western pacific. We used it in technology to leverage our capabilities. The program is yet another example of focusing on partnerships, technology, and so forth, to gain greater mission effectiveness. That's what it was all about and that's what our planning efforts and our mission analysis effort showed. We developed an international strategic plan accordingly. And, again, I took all of that kind of perspective and experience and reinforced it in PAC Area when I was transferred there later.

JD: As the Senior Coast Guard Officer in Hawaii, did you have a lot of foreign counterpart visitors see you, after visiting PACOM Headquarters?

TC: A lot of that Jim. For example, we had frequent and close contact with the Japanese Maritime Safety Agency (JMSA), which is the Coast Guard of Japan. By the way, General Douglas MacArthur had a Coast Guard 0-6 on his occupation staff in Tokyo after the war who was responsible for creating a US Coast Guard-like entity within Japan. This is the reason why, if there's one organization in the world that's a mirror image of the United States Coast Guard, it's the Japanese Maritime Safety Agency.

So, our two agencies had a very close and supportive relationship. There was great interplay between the USCG Far East Section people that were stationed at the US Forces Japan facilities and JMSA. We have a small staff of eight people in the Far East Section. Two of which were Japanese nationals—civilian employees. All of those relationships were priceless.

Back to the meetings. DOD and CINCPAC had specific responsibilities associated with the insular possessions in the Pacific from a national security perspective. We were frequently invited to periodic meetings held with these island states and DOD because of our continued involvement with the islands from all kinds of different perspectives (fisheries, shipping, SAR, etc). We also occasionally engaged with counterparts from South Korea, New Zealand, the Philippines, etc.

And, of course, Hawaii was a wonderful place to live. I had frequent visitors to the USCG command quarters at Diamond Head light. There was a little lighthouse right on the property with an attached guest quarters. I had frequent visitors like Vice Admirals Richard D. Herr,

Roger Rufe, and Jim Card, when they traveled for business purposes to Hawaii. It was business and pleasure mixed—a good combination. I would host a little reception for them and invite a number of the DOD leaders. So, we got a lot of mileage out of the facility—a beautiful location. You could sit there on the lanai and look out at Diamond Head reef during the winter, early spring, when the humpbacks would come in, when they would be calving and you could see them jumping—breaching. So, again, the point I'm trying to make is, it was a wonderful place, a great environment to live in and work in. Clearly, meaningful employment. One small downside was the large number of feral cats that inhabited the area around Diamond Head crater. They could be quite a nuisance.

JD: Speaking of cats, there was a huge quality of life issue at the time was the pet quarantine laws. Can you talk about that issue?

TC: Yes, it was a real issue for military families. It was a challenge for people coming out there that had orders, and would actually deter some of them from taking the orders because of Hawaii's six-month pet quarantine. This meant service members could not introduce their family pet(s) until it has been quarantined at a doggy prison for six months. It was a challenging issue for families with pets. I think there was some moderation by the time I left the Pacific theater.

JD: There was some, given the advances in technology.

TC: Oh, okay. Well, I'm glad it's changed. Glad they modified it because that was a major concern by many of our personnel and their families.

JD: One last fisheries question. You talked about the partnership with them on the vessel monitoring. How was the Coast Guard's relationship with the fisheries on other issues?

TC: I thought it was very, very positive. Of course, it was great with the National Marine Fisheries. They were strong allies and supportive of housing the vessel monitoring system in our operations center. They were likewise supportive of our efforts to reallocate C-130 hours and expand our reach into other areas of fisheries enforcement. We were a key player in the Western Pacific Regional Fisheries Council, and most of the fisherman wanted us there because we brought a very practical operational perspective to things. We were all about safety for the fishing industry.

JD: Can you talk about Super Typhoon Paka, which hit the island of Guam on December 16th, 1997?

TC: Yes. It was a powerful one—one of the biggest in the history of the Pacific. The wind at Anderson Air Force Base on Guam was clocked at a peak gust of 236 miles per hour. There were over 5,000 homes destroyed. Guam was without electricity and there was a growing shortage of fresh water. I'm incredibly proud of the work that the United States Coast Guard did in the wake of Paka. We were the very first emergency responders on scene.

We were there with our Barbers Point C-130s in the immediate aftermath with all kinds of supplies, especially water and generators. We aided FEMA and the Red Cross. I can remember when our C-130s were flying in on the initial relief mission, and they and they ran into landing clearance problems with Anderson Air Force Base. We were told, "You don't have clearance into Anderson for this." Well we continued on anyway given the storm emergency and needs of Guam. This is an emergency and we are landing. Ultimately, we received support from DOD leadership to utilize Anderson. Overall, I was very, very proud of the response that CG men and women provided to the people of Guam. We kept the support flowing, that supply link flowing for a good ten days in the wake of the typhoon.

JD: Can you talk about Korean Air Flight 801 which crashed on Guam on August 6th, 1997?

TC: Yes, it was yet another crisis that struck Guam. It was a 747 that flew into the side of Nimitz Hill in Guam killing 228 out of the 254 passengers onboard. Our local Coast Guard folks responded to that tragedy the best we could, alongside the Navy and everyone else.

JD: I probably should have asked this sooner but when you became District 14 Commander, what were your objectives?

TC: There were a number of key objectives. High on the list was the objective to enhance our readiness posture—how to use our assets most effectively, especially given the budget pressures we were experiencing service-wide. These were increasing imperatives across the Coast Guard. The Commandant, Admiral Robert E. Kramek, in response to budget reductions, had cut all of the fat out during streamlining efforts and we were getting into muscle. Readiness is muscle. That was a concern. Admiral Kramek's successor, Admiral Jim Loy had similar concerns and challenges. So, it was clearly my objective across all operational commands, to get the pulse of where we were relative to readiness—to ascertain the material condition of our assets, the competence of our people, the level of our training. *Were we ready to carry our missions effectively?* Above all else, the CG is a response organization and we had to be prepared to adequately deal with our response to our top contingencies. *What and where are they? Where are the risks? How are we prepared? If we are not, let's get prepared.* So, readiness was a huge, huge focus.

The second focus—and we have talked about it generally—is the whole idea of a strategic analysis, mission analysis of our entire area-of-responsibility. Really understanding our area of operations. *What makes it tick? Again, where are the threats? Where are the risks? Where are lines of business in that area?* It was a requirement to undertake a comprehensive strategic assessment—a systems look—of our AOR. So, our objective was to take a systems look via a regional strategic assessment, a look that would take us out to 2010.

Another objective, and we've talked about it extensively, was to expand domestic and international partnerships. Our collective assessment was that there was substantial payoff here. Ultimately we built on existing, and developed additional, solid relationships creating the forums to engage internationally, and leveraging the great respect we had around our AOR. It's a good combination. Again, we can talk about that more when we discuss later efforts at PACAREA.

A fourth objective was to use technology, innovation and, process improvement to do our business smarter and look at ways to do just that. We established had all kinds of quality action teams to examine our business processes. Some of these paid off, some didn't. But, you know, you travel down the road until you say, well, we tried this. It's not going to work. We will try something else.

Also, in the context of these objectives that I just mentioned, our goal was to ensure that there were specific and unambiguous connections between our areas of emphasis locally, and up the chain of command. We wanted to ensure, especially to PACAREA and the Commandant, that we were supportive of service-wide priorities. We wanted to have that very clear link so all of those documents—the strategic assessments, the risk assessments—are all tied to resources, either reallocated or new. So, how we support corporate objectives was embedded in most of our plans.

JD: When the phone would ring at three in the morning, what typically would it be about?

TC: Well, most frequently a law enforcement or SAR/safety crisis of some kind. It might be a foreign the fishing vessel who was illegally fishing with a high seas drift net and trying to ram the *Basswood* who was on scene. Or, it might be a single-engine plane overdue from Oahu to Maui with only the pilot on board who didn't show up at his destination/ETA on Maui. "We've got some bad weather. We've got assets. They are not making a lot of progress at night in this weather. We are going to hit it hard at first light and we will give you an update at that point." We found the pilot, by the way. He had crashed in the channel between Maui and Moloka'i. Our rescue swimmer deployed from our helicopter to a plane debris field in literally shark-infested waters—four or five 20 to 25-foot hammerheads swimming around the pilot—and hoisted the pilot to safety. He had a series of gashes on his legs. The sharks had been swimming around just kind of, you know, hitting him. The rescue swimmer was unscathed.

So, that's a typical day in the United States Coast Guard. Those are the kind of calls you get. And every day of the year, we were poised to do those kinds of assists to the people of the Hawaiian Islands. That's why Governor Ben Cayetano and his state agencies had such great respect for us. That's why Senator Inouye supported us so much. They recognized the kind of things that we give to the public in Hawaii.

JD: Can you talk about pollution issues in D-14?

TC: Well, there was frequently reports of pollution in the harbor, or runoff issues with people dumping stuff in ditches. The Coast Guard would have to investigate all of those things. There would be a problem with a fuel farm in a remote part of the Big Island, and who did they call? Well, if it had any impact on the water, that's us. There are pollution response plans, response contractors, and associated action groups between us and other agencies—federal, state, local—about who had jurisdiction, near or associated, with the navigable waters of the United States. If we couldn't identify a spiller, or if the responsible party was not effective, we could federalize the spill, taking complete charge of the response action and holding the spiller financially accountable.

One pollution issue we dealt with in American Samoa was a number of damaged/submerged fishing vessels rusting and slowly leaking fuel oils in the harbor in American Samoa. A hurricane, some fifteen years earlier, had destroyed these fishing vessels and now they started to leak. Local authorities could not gain a consensus on how to deal with these destroyed fishing vessels. The Department of Interior had some responsibility. It would involve significant funds to try to get the hulks out of there. The United States Coast Guard Captain of the Port in Honolulu brought people together, cajoled them, pushed them, and finally got an answer on how to do that with safety and the environment at the forefront.

JD: Other than lack of money and distance, other challenges as D-14 Commander?

TC: There's always challenges. There are always opportunities to make things better. In Hawaii they included, how we were going to afford to decommission an Omega station in Haiku Valley when we had no budget to do so; how we were going to afford to keep CG Air Station Barbers Point going, given the Navy was closing its air station which had provided all the key support functions to the CG's air station; how to maintain our footprint/facilities at Sand Island in Honolulu Harbor in the face of local commercial interests, and sympathetic state authorities who wanted the property for other port uses; and how we were going to maintain our governance/sovereignty of far flung islands/EEZs of the Pacific. For all these challenges and others, most of them had answers. You bring a talented team together, and you bang heads, and you think "crazy" if need be. *There may be different way to look at the problem*, and so forth. As a district commander, you almost welcomed these kind of challenges, because they exercise the staff and the staff gets energized in attaining a solution that makes sense, and they have a sense of satisfaction when you succeed. Sometimes you are successful, sometimes you gain partial victories. Sometimes you don't. Incidentally, the challenges noted all ended in a good result for the CG.

JD: Can you talk about the role of Coast Guard reservists and auxiliarists in the 14th District?

TC: The auxiliarists were tremendous. But, you don't have many of regattas, and all of those kind of activities, like you had in Long Island Sound, where you had regatta, after regatta, after regatta, after race, after race, after fireworks, after whatever. You don't have that same kind of thing in the Hawaiian Islands, given open waters, sea state, and other factors. But, the Auxiliarists provided excellent support in all the typical areas—public education, administrative support, and the like. They were dedicated. The reservists were indispensable, particularly in dealing with Maritime Defense Zone issues. We really leveraged their capabilities because that was the clear focus of the Reserves. They lined up with Naval Coastal Warfare really well because that was largely a Navy Reserve function. So, that utilization worked very, very well.

JD: How did your prior assignments at Group St. Petersburg and Long Island Sound prepare you to become District Commander?

TC: Well, they all line up. Of course, they are all operational command assignments, but on different scale and different layers of complexity, especially regarding the breath of CG missions and issues involved. But, dealing with people, motivating people, leading people, setting clear objectives, communicating them well, holding people accountable, maintaining a focus on readiness and safety—these factors, the command assignments had in common.

So, the experiences of one command builds on another with your assignment subsequent to larger and more complex organizations. The one thing that is very important to learn and build upon from one assignment to another are the dos and don'ts associated with how do you deal with people—how to effectively lead from a command assignment; how you get the most out of people; how you effectively build the team and get everyone on the same "sheet of music." And, a lot of it is intuitive. A lot of it is feel. Some things work; some don't work.

I tried to show throughout my career that I had a sincere interest in the well-being and the professional development of the people that worked for me, by getting them the right training and the appropriate work assignments. I required most of the units that I was associated with to have a professional development plan developed for every one of the junior enlisted personnel. The chief or the first class involved would have to sit down with the junior guy, and actually put pen to paper helping he or she plot a chart ahead regarding their professional development. In essence, it was a personnel development plan that motivates and professionally develops Coast

Guard men and women, and clearly demonstrates command interest and support. And, clearly, the accumulated experiences gained working and delivering results with CG missions, in the areas of maritime safety, security, and environmental protection, were indispensable in dealing with increasingly complex operational and administrative issues when moving from one command level to the next higher one.

Overall, you learn all of those things from one operational command assignment to the next, to the next, to the next; and you put your experiences, good and not so good, in your leadership toolkit, and you apply them. In looking back, I find that I focused on similar strategic issues—especially if I had had good results—from command, to command, to command. When I was Commandant, you know, my general priorities were people, readiness, and stewardship. It was the three buzzwords that I used and constantly emphasized, that people could remember and focus on. All of my strategic goals and objectives boiled down to people, readiness, and stewardship with a host of specific actions supporting them. I would like to think they served my commands and the Coast Guard well.

JD: What advice do you have for future district commanders?

TC: Essentially the same thing that I would have for a group commander. "You are an operational commander. Care about your people, build the team, have a clear vision of where you want to take your command and communicate it. Communicate it well and often, and hold your personnel accountable for their contributions to it. If people don't know that, if they don't know what you are promoting, and where you are going and what your emphasis is, you are never going to get there."

When I was first assigned to Hawaii, I held a two-day off-site so that everyone got that signal and stressed that, if they saw any course corrections that are needed in any of that, let me know. But, once we all agreed on it, we were going to march down the street and implement this stuff. Again, having a vision, having objectives, clearly communicating them, and holding people accountable to them are very important. And having and maintaining associated metrics. In addition to having a well-articulated and communicated game plan and a motivated team focus, a key piece of advice would be to maintain the highest ethical standards throughout the command and demonstrating the same in your personal actions every day.

JD: We are coming to the end of your tour as D-14 Commander. Is there anything else you would like to add?

TC: Thank you Admiral Kramek for the D-14 assignment; and thank you to my immediate bosses in PACAREA, VADM Roger Rufe followed by VADM Jim Card. They are enlightened leaders who provided great guidance and flexibility to me. I enjoyed the heck out of that job. I had wonderful people on my staff. A great place to work and live. We did so many interesting things. I got to see so many nooks and crannies of the Pacific that served me well later. It gave me a perspective that I would never have had without those two tours there. And, I think strategically, that area particularly had a lot of implications for where the Coast Guard is going—was going to be going in the next few decades. So, I was very humbled to get the assignment, very pleased to be immersed in all of the issues of the western Pacific. And when I left, I felt good about the road we had travelled. I did think I left it a little more capable and focused command. My predecessors did good things. I built on that and I think I left it in good condition for my relief. And, it was good for Coast Guard men and women, and the public we serve. So, that was a good feeling. But I must say, it was tough getting my wife out of there. After two tours there, she loves Hawaii. And, in an earlier assignment in D-14, my daughter Kate had spent two of her high school years there. But, you know, we were going to PACAREA.

The two best Coast Guard flag quarters locations in the United States are in Hawaii at Diamond Head, and in Yerba Buena Island in San Francisco. So, I lived in one of them and was going to the other. Someone was looking after me! It was a wonderful, wonderful transition. From my perspective, it was logical. Since, as D-14 Commander, I had gained a greater understanding of missions across the entire AOR, preparing me well for the area assignment. It also involved a transition from one star to three star. I left Hawaii as a one-star, pinned on two stars, but then I had a change of command that made me a three-star. So, I think I was a two-star for two days. So, it was a terrific, terrific experience and honor. When I first learned about my assignment to PACAREA, the CG was in another one of those transition periods. The Commandant position was changing from Admiral Kramek to Admiral Loy.

JD: How did you find out about your new assignment as PACAREA Commander?

TC: I was at home in my quarters one afternoon, getting changed for an event so I was out of uniform in just my skivvies, socks, and a t-shirt. My wife Nancy noted that I had a call waiting that had come through from the Commandant's office in Washington. Clearly it was a very important call to take, as it was in the middle of transfer season and the incoming Commandant, Admiral Loy, was building his new team. I took the call and he said that I was going to be a three-star, and I was going to go to PACAREA and was pleased to include me in his senior leadership team. It was my first choice, and so I remember walking out of the bedroom, and my wife Nancy was sitting in the living room while I stomped around in my shorts and I said, "Well, you are looking at the next three star in Alameda." So, we laughed together, me in my shorts and black socks. [Laughs] But, it was a thrill. And I was honored in Jim Loy's confidence in me. And I couldn't hope to work for and with a more terrific guy than Admiral Loy. So, I was humbled by it.

JD: Were you surprised about being a two-star for only two days?

TC: I was surprised, given that I clearly did not assume I would be going to a three-star assignment. I also thought there were a lot of very capable Coast Guard flag officers that Admiral Loy could rely on for PACAREA. But, for whatever reason, he decided to promote me and assign me there. It was a tremendous fit because I had so much experience given my previous assignments in D-14. I had been involved in innovations and process improvement, and strategic planning, as well as the best use of resources. All of these things factored into Admiral Loy's decision to select me as PACAREA Commander. He said, "We need more of that across the entire PACAREA."

JD: Who did you relieve as PACAREA Commander?

TC: Vice Admiral Jim Card. Again, it was a tough act to follow. He was a very, very successful Coast Guard officer. You know, he wouldn't be going to be Jim Loy's Vice Commandant if he wasn't. So, I had great footsteps to follow in, as he was a process improvement guy. He was into planning—business plans. Vice Admiral Card came from the marine safety world, which I think led the Coast Guard in terms of business planning, performance metrics, and those kind of things. So, that was part of his world of work. So, he had made a lot of progress at PACAREA. I had a great foundation to build on, and he was going to be Vice Commandant.

So, Vice Commandant and Commandant were my bosses. As you might expect, I thought it was a very, very good fit. By the way, Jim Card and Jim Loy were Academy classmates—class of 1964 CG Academy graduates. I graduated four years after them. I followed Jim Card to PACAREA and then, when he retired two years later, I followed him to Vice Commandant, relieving Jim Card twice. Clearly, I have high regard for him as a very professional CG officer.

JD: Can you talk about PACAREA's AOR?

TC: If you think the D-14 AOR is big, PACAREA is like D-14 on steroids. It goes from the Pacific Rim to the west coast of the United States. From the North Pole to the South Pole, including the Bering Sea. You have most of the CG's largest and most capable air and cutter assets, including heavy icebreakers. Right now, the United States only has one operational heavy icebreaker and that is USCGC *Polar Star* [WAGB-10]. *Polar Star* has the responsibility for breaking out Station McMurdo in Antarctica every Antarctic summer. You have Arctic research and Arctic issues, which are growing and growing astronomically. The Arctic research vessel CGC Healy supported operations there. You have Coast Guard District 17 that is headquartered in Juneau, Alaska. We also have a major presence in Kodiak as a base, both for ships and planes. Every CG mission plays out in a large way in the AOR, and you deal with the most diverse international players on the planet.

Kodiak was a blessing and a curse at the same time. We can talk about why that was. It was expensive because we had a tired old US Navy base and all of its infrastructure needed fixing. I can remember pouring incredible amounts of money into Kodiak to bring it to life when I was the AC&I budget coordinator at Headquarters, knowing I would never visually see the results. What I mean by that is, it was not visible because it was all infrastructure. It was like the plumbing, the drainage, the power supply, the basics—never mind the fancy buildings.

The area, headquartered on CG Island in Alameda, California, is made up of the 17th District in Juneau, Alaska, the 13th HQ'ed in Seattle, the 11th in California, and the 14th in Hawaii. The Area Commander is double hatted as the 11th District Commander. District subordinate units included Marine Safety Offices, small boat stations, air stations, patrol boats, and buoy tenders. We had cutter and maritime surveillance aircraft operations off the eastern Pacific, all the way to Colombia. We had operations in the Antarctic. We had ships frequently on the Pacific Rim. We had USCGC *Midgett* [WHEC-726], homeported in Seattle, deployed as part of USS *Constellation* [CV-64] Carrier Battle Group to the Persian Gulf. That was an experience—first ever that a United States Coast Guard cutter deployed as part of a carrier battle group.

JD: How did *Midgett*'s historic deployment happen?

TC: We worked with CINCPAC to make the deployment happen, to experiment with the concept and to learn from it. We certainly learned what additional capabilities we needed in future deep water assets. The carrier battle group moves fast at a very high rate of speed. WHEC's like the *Midgett* are a turbine and diesel combination. When you get the turbines on, you've got to be at the gas station all of the time because it eats a lot of fuel as these are old ships. The bottom line was that *Midgett* could not effectively keep up the pace with the battle group. It was ultimately deployed with an amphibious group and provided credible service in that capacity. The embarked helicopter, an HH-65 had limited hot weather airtime given its under-power engines and high fuel consumption. Engine replacement some years later has remedied this limitation.

JD: Can you talk about the platforms that you had at your disposal at PACAREA?

TC: Again, the greatest number of the Coast Guard's largest vessels, homeported in Seattle, Alameda, San Diego, and Honolulu; and largest aircraft air stations in Kodiak, Sacramento, and Hawaii were in the Pacific area. They were the longest-range assets, obviously, because of the distances that you had to deal with. So, we had the most C-130s. We had the bulk of the High Endurance Cutters (WHECs). They patrolled up in the Bering Sea. They patrolled in the far western Pacific. They patrolled in the far flung Pacific EEZs. The C-130s frequently supported cutter operations as maritime surveillance assets. Our icebreakers, homeported in Seattle, staged out of New Zealand or Australia for access into Antarctica.

By 2015, we had three of the new national security cutters operating in PACAREA. Eight High Endurance Cutters, twenty-nine patrol boats, twelve buoy tenders, eleven sectors. They weren't sectors when I served there, but, they are there now. Eleven sectors, ten air stations in PACAREA. Thirteen C-130s, twenty-six HH-55s, thirteen HH-60s, and, of course, there is also deployable teams that we have—LE teams, environmental response teams, etc.

Today, the deployable assets are now coalesced in separate command structure. Admiral Thad Allen accomplished this when he was Commandant subsequent to my retirement. The new commands were a positive change. All of the deployable assets are grouped together, managed together, and scheduled together, which makes a lot of sense because they are really AOR independent. They go where the business is. Those are the national strike force—the tactical law enforcement units, the marine safety, and security teams, which was a product I created after 9/11, for port security and coastal security purposes.

Obviously, far east section, maritime section, and Samoa are still part of D-14, but obviously, subordinate to the area. There are a number of helicopter air stations throughout the area, structured as district units. One is in San Diego, one at LAX, one at SFO. We were at San Francisco airport (SFO) with HH-65 Dolphin helicopters. CGAS Sacramento had C-130s and helicopters; one in Astoria, helicopters; Humboldt, Humboldt/Eureka area, helicopters; Port Angeles, helicopters; Kodiak, HH-60s and C-130s; North Bend, Oregon, helicopters; Sitka, helicopters; air detachments in Guam; air support facilities in Cordova; and, of course, I couldn't forget CGAS Barbers Point, in Hawaii. That's quite a line-up. *Why do you need air in the Pacific?* Time and distance.

JD: How many personnel were assigned in the PACAREA AOR and can you talk a little bit more about the geography?

TC: There were thirteen thousand Coast Guard personnel in PACAREA's AOR. The area-of-responsibility encompasses six of the seven continents in the world. Seventy-one countries, 74 million square miles of ocean, the Arctic and the Antarctic. Huge. When you line up that and line up resources, it's a challenge. The same challenges in D-14, only bigger. You better put the resources—if you want to really leverage the resources and get output, get results, you've got to put them where the business is. *How do you know where the business is?* Well, we've got to know what the business is. You've got to know the shape of the business. That's where strategic risk assessments come in. You've got to know the risks associated with them and you've got to have a good intel apparatus that helps give you MDA—maritime domain awareness.

MDA means actionable intelligence for the operator so that you can plan and deploy resources to get results. It's a magic equation. To get it involves partnering. It involves technology and it involves command, and control, and sensors, and aircraft. It involves Deepwater assets. That's what Deepwater recapitalization is all about. Attaining Deepwater capability gets you MDA. [It] gets you mission effectiveness. We can meet operational demands with less assets. If you measure all of the long-range assets before and after asset modernization, we can do more with less because included in the future is maritime domain awareness capability. And part of that is building our intel, established as a huge priority by me and those that followed. You know, one of your standard questions, Jim, that you ask me is, "What were your objectives going into this new tour?" It was about getting MDA and getting intel.

JD: And, how did you go about getting MDA and getting intel now that you are at PACAREA?

TC: We needed maritime domain awareness in PACAREA's AOR and it starts with having a good intel—having visibility/transparency regarding what was happening in the AOR. For example, we couldn't have done the *Cao Yu* 6025 without having elements of that. It involves partnering in both technology and mission assessment. Regarding counterdrug ops, we partnered extensively with my next door neighbor there on Yerba Buena Island, Rear Admiral Dave Belz, who commanded JIATF West. He had an automatic entrée as a defense command into the Department of Defense intelligence network. So, we leveraged that relationship with relationships that we had built with the Joint Intelligence Center Pacific (JICPAC) in Honolulu. That input was very helpful in dealing with cutter patrol scheduling both for drug enforcement efforts in the eastern Pacific and fisheries enforcement in the western Pacific and Bering Sea. We also got better professionally regarding intel processes and analysis. I imported people from JICPAC to PACAREA to train a number of my staff. What we did in PACAREA was a start. It continued in earnest throughout the CG after 9/11 and continues to the present.

Good analysis and intel allows better use of scarce operational assets. It helps answer the question as to whether we are using them effectively. That was one of my first questions when I got to PACAREA. *Are we using these resources to our greatest advantage, particularly our large long range assets?* The other questions I asked, *Why aren't we doing any substantive counter drug operations in the eastern Pacific? Why aren't we scheduling ships there? Why are our drug interdiction results so paltry? There has to be a way to do better there. Why aren't we scheduling more resources there?* The initial response from staff was that there were no choke points—big expense, little intel, too hard, high-speed smaller vessels, not a lot going on there. My reaction was to rethink the eastern Pacific counterdrug operations equation. Ultimately, we wanted threat-based cutter and surveillance aircraft scheduling based upon MDA and intelligence which required us to think about the threats differently.

One key factor was to understand what the drug smuggler network needed to be successful in moving contraband from Colombia north, up the west coast of Central America. *What does the bad guy need to operate in the great distances of the eastern Pacific and get from Colombia to Guatemala and southern Mexico? So, what were the key elements they depended on?* The platforms used were a combination of ocean go-fasts and fishing vessels to resupply the go-fasts along the south to north route with fuel. The fishing vessels were staged along the route and basically served as floating gas stations.

Given this, we changed the approach and started putting greater emphasis on tracking the fishing vessels. We take that away, or we track it, and we are going to find the go-fast. It's easier to track the fishing vessel. So, working closely with JIATF West, we developed better intel based on a different focus. Our acquired MDA made effective scheduling of cutter and aircraft deployments much easier. We started seeing results too. In the first year of threat-based scheduling, we seized fifty-five tons of cocaine. We were seizing more cocaine than in the Caribbean. Staff got energized because we were getting results. The cutters were motivated by getting results.

I recall that we had two of our 210-foot cutters deployed on counter drug eastern Pacific ops one late fall/early winter. One was on patrol over Thanksgiving and over Christmas and they were coming into port just before New Year's, coming into San Diego to offload their seized contraband and arrested drug smugglers. They had a very productive deployment based on threat-based scheduling. They had tons of seized cocaine stacked up on the flight deck. They had bad guys in handcuffs and leg-irons. I met them in San Diego to recognize their superior operations. But they were complaining to me, "Admiral, why did you bring us in?" They already had missed two holidays. They would have missed a third if the patrol was extended, but they were more interested in keeping their productive patrol efforts going then returning to port.

It clearly is a motivator when you do things smart and you get results. That experience made my day and, I think, the staff's day and the unit's day. We turned around the whole counterdrug mission in the Pacific and it continues to the present. It's about MDA.

JD: Can you talk about Colombia?

TC: Colombia, of course is a primary source country in our nation's fight against the introduction of illegal drugs into our country. We have been working with Columbia for a long time in their fight against drug trafficking which has been complicated by their very long standing internal conflict with rebels, the FARC. Much progress has been made with them over the years. I visited Colombia to reinforce cooperative government-to-government efforts regarding drug law enforcement subsequent to my assignment as PACAREA. The west coast of Colombia in particular was a high threat area regarding illegal drug distribution. The government didn't have sufficient control over that area and that's where a lot of the drugs were being shipped from. The topography was challenging with mountains right down to the ocean. A lot of jungles. Rebel elements. And the indigenous population was not terribly supportive of the government.

I was down to discuss our law enforcement partnering efforts and the possibility of additional excess US military equipment and platforms to Colombia. In addition, I stressed the priority to get control of Colombia's west coast through a greater Colombian Navy presence there, with additional ships and bases. I met with the President, Minister of Defense, and the head of the Colombian Navy. We made some progress in ensuring the necessary priority regarding the west coast and reinforced our collective emphasis on cooperative drug enforcement operations. Clearly, an effective partnership with the Colombian government, Colombian Navy, JIATF West, in country USA DEA, and others was, and is, essential in keeping the pressure on the drug distribution network. Cooperative efforts included sharing of key intel for our patrol efforts, joint drug LE operations, and the authority to access their territorial maritime areas in pursuit of drug traffickers without gaining permission first. That partnership has continued to grow over the years. The recent peace agreement with prior rebel elements will help in the continued fight against illegal drug networking elements.

JD: Why was the PACAREA Commander dual-hatted as the 11th District Commander?

TC: Well, it was part Coast Guard's streamlining plans of the 1990s, where selected Coast Guard districts were converted to district "lites," i.e., smaller staffs with a dual-hatted commander. D-11 staff was reduced in size and collocated with PACAREA staff on Coast Guard Island in Alameda. It was a way to deal with Headquarters staff and cut out what could be perceived as fat while preserving the muscle—that is, ships, aircraft, boats, etc.

JD: How did you divide your time between the two commands?

TC: Sometimes it was awkward but I had a very strong staff at both the district and area levels. Much of the D-11 issues were dealt with by very capable O-6s on the staff. And the collocation of the respective staffs facilitated effective coordination between them—joint briefs and meetings were the norm. PACAREA was clearly the more dominant command responsibility for me but, as appropriate, I was very engaged at the district level as well. One of most extensive search-and-rescue cases during my tenure was in D-1—the Alaskan Flight 261 tragedy, with well over a week of concentrated oversight and effort on my part.

JD: Can you talk about Alaskan Airlines Flight 261?

TC: On January 31, 2000, Alaskan Airlines Flight 261 was flying from Puerto Vallarta, Mexico en route to Seattle, Washington with a scheduled stopover in San Francisco, California. Alaskan Airlines Flight 261 was an older MD-83 aircraft. So, it was on her way to San Francisco when it began to experience problems with the maneuverable tail section, thereby losing control. It then literally fell out of the sky into the Pacific Ocean off Santa Barbara killing all 88 passengers and crew onboard. We mobilized quickly. I received an emergency call around eleven o'clock at night. In short order, I departed for LAX, set up command posts—one at an LAX hotel and one at NAS Point Mugu, relatively close to the crash site. We immediately mobilized every asset we could—small boats, patrol boats, aircraft—and coordinated with the county.

Shortly after the emergency notification, I talked with Vice Admiral Denny McGinn, Commander of the Third Fleet. Denny is a true professional and really a wonderful guy to work with. No institutional parochialism. We knew each other from previous assignments in Hawaii. In our conversation, he offered any assistance that the Third Fleet could provide. A Navy surface combatant and helicopters were ultimately made available to join the search, and then, the recovery operations.

A priority was to set up a command presence at an LAX hotel because that's where ultimately I felt that families of the crash victims would gather—not at Point Mugu, but at LAX. I positioned my O-6 search-and-rescue head from D-11 down at LAX at the hotel with the families with an emphasis to keep them informed of search and recovery efforts. The goal was to ensure they had complete, accurate, and timely information.

The pre-need relationships we maintained with the Navy proved invaluable as we positioned for effective response operations. Having access to Point Mugu as a command post proved critical with its built-in security, crowd control, press control—everything that the Navy can provide on a secure base. Instant control. So, all of my press conferences were from there, which I did on at least a daily basis. As you might expect, the crash became a national event very quickly. The engagement with the national media became intensive and extensive, and most of that fell to me. There was also an insatiable demand for timely information back to Washington—to CG leadership, the Secretary of Transportation, and the White House.

It clearly was a tragic experience for the loved ones involved, and we tried to be very sensitive to their grief and associated needs. They received frequent updates via our LAX command post where they gathered. It was also hard on our boat crews, mostly very young men and women dealing with the very gruesome sights at the crash site. Part of the thing we did right away was to have crisis counseling available to them in the post-search phase.

Another thing that was interesting about that case, and a lesson learned by me, was that time zone differences presented a challenge at times—a challenge because Washington, appropriately, wanted to be briefed on a daily basis early in the morning, their time. So, we found ourselves working until about midnight or one o'clock west coast time and then getting up to prepare for a briefing to the Secretary of Transportation and the Commandant, and others that had to be briefed every morning on exactly what we were doing, and why we were doing it, and the status. So, I came to understand really early on that, on these type of big cases, there is a fatigue factor that sets in because of the time zone and the demand for information. There is a huge, insatiable demand for information that you can't avoid and must program into the schedule. From my perspective, it was a very effective operation and information dissemination effort. We did good, but there was a huge fatigue factor involved that had to be dealt with.

Dealing effectively with loved ones was a high priority for us. Particularly difficult was notifying them at the point we were not searching for survivors anymore. You know, that's difficult. But, we were careful to lead up to that point with factual information with each sequential brief that we gave them. I would always brief them at the conclusion of each day's efforts. I briefed the families on how many hours and how many resources were involved in the search for their loved ones; how we were exhausting all of our options; how high the probably of detection was; why it was a challenging recovery effort, etc. We attempted to provide every meaningful detail of our efforts. You try to effectively deal with the information flow and try to be as professional as you can while being as understanding and compassionate as you can. They clearly wanted closure when trying to accept the inevitable regarding the death of their loved ones. It was impossible to give them the closure they wanted—i.e., actual recovery of the deceased. The plane basically disintegrated upon impact along with its passengers and contents. Ultimately, we attempted to provide supporting/comforting things for the families. We had a memorial event very soon after closing search and recovery efforts. We had a memorial ceremony on the beach a mile or so from the crash site for families and loved ones. We had a helicopter land and we had a big basket of roses, one for every person on the plane. The helicopter landed and we had a few words said by a chaplain and families would gather there right by the water. Then we loaded the roses onto the helicopter, it took off, circled the families, and then flew out to the crash site and dropped the roses there.

I think they were very appreciative of those efforts. We then had, of course, a larger memorial ceremony at Pepperdine University a few days later. Secretary of Transportation Rodney Slater came out to that and several White House folks came out. Several family members came up to me afterwards and were profusely thankful for our efforts. The incident was clearly an incredible tragedy—a heartbreaking event. But, that's the business we are in and we put our best foot forward in all respects.

The following week, I was at several business meetings over on the Oakland side of the Bay and I was in my service dress blues. I was hungry so I stopped at a local sandwich shop. I got in line in the sandwich shop to get a sandwich on the run. The lady behind me in line tapped me on the shoulder and said, "Pardon me. Were you the Coast Guard admiral that was on TV for the press conferences about the crash?" I said, "Yes. I was. It was an incredible tragedy and loss of lives. Our hearts go out to the families there. We clearly put our best foot forward in everything that we could do, but it was ultimately a lost cause given the nature of the accident." She said, "I just want to tell you, you came across as so understanding, so compassionate, and so professional in those meetings." It made my day! It was better than a great fitness report because it came from Joe Q. Public. At least, I felt good that we had tried to respond to the tragedy in the best way possible, while being be understanding and compassionate. That was a long response to your question, but it was a huge issue on the west coast and national, and impacted me personally.

JD: Did you have any crisis media training to prepare you for these types of situations?

TC: Well, I go back to St. Petersburg and the Blackthorn tragedy. That was a huge crisis. A lot of loss of life. I had not reported to St. Pete by the time of the collision, but I thought my boss, then Captain and later Rear Admiral Ed Gilbert, had put together a good crisis response effort—how to do it; how to shape it; who to use; how to use your best expertise. And he wrote a number of articles on crisis management in the maritime arena. I discussed the incident with him and read write-ups on the tragedy. I think that helped me understand the demands of a crisis event a bit better. But, you learn by doing. For example, you learn by studying CG experiences with TWA Flight 800 that crashed off of Long Island on July 17th, 1996. Remember that one?

Go to school on that one. *What did we do good? What did we do not so good? How do we get better, especially in the area of information flow and media relations?* And dealing with survivors or the relatives of those that didn't survive. Dealing with the families. Having unfettered communications, open communications, and a full look at what's going on. Take the mystery out of it. Demonstrate how professional you are dealing with it. There are several types of demands for information. There's a media demand for information, loved ones' need for information, and there's governmental—your chain of command and up, and beyond the political chain that wants or requires information. Insatiable. No complaints, it's just a matter of fact. You've got to be prepared to deliver on that.

JD: Can you talk about the tank vessel that left an oil slick behind in San Francisco, that you tracked off the coast of Guatemala?

TC: There was a vessel, a tank vessel command, and it pumped oil and debris out of its tanks offshore in San Francisco, near the Farallon Islands about seventeen miles off the entrance to San Francisco. We discovered the slick. We did detective work. We saw it was oil discharge; we tracked when vessels left port; what was their likely route. We felt that, probably, the tank vessel in question was en route to Panama. This was a Captain of the Port, marine environmental protection mission—an enforcement mission where we were acting as a port state control authority since the suspect vessel was foreign flagged. There was a violation of environmental law in our waters by a foreign vessel and we didn't want to let it go. The challenge was that the vessel had cleared our waters, was a foreign flagged vessel, and was in international waters. However, we were very motivated to hold the vessel accountable and send a strong signal to the entire international maritime community. We used intel and surveillance aircraft to locate it off Guatemala in international waters, where we diverted a Coast Guard cutter that was on counter-drug ops to interdict the tank vessel.

The Coast Guard is multi-mission—one of our strongest points, by the way. No one unit, no one asset does just one thing. There is a great deal of strength in that characteristic. But, anyway, we diverted the cutter. We interdicted, came onboard, and stopped it. [We] said, "Standby to be boarded. We are enforcing port state control authorities in international waters." This was all a first. What were the factors for success: technology and MDA, sensors, partnerships, coordination with the State Department, a Presidential Directive 27 (PD-27) process. PD-27 was published under the Carter Administration initially and it provided a process for interagency coordination with the State Department for various actions involving the international arena. It was really the predecessor to Homeland Security Presidential Directive 13 that was done post-9/11 which created MOTR, the national Maritime Operational Threat Response Plan.

This case is all about how the interagency works in an international crisis, and about who has the authority to do what. Again, PD-27 needed a little more work, but it served the purpose here. We coordinated our approach through the State Department and documented it by putting an evidentiary package together. We executed the LE boarding off the seacoast of Guatemala and also met the vessel with another enforcement team in Panama when it docked, with the cooperation of the Panama government and our State Department. The vessel was ultimately fined about $10 million. This was a unique operation—a law enforcement case, a marine environment protection case, a port security case, all with coordinated action—interagency, international, and involving several Coast Guard programs. In addition, it sent a huge signal to the shipping community—that the Coast Guard is going to enforce its port state control authorities, and foreign flag vessels that are in US waters had better abide by every law and rule. Bottom line, being aggressive here was the right thing to do. I was very proud of our staff that worked on it.

I might note one other thing. Having skilled, experienced lawyers on your staff is really crucial for the operational Coast Guard because our authorities are very complex and expansive. Many of the operations that we conduct have a legal dimension to them, in terms of domestic and international laws. In D-14, at every morning operational brief, I insisted that the staff's lawyer be there as well. You asked me earlier what advice I'd give—ensure that your lawyer is an indispensable part of your operations. We're a law enforcement agency with expansive law enforcement authority, so we need to have that legal advice always close at hand. It certainly was critical this case.

There was another case that occurred up off Coos Bay area, on the Oregon coast. It involved a 639-foot freighter, the M/V *New Carissa*, which ran aground on the North Spit near North Bend, early on February 4th, 1999. Beautiful, beautiful beach, with lots of wildlife, now with a stricken vessel, beached and threatening one of the worst oil spill disasters in Oregon's history. We activate our formal Incident Command System (ICS) to deal with it. The ICS had been incorporated into the CG by our marine safety staff as a standard way to respond to spills. These processes and procedures had originally been developed by the US Forest Service to fight wildfires. We ensured that all our crisis action plans involving large scale operations include an incident command system-like structure and approach. We instituted such a system in D-14 when I was there, and then in PACAREA when I was assigned there. In a way, the ICS approach is one of the building blocks of the sector concept—to be developed and implemented later, during my time as Commandant Sector Command.

Think about it. The Sector Command was about integrating marine safety business, Captain of the Port business, Officer in Charge of Marine Inspection business. The ICS came in handy when we planned and coordinated a controlled in situ burning of the oil onboard the *New Carissa* so as to reduce the risk/impact of spilled oil. To do an in situ burning of the oil required a really close relationship with the state of Oregon and its environmental departments. Unfortunately, the burn did not work terribly well, with difficulty in getting the cargo to burn. They tried to get the thing lit off, and it's not as easy and get the whole thing burned. Ultimately in the process, one of the bulkheads collapsed and the vessel broke in two on the beach. At that point, the consensus amongst everyone was, "Let's try to tow the hulk offshore and sink it," effectively getting the bulk of the fuel in very, very deep water because it's where it wouldn't do damage to the coastal environment. The largest portion of the vessel, and the part with the greatest fuel onboard, was planned for towing and offshore sinking. But sinking the vessel offshore was, in itself, a challenge. There are many void spaces and air pockets throughout the vessel that act to keep the hulk afloat. The Navy's Third Fleet, led by Vice Admiral Denny McGinn, came to our assistance here. When I asked if the Navy could sink the vessel when we got it offshore he said yes, but recognized the difficulties. He offered that, if the Navy signed up for that job they were not going to fail at it, so he prepared to provide plenty of fire power. He offered that the *New Carissa* was going down! So, on March 11th, 1999, once the *New Carissa* was offshore in deep water, he had USS *David R. Ray* [DD-971] fire it's five-inch guns at the *New Carissa* and it didn't go down. But the Navy had backup—ultimately USS *Bremerton* [SSN-698] fired one of its torpedoes and the *New Carissa* went to the bottom.

This case is an example of large operations with plenty of media attention. It drew upon contingency plans we had in effect, extensive partnerships with the state trying to get consensus on environmental issues, and relationships with the Third Fleet and Department of Defense. It was an example of a case where, if you haven't established pre-need relationships and pre-need plans, it's not going to go well. The *New Carissa* was a tragedy for the northern Oregon coast and there was damage to wildlife and the environment, but it was mitigated to the greatest extent possible. The remaining wreckage of the *New Carissa* that wasn't sunk lasted there until September 2008.

Other interesting operations during my tour, included a number of cases off Central America involving Chinese migrant ships. The smugglers would pack these boats full of poor Chinese and get them in Mexico and Guatemala, and up through the border. When I was out in D-14, we had a Chinese migrant ship trying to get into the Hawaiian Islands and two or three ships trying to get into Central America. We located interdicted them through the development of good intel, good maritime domain awareness. Intel networks. We had an active intel network. The kind of emphasis that we placed on operations, they were the right emphasis—partnerships, technology, intelligence, planning, understanding your AOR, regional strategic assessments—those were all the priorities within PACAREA. In the end, they all contributed to successful operations.

The other initiative I'm incredibly proud of is the North Pacific Coast Guard Forum. It was incredibly, incredibly productive. It started out with the Canadians, the Japanese, the South Koreans, and the US Coast Guard. But it ended up including other countries, including China and Russia. There were several nations in the forum that had a great deal of historical baggage with lots of animosity. We brought them all together in a very, very, cooperative way, focusing at first on noncontroversial operational matters, including SAR. Everyone can find a common bond when it comes to search-and-rescue, developing communication protocols between operations centers of Coast Guard-like entities or border control-like entities, for search-and-rescue purposes. Then next we expanded to marine environmental protection and vessel safety and navigation. Pretty soon, we had a large portfolio of issues with a formal related agenda for the annual meeting. We created intersessional working groups to work on the specific agenda items between the annual meeting. The Forum developed useful operational protocols among the nations involved and, most importantly, developed credibility and trust among the nations involved. And, oh, by the way, the concept of such a forum has been expanded. Now, LANTAREA has the North Atlantic Coast Guard Forum based on the PACAREA model, and an Arctic Forum.

It was important to have both Russia and China as members of the Forum, [as] there were a number of issues that needed close coordination. With Russia, we had fisheries law enforcement operations going on up in the "doughnut hole" on the Bering Sea US-Russia maritime boundary. With the Chinese, we shared responsibilities associated with the UN High Seas Driftnet Moratorium. We worked closely with the Chinese for High Seas Driftnet enforcement and other

High Seas Fisheries enforcement, working with their fisheries agency. To be effective, since most of the illegal fishing was done by rogue Chinese fishing vessels, we needed Chinese governmental authorities and their language skills. We developed a "ship-rider program" where Chinese fisheries LE members would ride our ships to help enforce the international high sea driftnet protocols. They'd fly to Kodiak, because all the patrols, all the high-endurance CG cutters, would stage out of Kodiak. They'd go up to Kodiak and get a week training in latest fishery enforcement issues, current intel on the fishing grounds, then deploy with our ships. The patrols were very productive. We'd get the benefit of their LE authorities relative to Chinese flagged fishing vessels, we'd get their language skill—all of which led to joint arrests of offending fishing vessels and, ultimately, large fines and loss of fishing permits. I went over to Shanghai and had a meeting in the wardroom of one of their fishing agency ships. We reviewed the program and committed to the next step which involved the Chinese deploying their ships to the LE effort. And we agreed to have CG surveillance A/C provide sighting data to their vessels, and an A/C rider program.

It was impressive to have that kind of cooperative action happen in operations between China and the US, and it all feeds off the Forum that we established—the annual forum, and everything else.

JD: Whose idea was it to establish the North Pacific Coast Guard Forum?

TC: Both Jim Loy and I had a hand in it. When I was out in D-14, we gave priority attention and talked to the Japanese Safety Maritime Agency, and they were supportive. I had assigned one of my staff members as the coordinator of it, and it soon took hold. The countries would have the annual meetings at different locations. We had a Forum meeting in Japan once, one in Korea once, one I had it in Hawaii, one in Canada. Everyone tried to show their best footing in terms of the location, and cultural events were included along with the business agenda.

JD: How did you prepare for these international forums? Your job is almost like that of a diplomat, dealing with different countries and cultures. How did you learn what to do, not to do?

TC: We did have an international affairs staff in Washington Headquarters that supported the Commandant and Vice Commandant on international matters. There was always a preparatory meeting on the dos and the don'ts about who we were going to meet with, and how you address them and so forth. Typically, the first engagement in any foreign country was the US Embassy in that country. You'd meet with the country team and you'd get briefed on what's going on, and you usually have linguistic support out of the embassy, and usually there would be an action officer from the embassy who would go with you. It was a planned trip—planned engagement with objectives. And then we'd assess the trip after we returned, after every trip as Vice Commandant or Commandant. I would provide a trip report for the Secretary detailing every aspect of the trip, including objectives, activities, accomplishments. We can discuss trips as Commandant later in the interview process.

JD: Looking forward to that.

TC: I really prized the relationship we established with China, and I continued that as Vice Commandant and Commandant. I thought there was huge benefits developing the relationship. We knew the differences of opinion/values each country had, but to develop a trusting relationship with our counterparts had benefits. I was frequently engaged with four or five Chinese ministries and, of course, the embassy was supportive in these engagements because [they] recognized the access potential. The Chinese wanted to meet with the USCG and pursue issues of importance to both countries.

JD: Okay. Given the time differences in your AOR, how did you keep in touch with your major commands?

TC: Frequent flag conferences were a great way to gain alignment at the senior levels. And, fortunately, I had a very competent staff. I relied on staff to do a lot of the day-to-day communications. I was out and about frequently. One of my first internet initiatives was to have internet connectivity on all of our cutters. If I'm sending them to the maritime boundary, far-flung EEZs, or I'm sending them way down off Guatemala and Costa Rica, I wanted to be able to contact us all the time. I wanted to be able to contact home. Seventh Fleet can do it. The Third Fleet can do it. Why can't we do it? So, we slowly developed that capability. I think we were ahead of our time within the Coast Guard, trying to push that. We made some progress and did improve that capability. That was one way you could keep people tuned into where PACAREA was going and why.

Everywhere I went, I had town hall-type meetings, all hands. I tried to be approachable. PACAREA, a big AOR with many units, so you only can do so much of that, but I spent a good deal of time doing just that, trying to be an out-and-about operational commander. I wanted to be out, learning and listen to what's going on in the field, and we did that. Much of what I was trying to communicate was the same as in D-14—understand our business; do thorough planning and regional strategic assessments; pursue things based on fact; allocate resources effectively to high priority issues. We focused on business plans and balance scorecards and how you measure your performance, how you report your performance, and how you link up with corporate goals and objectives. I probably drove the staff crazy doing all that stuff, but it was terribly important. And it was exportable to the rest of the Coast Guard, especially the leadership council—the two area commanders, the Vice Commandant, and Chief of Staff. We'd meet three or four times a year, and I would always speak to what we're doing in PACAREA and regional strategic assessment. And all PACAREA district commanders knew these matters were of high priority.

Another big issue I had with PACAREA leadership was getting them to work toward an environment that fosters professional development. I stressed teamwork as a way to get things done. The team is a wonderful thing. The team is a powerful thing. A really empowered team, there's nothing better, and I tried to preach that, implement that. I guess it was my TQM heritage.

I was concerned about what was happening in High Endurance Cutter fleet in terms of personnel. I was concerned about sexual harassment. I was concerned about the use of alcohol. Personnel were deploying up to the maritime boundary, stopping off in one of the Aleutian Islands, and going on liberty and getting in trouble. That sexual harassment existed and a couple of instances of rape allegations really concerned me, so I had my human resources and legal folks closely examine these issues. *How do we make this better? What are some of the root causes?* In the final analysis, it's a leadership problem. I felt when it all came down to it, there was a serious leadership problem on certain units where there were improper personnel incidents occurring. In several instances, people were not being held accountable—whether a leading first-class petty officer in a division, the chief, or the wardroom. Sometime they saw something going on and didn't do anything about it. They saw the early stages of something happening and didn't jump in. So, that was one issue. The other was sexual harassment, the inappropriate use of position to be powerful over a person of another gender. And alcohol certainly wasn't the sole reason, but it was a contributing, exacerbating influence on the issue.

We tried to attack all parts of inappropriate relationships from various aspects. At COs' conferences, we underscored command responsibilities in the very, very strongest terms—about what their responsibility is as leader. You need to have MDA of your ship. You need to have domain awareness—what's going on, what's not going on. *Do you have a favorable climate? Are there the beginnings of improper relationships?* As a leader, you need to know. No excuse, you didn't know. It's your ship. You need to know, and your wardroom needs to know, and your Chief's Mess needs to know, and you need to intervene. That was a very, very strong and continuous message.

Responsible use of alcohol abuse was also stressed through policy statements, conferences, and other guidance. Not that we eradicated the problem. It's a persistent issue, and it's like a journey, not a destination. You've got to be on top of it all the time. But it's a leadership issue more than anything else. We stressed that, we worked that, and [it] continues to be worked in all the services. Our service is not the lone stranger regarding these personnel challenges. In fact, our service when you look at stats, it's better. Not perfect, but better. We had people issues to be concerned about. And it happened to manifest itself mostly in the High Endurance fleet.

JD: And why was that?

TC: Well, I think they're away a long time. They're deployed a long time. Then they were either bouncing around, rough weather, doing their business, and then they'd go ashore on liberty, and then blow off steam. They are young. And at times, they didn't have "adult supervision" ashore. That was part of it, I think. Now again, alcohol—that's not a justification for bad things happening, but it's an exacerbating factor, a contributing factor. Too much alcohol and, sometimes, unwanted behavior occurs. But, again, that's a leadership issue and it continues to this day because the current Commandant is on top of that. In all the five service branches, it's become a greater and greater focus, as it should be, especially as more and more women are joining the armed forces. We were the first service branch to have basically open, unrestricted assignments for women. It was basically no restrictions for women except if the facilities themselves couldn't accommodate some basic level of privacy, like berthing areas, the size of the ship, or their configuration. From my perspective, it enriches the services to have gender diversity. You've got to do it right—have the proper policies and leadership in place, and foster the right type of climate. But anyway, I had to talk about that a little bit because it's an important issue.

JD: We've crossed the four-hour mark. You're a champion gold-medalist interviewee. So, I think this is a good time to stop.

TC: Good. Again, we may have left a few things to be discussed. Let me think about them a little bit. If we need to retrace our steps a little bit next session, we can clean up.

JD: We'll do that.

TC: We can clean up some of the things. But, look, I was blessed and so fortunate to have two incredible operational assignments back-to-back. First, as a one-star and then, as a three-star. I loved the San Francisco area—what a wonderful, wonderful city that is. My spouse also loved San Francisco—a great community, a very supportive community. When I arrived, DOD had left or was in the process of leaving San Francisco vis-à-vis BRAC, and other reasons. Presidio closed; Mare Island Naval Shipyard closed; Oakland Army Terminal closed; Hamilton Air Force Base closed. So, the USCG was the only armed services game left in town and, fortunately, the Navy League just absolutely adopted us. The Navy League support was just "out of sight" with great they support of our men and women. They were just terrific. All of these made for a great and wonderful assignment.

The assignment was professionally rewarding. There was a culture of mission analysis, planning, measurement, performance metrics, and risk assessments that we created there, and I think it spilled over into other areas of the CG, so I feel good about that. It's been fun reviewing the tank vessel Command, and the *New Carissa,* and those kind of operational experiences. That brought back some memories of a very dedicated staff working very, very hard to achieve good operational outcomes. And I was privileged to be their boss. They were great folks.

My deputy in PACAREA was Charlie Wurster and he later was picked up flag. He had been CO of a LORAN [long range navigation] station in Alaska. He was a civil engineer. He was shocked when I picked him. "Well, I'm not an operator." He had some operational experience but he was mostly a civil engineer. I said, "Well, I need your brain cells, Charlie. That's what I need." He was a smart guy. He was very good with people. "I need a team builder and I need your brain cells." He was good at both of those things, and he was a great, great, loyal deputy. Commander Mike Sullivan was my very talented Executive Assistant. Lieutenant Dave Burns was my aide, followed by Lieutenant Lynn Soleto, who had a legal background. Terrific support all around and great front office in PACAREA.

We didn't talk about Coast Guard Island, our island base located in an estuary between Oakland and Alameda. That's where all the WHECs tied up. MLC Pacific was also located there. It was Coast Guard heaven. We had great relations with city of Alameda and we had many community support things there. Anyway, we could talk about that some more, but we need to probably take a breather here. You've got things to do and I've got things to do this afternoon, so we'll halt. Thank you for letting me go down memory lane with all these things. I have, as you can see, fond memories of these experiences, and the people I served with. I still bleed Coast Guard blue, even though I've been retired for some time.

JD: Thank you for sharing your wisdom. This will benefit generations of Coast Guardsmen for decades to come. This is a wrap.

End audio file Collins4.2.Dolbow.USNI.2.23.16

Interviewer: Jim Dolbow (JD)
Interviewee: Admiral Thomas Collins, USCG Ret. (TC)

Begin audio file Collins5.1.Dolbow.USNI.4.17.16

JD: Good afternoon. This is Jim Dolbow. Today is April 17th, 2016 and I am in McLean, Virginia with Admiral Thomas Collins. Admiral, can we talk about your role as Commander of the Pacific Maritime Defense Zone and what that entailed?

TC: Sure. In a way, we acted as the executive agent for CINCPACFLT for Naval Coastal Warfare and we had the planning role for many of their exercises. Reservists clearly played heavily in that role. There has been a long-standing relationship with our Port Security Units (PSUs) and the EOD folks in the Navy. So, it was a logical lash up, reserve to reserve, and they played significantly in the development of appropriate defense plans focused on harbor and coastal areas throughout the Pacific Rim. We had a Coast Guard liaison officer in South Korea to coordinate our participation in bi-lateral military exercises in South Korea. During my tenure at PACAREA, I committed Coast Guard assets to these exercises and I did make a visit out there to support that exercise and to continue our relationship with the numbered fleets.

All this was in keeping with the contingency plans. We had a number of exchange programs where we would exchange officers supporting the overall relationship with the Department of Defense and the Navy. We supported CARAT*** and that was because CINCPACFLT frequently sought Coast Guard assets to engage on the Pacific Rim, since most of the navies of the world are often more like Coast Guards than they are like navies, in terms of the scale, the size, capabilities, and the functions that they performed for their government, i.e., largely supporting their sovereignty in the maritime domain and protecting their borders and so forth. So, we committed a ship to CARAT on a frequent basis.

We programmed about 185 cutter days a year to the CINC. So, our relationship with the DOD/Navy was fairly robust, more than in Coast Guard's Atlantic area, largely because the Pacific is the Navy's playground.

*** Cooperation Afloat Readiness and Training (CARAT). CARAT is a series of bilateral naval exercises between the US Navy, US Marine Corps, US Coast Guard, and the armed forces of Bangladesh, Brunei, Cambodia, Indonesia, Malaysia, the Philippines, Singapore, Thailand, and Timor-Leste.***

We had liaisons at PACOM. We had liaisons at CINCPACFLT. We also maintained a small staff at US Forces Japan that performed Merchant Marine inspection activity on the Rim. So, I had very extensive interplay with the Department of Defense when I wore the PACAREA hat and later, in subsequent assignments, those relationships served me very, very well in my future roles as Vice Commandant and Commandant.

JD: Can you talk about the interaction between yourself as PACAREA Commander and your District Commanders?

TC: It was a frequent interplay given our distributed operational model and it served us extraordinarily well. The way the Coast Guard is structured, it gives a great deal of operational leeway to our field commanders and local commanders. There is not much rudder order commands to district commanders, or from them to their subordinate commanders in terms of operations because they have assigned responsibilities. They have plans. They've nurtured the plans. They are held accountable to the plans—operational standards—and they are held accountable for their performance. But, we are not in their sandbox, micromanaging them. That is clearly not our model in the Coast Guard. The model fosters a bias for action and to spring on mission requirements at the local level and they have full authorities to do that. Having said that, to answer your question, there was frequent interplay, and back and forth, and information exchanged.

There were semi-annual senior officer, flag officer conferences. There was extensive dialogue on requirements and associated budgets/budget development. There was guidance that was given to them in terms of strategic planning factors and issues, and those type of things, and they were held accountable to performance. So, I assure you, if there was a problem that was on their plate and they needed resource help or other type of involvement, that needed my immediate inclusion in whatever the event was, they were not hesitant to let me know. But, we had good district commanders. In a nutshell, there was productive interplay and frequent exchange of information.

JD: How often did you talk with the Commandant or the Vice Commandant?

TC: Periodically. I probably talked more to the Vice then I did to the Commandant just because the Vice was into some of the day-to-day processes. The Commandant would occasionally come out to PACAREA to visit a particular unit or send a special message on some issue. We also had a leadership council that consisted of the two area commanders, the Vice Commandant, and the Commandant, which met twice a year. Basically, the meetings involved a good deal of strategic planning that was going on. It was started by Admiral Kramek and further pushed along by Jim Loy and Jim Card. We needed to get better at strategic planning in the Coast Guard. We needed a family of plans that provided an integrated approach to planning and risk, as well as developing an up-to-date environment where we strategically knew our business, and then matched budgets and resources to those strategic objectives. The greatest interchange with the Commandant took place at the leadership council meetings. I will talk a little more about leadership council when we get to the Vice Commandant because the Vice Commandant acted as an executive secretary of the leadership counsel.

JD: What was PACAREA's Headquarters like in Alameda?

TC: By Coast Guard standards, it was good. Everything about San Francisco in terms of location was terrific. Where I lived on Yerba Buena Island was awesome. There was a little CG industrial base on the island as well. The buoy tenders tied up there, but the main base was over at an island in an estuary between Alameda and Oakland. The name of the island was Coast Guard Island and it was home to major commands like Joint Interagency Task Force-West (JIATF West), the Maintenance & Logistics Command Pacific, and major CG cutters, and our Pacific area operations and intel centers.

Rear Admiral Dave Belz commanded JIATF West—a joint component of US Pacific Command. He was my next door neighbor on Yerba Buena Island. Rear Admiral John Parker commanded the maintenance and logistics command at one point there. We also had four High Endurance Cutters tied up there. We had major support responsibilities there, including housing responsibilities for all of the Coast Guard in the area.

In that timeframe, DOD's huge presence in San Francisco disappeared because of base closures and other issues. So, we were busy strategically planning where we could get some of DOD excess facilities with the first priority being housing for our people. It was a very expensive area to live in. The preference of the Coast Guard was, at that point, "If you don't have to own homes, don't." In other words, if you can manage to live on your paycheck on the economy in a given area, then do it. The last preference would be to own because when you own, then you have all of the life cycle costs, maintenance, and administrative responsibilities associated with housing. But, having said that, our goal in San Francisco was to own the housing because it was scarce and expensive—both a burden on our members. The expensive nature of housing in the Bay Area continues to this day, placing it as one of the nation's most expensive places to live. So, as a result of base closures and other downsizing of the DOD, we were able to get a number of fairly decent housing units in Concord, and also up in Hamilton.

So, anyway, that's the CG landscape there in San Francisco. Senior housing units and a small industrial base on Yerba Buena for buoy tenders and buoy maintenance and the rest of the presence basically on the Coast Guard Island near Alameda and Oakland. We also had a vessel traffic service on the top of Yerba Buena Island. Yerba Buena is a mountainous little island with a flat top appendage to the north, Treasure Island, which used to be a Navy base.

JD: Can you talk about the importance of the international partnerships in PACAREA?

TC: Sure. Our goals going forward were to enhance mission performance. *How do we maintain our readiness? How do we optimize the scarce resources we have especially considering the huge AOR and its expansive responsibilities? How do we manage our scarce resources that are readiness challenged because of the increasing number of days lost to casualties and maintenance?* We plotted the time lost to casualties and maintenance for some of vessels and aircraft and they were all going up. Jim Loy called that the turning of the "dull knife" because we kept using a "knife" and didn't have the resources to "sharpen" it, and pretty soon it gets pretty dull. We were becoming dull knives. So, we had our dull knives, a readiness issue, and a big AOR with increasing responsibilities. So, it was critical that we put metal on target. *How do you assure you are getting the most out of your resources? Do you truly know your AOR?* So, we did a strategic assessment of our AOR and required every district and the area to do strategic assessments.

One of the critical factors in attaining our enhanced mission effectiveness goals—one of the answers was partnering with friends, allies, and others. Leveraging competencies and capability across your AOR, including international. It was a target-rich environment to leverage these relationships whether it was with Canada, Japan, South Korea, Russia, China, Singapore, etc. These are all some major players that were targets and we developed specific objectives assigned to each one. *How can we use a particular partnership to further our productivity?*

We also stressed the application of intel and technology. We developed better intelligence by having a greater maritime domain awareness so as to optimize the deployment of platforms like cutters and aircraft to be most productive. We wanted intel-driven operations at PACAREA.

We developed regional risk assessments based on up-to-date intel and coordinated asset deployments accordingly with our interagency and international partners. Multilateral and interagency partnerships were essential to enhancing capabilities and asset productivity.

There are a number of examples where we were successful with this—working with China on a ship rider program is a great example. We created a ship rider program out there in response to our responsibilities under a UN resolution on high seas drift net enforcement, which was illegal by international convention. The signatories included China, Japan, and Canada. So, with a partnership with those nations, we would be more effective in stopping illegal high seas drift net fishing. This was multi-mile–long gill net-type fishing that was very effective fishing, but it killed indiscriminately. It killed everything. So, that had to be stopped. Most of the illegal fishing done in this area was done jointly by Taiwanese and Chinese fishermen. The answer to attain effective enforcement was to partner with China. We developed a ship rider program with them where we had Chinese fisheries enforcement agents riding our High Endurance Cutters that we deployed to the western Pacific to stop the high seas drift net fishing. So, we had the legal authorities of the Chinese government right onboard. We had language skills right onboard. There was a payoff for both our countries and, when that program finally matured, it included them providing their ships in partnership with us and we supporting their ships with our C-130 aircraft to give them spotting, because it's a big ocean and you need aircraft support to vector you in to the alleged violator. So, all of that international partnering paid huge, huge dividends and furthered US-China relations at the same time.

We also started the North Pacific Coast Guard Forum (NPCGF) which was initiated in the 14th District and further grew at PACAREA, when I got there with the goal of bringing the international Pacific coast guards together on an annual basis. Our efforts brought them together with non-threatening issues like, *How do you communicate better for search-and-rescue if that happens in international waters, but is close to your countries? How do you collaborate and communicate when there is a disaster at sea? How do you communicate when there is a major spill in your AOR?* All of these things are important to each individual nation. And you don't want to start exchanging business cards in the middle of a crisis. So, this was a way to identify those common issues and work them together, to develop communication protocols so our ops centers could all talk to each other, to develop contingency plans jointly. It was a very productive undertaking. Participants from all the countries involved were very enthused about it. To add to the enthusiasm, we tried to hold the annual meetings in really great places with respective countries taking turns hosting.

We would have a working agenda that we would create and then we would establish communication groups that would work these issues between annual sessions to be presented to the next meeting. Over time, the agenda grew from search-and-rescue, to marine environmental protection, to other issues confronting the respective agencies. It leveraged everyone's capabilities and engendered respect between countries that never existed before. I thought it was a tremendous model. It has been duplicated in the North Atlantic Coast Guard Forum as well as with the Arctic Coast Guard Forum. It's a multilateral approach to issues and has paid huge dividends for the USCG and our nation.

Another example of international cooperation was the annual search-and-rescue exercise that we held in Hong Kong every year. It initially started in the 14th District, and then continued when I was in PACAREA. This was an annual exercise with the goal to ensure adequate and coordinated response to long-range SAR cases in a huge AOR with multi-million square miles of ocean. The exercises helped raise the competencies of all the smaller countries in the Pacific Rim. We, meaning the United States Coast Guard, would set up the exercises and would act as the controllers for them. Each year we would commit at least a C-130 to the exercise. There was an inshore exercise and there was an offshore exercise, coordinated locally there by the Hong Kong Civil Aviation Department. They would do the offshore every other year and we would commit a High Endurance Cutter to the Hong Kong SAR exercise, on the backside or front side of a deployment of a cutter that was supporting DOD on the Pacific rim.

The foregoing are just a few examples of efforts to leverage international partnerships. Mexico is another example. *How do we get greater cooperation with Mexico for drug enforcement? How can we gain Mexican approvals for our cutters making port calls in Mexico?* That's a very sensitive issue in Mexico. But, we started with Mexico with benign things. Search-and-rescue coordination, pollution exercise, and so forth. Ultimately, we developed a more cooperative role with the Mexican Navy who is one of the more competent, honest, and forthright elements in their whole government structure. Partnering with them to further our drug enforcement efforts was critical.

We worked with Guatemala to gain forward basing of our C-130s because it was a long run every time from Sacramento, to go down to support a counter-drug patrol out in the eastern Pacific. We partnered internationally, built relationships to forward base a C-130 in Guatemala and to materially enhance mission success. Presto, done. Embassies like to see us coming because of these relationships that we built.

JD: Can you talk about who originated the North Pacific Coast Guard Forum?

TC: It was a discussion initially between the Coast Guards of Japan and the United States that centered around better communication, mostly on SAR. *How do we communicate better on SAR?* "Well, we need some communications protocols." *Well, how do we get it?* "Well, let's meet." And the thing grew. We just kept leveraging. *How do you deal with a maritime disasters like a large capacity cruise ship that's in international waters and those kinds of things?* So, it almost grew naturally and I'm glad it did.

It was exciting at the same time because you developed some good relationships with some of the players. I remember visiting Shanghai when I was at PACAREA, to meet with their fisheries leadership onboard one of their fisheries enforcement ships. It had a huge banner on the side that read, "Welcome Admiral Collins." I mean, it was two hundred feet long. During the meeting in the ship's wardroom, some of the Chinese hosts were wearing t-shirts with United States Coast Guard Cutter *Dallas* [WHEC-716] on it. I thought I was in Alameda, for Pete's sake. It was rewarding to see the trust, and credibility, and the working relationships that developed. The Chinese fisheries agent that was wearing the *Dallas* t-shirt was a ship rider on the *Dallas* during a prior successful high seas drift enforcement mission. He came up to me and said, "I attribute my ability now to get command of my own vessel from that experience." Trust and credibility results from these types of engagements.

JD: What was your initial reaction when the Russians asked to join the Northe Pacific Coast Guard Forum?

TC: My reaction was "Come on down." You know, we need a good relationship with them and they probably need a good relationship with us. Now, it was a little different because there were many ex-KGB ground pounders, if you will, in the Russian Border Guard. The Russian Border Guards were into tanks, and bazookas, and things like that, but they also had responsibility for maritime safety and security. I saw it as an opportunity to engage, build more trusting relationships, and enhance missions in areas where we could find mutual benefits.

After a member is asked to join the forum, we ask them to be prepared to deliver a little "roles and organization" brief at our annual meeting. For the Russians, it was basically "Russian Border Guard 101"—describing their missions, organization, goals, why they wanted to join, etc. The Russians had pictures of tanks shooting things and all of that. Anyway, I just whispered in their ear afterwards, "You might want to try a little different approach qith this group." So, they tempered their approach a little bit. But, hey, in the final analysis, they turned out to be productive players. And, most importantly, it allowed us to develop a relationship well before a crisis developed.

Why did I want the Russians in this forum? One of our major problems was the maritime boundary line in the Bering Sea. Foreign fishing vessels are not supposed to fish on our side and vice versa. Well, all of the violations were Russians coming across the boundary line. I needed a hot line to the Russian authorities. I needed good 24/7 communications into their ops center when I had these fishing problems. I didn't want to see an escalating crisis over a Russian fishing vessel intrusion. So, a government-to-government relationship was really important. I could work it through the forum, which we did.

JD: I guess it would be fair to say that this forum was a great tool of Coast Guard diplomacy.

TC: I think it was and, from my understanding, continues to be. But, it was started with operational practicality in mind, and how to get the job done in a vast and challenging AOR.

JD: Can you talk a little bit about the historical baggage between Japan and China? How did you manage all of that?

TC: Well, it's a matter of having a practical operational focus, along with some continuity in the people that are involved so that you don't have to reinvent the wheel every time, annually. Then, pick talented staff that are diplomatic—adept at sensitive areas and sensitivities, and then inclined to treat everyone with openness and honesty upfront. You do what you said you were going to do, and there are no hidden agendas. So, you build that kind of credibility.

Again, we were into mission areas of apple pie and motherhood. I mean, who can't attach themselves to common search-and-rescue issues? You know, why wouldn't you want to cooperate? So, once you build off that, I think that people got to know each other and got to have better trust. I had an incredibly positive relationship with counterpart elements in China. They understood the importance a productive relationship, so much so, they came to my change of command. They came to my retirement ceremony. In all our dealings, we were sensitive to our differences, but at the same time, we were not "giving away the store" at all. But, we just had positive, professional exchange, and there was an element of trust that was developed. And we attempted to keep the Japanese-Chinese interaction a professional, practical one.

JD: Can you talk about the optics of a Coast Guard cutter painted white with a red racing stripe, contrasted with a grey US Navy hull?

TC: I think Jim Loy might have coined the term that the Coast Guard is a distinct instrument of national security, and it's pretty accurate. We are a unique thing in the United States of America, that we are both an armed force by statute, and we are a law enforcement agency, and have a wide array of day-to-day missions that serve the public. I think we are less threatening to a lot of foreign entities that see us as lifesavers. I love the CG to be known as the lifesavers, quite frankly. That's the best thing to be tagged with that I can think of, and that's how a lot of people see us and they also respect our competency, our professionalism. If you go to IMO and you ask people who they think is the most professional seagoing entity, they will all say the United States Coast Guard.

You know, in Japan our counterpart organization used to be called the Japanese Maritime Safety Agency. They are not called the Japanese Maritime Safety Agency anymore. They are called the Japan Coast Guard. The Philippines created a coast guard in the image of the United States Coast Guard. Chile, same thing; Argentina, same thing. Japan—I can remember being way back when, a lieutenant commander in the Office of R&D and a large Japanese delegation visiting Coast Guard Headquarters and going to every office and taking copious notes because they wanted to go reengineer their Japanese Maritime Safety Agency, and they wanted to be more Coast Guard-like, US Coast Guard-like. So, I think there is great respect for the things that we do and, because we are not under the Department of Defense, we are a little bit less threatening and we have this dual capability armed force/law enforcement authorities.

JD: Did you ever go visit USCGC *Polar Star* [WAGB-10] off Antarctica while you were at PACAREA and what was it like?

TC: Yes, I went down to see *Polar Star* to ensure I was up to date on that mission. We staged out of Christchurch, New Zealand, 2,300 miles from Antarctica. You fly down in ice-equipped C-130s, which would use huge skis to land. There were penguins everywhere. I mean, it's an amazing place.

Well, we rode *Polar Star* while she was doing channel work. Went up in the ice conning tower to observe the icebreaking. Sometimes, it is "Come left a bit to the next fissure in the ice." You use that to help us break. Sometimes it's backing and ramming. Sometimes it's straight breaking. Pretty amazing. Also, got a trip to the South Pole. That's another almost 1,000 miles from McMurdo Station to the South Pole. The Pole facilities were in the middle of a rebuild when I visited. We flew up and over the Transantarctic range over the Antarctic ice cap to the South Pole and it was "only" -50 degrees. When we were in Christchurch, they outfitted us with all kinds of extreme cold weather gear. The Pole is at 10,000 feet. It's a huge ice cap and the thing is, it doesn't snow all that much in Antarctica, but when it does snow, it never melts. So, this big huge ice cap has built up over time and the reason that it is such an important research area is that the ice cap is like a time machine. You go drilling down through it and come up with findings that support the study the history of the planet by going down and taking samples of different stuff.

The South Pole is one of the best places in the world to go for scientific research. I asked their chief head scientist, "How do you determine what projects to do down here?" He said, "The first question is, can it be done anywhere else in the world? And, if the answer is 'yes,' I tell them, you are not doing it here just because it tends to be expensive given all of the challenges you face in that environment."

But, having said that, it's one of the best places on the planet, if not the best place, to study the universe. It's so clear you have, optically, the best viewing point and so a lot of astronomy is done there. But, anyway, it was a very interesting trip. I'm glad I went. I understood much, much better the demands on the crew, on the ship, and made connections with the interagency people that we have to work with down there and so forth.

JD: Can you talk about PACAREA's preparations for Y2K?

TC: Yes. Coast Guard Headquarters had the lead, backed by a Commandant instruction on it. We had a parallel PACAREA directive to our PACAREA staff and our subordinate districts on what to do—the process by which you identify vulnerabilities and how you would address them. We also set up at PACAREA "tiger team," if you will, of experts that subordinate units could draw on to more fully understand the challenges associated with Y2K. We didn't have any problems. I think the process was a good one. Everyone was attentive to it and we followed the game plan.

JD: I guess you are glad to see Australia ring in Y2K without any glitches.

TC: Right. Absolutely.

JD: In 1999, USCGC *Midgett* [WHEC-726], homeported in Seattle, deployed as part of the USS *Constellation* [CV-64] Carrier Battle Group (CVBG). This was the first time a US Coast Guard cutter had sailed with a Carrier Battle Group. Can you talk about the historical significance of this?

TC: Yes. It was a big deal because we had to spend some scarce budget on selected upgrades for *Midgett* so it could be considered a legitimate player in the Carrier Battle Group. So, there was a lot of prep work. There was a special team put together to do it.

Midgett sailed with the CVBG, but it was tough going. The reason being is that the CVBG proceeds at a high clip because it doesn't lollygag around. *Midgett* had a tough time keeping up with the CVBG because of her older plant. The turbine-diesel combo on the 378s like the *Midgett* had to run at the speeds on a continuous basis, so it was a tough time keeping up the speed. So, we ran it across the Pacific and, when we got close to the Pacific Rim, *Midgett* shifted to an Amphibious Readiness Group from the Carrier Battle Group. It was a better fit. I think what we learned was it was a good experiment and it was good for the crew. But, just the day-to-day working back and forth with the battle group, we just didn't have the platform that could routinely deploy/run with a Carrier Battle Group. Clearly that was the conclusion.

The other thing that we didn't have going for us on this deployment was the right helicopter even when we were with the Amphibious Readiness Group as it deployed in the Arabian Gulf. The Coast Guard has always had problems with the HH-65 Dolphin Aerospatiale helicopter because of its engine. We are mandated by Congress to put a US-manufactured engine in that helicopter. The Honeywell engine didn't have the power that the airframe needed, and when you get in an environment where it is 120 to 130/140 degrees, it zaps power/fuel. So, the helicopter just couldn't function very well.

One of the first things I did when I became Commandant was to finally fix that engine problem with an engine replacement—a foreign engine that was optimally mated to the helo. Now, I got beat in the head and shoulders on Capitol Hill and I needed reinforcements from Governor Ridge to make that change. But we were successful in changing out that helicopter, and we installed the Turbomeca Arriel, which was originally mated to that aircraft. Finally, it was the perfect power relationship to the aircraft. Governor Ridge convinced the Hill to not fight us on that, and we changed out all of the old engines. I had aviators running around with big happy smiley faces because finally this aircraft could do what it was supposed to do originally.

But, in the terms of the *Midgett* deployment, we found out those limitations up close and personal. So, it was a good experiment.

JD: I want to get back to the helicopter engine. Did the engine failures cost any lives?

TC: No, but at times an aircraft disaster was close at hand. Our in-air power failure rate/power losses were incredibly high. When Secretary Ridge saw our in-air failure rates, he became very concerned. He said, "This is not right. This is dangerous stuff." I replied, "Absolutely. This has to be fixed. This is not only hazarding our aircrews, but the people that we go to assist." This had to be changed and we did it post haste.

JD: Okay. I want to go back to March through June of 1999. There was a surge of Chinese migrants on Guam. More than twenty vessels with 75 to 100 migrants on board. What impact did that contingency have on Coast Guard readiness throughout the rest of PACAREA?

TC: Well, it was one of the surge things. I think there is a good story here. Number one, we weren't surprised by it. We had intelligence from the interagency and knew what these migrants were working on. It was all from one province in the southeast part of China. There were some hard times there and people were looking for a better life. So, we built up assets and prepared for this contingency and there was really good on-the-ground interagency coordination between INS, FBI, and the state of Guam. So, we were poised to respond to that and the story is that none of those got onshore illegally. It was like someone had turned on a spigot wide open and they had these vessels planning to come one after another, but the strong deterrent effort stopped it as fast as it started. Again, I think it was because of the deterrent position that we had.

JD: What kind of warnings did you have that they were going to be doing this?

TC: Mostly through INS, and there was also some communication with the Chinese border guard folks who we had built a relationship through the North Pacific Coast Guard Forum. So, all of those things play out on that.

JD: Can you talk about the advent of go-fast boats?

TC: Yes. I was interested being successful in putting metal on target regarding our cutters and aircraft, instead of historical driven scheduling for cutter deployments. We wanted risk-based, intel/threat-driven scheduling of our major assets. When I first got to PACAREA, I asked for a review of the counter-drug mission in the eastern Pacific. We had very little ship days scheduled there, largely due to a perceived chance of success—limited choke points for interdiction purposes, along with limited assets. We did some more homework to get a better handle on the mission/AOR. The ocean-going go-fast was the smuggler's platform of choice—fast but it used a good deal of fuel to get up the eastern Pacific. They had to be refueled several times on their way north by Logistic Support Vessels (LSVs), as we called them. They were fishing vessels with drums of gasoline on deck.

We concluded that the LSVs were a lot easier to track down than the go-fasts, so we started to focus on them using intel on when the LSVs were departing home port. We worked with JIATF West, and DEA, and others that have people in country to gather more info on the LSVs and track them. When we knew where the Logistic Support Vessels were, that's where the go-fasts were going to eventually be. I said, "We deployed our cutter and A/C assets accordingly."

We turned things around with some incredible results. We increased ship days down there by over 50% and, by the second year, we were seizing more drugs than in the Caribbean. We were getting 80% of the drug seizures because we materially changed the way we were doing counter-drug operations. We looked at the process and thought a little bit more innovatively. It's just another example that thinking outside the box sometimes produces a better outcome. Use of force from helos was another tool the CG had, but at that point in time it was used exclusively in LANTAREA and was not available to us.

JD: Can you talk about the controversy over armed helicopters by a few of the pilots because they joined the Coast Guard just to save lives?

TC: Change is hard and there are a number of things that you try to do, whether it's organizational change or policy change. Sometimes you've just got to do it. Damn the torpedoes and do it. You study it, and you look at all different dimensions of it, and if the consensus is it's a good thing to do, and it's going to help us in mission performance, then you do it.

We also prepared and trained extensively to operate with the new capability. We were charged by the President, and Congress, and our Secretary to do this mission and it's our responsibility to do it as efficiently and effectively as we can. And arming the helicopters was one way to do it. Now, if a particular Coast Guard officer or crewmember doesn't like it, they have a choice. They can go and find something else to do. But, it was the absolute right thing to do, and is the right capability to have, and I'm glad that we did it and we are still doing it. Adding that capability has been terribly effective for the USCG in interdicting illegal drugs, especially in dealing with the go-fast threat.

JD: In the late 1990s, the Coast Guard was behind its DOD sister services in funding quality of life issues such as childcare, housing, medical, tuition assistance, and some bonuses. Can you talk about this impact the disparity had on recruiting and retention of Coast Guard personnel?

TC: Whenever you can't provide the basic quality of life issues, it is going to have negative impact across the Coast Guard. Particularly hard hit was childcare. I can remember visiting units and talking to female enlisted personnel that had a couple of children and they said, "I can't afford to be in the Coast Guard. My whole check is going to pay childcare." So, that was a hardship, clearly. But all of those things added up. The pay and benefits, tuition assistance, all of those things add up to impacting retention. Now, one of the initiatives that we can talk about later when we discuss my assignment as Commandant, my slogan as Commandant was "readiness, people, and stewardship." I can talk about what that entailed but, on the people side, one of it was worrying about the workplace, professional development, and benefits. *What made for a dynamic, energized, and innovative workforce?*

In PACAREA, clearly one of the important quality of life things was improving housing, and we made huge gains especially in Kodiak, Alaska, and in the Bay Area. Kodiak was a priority and so where I could influence the leadership council, and the programming and budgeting empire network, I would twist arms. We built hospitals, clinics, and childcare centers when I was PACAREA. So, those were huge improvements.

The other thing was connectivity. I was worried about men and women on the fleet. They had long deployments in the Bering Sea. It's not a lot of fun in the Bering Sea. It just is not. It's nasty. It's ugly weather/seas, and the crews are away for a long time. There are no good liberty ports. I'm sorry, but Adak, Alaska is not a great liberty port. They tend to just go hit the local bar and have a risk of getting in trouble. So, I tried to change the dynamics of that, and change onboard life, and do it by connectivity back home. We were way behind the Navy on this capability for our folks. But some progress was made, and more was made several years later. I will talk about that as we get into my assignment as Vice Commandant and role with the Innovation Council. I should note that although we lagged the Navy in a number of work force benefits, our retention rate and enlisted numbers did not drastically suffer. From my view, the attractiveness of our missions to young men and women far offset some of the quality of life shortcomings.

These are a couple of examples of things we did focus on during that timeframe, and that meant substantial differences to our men and women. Clearly, retention is a very important thing. It's better to retain. Once you get someone trained, you don't want that person to go out the door because of the investment made. I might have to say, jumping forward a few years here, in post 9/11, our retention rate was over 88.5%. It was the highest of any armed service, and it stayed that way during my time as Commandant because we did a great deal for the workforce.

We had a program called Future Force 21, and that was started by Jim Loy to his great credit—to look at how do we train, how we develop, and how we retain our workforce. People worked really hard on that, looked at it every which way. Rear Admiral Fred Ames was the Assistant Commandant of Human Resources, followed by Rear Admiral Ken Venuto. They did a masterful job in dealing with those issues. I think there was substantial strong signals sent to our workforce. It was started under Jim Loy and continued with me, and Thad Allen continued to work on those workforce issues because there is nothing more important.

JD: You mentioned previously during your travel to foreign countries that among your first stops would be the US Embassy. For the benefit of Coast Guard personnel visiting US Embassies overseas, what are some of the questions they should ask of the ambassador and the country team?

TC: Well, the reason that you do that is because it is a matter of protocol. It's the right thing to do. It's also the required thing to do. You don't go into the foreign country without the ambassador and the country team knowing. In addition, they are very helpful furthering the purpose of the visit. So, whenever we planned a trip, it was always preplanned with the embassy staff. One of the questions that you should always ask, "What's on the ambassador's agenda?" I always did a little research before I left. And, when I went to talk to DCM or the ambassador I would say, "This is why we are here. But, I know you are interested in X. How can we help you on those issues?" A country visit must be done with adequate planning and so it's good for the country team, to be consistent with their objectives and constraints, and good for you and your mission.

JD: Any memorable country visits?

TC: The trips of China were most memorable quite frankly. I made a couple of visits when I was at PACAREA, and then later as Vice Commandant and Commandant. I have always been impressed with how smart the Chinese are. Clearly, we don't agree with a lot of the things that they do, but they are smart. I don't believe in—I don't like their human rights policy, their lack of freedom, their limited choices, and their authoritative approach to their population. But, having said that, they are of substantial import globally and rub up against many of the issues of great importance to the US. As such, productive engagement with them is paramount from my perspective. In that light, and in furtherance of USCG missions and goals, I had some very interesting trips with them. And they are great hosts!

JD: Admiral, of all of your accomplishments as PACAREA Commander, what would you say would be the most significant?

TC: I think from an operations perspective, clearly, the migrant issue in Guam, the M/V *New Carissa* off the Oregon coast, and the crash of Alaska Airlines Flight 261 on January 31st, 2000. Flight 261 had a tragic outcome with 88 fatalities. I thought the Coast Guard did incredible stuff, and particularly handled that so delicately all the way to the memorial service that we orchestrated at Pepperdine University, where Transportation Secretary Rodney Slater came out. I was very, very proud of what the Coast Guard did in that and how we dealt with that one.

Another case of some significance was the tank vessel command—a first. That's the case where a foreign tank vessel had overboard discharge and polluted the waters off San Francisco and continued on its way down off the eastern Pacific, past Mexico. We put two and two together, and played detective assessing what ships went in and out of port at the time, and when did the discharge get noticed. We pinned it down to the tank vessel command. We chased it several thousands of miles and seized it exercising Presidential Directive 27 (PD-27), "Procedures for Dealing with Non-military Incidents." This was the process by which you communicate interagency to respond to a significant national issue. We had the Justice Department involved. We had the State Department involved. From my view, we did everything right. We were acting as a port state control agent in that case. It's not a flag vessel that we are after. We were the port state. We were in pursuit of a foreign vessel that had committed a crime. It was the first time that anyone had tracked down a ship like that in international waters and held them accountable to the tune of an $8 million fine against that vessel. And it sent a clear signal of accountability to the maritime world.

Apart from operations, I think the efforts we made in strategic planning and associated resource utilization was particularly noteworthy, as was the development/furtherance of critical international and interagency partnerships.

So, these were just a small number of these operations and accomplishments. There were many, many more. I was very, very proud of the men and women in PACAREA and how they performed across the board on so many things. I couldn't have been prouder and it was so much fun. I mean, so many unique things happening there between the 14th District and PACAREA. I admit, I am a non-objective player, but I would have to call it a success. From my view, PACAREA was the most challenging area that we had, and it was strategically important because it was at this very time the Coast Guard had a study going on validating all of our missions and validating the Deepwater project in the late 1990s. It showed all of the responsibilities, and the demands on our service, and the requirements for our nation in the deep water environment, and why we needed these assets. So, I was proud of that, and in what we did.

We left PACAREA better than we found it. It was handed off to us from Vice Admiral Jim Card who had done a lot of great things. We built on that, but we left it better off in many ways. One of it was the operational performance; one was threat-based use of resources. I also created a highly productive resource management staff. When I went to a High Endurance Cutter commander or base commander, I stressed that he or she was a resource manager in addition to being an operator. I expected the COs to be a good steward of resources. I held people accountable for that, so I think that culture changed at PACAREA, in the spirit of innovation and the strategic use of assets, while developing integrated strategic plans that were linked all the way up in support of the Commandant's objectives. We developed resource and readiness metrics that became the benchmark for the rest of the service.

So, all of those things—effectively using resources, building our intel capability. I didn't have a lot of folks with intel experience so I imported folks from CINCPAC who then augmented our staff and trained our staff on what systems to use and how to be better at intel. So, it was those innovative things that we did that I particularly have good vibes about. Strategic planning, resource utilization, the partnerships that were created, and pretty extraordinary operations. We had an aggressive enforcement of the Bering Sea as well. We had a number of confrontations with illegal Russian fishing vessels trying to ram us and our COs did a really good job during those situations.

JD: What advice do you have for future area commanders?

TC: Articulate the need for solid assessments, strategic assessments. Think strategically. Think as a system. Know your AOR. Demand that your staff really dissects things and understands the mission and the constraints and the threats in your AOR. That should be business number one. Business number two is to energize and enable your staff. Give them a long leash. Let them think crazy. I used that phrase before with you. But, let them think different and they will be energized accordingly. But, the other thing is to engage, engage, and engage. Part of your responsibility is to think outside your own organization. Sometimes you get tunnel vision and you only think within the Coast Guard. The area commanders need to build interagency and international relationships so that you can work together in a unified way and get things done. That should be high on any PACAREA or LANTAREA commander's agenda. Know your people. Know your area. Engage, engage, and engage. And lastly, lead by example, show integrity in all you do.

JD: How did you find out that you were selected to become the next Vice Commandant of the Coast Guard, and what was the selection process like?

TC: Well the selection process involves the Vice Commandant and the Commandant getting together and figuring out positions in the next flag slate. The Commandant also gives a courtesy looksee at the next slate to the Secretary and the Deputy Secretary to say, "This is what I'm thinking. This is why and this is a very good choice. You know him or don't know him or whatever." We grow our own. It's not like we are taking someone from outside the service and plunking them into Vice Commandant or Commandant. I worked with Jim Loy on a number of occasions in Headquarters staff. We both served as instructors at the Coast Guard Academy. There was some overlap, not all for years, when we were junior officers. So, I had worked with him off and on, on a number of occasions, so we were known entities to each other. I had been in the leadership council in PACAREA for two years, meeting twice a year, going back and forth with Headquarters, and the Commandant, and Vice Commandant. And apparently, I had the right résumé.

I got notified by the Commandant that he would be pleased to have me serve as his Vice and I thought that was a very attractive thing to do in an important time in our service's history. I was sad to leave such a wonderful place as San Francisco, the quarters I had on Yerba Buena Island, and the great job that was just action-packed at every twist and turn. So, we were a little sad about leaving that but, at the same time, enthused about getting back and helping the organization to work to huge challenges at that time. The challenges were, *How do we get out from under recurring, declining budgets while continuing to adequately perform missions critical to our nation?* We'd been trying to do more with less for over ten years. Well, more than that—into the 1980s. We had lived on just dimes and nickels and our asset base was showing it, and I said we needed help. I hoped to be part of the solution. So, I wanted to see if I could jump into that inside the beltway game and make things better for the organization. So, I was honored with the call from Jim. I was glad to be working as his number two. I thought very, very highly of him and had for a long time, so it was good prospects.

JD: Who relieved you at PACAREA?

TC: A classmate from the great Coast Guard Academy class of 1968, Vice Admiral Ray Riutta. I believe he was Chief of Ops in Headquarters when he came to relieve me out in PACAREA. And, he had been a PACAREA guy. He had been a ship driver out there, and he also been 17th District Commander when I was 14th District Commander in Hawaii. So, he had great familiarity with PACAREA. He really, really wanted that job. It was a good fit. Very capable guy, so it was a good transition.

JD: We are finishing up on your tour at PACAREA. Is there anything else you would like to add before we move on to Vice Commandant?

TC: No. I was thrilled with getting that assignment. PACAREA is a fascinating area. So many different cultures, and peoples, and challenges in that AOR, that it made it really a kick to be involved. And my family enjoyed it as much as I did.

JD: We are moving on to your role as Vice Commandant. What was the transition period like for an incoming Vice Commandant of the Coast Guard like yourself?

TC: In terms of overlap, it was short. It would have been very, very different for someone outside of the organization coming in. But in the Coast Guard the senior flag positions are held by seasoned individuals who, as junior officers, have typically come in at the bottom of the officer personnel pyramid and have risen upward based on performance. I had been engaged with Jim Loy and his whole staff from the get-go while on the leadership council, when I was PACAREA Commander.

The other thing, from a family perspective, was that my wife and I had lived in the DC area before. We had a number of assignments at Coast Guard Headquarters and quarters were provided out in Bethesda on Goldsborough Avenue. Called it "the gas station," big flat roof-type private home on Goldsborough Avenue. So, there was no worry about buying a house and both of my children were out of the house by then. So, it was a pretty easy transition and in terms of overlap, the transition process took four or five days.

JD: Please tell us about Admiral Loy. What kind of officer and leader was he?

TC: A great guy to work with/for—gives you a long leash, but holds you accountable. He has a good manner about him, treats people properly. He has an extensive knowledge of our service and is a solid leader who communicates very effectively, both up and down the chain of command. So, I have great respect for him and so do others. He went on from the Coast Guard to run the Transportation Security Administration (TSA) and later served as Deputy Secretary of the Department of Homeland Security (DHS). He has been a very successful professional in everything that he has done. So, I really looked forward to moving from PACAREA to be his number two.

When he wasn't driving ships, he had a number of human resource assignments. He was head of the Office of Human Resources at one time. He was also chief of the OCS School down at the training center at Yorktown in a previous assignment. He was also a senior detailer. He ran the Officer Assignments Division in the Office of Personnel at one time.

Leadership, personnel development, and operational expertise was a wonderful combination for our Coast Guard. He was really into leadership issues and how to develop folks. He even co-authored a book on leadership with best-selling author Don Phillips, titled *Character in Action: The US Coast Guard on Leadership*.

JD: Great book. It was published by the Naval Institute Press in 2003. What guidance did you receive from him about your new duties as Vice Commandant?

TC: General strategic guidance, not rudder commands. He was clearly interested in pushing the strategic plan and his stated agenda. And, as part of the leadership council while at PACAREA and before I became Vice Commandant, I had figured materially in the development of the strategic agenda.

The big thing for him was the Coast Guard readiness posture. The readiness of our cutters and aircraft was a huge challenge for us. Prior to 9/11, we were tying up ships. We didn't have any money to buy them fuel—grounding and putting aircraft in storage at Davis-Monthan Air Force Base in the Arizona desert because we didn't have the necessary funds to maintain them. We were in pretty desperate budget straits after years of declining budgets, so readiness had to be priority number one. Another priority was positioning the Coast Guard for the future. He called it shaping for the future, with an agenda, with specific strategic objectives addressing those issues.

Admiral Loy also wanted me to help/provide senior oversight of the Deepwater program since I had been so involved with it in prior assignments. I had been involved in capital acquisitions as Chief of Office of Acquisitions and as a program analyst and division chief in the Coast Guard's Programs Division in the Office of the Chief of Staff. He also wanted me to take a leadership role in quality management, process improvement, innovation, and application of technology, given my past experience in these areas.

JD: How often did you meet if both of you were at Headquarters?

TC: Our two offices were collocated. In the front office, there was a little bull pen. The secretarial bullpen is in the middle and the doors open up and you go to the left to the Commandant's office. You go to the right to the Vice's office. You could throw darts across into his office from my office. So, we were interacting every day. Almost every meeting that he went to in Headquarters, I was there. Of course, Headquarters is meeting central. There was also a daily ops brief usually in the morning. If we were both there, we both went. If he wasn't there, I would go.

JD: Can you talk about what an average ops brief was like?

TC: It was a review of daily operations throughout the Coast Guard and associated issues that had to be addressed. If there was a problem, the op cen would flag it as something that needed our intervention; something that was of interest to the Secretary; or something that had resource or policy implications, or a legal issue associated with it. There were frequently legal issues that needed to be addressed. We are a law enforcement agency dealing with jurisdictional issues—proper application of our authorities and all of those kinds of issues that have to be talked through.

JD: What was the criteria for something for you to handle, and what was the criteria to send it up to Admiral Loy?

TC: Anything that fell in my job description I would work. There was one Executive Assistant at the time—the Commandant's. So, it was the Vice Commandant and the Executive Assistant that really ran the front office staff. Protocol, secretaries, schedulers, speech writers, all of that stuff, and all of the correspondence that was coming into the Commandant didn't go into the Commandant's inbox. It went into the EA's inbox. It went from the EA's inbox and went to mine as the Vice. So, we were the masters of the paper product and I was the last stop between something that would go into the Commandant. If I felt it was fully matured, well-staffed, ready for his looksee, then I would send it in. Obviously, I would also send it in with my comments. I wouldn't send it in if it wasn't staffed properly and didn't give him recommendations. Don't just give him a problem. Give him a staffed issue with options and recommendations. So, in a way the EA and I were gatekeepers.

JD: Were there some major culprits that were like, "Do an end run around the system?"

TC: Well, yes. I think any organization has people that are like that and it's fine. Sometimes there is a reason for it. Sometimes, an issue would come up and he would say, "Tom, I need the Chief of Staff down here. I've got this budget thing he's working on that I'm not comfortable with." So, that would be a spur of the moment thing, and he'd come down and talk about it. I think it is common and necessary for most organizations. It's not the standard way of doing things, but there are always exceptions where the boss needs immediate access to people and urgent issues.

JD: Right. At the time, you became Vice Commandant, did you think that assignment was going to be your last assignment, since the last Assistant or Vice Commandant to be selected for Commandant was Admiral Edwin J. Roland in 1962?

TC: Absolutely, yes. I thought that this was a great way to continue to contribute, and then end my career. In fact, I didn't even have thoughts of putting in for the Commandant's job. I know the tradition is that the Vice comes in and goes out with the existing Commandant and that's the way it's going to be.

JD: What was an average day like for you as Vice Commandant, pre-9/11?

TC: Well, pre-9/11, working the policy and programmatic issues; working my job description, tending to meetings; and minding the store when the Commandant is traveling, or is on leave, or is out. The Vice is the acting Commandant or filling in for him when he's traveling, when he's out of the office, when he is on leave, or out CONUS and that was often. I would say maybe I would find myself 25% of my time in that modality. The job frequently involved fighting fires since, frequently, when an issue rose to the VC or C level, it was a problem to be solved.

JD: How often did you have to represent the Coast Guard in sessions at the National Military Command Center, where the members of the Joint Chiefs were in Admiral Loy's absence?

TC: Not infrequently.

JD: And, what was your impression of JCS tank at the Pentagon? Is it anything like what Hollywood makes it out to be?

TC: I am not quite sure how Hollywood makes it out to be. It's a large scale, professional operation that is very well staffed. Everything is prepped and prepped and dry-runned three or four times before it gets presented into the tank. But, I was impressed. There are meaty discussions that occur, focused on a specific agenda. Every issue on the agenda usually started with a power point-type presentation. I was impressed that people were willing to think and speak their minds critically about things. And it was a very joint type of a setting as it should be.

JD: Did you feel that you were at a certain disadvantage because the Vice Commandant had three stars instead of, in comparison, to the four-star vice service chiefs?

TC: No. I think that made us just about even. I'm saying that half-jokingly. I didn't feel slighted or anything else particularly after 9/11. I thought they treated the Coast Guard well and gave us our due. Most of them understood who we were and what we did. We were treated with dignity, respect. And I had established solid relationships with DOD senior officers from my time in the 14th and PACAREA. By the time I was Vice Commandant, and then Commandant, many had found their way to the Pentagon. We did things in a coordinated way—it was all about the mission at hand more than it was about four-star vs. three-star—i.e., *How do we work together and how we use respective competencies and authorities?* For us, it was involvement in certain niche areas in support of DOD. In fact, the Coast Guard and its distinct missions and authorities were in frequent demand by a number of combatant commanders.

JD: Can you talk about the Vice Commandant's living quarters? You mentioned it looked a little bit like a gas station.

TC: Yes, it was referred to affectionately as the gas station since it had that type of look—a couple of square modules put together with a flat roof located on Goldsborough Avenue in Bethesda, Maryland, in a fairly high end neighborhood. Actually, they were very decent quarters. It had a great lot and was very well laid out inside with a very good kitchen.

I had a quarter's manager which we did in all of the quarters, be it District 14, or PACAREA. It was an easy transition, family-wise, into those quarters. Bethesda was a very nice place to live, with restaurants and malls galore close by. The Coast Guard no longer has those quarters. Both the Commandant's quarters and the Vice Commandant's quarters were sold after I retired, as were the Chief of Staff's quarters located near Montgomery mall. Admiral Thad Allen initiated the transition away from the three homes, and Admiral Papp realized the benefits of it. It involved the building of brand new homes on Bolling Air Force Base dedicated for the Commandant, Vice Commandant, and Chief of Staff and managed by the Air Force. The CG benefited from built in security at Bolling as well. And the quarters are very close to the new CG HQ. Further, the money realized from the sale of those three homes were added to enlisted housing funding.

JD: Did you have to entertain much, as Vice Commandant, in our quarters?

TC: Yes, I did, but not as much as when I was Commandant. But, there was some entertaining to support engagement with marine parties of interest—foreign dignitaries, the interagency, as well as CG personnel.

JD: Can you talk about your role as agency acquisition executive and what that entailed?

TC: Yes. That's one of the critical job elements for the Vice Commandant. As agency senior acquisition executive, the Vice's role is to oversee all recapitalization efforts. I also oversaw the requirements definition for some of the subordinate systems. Being a source-selection official is a formal title for major systems contract awards. So, ultimately who signed on the dotted line would be the source selection official for the contract award. Most of that was a responsibility of the Vice Commandant, and not only for Deepwater, by the way, but all major systems acquisitions. It was familiar territory. I had been Chief of the Office of Acquisitions. I had been deeply involved in our service's capital planning and budgeting efforts.

JD: Do you recall how the Deepwater project got its name?

TC: I didn't name it. As I recall, it was named by the requirements people in the Office of Operations. It was a good name because it reflected the mission focus of those cutter and aircraft assets—our offshore assets. It was a good name and Integrated Deepwater Systems was an integrated approach. It was a systems approach to recapitalizing—necessary since all of our assets were coming to the end of their service life at the same time. And very importantly, OMB always made us do tradeoff anyway. A systems approach facilitated that. So, we took an integrated systems approach and issued a performance-based specification for Deepwater. What did we mean by performance-based? We didn't say, "Build a ship this long that looks like this and has this system in it." We didn't define the piece parts of the system or its design but instead specified what operational performance, what operational output we wanted from the entire system of systems. The program was supported with a great deal of operations research modelling and simulations, so as to achieve a future state that is more efficient. The best performance at the best value.

So, it was not a one-for-one replacement of the existing platforms/systems. It looked at the total system and what it could perform. It was a unique approach. I think it was a good approach and the overall architecture of the system of systems—i.e., the mix of aircraft, cutters, boats, and systems—the system of system design, and its individual asset types were solid. The one major problem that Deepwater encountered later was the use of a systems integrator to run the program under one large contract. This approach was driven by the fact that we did not have the staff—numbers or the expertise—to run the Deepwater program as a bunch of individual contracts. The whole integration of all of the systems pieces were under the governance structure of one Deepwater integration effort—a joint venture between Northrop Grumman and Lockheed Martin under a contract awarded on June 25th, 2002—my birthday, by the way.

JD: Nice present for you.

TC: It just happened that way. Now, would we have rather had a number of separate contracts run by/integrated by CG personnel? Probably, yes. Again, we really didn't have a choice at that time. We didn't have the capacity to run them. We didn't have the capacity or the skill to run multiple contracts. In fact, our acquisition staff was frequently cut by OMB and the Hill, not added to. So, we went with a contracted systems integrator which ultimately proved to be a challenge from a cost/schedule/performance perspective. That governance structure didn't work very well. The CG ultimately stepped away from individual contracts and CG governance, which was a good move.

JD: Can you talk about some of the operational requirements?

TC: The operational requirements were substantiated by two things. It was substantiated by the 1999 Interagency Task Force on the Roles and Missions of the US Coast Guard and OMB's A109 circular which required major acquisition programs to have a mission analysis associated with it. So, you needed to do a very formal planning mission analysis that defined all of the mission set of the asset that you are trying to buy. The validation of the systems of systems design was also supported by operations research modeling. The ultimate design includes three classes of cutters, cutter boats, fixed wing and rotary wing aircraft, sensors, and supporting sub systems. The performance capabilities of these systems—range, speed, etc.,—were also defined in the program specifications.

JD: Another role as Vice Commandant is that you served as the liaison to the Coast Guard Foundation and the Alumni Association. What did that entail?

TC: These roles included being the point of contact for the Alumni Association and CG Foundation in the front office. So, if they needed to come knocking on the door of the front office, they came to the Vice Commandant. We reviewed the budget that they created and the people oriented projects that they wanted to do. The role also included representing the US Coast Guard at Foundation events. Vice Admiral John D. Costello, was the Chairman of the Board of the Coast Guard Foundation. I had known him when he was on active duty. I would go to most of the regional award dinners to represent the service and the Commandant. I would usually meet with all of the directors ahead of the award dinner and give them an overview of current goings-on in the Coast Guard. So, most of the representational work with the foundation would be done by the Vice Commandant. It is a great organization that does terrific things for our personnel—scholarships, recreational projects, etc.

JD: Can you talk about your role pre-9/11 as Co-Chair of the Navy-Coast Guard Board (NAVGUARD Board) that you co-chaired with the Vice Chief of Naval Operations?

TC: The Vice Chief of Naval Ops and the Vice Commandant were co-chairs of the NAVGUARD Board which included key senior operational and support staff leaders from each service. Most of Coast Guard's staff that worked those issues for the NAVGUARD were from the defense readiness staff within CG Operations. They would be the ones that would be my staffers for the NAVGUARD Board. The agenda of the Board focused on the coordination of the services' respective roles and assets—how we work together, how we develop and leverage our respective capabilities and assets—all in the national interest.

A major initiative involved the idea of the National Fleet concept with a heavy focus on the direction of Deepwater. We wanted to plan, construct, and operate our Deepwater assets so as to be compatible and in support of US Navy responsibilities. That dialogue started early in the life of Deepwater. As we created the requirements for our Deepwater assets, we asked the Navy several questions. What requirements would the Navy like to see in them? How would they use them, when and if we augment the Navy? It was a collaborative approach to the requirements development of the systems and capabilities that would be put into those platforms. And many of the subsystems—weapons systems and sensors in particular—would be funded by the Navy based on agreements developed within the NAVGUARD Board. That was the initial major thrust of that body and then it matured over time to be a focus on this concept of a National Fleet. We examined how does our mission responsibilities and capabilities meshed together and how we should acquire, develop and operate our respective assets in a non-redundant, but complimentary way. Heaven forbid, you know. I mean, that is a logical thing.

To this end we created a formal National Fleet concept supported by documentation. When I was Commandant, Admiral Mike Mullen and I signed a formal National Fleet document that outlined how we are going to manage, maintain and operate our fleets together in a complimentary way. It is a great concept and I think it's still alive and well, as we speak, and it's the right thing to do. In the final analysis, Navy and CG major assets are the nation's maritime security and defense assets. They should be managed, planned for, cared for, collaboratively all in the national interest. And that's what the National Fleet concept is all about.

Clearly 9/11, influenced the Board's agenda with a focus on reviewing how we work together on defense of the homeland and where does our respective responsibilities begin and end. So, it was one additional forum by which the Navy could provide input to the development of planning documents that were going outside the DOD.

JD: Can you talk about the state of Coast Guard readiness the summer of 2001?

TC: Well, it was not only bad in 2001, it was bad in 2000. Bad in 1999. Bad in 1998. It was getting worse all of those years. Jim Loy's number one priority was to restore our readiness. There is a people dimension, there is a hardware dimension, a training dimension, and a system dimension to the readiness equation. And they are all going in the wrong direction during that timeframe. It had everything to do with aged cutters and aircraft and getting the little budget support that we needed.

Due to aging platforms, the proportion of the operating expenses that had to be allotted to maintenance budget kept increasing as were the number of cutter days lost to casualties—that's when you have a vessel that is supposed to be scheduled to do mission X in location Y, but can't do it because of a casualty. The overall situation was aggravated by years of declining budgets and organizational streamlining to try budget savings awhile meeting mission responsibilities.

You can ultimately streamline yourself to death. You consume your assets and erode your capabilities. That is what we were doing. We had been streamlining, streamlining, streamlining. We couldn't squeeze anything more out of the budget. That is where we were prior to 9/11. We were literally tying up ships to the dock and cancelling patrols, because we didn't have enough budget to buy them fuel. We were also laying the older aircraft up and putting them up in long-term storage in the desert because we couldn't support them. We had serious maintenance challenges with our C-130, HH-65 fleets.

Admiral Jim Loy used the metaphor of a dull knife when talking about readiness. You keep using it and keep using it and keep using it and you never sharpen it. Pretty soon, you have a pretty dull knife and by the year 2000 our Coast Guard knife was really dull. He continually made the readiness case with the administration and on the Hill. He stressed to them that they needed to know the consequence of declining readiness—that it was his responsibility to tell them. very frankly, what the CG can do and what we can't do due to readiness impacts. Frankly, deteriorating readiness was impacting our ability to perform. That was our message. That's where we were the day before 9/11.

JD: Can you talk about the morning of 9/11 and where were you when you first heard about the World Trade Center?

TC: I remember it like it was yesterday. I had an annual physical appointment at the Bethesda Naval Hospital and I was coming back to work when I heard on the radio that there was a plane that hit the World Trade Center. I thought, "What a tragedy. It must have been some small private plane in the air that just had a problem." I remember walking through the double glass door into the front office and the staff was gathered around a wall mounted TV. Just as I walked in, the second plane hit. Immediately, the thoughts were, "These hits are no accident." The Commandant and I met quickly thereafter. And, of course, the Pentagon hit followed the hits in

New York. From our office windows, we could see look across the river and see the smoke rising from the Pentagon. I should note that Rear Admiral Jeff Hathaway was assigned over there on the Navy Pentagon staff as Director of Anti-Terrorism and Force Protection. Unfortunately, he lost a substantial part of his Navy staff.

Jim Loy and I got together quickly and talked through what was in front of us. Of course, we had a real sense of urgency about this. It was a sad morning. But, prompt action was called for. We recognized that the nation and the Coast Guard, with the 9/11 tragedy, were facing transformational security issues/challenges. The focus of 9/11 was on the aviation part of our transportation system. But we recognized that the maritime part of the system was just as vulnerable or more so. We knew that, at least, the aviation part of our transportation system had a security regime and had protocols, processes, and access control, and all of these things. At that point in time, except for large capacity cruise ships, the maritime component of our transportation system did not have a security regime in place.

Of course, what put everyone at unease on 9/11 was not knowing if there were more terrorist actions yet to come. For the maritime part of the transportation system, we quickly decided to shut everything down nationwide. We issued Captain of the Port orders to close down the ports until the threats were more clearly understood. We reached out to Rear Admiral Dennis Sirois who was in charge of the Coast Guard Reserve at that time. He later became Assistant Commandant for Operations when I was Commandant, and I directed him to prepare for a Reserve call up so as to have a greater presence in our ports and waterways, all in coordination with our Captains of the Port around the nation.

There is a Title 14 call up and Title 10 call up. Title 10 requires a presidential decision to call up the Reserves. However, the Secretary of Transportation has Title 14 authority to call up the Reserves—the only Secretary that has its own authority and didn't have to go to the President. However, clearly, it's prudent to give the President a head's up. So, we agreed on the need to quickly communicate with the Secretary to that end. Jim made a call to Secretary Mineta that morning asking for his permission to call up reservists, which we got. So, we had a massive call up of the Reserves. It was an unbelievable response by the Reserves. They were awesome. It was a large number within the first couple of days, and then we doubled and tripled it. It was the largest call up of the Reserves since World War II. And, you know, they have filled the holes in so many ways—and not just in the days and weeks following 9/11, but in the months and years following 9/11.

Also, was the need to get with DOD quickly and to talk about our respective roles. Jim about getting to talked to CNO Vern Clark that day as well including the need to share and coordinate resources where we need to and to work together collaboratively where we need to. Then, within a few days, Jim and I met with Vern Clark and the Secretary of the Navy, Gordon England, to discuss the way ahead to enhance security in our ports and waterways. Basically, they said, "Whatever you need, you've got." Our relationship couldn't have been anymore collaborative. It ended up, ultimately, being a two-way street. They provided several patrol boats to us and other types of support that we needed and ultimately we provided them, during OPERATION IRAQI FREEDOM, with patrol boats, people, buoy tenders, and High Endurance Cutters. So, 9/11 was the start of a more activist type of relationship in terms of mutual support, back and forth.

JD: Looking back at that time, did the days run together?

TC: It was a busy time. We knew we had huge, huge gaps in the maritime security arena. What if the terrorists had struck the maritime sector instead of the aviation part of the transportation system? From our view, the maritime sector was much more vulnerable, and much more valuable. I mean, the amount of goods coming into the country by ship, is over 90%. We have tens of thousands of miles of coastline. Hundreds and hundreds of key facilities like nuclear power plants on waterways. Chemical plants. Refineries. Take the Houston ship channel. A wide array of chemical plants are located there and, as I recall, nearly 50% of the nation's petroleum is refined there. They can become substantial target-rich environments.

Prior to 9/11, 2% of the Coast Guard's budget was spent on port security. Two percent. Right after 9/11, we were allocating 50% of our assets—people, boats, etc.,—to that issue until we attained a clearer assessment of risk. As things became clearer resource allocation moderated down to about 20%. As I recall, by the time I left as Commandant that figure had dropped to slightly below the 20s. In any event, it was a very significant shift and we had much on our plate to make the transition a successful one. We didn't have the capacity. We didn't have adequate plans in place. We didn't have the processes and procedures in place. We recognized that we didn't have the capabilities and capacity in place to deal with these new threats. We had a great deal of work ahead of us.

If my memory serves me correct, Admiral Loy traveled to the International Maritime Organization (IMO) in London that fall because we had quickly concluded that this was not only a domestic issue, but it was also an international issue. The vast proportion of maritime traffic coming into US ports comes from foreign ports under foreign flag. Ensuring that they posed no security risk was essential. All international maritime issues had to go through IMO who had heretofore been involved primarily in ship safety, ship design, pollution, and safe navigation of ships. Security was not part of their primary agenda, and both Jim and I agreed that security must be front and center regarding the IMO agenda. Jim addressed the IMO session that fall in London and spoke strongly about making maritime security an international priority. That's one of the batons he passed me when I relieved him, making an international maritime security regime happen.

We are getting ahead ourselves, but when I took over as Commandant in the late spring of 2002, know, a maritime transportation security act was passed that required us to do all kinds of things domestically to secure the maritime system. It essentially required us to build an elaborate maritime security regime. It also required us to go inspect all of the ports of our trading partners to ensure that they had the proper security around, including security plans for every port facility. I should note that the CG played a major role in working with congressional staff to shape the legislation.

We also had Homeland Security Presidential Directive 13 (HSPD 13)*** which required us to develop a national transportation security plan and maritime security plan. There was a requirement for a major plan and about eight subordinate plans to be developed, and these required extensive interagency engagement, to make happen. These weren't Coast Guard plans. These were a national plan. So, we had both international and domestic requirements to craft so as to finally achieve a security regime in the maritime sector. There were huge implications for our service—how we are organized; how we are staffed; what the competencies should be; what capacities we needed; associated standards and doctrine—all of that. Huge.

I think looking back on it, it was one of those really transformational times for our service, like no other. There were a few of those really big transformational periods where you can fundamentally mold the character of the organization going forward, and I think 9/11 was one of them. If you add the post-9/11 impact, then you roll in the integrated Deepwater systems with new technologies—with all of your systems to be changed out, all at one time. Huge, huge transformational issues. What helped me as Commandant was being Vice Commandant at the time of 9/11, and being on the ground floor of most of these things, and collaboratively working them with Admiral Loy.

We can talk about the selection process, if you like. I don't know what was the Secretary's reasoning for selecting me to become the 22nd Commandant. He never said, "This is why I picked you, Tom." I didn't ask either. I liked the outcome and I think it was that continuity thing that made sense to the Secretary.

HSPD 13: Maritime Security Policy outlined President Bush's vision for a fully coordinated US Government effort to protect US interests in the maritime domain. This document aimed to integrate and align all US Government maritime security programs and initiatives into a comprehensive and cohesive national effort involving appropriate federal, state, local, and private sector entities.

JD: What advice do you have for leaders that find themselves in a crisis like this to stay mentally sharp, given the long hours and a lot of stress. How do you balance everything?

TC: Well, number one is you surround yourself with good people. You can't do it all yourself. So, there was a heavy reliance on the ops guys. There was a heavy reliance on the Reserve guys. There was a heavy reliance on the legal guys. It was a team effort, everyone on board, GQ [General Quarters] type of operation and I think everyone had a sense of urgency about this. We invoked a team to come to grips with these things and all of the plans that had to be developed. And the plan is more than just the plan. It's thinking through the whole thing. Assigning responsibilities and everything else. My concern with the sense of urgency is you move further and further away from that tragic event of 9/11, and the sense of urgency about how to close gaps goes away, and people are not providing necessary funding and so forth.

But I think, as a team effort, a focused effort, you draw upon your professionalism and your experience, and it is just fundamentally good leadership and we had a lot of good leaders in the Coast Guard at that time, thank goodness. Jim Loy being one of them. I added my two cents, whatever that was worth. But, we had a good team effort and people worked long hours and worked hard to make it happen. It was one of those, "Coach put me in the game," moments. There was a lot at stake.

JD: How surprised were you that there was not an attack in the maritime arena following 9/11?

TC: I have been surprised that we haven't. Like I said, we have some very, very valuable assets. They've gotten a lot more secure since 9/11 thanks to the regime that we put in place in response to the Maritime Transportation Security Act and the International Ship and Port Security Code. Both are results that came out of our work with the International Maritime Organization. So, we've got a global security regime in place for the maritime. We didn't have it. Now we have it and we had it in short order.

I was amazed that we pulled that off and by we, I mean, the staff. They worked so hard in getting the International Port and Security Code through the IMO. It required a whole bunch of new security requirements for ships and ports. Ports had never been before in the IMO and now we have IMO with international standards for ports and we got that all approved by December 2003. So, yes it could happen in the maritime. Less risk of it now. This is a risk equation. It's managing risk. We have better response. We are better prepared. We launched things. That is all part of the maritime strategy that we developed. So, we are in a much better position. It's not 100% full proof. Neither is the aviation, as we have seen. So, this is not a destination, it's a journey. It's going to be an ongoing thing. I just hope that the nation keeps in the forefront all of the risks involved here. The recent terrorist activities, although not pointed at the maritime transportation system, show that the aspirations of the terrorists are still there. So, all of that foundation work that we put in place is very, very important.

JD: What do you recall about the atmosphere at Coast Guard Headquarters after 9/11?

TC: I think there was a sense of going to General Quarters (GQ) battle stations. That was the mentality of clearly the first six months to one year. It was GQ, man your battle stations. From a staff perspective, people were willingly putting long hours in because they knew how important it was.

We had mandates from the President of the United States of America. It was a presidential directive that says Coast Guard will work the security issues. We were the lead federal agency for maritime security. Accordingly, I think people had a sense of urgency about it. It was noble business and the risks facing the nation were and are real. So, 9/11 was transformational for the CG and it impacted my focus as Vice Commandant from that point on. My highest priorities were 9/11-related and Deepwater related.

One of the new mandates came from the White House and Secretary Mineta's office. At that juncture, the Deepwater specification was based on pre-9/11 requirements. The administration wanted us to review those requirements in the face of 9/11. Were there things now that we needed to be included into the systems/ship design in a post-9/11 environment? Another mission analysis was required to refine the requirements, which we did. The current design did not have chemical, biological, radiological protection capabilities built into the platforms and the cutters didn't have a skiff, the ability to handle top secret information and classified information, and so forth. Those are absolute necessities in the post-9/11 environments, and so we had to make some of those adjustments which had an impact on the contract, and the cost, and so forth.

JD: Can you talk about, in the days after 9/11, you and Admiral Loy's interactions with the area commanders, district commanders, and the Captain of the Port of New York?

TC: All our district commanders and COTPs rose to the occasion and provided a timely response to the situation. Vice Admiral Thad Allen was LANTAREA Commander at the time. In the immediate aftermath of 9/11, we depended on him a great deal to address day-to-day operations associated with New York City. Clearly, the focus was in New York because of the impact of the World Trade Center and the evacuation of the tip of Manhattan.

There was a mass evacuation of 500,000 people from Battery Park in southern Manhattan and it was mostly by maritime—everything that could float. It was a great example of people stepping forward—private interests, local agencies, law enforcement, first responders, COTP etc.—in a time of crisis and taking the bull by the horn. It was coordination on the fly between the Captain of the Port and marine interests like the ferry operators, tug boat operators—you name it. It was an incredibly great performance up there in New York by all involved, not just Coast Guard. We obviously had a big role, but credit goes to all of the maritime professionals in the Port of New York that stepped up to the plate. They made that happen. It's pretty amazing.

JD: Yes. It was like the largest maritime evacuation since the Dunkirk.

TC: Yes, and done on the fly. I mean, that's what is so amazing about that.

JD: Is there anything else that you would like to add about 9/11?

TC: Well, again, we are going to be talking about 9/11 when we talk about my assignment as Commandant because that just dominated our agenda in terms of dealing with the perceived security gaps at the time. The one thing 9/11 did was to identify capability and resource gaps, and subsequently resulted in budget and headcount increases. We had been budgetarily challenged for so long. Things turned around quickly. For years and years, we were just challenged budgetarily. If it wasn't for certain senators on the Senate Appropriations Committee that gave us supplemental appropriations out of the DOD bucket, we would have been even worse off. What happened after 9/11 was a realization from outside our service that the Coast Guard was right in the middle of our nation's security challenges—recognition that new legislation was passed with extensive requirements for the Coast Guard, and that our service needed to be resourced to do that.

So, we were in the growth mode after 9/11 and that was one of our challenges. You can grow well or you can grow not well. I mean, you can unintentionally change the culture of the organization, which we did not want to do. You can invest in the wrong things. We wanted to budget with strategic intent. In other words, *What is our strategic objectives and how do we match the resources to them? How do we make sure we are putting the right dollar on the right thing to do in order to reduce risk?* So, it was one of the things that was heavy on our plate. Our Coast Guard culture is a wonderful thing—it has served us so well over the years and we didn't want to change it, yet we needed to transform many parts of the service.

So, my job/our job was to orchestrate change. Every time I peeked under the covers, there was change. There was nothing staying stable. Organizational change, budget change, resource change, platform change, policy change, process change. So, it meant for a busy schedule for everyone. But, there was a no greater time to be in the senior leadership slots of the Coast Guard so as to answer the mail.

JD: Was it frustrating that it took 9/11 for the Coast Guard to receive significant increases to its budget?

TC: Well, no. It is just the way Washington works. Sometimes crisis brings resources. I should note that the increases did not involve an unlimited spigot. But, the budget did improve and allowed us to achieve some momentum under Deepwater, and allowed us to add some additional blocks of our maritime strategy. We reduced threats we have; we'd managed risk and reduced them by our security initiatives. But, the input to this sort of security input-output model were authorities. *Do you have the right authorities to reduce risk? Do you have the right competencies needed? Do you have the right capabilities and do you have the right capacity to do it?* In other words, headcount, number of boats, number of planes, etc.—capacity, competencies, capability, and authorities, that is the input to the strategy. So, we reviewed all of those things and we worked on all the inputs, including their resourcing.

JD: How did you even know what inputs to consider?

TC: Well, we knew there were some gaps. In the face of threats/vulnerabilities, we reviewed all of our authorities and tried to identify necessary changes. By the way, most of our authorities were largely sufficient. There were a few tweaks. Most of our port security authorities go back to World War II and are extensive. Where we were lacking was in capacity and capability. We didn't have enough physical presence in our ports. That's a capacity issue. We didn't have selected competencies and the intel. So, I think we began to understand where those respective gaps were, and then we went about trying to fill them. Now some of the things added have been adjusted since, and appropriately so because, as time moves on, the risk gets changed over time. I think the maritime strategy was a good one and it's largely intact to this day. I think we got it right and we can talk about that in detail.

JD: How do you prioritize risk?

TC: We actually had a model for this, and hats off to the marine safety folks. They actually developed the risk matrix and a threat assessment, and that was part of the planning. We put a mandated planning process in place for developing a security plan for facilities. Every facility had to have one, and they had to go through the mechanics of assessing their vulnerabilities and then come up with a risk assessment and a security plan that addressed it. So, every facility, port, and ship had to have a plan.

We used to be a flag state. In other words, we had a lot of ships under our flag. Now, we are largely a port state. In other words, all foreign bottoms come in and foreign flag vessels come in. There is a reason for that. I mean, it's cheaper to run the vessel with a foreign flag. *But, how do you control them? How do you know what's coming into your port? How do you know about the people onboard? How do you know who owns it? How do you ensure there is not a biological, radiological, or nuclear thing on those? How do you know?* So, we had to address that, which we have. We really tightened up the scrutiny of all inbound foreign flag ships. We have advanced notice of arrival. Mandated information that comes with it regarding ownership, financing, etc. We've attempted to take that veil of secrecy off international shipping so there is greater awareness of the crew list, the manifest, and the ownership. And, if there is anything that peaks our interest, we then have a "vessel of interest," and the level of scrutiny goes up accordingly.

It's all threat based and intel based. You've heard me say this before. A threat-based use of resources pays dividends. We wanted to put intel against the things at the greatest risk, so we developed an international vessel movement center that monitors the movement of vessels, particularly incoming. It's jointly staffed with the Navy at the National Maritime Intelligence Center in Suitland, Maryland. We jointly do it and there's US Customs participation as well. We monitor all shipping. We dissect it and where there is an issue, there's graduated response depending upon what we perceive the level of risks to be. That ranges from getting boarded, ordered to remain offshore, escorted in, or whatever.

JD: After 9/11, how often would you get the late-night phone call that began with something like "Admiral, we are concerned about this or that ship?

TC: We had a number of those. There was one coming into New York. There was something curious about the manifest. We had Geiger counters out there and they detected something so we held it offshore until we got better information on the manifest. We had to coordinate with the Governor of New Jersey and others about allowing the ship to come in. To make a long story short, it was held offshore a long time. We examined some of the cargoes offshore and we finally made a determination it was from ceramics. It was a big cargo of clay ceramics that give off the Geiger counter readings and so forth.

JD: On December 28th, 2001, President George W. Bush signed the Intelligence Authorization Act for FY2000 that made Coast Guard a member of the intelligence community. Can you talk about what that meant for the Coast Guard?

TC: It was huge—another transformational event for the Coast Guard. I've said over and over again how important it was to have awareness of your AOR, awareness of your business, transparency of what is going on in your AOR in order for you to manage risk and make the best use of your operational assets. To have maritime domain awareness is the term we have used and now it's kind of a term of art. Maritime domain awareness is the ability to have that level of transparency. You can't have it without a competent intel establishment and until you are part of the intel community. Without it, you are not going to be able to have the inside view of certain things, and with that designation comes access to the information you need as a high-performing law enforcement agency. So, it was a huge change for us and when we became a member of the IC, I can recall Fran Townsend saying, "We should be careful what you are asking for too because with it comes substantial responsibilities, and effort, staff, and increased competencies that you have to develop in order to be a thriving, legitimate, contributing member of the intel community." So, when we signed up, we signed up to that. A good portion of our post-9/11 budget uptick went to intel. It went to maritime domain awareness (MDA). Maritime domain awareness requires intel. It requires sensor systems. It can be National Vessel Movement Center. It could be a VTS system in a port that's going out and surveying the port. It's all of those things that develop a common operational picture of your area to enhance both security and safety. One of our highest priorities has been MDA. And the funny thing is, as Jim or I travelled around and visited counterpart organizations around the planet, everyone wanted MDA. They didn't call it MDA, but that's what they were after. When we were in the Mediterranean, they wanted MDA.

In the Baltic, they wanted MDA. In Malaysia, they wanted MDA. Singapore wanted MDA. Japan wanted MDA. North Pacific Coast Guard Forum wanted MDA. They all wanted MDA and we all have worked hard at that.

One of the things I did was represent Admiral Loy at the International Sea Power Symposium (ISS) at the Naval War College in Newport, Rhode Island hosted by the CNO, Admiral Vern Clark. I attended and spoke. Then, each morning, Vern and I would have breakfast together and we would compare notes. I can recall Vern noting that so many of the world's CNOs were interested in the things the USCG does. They wanted to talk about, *How do they secure their borders? How do they regulate their fisheries? How do they find out what's coming into their country?* Maybe it was because many of the navies of the world have a number of Coast Guard type missions. In fact, the USCG is bigger than many of navies of the world in terms of ships and planes and so forth. I found it very interesting to participate in that symposium and deal with other nations trying to grapple with similar security problems—clearly, high on their agenda was MDA.

JD: What do you say to the critics at the time that said Coast Guard membership in the IC was just to get more funding?

TC: There were? Maybe they understood the budget we were in and they said that these folks are desperate and that is what they are doing it for. But, I think that would be very shallow thinking. The fact of the matter is, we are a law enforcement agency responsible for the maritime security of our country and we didn't have adequate intel, infrastructure, and capabilities commensurate with that role and that gap needed to be closed. So, we got some additional funding support but it wasn't disproportional to real needs. Frequently it was on the margins. It certainly didn't solve our overall budget problems. We did not join to gain budget advantage, we joined to enhance our ability to identify and manage risk, and do better things for the nation. So, clearly, it was a good decision. It was the right thing for the country. Right thing for the department and the agency. We are better for it.

JD: Did you have much of the role behind the scenes dealing with Congress on this issue pre-9/11?

TC: Mostly, it was staff-to-staff with our intelligence staff working the Intelligence Committee staff on Capitol Hill.

JD: It really accelerated after 9/11.

TC: Absolutely. 9/11 gave it the huge push.

JD: What do you remember about the selection process for Commandant and when did you decide to put in a package?

TC: Well, the selection process was basically open to two-stars and above, and they were invited to, if they wanted to be considered, to provide a package to the Secretary via the Commandant. It had to include your background, your assignments, your experience, and a little essay on what you wanted to do if you were Commandant. Actually, I wasn't planning to put one in. My youngest daughter, Kate, asked me about it, and I said, "Well, no, I'm just going to retire," and she said, "Dad, you need to at least run through the process. You would be forever second-guessing yourself. You've put so many years into this organization. You love it to death, so why wouldn't you throw your hat in the ring, plus you could probably add a lot of value. So, you need to do it."

So, I thought about it and I thought to myself, *Well, she's probably right.* I needed to compete for the job. I would be second guessing myself and I still have some fuel in the gas tank to do this, and I knew what kind of energy was required of the job. I was interviewed by Deputy Secretary of Transportation Michael Jackson, who is a great guy—a very competent professional. Had the interview. The Deputy and the Secretary ran through all the applicant packages and selected who they wanted to interview. They ultimately interviewed four or five finalists and made the selection. Then the Secretary notified me of his decision.

JD: So that was an important essay.

TC: It was an important essay and it was all about managing change within a structure of continuity. I said, I want to keep the culture of the Coast Guard. I want to keep the major characteristics. I don't want to change that. The fundamental characteristics are terribly important to our organization. I don't want to change them, but there is a whole bunch of things that need to be transformed given where we are post-9/11. Here they are and here's my transformation plan for all of them. It seemed to resonate with him and the deputy. So, I got selected and a whirlwind four years followed. I was thrilled with the opportunity and I was thankful to have served with such a great current Commandant, Admiral Loy.

JD: Do you remember any of the questions that Secretary Mineta asked in that interview?

TC: I don't remember the specific questions. They included some of the typical things that you get asked in a job interview. It focused on my experience to date, how I would deal with certain matters that were before the CG, a number of personal character-type things, and so on. But, it was a very positive interchange and the decision followed in a couple of days.

JD: Was there any family celebration after you found out the good news?

TC: We sat back and drank a glass of wine to celebrate. A toast. We knew that the new job was going to dominate our life for the next four years. We both knew that going in. And we were all in. My wife Nancy knew the demands of the job and had agreed to taking them on, or I wouldn't have put in for it. It was really a commitment for both the spouse and the principal. She clearly signed up for it. Also, it meant that we had to move. So, we moved from the "gas station" there on Goldsborough, literally right around the corner to the Kenwood Estates neighborhood to the Commandant's quarters.

JD: Now the fun began and you had to prepare for your Senate confirmation hearing to be Commandant. What was that like?

TC: A priority was to review prior confirmation hearings to see what kind of questions would likely be asked. And current USCG issues were likely to be part of the hearing. Fortunately, as Vice Commandant, I was up to speed on almost all current matters facing our service. So, there was not a great deal of study needed there. Also as part of the process, I had to prepare and submit a financial disclosure document since finances and associated matters were reviewed by the Committee. I had to appear before the Senate Commerce Committee chaired by Senator Fritz Hollings for my confirmation hearing. So, we prepped. Coast Guard Congressional Affairs had developed, as they always did, a hearing book full of potential questions with suggested responses that were prepared with the assistance of Headquarters staff.

As it turns out, it was a very pleasant experience because I was honored to have Senators Ted Stevens and Daniel Inouye as my two sponsors, both senior and very influential statesmen. They weren't members of the Commerce Committee but had arranged with Chairman Hollings to be my official sponsors. They both showed up to speak on my behalf. They spoke first and their very positive comments paved the way for a very non-contentious hearing. I was very fortunate to have served in the Pacific—D-14 and PACAREA—at senior levels, and had frequent interaction with both senators in matters that they had great interest in. It appears I had gained their confidence. There was not a great deal of pointed questions for me from the committee members after the statements by my two sponsors.

JD: Now, how did your role as Vice Commandant change from the time you were nominated as Commandant, until you became Commandant?

TC: I fulfilled the same duties and responsibilities. Clearly, there might have been a different reaction from the staff to me, recognizing I was not going to disappear from the scene as is normal regarding the end of a Vice's tour. I was also very busy. The Secretary's choice has to go up to the White House and the White House has to approve it before it's announced, so that takes you into the new year. Then you are working your flag assignment slate including decisions regarding who was going to be the next Vice Commandant; who were going to be the next area commanders, etc.? So, I was engaged in working the flag slate, and meeting with my new prospective leadership council, laying out our specific goals and objectives for the years ahead in a document referred to as the "Commandant's Directions," and defining how we are were going to communicate our vision of where we want the Coast Guard to go, both internally and externally.

JD: Did it help to have Transportation Secretary Norman Mineta stay over between administrations because he was originally appointed by President Clinton and he remained in the post under President Bush?

TC: Yes. And his Deputy, Michael Jackson, was also, and had been, of great help to us in meeting our mission priorities. Without the support of these two accomplished public servants, it could have been a very different outcome for me.

JD: And just the Coast Guard in general.

TC: Yes, for me and then for Coast Guard too. Both had great, great regard for USCG and the professionals who make it up. So, yes, I think, having him in place during this time of great transition for the Coast Guard, not only with the Commandant changing, but with all new security mandates and new responsibilities—like being a member of the intel community which now had to be matured, or putting security on IMO's agenda, or meeting the requirements of the Maritime Transportation Security Act, etc.

JD: And as a change agent, how do you make things happen?

TC: Well, you've got to get both external and internal buy-in of clearly articulated goals and objectives. You've got to assign responsibility and make sure you've got the right people attached to the right thing. Hold them accountable with clear metrics. You have to hire the right people to do the right thing and then you hold them accountable.

I can remember meeting with Secretary Ridge at a CISCO-sponsored managerial workshop—a symposium on how to plan and manage significant change. It was down in Florida. He planned to attend and speak at one of the sessions. I attended with him. We flew down together and had lunch with some of the CEO kingpins of the time who were involved in massive changes within their organizations. There was John Chambers himself, the head of CISCO. There was Carly Fiorina who was HP at the time. There was Jamie Dimon, CEO of JPMorgan Chase. Secretary Ridge went around the table and asked, "I'm orchestrating change associated with the new Department of Homeland Security. What are your words of wisdom I can get from all of you, since you have gone through driving major changes in your private sector companies?"

Jamie Dimon stressed that you to just pick the precious few elements of change that you are personally going to be involved in; sort of a top ten list of changes, and to make sure you assign people that's a good fit for the tasks at hand, but hold them accountable and ask for metrics frequently and every time you meet with that individual. That's all you talk about. He said his top ten list was always on his desk at work. It was on the bureau in his bedroom and that's all he talked about when he met with the staff elements responsible for making it happen. It is a straight forward way to manage change. He made it imperative across his organization and I think that is part of the secret. I took his message to heart.

JD: When you were nominated to become Commandant, was it like, *Now I finally have the opportunity to finish making changes on things that I've been working on my entire career*?

TC: I had a number of priorities that I wanted to tackle and some of them were just continuations of these seeds of change that had already been planted, but some were new seeds that I wanted to plant. One of them was how our field structure was organized, and I tried to get that change in my previous assignment at lower levels and I was never quite successful. I always ran into roadblocks up the chain. But, I thought in the post-9/11 environment, there is nothing more important than to have greater effectiveness and greater efficiency for the "pointy end of the spear"—what I mean by that is, the point of the organization that delivers service to our customers. Organizations have a tendency, when they do organizational changes, to rearrange the "deck chairs" up at Headquarters. Okay, sometimes that is needed—but the real difference, where you want to optimize things, is at the service delivery point. And I thought there was room for improvement, both greater effectiveness and efficiency. So, that was one thing that I had salted away and thought that maybe I can get this done now.

JD: We've talked about the passing of the batons. Were there any other batons that Admiral Loy passed onto you?

TC: Mostly, unfinished business that we needed to slug through and clearly the IMO business we needed to slug through. We needed to fix readiness and Deepwater was a big part of that. So, we had to keep the ball rolling on Deepwater, and keep filling out the wiring diagram on maritime security strategy, policy, resources, and organization, and how we deal with that.

JD: Can you tell us about the change of command ceremony at Fort McNair when you relieved Admiral Loy?

TC: It was a wonderful, grand ceremony. I was pleased to have Secretary Mineta and General Richard Myers, Chairman of the Joint Chiefs there. A good number of high ranking officials attended to help celebrate the great job that Jim Loy had done, while wishing me well on my new job. *Eagle* was the backdrop.

JD: I was there. It was a nice day.

TC: Yes, and we had a lot of the cabinet-level type people invited. Secretary Mineta had a reception on the *Eagle* for the dignitaries—ate in the wardroom and that kind of thing, which is a great setting. All the VIPs thoroughly enjoyed that venue. It was also a nice day for my family. Unfortunately, my father had passed on right after 9/11, several years after my mother had passed away. They would have been ecstatic at the event, very proud. My mother's brother and his wife, Finn and Peg Hansen, were in attendance. They offered that they were standing in for my parents, which was kind of nice.

JD: I'm sure they were smiling down at you.

TC: Yes, and my brother and sister were there. Of course, my daughters were there. So, it was a big day.

JD: Did your daughter say anything about applying for Commandant?

TC: She said, "See dad, you took my advice." [laughs]. It was clearly a big day and the staff did a great job putting everything together from the *Eagle*—the Secretary's reception, and a reception before the change of command with all of the trappings—the tent, the bands, and the protocols. There is a great deal of work to pull these type of events off, and everyone stepped up to the plate. I think we hit a home one!

JD: And to get the weather to cooperate.

TC: Yes, it was perfect. Something you remember for a long time. And then, in my change of command at the end of my tour, President George W. Bush attended. I can't remember another Coast Guard change of command where the President of the United States attended.

JD: I don't know of one either.

TC: And it was a reflection, I think, of the great respect President Bush had for the Coast Guard, and his respect for Admiral Thad Allen, who had done such a great job in the aftermath of Hurricane Katrina as the principle federal official. Again, not running the Coast Guard end of it, but running the entire effort of the federal government as the principle federal official. Steeping in fix a number of things, he became the face of the recovery to that effort, and did such a good job. So, I think it was recognition of, thanks to me for things the USCG had accomplished over the four years, and recognition for Admiral Allen. So, we experienced really fantastic ceremonies on the front end and back end of my assignment as Commandant—either end. The Chairman of the Joint Chiefs also attended my outgoing ceremony—that was General Peter Pace at that time.

JD: Did you know that Admiral Loy was going to get that job at TSA prior to the ceremony?

TC: [head nodding] Yes, the Secretary held Jim in very high regard and sought his leadership to enhance the functioning of TSA. A leader and a manager is basically what they needed. Jim Loy did great things for them.

JD: Now that you are Commandant, did you get picked up now in the morning?

TC: Yes, I did have several drivers. It was a good thing to have. I had secure communications from the car to make business calls and everything else, going back and forth. I also had a security detail that followed me everywhere. Post-9/11, I had four people in a security detail. Not serving all at one time, but that would rotate.

Another critical support benefit was the GV [Gulfstream V]. What an aircraft that is. It had been acquired with congressional support during Jim Loy's tour as Commandant. It is stationed at the Coast Guard Air Station at Reagan National Airport. It also supported the transportation needs of the Secretary of Transportation and now the Secretary of Homeland Security. It made business trips more effective, more productive—especially as it had global secure communications. In dealing with counterpart agencies in other countries, I often flew internationally on official travel to New Zealand, Colombia, Greece, Singapore, China, Japan, Korea, Peru, Chile, Guyana, Argentina, and all through Central America. Not the Commandant, nor the Secretary, could function as efficiently as they do if they had to fly commercial.

JD: Did it take some getting used to, having a security detail?

TC: It did because they were everywhere with you. But, that was part of the deal. And quite frankly, they were very helpful, particularly on foreign travel. They facilitated a great deal of the coordination with the respective country teams in terms of logistics throughout the course of the trip.

JD: Can you talk about some of the aides on your staff and their roles?

TC: The Commandant's aide is really important and I had two great ones. I had John O'Connor, who is now an O-6 executive assistant to the Vice Commandant. He was a lieutenant commander when he was my aide the first two years. Incredibly competent guy—loyal, smart, now a Captain in the Coast Guard. John was followed by Cindy Letterer, another lieutenant commander, who was my aide the last two years—another very, very competent professional. Both really added to the productivity of the front office.

My staff was much smaller than [those of] my DOD counterparts. I had a protocol-type person, a speech writer, scheduler/secretary, an executive assistant, and a flag aide. Given the many presentations and speeches I gave, if I had to write them all, that's all I would do. So, in terms of representing the service, and getting your message out for the benefit of the agency, the mission, and the people it serves, you have to have that level of support. You can't physically get as much done without that staff support.

JD: On days that you were in DC, what time of day would your day start?

TC: Whenever I needed to be there, but normally, I would get in there 7:30, 7:00. No later than 8:00, frequently earlier. I would be working until 5:30, 6:00, 6:30, 7:00. It was frequently a seven days a week job. There was something going on most weekends.

JD: Did you take the job of Commandant home with you? Was there work/life separation or was it like 24/7?

TC: You almost never get away from it. I'm not saying that critically. I mean, it's just that was the way it was. I probably would have had it no other way. It was a whirlwind and you're totally immersed. There were weekend events. Frequently, business travel over weekends. There were representational things and things with the DOD folks—frequent interaction with them. I would attend all of the combatant commanders' conferences. I'm there with them when they meet with the president.

I was always connected with the USCG OPCE, 24/7.

JD: What did you do to relax or what did you do for recreation?

TC: I worked out. I ran. I walked. Occasionally, I played some golf when I could get the time. Nancy and I did take a vacation here and there, but not very long ones. It would be a couple of days to go to the beach or something. We had not been on an extended vacation those four years. That's why when I did retire, we had a long one. We had like a three or four week one when we went to Europe, and that was a good thing in terms of winding down.

JD: In preparation for this interview, I reviewed Admiral Yost's oral history interview that was conducted by the Naval Institute a while ago and he referred to the job of Commandant as being in an ivory tower and remarked that you begin to miss things regarding the personnel who are serving around the country and the world. Agree or disagree?

TC: I think you can get caught up in that type of situation and you've got to watch for that. But, I tried to get out. I did many, many all-hands sessions around the Coast Guard. When I was PACAREA, I would try to make a point to visit each district to update them on current issues facing the field commands and our personnel. I tried to do the same thing when I was Commandant because you can get so caught up with just hearing selected views on things. It's terribly important to go talk to the deck plates; seek out people in the trenches and ascertain what they think, and what they are doing. I did that during Katrina and Rita, and I did it throughout my time as Commandant, and I got invaluable feedback that I took back to Headquarters. On all of those trips, I always had action items that I would come back and pepper the staff with. *What about this? What about that?* So, you try to avoid the ivory tower syndrome.

JD: Admiral Gracey also stated that he had trouble getting other flag and senior personnel at his daily briefs to talk openly and honestly with one another when the Commandant is sitting there. Was that your experience?

TC: I think that there is always some element to that. But, I tried to be open and allow dissenting views to come to the table and encouraged it. Remember, as Vice Commandant, I was charged with trying to encourage innovation.

We didn't talk about that role much, but I started the Innovation Council. I required the areas to have an Innovation Council and I required districts to have one. We linked them all together so that the Innovation Council would review suggestions throughout the Coast Guard, and allow our personnel to think creatively and openly about things. We would then set priorities for funding certain IT web-centric initiatives. In fact, we were working to create an e-Coast Guard. We first defined what that meant, and we supported the various innovation initiatives. And we made a lot of progress. We focused on developing connectivity onboard, among our ships and ashore. We connected all our High Endurance Cutters with email. We worked on getting PDAs and laptops in the hands of people to increase on-the-job productivity. We worked to automate the boarding process so our coxswains didn't have to come back after spending four or five hours on the water, and then spending another hour or two manually filling out the boarding reports and violation reports. Huge. Those are the kind of things we did in the Innovation Council.

We tried to encourage this idea of working smarter, not harder. We also sponsored an annual innovation expo where you could come and submit an idea that you had. It involved many display booths where you could show your innovation initiative. It's all about creating an atmosphere that encourages change when change is appropriate; process improvement when process improvement is appropriate. Not change for change's sake, but change with a purpose. Change with strategic intent. When you do that, people have the spirit of wanting to speak out.

Hopefully the Coast Guard has changed over the years and is continuing to change in regards to innovation. I saw it up at our Coast Guard Academy. I had made a purpose to do an annual leadership speech up there and meet with cadets as Commandant. I also visited more frequently than that, where I met with cadets and discussed current events with them. They are impressive, not bashful. They are poised; they are articulate. They aren't afraid to express their views.

So, I think our society has changed regarding expressing themselves for the betterment of the service. I think the atmosphere within respective services has changed, and our society has changed, and the people that we are getting are more apt to speak their minds and that is a good thing.

JD: Admiral Gracey also commented that he paid attention to what the commandants that came after him did. Did any retired commandants offer their advice or opinions to you and did you seek out any?

TC: I talked to Admiral Kramek on several issues. I also had an annual retired commandants-type of a luncheon at my quarters and there would be a lively exchange of ideas there. Some of the former vice commandants at alumni association gatherings or Coast Guard Foundation gatherings would approach me with something to say. One of them was former Vice Commandant Bob Scarborough—a great guy. He was terrific because he had so many good ideas and he was not bashful about expressing them. But, yes, there are many pearls of wisdom out there that you can gather. And the one thing you've got to learn really quickly is that you are not the source of all answers. You need to have a lot of support on the bench to pull things off, and you've got to nurture that support and allow it to flourish. That's one of the ways to increase the chance of being successful.

JD: How much of your job as Commandant was being a good diplomat, politician, and actor?

TC: I think you have got to be all of those things. I think you've got to be true to yourself and true to your principles. You also have got to have unbridled integrity. When you go on the Hill, you've got to put your best foot forward there. But, you've got to be honest, forthright, and full of integrity—in whatever hat you are wearing.

JD: How much entertaining did you have to do as Commandant in your quarters, and did you feel it was too much?

TC: There were numerous occasions for representational events at Quarters One. I don't think it was too much and we had help. We had quarters managers and I could import other quarters managers. There was a flag mess at Coast Guard Headquarters that serviced the flag corps for lunch and so forth. We could draw on them. There were also specialists that were the source of the Secretary's mess. So, it was a whole bunch of folks that you could draw on for special events and that really helped. It's still in your house and you are devoted to the event in every regard, but you couldn't do it without them, especially the cleanup part. Sometimes, the Coast Guard Band would come out and there would be a little entertainment thing going on. All of these things are why you have aides to help put all of that together. Of course, my spouse, Nancy, was in charge when it comes to engagements at the quarters. She was the brains behind most of that. If it comes off, it's because she made it come off—not anything that I did. Nancy was a spectacular hostess and knew all the proper etiquette—way more than I ever did.

JD: What did the neighbors think about having a Coast Guard Commandant live in their neighborhood?

TC: We had good relations with them all. We were very reasonable. We weren't too rowdy. It was kind of nice to be out in the community because it gets you away from total military immersion. Now, post-9/11, it became a security issue about where the Commandant should live. Since I retired, it was decided there was more benefit being on Bolling Air Force Base from a whole host of perspectives. One was to get out from underneath the cost of managing and owning a home and having to manage. Those functions are all done by the Air Force now. But, it's a very nice arrangement and the Air Force was very, very cooperative and terrific in making that happen. There is now dedicated housing with built-in security, and it's a stone's throw from the new Coast Guard Headquarters right up above Bolling AFB, off Martin Luther Boulevard. A step forward from my perspective.

JD: You mentioned that you had to give a lot of speeches and talks. Is it important to the job or do you feel that it detracted from everything you had to do?

TC: Well, I will tell you, I tried to plan speaking engagements with an objective in mind—things that would further the CG's overall goals, whether I was trying to articulate a policy change or motivate an audience toward our specific issue. And to both external and internal audiences. The message to the internal audience is a lot about what page we are on and we need to all be singing from the same hymnal. I would usually try to combine internal speaking engagements with an award ceremony or recognition of some sort.

The external speaking engagement is all about telling the CG story, seeking support, and gaining alignment. You can't live like a mushroom in a dark room somewhere. You have to have the customer support to be able to do your mission effectively. To get your interagency and international partners to support you, you've got to go out and kick the tires and engage with people. So, I think it is terribly important for the Commandant to get out and communicate the message—very, very important part of his job.

JD: Can you talk about the role of your speech writer? Would you give a broad outline, or would the speech writer write it for you?

TC: I would talk about it ahead of time. I would stress the kind of emphasis I wanted to make. If some of it was about a subject that I had given before to a similar audience or something, I would customize it for another group. There were additional iterations of it and they didn't write all of the speeches. Many of the speeches were drafted by the CG program office that had responsibility for the issue in question. We had a guide for speech making for the Commandant. How a speech is constructed it, how it should be put together. The speech writer would coordinate with the respective program office to get the speech written.

JD: Can you talk about your precepts for selection boards? What are you looking for?

TC: Obviously, I was looking for people that were creative thinkers, with good character, that had demonstrated superior performance under difficult circumstances, and demonstrated both good leadership and managerial skills. All of that, which was clearly spelled out in the precepts.

JD: What kind of things did you think the Coast Guard should look for in selected flag officers, and did you write any flag officer evaluations?

TC: Yes, I did. As PACAREA Commander, I wrote flag evaluations. I should note that a job of the Vice Commandant was flag corps administration. So, fitness reports, evaluations, assignments, all of those things were communicated from the Vice Commandant. I would also draft the next assignment slate for the Commandant, and that would be something we would work on collectively. There was also the whole idea of professional development of flag officers--what kind of courses to offer them, and sponsor for special development, both SESs and flag officers. We experimented with 360 evaluations for flag officers, not only your boss would evaluate you, but your subordinates would.

JD: How active as Commandant were you in the budget process for the Coast Guard, and at what point did you have to negotiate with OMB?

TC: Many of my staff assignments during my career involved planning, programming, and budgeting (PPB), so I was naturally drawn to these functions. However, the Chief of Staff, the Resource Director, and the Programs Division had the lead in the area of PPB. Much of the interplay on these issues would be staff-to-staff, whether that be with the department, with OMB, or the Hill. Frequently the hard work, staff-to-staff would lead to a principal's meeting where final issues/levels would be discussed. But, clearly the Commandant has a very big role in program priorities and the associated budget. Before submittal to the department, the Commandant articulates the overall strategic objectives of the budget and also approves the priorities in the various budget cycles.

The Commandant is right there during both secretarial, OMB, and congressional budget engagement. After the Secretary approves the CG's budget, the Commandant then meets with OMB senior level staff following staff-to-staff (CG and OMB) discussions/Q&A. When the budget goes to the Hill, he testifies on the Hill before all of the committees—both authorization and appropriation. Again, there is extensive interchange between CG and Hill staff prior to budget hearings. The Commandant is kept up to date on this interchange. So overall, PPB is a huge, time consuming role for the Commandant. Always has been, and I think it always will be.

JD: Did you participate in what they call murder boards, prior to a congressional hearing?

TC: Yes. I would go home with three or four mammoth hearing books—three- to four-inch binders full of brief issue papers—major talking points and background on a whole host of issues associated with the budget and authorization issues. When I was a young PPB staffer, we would research the questions asked at previous hearings to speculate on what follow-up questions would be asked of the Commandant. So, there is a paper trail of all of these issues through various correspondence between Congress and the Executive Branch, and we would try to capture all of those things so that you avoid surprises for the Commandant when he goes up on the Hill. It's called a murder board because you run through all of these questions in front of the Commandant who would likely have many pointed questions. The murder board frequently involves a meeting with a number of flag officers involved on the subject of the specific hearing in question, budget hearing and otherwise. The murder board would clarify various issues and, in the final analysis, ensure the Commandant is well prepared for the hearing on the Hill.

JD: Did you prefer to be given options on an issue or to have a solution presented to you?

TC: I wanted the issue clearly specified and, if appropriate, alternative approaches articulated with a concluding recommendation. So, it would be a combination of both.

JD: Can you talk about your selection of Frank Welch as the 9th Master Chief Petty Officer of the Coast Guard (MCPOCG) and how important is the MCPOCG position to what you wanted to do as Commandant?

TC: Having a talented MCPOCG helps in fighting that ivory tower problem we talked about earlier. As Commandant, you need feedback on the enlisted workforce and associated personnel policy matters under consideration. You need someone that has been there, done that, and is respected amongst the workforce communities. And that is certainly what master chief petty officers are. They are clearly the backbone of your organization. So, it is really critical to get that input when dealing with a numerous HR, budgetary, and policy issues. He always had a seat at the table. I wanted to listen and see what his perspective was because he had a pulse of what was going on, and what the workforce felt. When I chose him, I was looking for someone that had that a good skillset relative to dealing with people, was a good leader, and had a solid operational background—all of those things. And he fit the bill.

JD: How would you describe your working relationship with him?

TC: You'd have to get the Master Chief's input on that, but I think it was very positive. It was open. He spoke his mind. He wasn't reticent about saying what was on his mind and he stood in a long tradition of master chiefs that are like that. I have learned to give chiefs a little room and you will get great info from them. Chiefs speak their mind. Another example of that was reflected in the performance of John O'Connor, my military aide. He was prior enlisted. He was a Quartermaster, had a number of operational assignments, and made Senior Chief in record time. He then went to OCS, got a commission, and then went to Harvard where he attained a Master of Education degree and a Doctorate in Human Development and Psychology. Given all that background, he frequently provided down-to-earth, useable, invaluable input.

JD: Talking about the Vice Commandant, what factors led you to choose Vice Admiral Thomas Barrett and Vice Admiral Terry Cross to serve as your Vice Commandants?

TC: Well, number one, I like them both personally. They had superior résumés. They were humble, effective, of high ethics and values, people oriented, and results oriented. They had both been important contributors of my agenda development. They are very reasoned thinkers. I had also worked with both of them on a number of occasions, particularly Terry Cross. I thought they were both great choices.

JD: What sort of division of labor did you set up with your Vice Commandants?

TC: Not too unlike what existed with Jim Loy and myself. You know, there were those basic functions. The agency acquisition executive. The leadership council. Stand-in for the Commandant—all of those basic critical job elements, and he had the same ones.

JD: How often did you interact with the area commanders, now that you became the Commandant?

TC: When there was an issue that either they addressed, or one they felt wasn't getting the right attention at Headquarters, they would give me a call and vice versa. Sometimes, there was a special initiative they were working on—either under the cognizance of the leadership council (LC) or otherwise—and they would come in to give a brief to me on it, or a special appeal to me. We would also have our bi-annual flag conferences that they would be involved in. The LC was a key venue for our interaction.

JD: What were some of the agenda items on your bi-annual flag conferences?

TC: All of the ten or twelve things on our strategic agenda—our Commandant's Direction—that we were working on. *Where do they stand? How, as a flag corps, do we push them down the road?* Agenda items included implementing the Maritime Transportation Security Act; pushing security requirements through IMO; transitioning to the new DHS; building out new security capabilities and capacities; developing our role as an official member of the intel community; developing and implementing the sector concept; moving Deepwater ahead successfully, etc. Basically, the agendas included those items critical to the CG's transition into the post-9/11 world.

Our conference agenda at the end of 2005, which I called the fourth quarter agenda, was an important one, to both myself and the CG. I noted to the flag corps, "Okay, a team can play really good for three quarters, and then really flunk the last quarter and lose the game. We are in the fourth quarter and here is my fourth quarter agenda. These are 'got to haves.' I've got to have these at the end of the tour here. This is the end of our collective tour. This is the flag team for the four years that I've been working with, and we need to bring home the bacon the last quarter, and these are the key items." So, we talked through how we were going to get that done, and who is responsible, and that kind of thing.

JD: Can you talk about the role of the Admiral's aide, and what makes a good flag aide. and any advice you might have for anyone becoming a flag aide?

TC: You have to have a good personality and be effective working both up and down the chain of command. The chemistry must be right. You are also looking for a proven performer, in addition to a person that is results oriented and attentive to detail. You are looking for someone that is incredibly loyal. Those are some of the traits you are looking for when you go pick an aide. The Office of Personnel will present four or five candidates whom they evaluate as proven performers that have excelled in all of their jobs. They will give you a well-staffed package on each one and they will make a recommendation to you. The aide is important to the effectiveness of the Commandant, ensuring coordination of external engagement activities, total coordination of business trips, and working with the rest of the staff to insure all aspects of the Commandant schedule, including the planning of it, comes off well.

JD: Rounding out a series of questions on personnel, can you talk about the benefits the Navy chaplains bring to the Coast Guard?

TC: They are an important resource to work personal matters, formal events, etc. They get transferred temporarily to the Coast Guard. They serve in a whole bunch of different capacities. Ceremonies, dealing with crisis issues, family issues, and otherwise. They are a great source of counsel for our command leader regarding personal issues and problems. They provide support on the human resource front, they can support ceremonially, and they can provide yet another perspective on people programs and associated policy. They are valuable assets, clearly.

JD: When you became Commandant, what guidance did Transportation Secretary Norman Mineta give you?

TC: I was a known entity to him, so there was not a great deal to cover to get acquainted. Basically, he said "Welcome aboard." He noted that he looked forward to working with me to carry on the agenda and work the issues that are confronting the Department of Transportation. It was a general welcome aboard. Since 9/11, a new cabinet department focused on homeland security was an issue that was on the table and kicked around, but exactly how it was going to manifest itself had not been articulated. However, after week two of being Commandant, I received a call from Secretary Mineta that was very specific on the matter of DHS. He said that he had just gotten back from a meeting with the White House Chief of Staff, Andy Card, and that President Bush had decided to go ahead and create the Department of Homeland Security.

Since 9/11, there was a Homeland Security Council established in the White House led by former Pennsylvania Governor Tom Ridge and his deputy, Richard Falkenrath. They were the ones putting together options for the president on how to create this new department, and obviously had made a decision to do it. And the Secretary was notifying me and asked me to drop by to meet with him. So, that was the first really substantive, "Here is what we've got to do. You are going to be moving to DHS. TSA and Jim Loy is going to be moving with you." He stressed that he thought highly of the CG, but given the direction the president was going, to salute smartly and make it happen, we had to work together to make this the best transition for the Coast Guard that it can possibly be. He stressed that I could count on him to make sure that good things will happen for the CG. Well, that was my first substantive give and take with him. An issue of great impact for the Coast Guard.

JD: Not quite what you hand in mind probably, for your first two weeks on the job as Commandant.

TC: No, I hadn't figured that two weeks in, I would be overseeing the move to a new department—the third department for the Coast Guard since 1790. Incidentally, in my career, I was in all three departments (Treasury, Transportation, and Homeland Security). I was an ensign when the Coast Guard was at Treasury before being transferred to the newly created Department of Transportation.

JD: I think this a good place to wrap.

TC: Why don't we call it a wrap here.

End audio file Collins5.2.Dolbow.USNI.4.17.16

Interviewer: Jim Dolbow (JD)
Interviewee: Admiral Thomas Collins, USCG Ret. (TC)

Begin audio file Collins6.1.Dolbow.USNI.4.18.16

JD: It is Tax Day, April 18th, 2016, and there is no better way to celebrate it than by interviewing Admiral Thomas Collins. Admiral, can you talk about the guidance you received from Secretary Mineta and any expectations he might have had?

TC: Yes, of course. 9/11 was a genesis of a sea change for the Coast Guard's security mission, and it resulted in a considerable shift in focus and emphasis, along with resource adjustments. The Secretary had to consider how I would position the Coast Guard relative to the post-9/11 challenges. It was part of the interview process. He had a package for each one of the candidates for Commandant, which included our past experiences and assignments. It also included a short essay on where we wanted to bring the Coast Guard over the next four years, as Commandant. My essay's theme was all about dealing with this change and how the Coast Guard would confront significant externalities that were going to impact the Coast Guard and, most importantly, how we would deal with those challenges and still retain operational excellence across all the statutory missions. In my short essay, I addressed where my focus would be on transformational change in the Coast Guard but all within a framework of continuity. What I meant by that is that it was critical that we didn't change the fundamental character of the organization, especially in terms of the United States Coast Guard being a maritime, multi-mission, and military service. They represent the core and time-tested characteristics that we hold dear as an organization. They make us who we are.

So, I attempted to lay out how we would preserve our character, and our operational excellence in a period of great, great change. I believe the message resonated with him and served as the basis for our relationship going forward. The change we dealt with for the following four years was substantial. We developed, promulgated, and implemented the largest regulation in Coast Guard history, regulations supporting the Maritime Transportation Security Act. We had the biggest recapitalization projects in our hands, with the greatest technological changes in the history of the Coast Guard—Deepwater and Rescue 21 in particular. We then had to re-baseline our service, and justify our modernization program to the Secretary, the department, and Capitol Hill.

We had one of the most impacting, top-to-bottom restructuring of the Coast Guard in its history, or at least since 1915—reshaping our field structure in keeping with the new mission environment. The new organizational entities were called sectors. They had a major and enduring impact throughout the administrative and operational chain. We undertook to optimize the service delivery point, the field level, and then forced PACAREA, LANTAREA, and Headquarters, as well as the districts, to adjust themselves to the sectors—a whole different concept and a massive undertaking for our service. And I should note, we changed cabinet departments in the middle of all of this, and we deployed High Endurance Cutters, buoy tenders, port security units, maintenance support teams, and patrol boats to the CENTCOM AOR in support of Operation Iraqi Freedom.

We had to expand our international relationships to get all our work done to meet the mandates of the Maritime Transportation Security Act, as well as the global changes to vessel and port security. We probably made the greatest change ever in the history of our service relative to our ability to acquire, analyze, and take action on intelligence. We had substantial augmentation of DOD missions using not only active duty, but unmatched deployment of Reserves. At one time, we had close to 70% of our Reserves recalled to active duty. We also had to manage readiness issues with the legacy fleets. I'm referring to current WHECs and our patrol boats, which both had severe readiness issues in terms of their age and lack of budgetary support. We launched major mid-life mission effectiveness projects to keep them alive. All of this was a huge, huge undertaking and I could go on, but the external environment, external mandates, internal change that we felt was necessary truly made this a transformational period.

It was a time of great demand on our service. Great challenge, but great opportunity to have the privilege to wear the uniform, and be in this position and have such talented and dedicated people to help make all this transformation work, and make sense out of it. I was quite honored and there was great team that came together. I had Tom Barrett as my Vice Commandant. Thad Allen had been LANTAREA Commander, and subsequently was assigned as Chief of Staff. He served as Chief of Staff for the four years that I was Commandant and he's a workhorse—very effective in dealing with both the Headquarters staff and the interagency. So, a great deal of credit for many of the organizational advances that happened during this period go to him.

Terry Cross came in as Vice Commandant after two years. Jimmy Hull, followed by Vivien Crea were down in LANTAREA. Terry Cross, followed by Harvey Johnson out in PACAREA. But, the point is a very, very talented team. I met with this talented team in advance of my change of command, to refine and expand on my three- or four-page essay that I had prepared for Secretary Mineta. I wanted to give it some more life, put more meat on it, and develop it into a Commandant Direction, which is a formal Coast Guard planning document that every Commandant has when he comes onboard, that lays out a vision for the future with emphasis on the next four years. The Commandant's standing orders, if you will. It usually is thematic in content, and incorporates specific strategic objectives and goals.

The first key north star was readiness. We had to be true to our motto of *Semper paratus* and deliver operational excellence in a challenging environment. The Coast Guard has probably the highest state of readiness requirements and standards of any armed service. We are, in essence, a maritime operational firehouse. The challenge was to meet expanded readiness requirements with expanded missions, especially regarding maritime security. So, in the face of an aging capital plant and expanding missions, readiness had to be a key theme—maintaining, extending, and improving our readiness.

The second key north star was stewardship. *How do we manage your assets well? How do we give the best return to the American people?* Fortunately, we did get some budget relief in the wake of 9/11. The key question was how to employ those resources effectively and efficiently, and get good outcomes for the American people? So, stewardship is the key thing that involves being innovative, being good managers in managing your people well, etc.

The third and probably most important north star was people—how to best manage our personnel and utilize personnel resources; how to best you retain personnel; how to best recruit; how to best develop; how to do these tasks in a transformational environment.

So, readiness, stewardship, and people were the themes of my Commandant's Direction. The document specified the things that we would have to tackle within these major areas. I've often used the metaphor that we are taking a nautical navigational fix on our operational excellence, on these three lines of position (LOPs) as we go through readiness, go through people, and go through stewardship. But anyway, I think they were the right themes and we measured everything against them for the next four years. *Where are we in terms of readiness? Where are we with people? How do we manage our workforce? How do we not lose the things that have made the Coast Guard such a great and respected service?*

The Commandant's Direction is a useful document because it forces you to codify where you want to go, and then it's a great communications vehicle because, internally and externally, it is our blueprint for action. We budget and manage to the strategic intent of that document when we put budgets together for the Hill or whatever—it all ties in. We clearly felt that dealing successfully with our three major themes would yield operational excellence in a new and challenging environment. That was what we had to deal with and it meant that you needed some talented folks to step up to the plate with a lot of energy to make it happen. We were quite fortunate we had that in our cast of characters when we put the team together. And, from my perspective, these goals and objectives directly addressed the expectations of Secretary Mineta.

JD: Can you talk about the development of the Maritime Transportation Security Act?

TC: The whole idea behind the Maritime Transportation Security Act was to establish a security regime for our ships, ports, and waterways in light of increased security concerns in the aftermath of 9/11. It was a concern shared by Jim Loy and I, the Secretary, and the Congress. 9/11 did not happen in the maritime component of our transportation system but it could have, and the maritime had significant security vulnerabilities. 9/11 happened in the aviation component of transportation which, by the way, had an established security regime in place, regarding access control and the like. In the maritime, apart from large capacity cruise ships, the maritime did not have a security system at the time of 9/11.

In the maritime, we wanted a system that would enable us to manage risk, as the maritime transportation component is valuable and very vulnerable to a security incident system. The fact of the matter is we didn't have all of the Captain of the Port security authorities we needed, and we didn't have in place a process to manage facilities, ships, and ship crews from a security perspective. Congress recognized that as well, and that is the basis for Maritime Transportation Security Act. We worked hand in glove with Capitol Hill staff putting the legislation together. That was critical because we wanted the domestic legislation to be in sync with the international effort that we were developing through the International Maritime Organization.

We had made a trip the fall of 2001 to IMO in London to get security standards on the international maritime agenda. This was important because we are a port state, not a flag state. By that I mean we have a great deal foreign bottoms, foreign crews, foreign flags coming into our ports—the bulk of our trade was with foreign-flagged vessels. We wanted to know what's coming in; what's the cargo; who are owners. *Is there a security risk associated with that? What about the facilities? Are they prepared to handle cargo in a secure way, etc.?* So ultimately, two governing directives were developed for maritime security—the domestic one under MTSA, and an international one that was ultimately called the International Ship and Port Security Code when it was passed. We had to get those two things in sync. They had to be mutually supportive. We drove that approach both in London at IMO, and in Washington on the Hill. We partnered with flag states and port states around the world to help get that through.

JD: And that's a huge accomplishment just in and of itself.

TC: Look, we are a little ahead of ourselves but, maybe it's a good time to talk about it. Both of the two initiatives were massive, massive undertakings. As I mentioned, it is a largely regulatory effort because it doesn't end once you have a piece of legislation. The domestic legislation is authorizing you to develop a regulation, and there is budget authority that is also specified in that legislation. But, the work is just starting when you get this piece of legislation. Now you've got to develop the regulation so that you can later promulgate it and implement it—a demanding undertaking since, at the same time, we were launching the international security initiative. We had to get over 140 nations to approve the international security requirements for both ports and vessels. Oversight of ports was a relatively new thing for IMO and took a great deal of work in the trenches to move it along. I led three or four US delegations to IMO sessions to get the work done. That International and Port Security Code was approved in December of 2002. That means the essential issues had been identified—all of the piece parts of an international security regime had to be created and developed. They were socialized and run through various committees and voted on and approved in about one year—a year and a couple of months. That may be a Guinness Book of Records item for the International Maritime Organization or any international body, since there is frequently a lot of inertia in international groups with all kinds of different perspectives and agendas. To get that done in a little over a year is just mind-blowing to me, looking back on it. And to get the domestic version of it done as well.

We also were successful in getting a special version of MTSA done with Canada because we wanted to ensure that, because of the joint waterways and so forth, Canada had a parallel piece of security domestic legislation—which happened. My hats off to the Marine Safety Coast Guard folks that worked so hard on this by burning the midnight oil. Lock them in a room, shove a pizza under the door, work, work, work. These two security initiatives are truly transformational for our service. Just those two things alone, never mind all of the other things I mentioned previously. So, it's an immense accomplishment and it took a team effort. I might have been a cheerleader. I might have shaped some of the broad dimensions of it, but the hard work in the trenches goes to the staff who made that happen.

I can remember being there in December 2002. Upon an approving vote at IMO, each country had a team representative go up to shake hands with the presiding officer of the chamber. One of our commanders went up there with tears running down her face. That shows how much of a personal commitment our folks had, how hard they worked, and how much it meant to them. So, again, I have very, very fond memories of, and respect for, those that worked on this. And it was an essential step for the security of our country. We developed and led a comprehensive maritime security strategy and regulatory regime for our nation. as well as internationally. And got it done by very early by summer of 2002. Record time!

We were also developing and publishing a national maritime security strategy. So, it was not only the regulation and the international standards, but there was a policy framework that was needed for the Coast Guard and the interagency. And this architecture, this policy and procedure architecture, had to be developed as well. We were also designated by Homeland Security Presidential Directives as the lead federal agency for maritime homeland security. The associated governing policy directives were challenging to build because the different agencies involved had different agendas and different priorities. We needed an integrated and over-arching national maritime strategy and policies to deal with maritime threats and vulnerabilities, and especially as regards to a coordinated federal response to a specific threat at hand. *Who has what authorities? What responsibilities and what is the procedures?* It also had a maritime domain awareness component—how to get transparency of cargoes, ports, waterways, vessels etc., so as to adequately assess risk. *How do you improve that and how do you integrate maritime intelligence across the interagency?* So, those were big piece parts of the National Maritime Strategy that we had to develop.

Clearly, there were a number of domestic and international policy wheels in motion. And, at the same time, we had current operations to conduct—deploying new security teams in our ports and waterways, directly overseeing security initiatives of domestic port facilities, developing teams to monitor overseas port security measures, sending people and ships to the Arabian Gulf, and doinh all of those other things that I mentioned earlier. It was really a continuous all hands on deck-type of a time in trying to keep these parts moving in the right direction.

JD: And, how did you keep them moving in the right direction?

TC: Well, we had the various initiatives clearly identified with key staff designated as responsible, metrics associated with those efforts put in place, and recurring review points to ensure all were kept on track. Staffs were held accountable for performance relative to moving the various initiatives along. Heck, it was a dynamic process. I mean, even after we developed both the Maritime Transportation Security Act and the ISPS Code standards and regulations within a year or so of 9/11, they weren't immediately enforced. They didn't go into effect right away because we had to give time for the impacted customer—facility, ship, nation or whatever—to get their act together to be able to meet those requirements. Part of MTSA required designating the various Captains of the Port as the Security Coordinator for a given port. He owned the security regime. He had to review all ship and port security plans. There had to be a vulnerability assessment done. There had to be plans established. There had to be a training regime for the facility, etc. Those were all reviewed and approved by the Captain of the Port, and then there was an area security committee that covered specified areas all led by the Coast Guard.

And, there were also additional initiatives to further minimize risk which we called "America's Shield"—a whole host of things that fit into our overall national maritime strategy. We had four major areas of our security strategy. The first, one of the most important, was to enhance maritime domain awareness. Number two was to build and administer an effective domestic and international security regime. Number three was to increase operational presence in our ports and waterways and leverage state, local, and private assets for that kind of presence as well. Number four was to improve our response and recovery posture in the event there was a terrorist incident or emergency.

So, those are the four buckets that all our initiatives fit into. Enhanced maritime domain awareness was an essential and cross-cutting piece of the strategy. The whole transformation of our intelligence establishment fit into that. It goes beyond situational awareness, just for one situation, but includes the whole awareness of what's clicking in your AOR. *What's coming your way? What isn't coming your way? How do you become well informed before a threat emerges in your AOR?*

One of the concepts was defense in depth, or pushing the borders out and finding what's coming your way well before it gets to you. It meant developing good actionable intelligence especially now that we were a part of the intel community. We now had access to intel data from the intel community. We created the National Vessel Movement Center (NVMC) as the single clearinghouse for submission and processing of notice of arrival and departure (NOAD) information for vessels entering US ports and facilities. The Intel Coordination Center and its NVMC in Suitland, MD was tasked with vetting the manifest, crew, cargo, and ownership, before 96 hours of arrival. Before any vessel came in, they had to give information on all those requirements and it was scrutinized both by Customs, and Navy, and Coast Guard. It was a joint interagency effort and it was a risk management issue. And we sorted those things coming at us, and we identified where risks might present themselves. We labelled the highest risks Category-1 risks, where the highest level operational response would occur, including a ship being held offshore, boarded, and investigated by a specially trained boarding team. We had developed a sea marshal program along with MSSTs, Maritime Safety and Security Teams, to provide that on-scene control.

JD: Can you tell me about what vessels would fit into Category-1?

TC: Any vessel that had some risk, or uncertainty, or increased level of risk, we felt based upon the intel screening that we did. It could be a crew member. It could be a suspicious cargo issue. It could be an owner/finance issue. It could be a whole host of things. It all started with maritime domain awareness and Deepwater. Deepwater was a network-centric offshore-type of system. It was planes, and helicopters, and ships, and boats, and we were in a network, tied together with enhanced command, and control, and communications. They were very MDA. They were about pushing the boarders out.

Deepwater was MDA and so clearly that fits into our integrated operations centers in various ports that were often multi-agency in nature—engaged in developing a common operational picture. That's very MDA-ish. Developing field intelligence support teams was part of it. We ultimately developed over thirty of them, so the sector commanders would have intel expertise right there that could service their need as an operational commander to help answer the questions he may have about utilizing his assets in the most productive way to manage/reduce risk. *Where do I put my boarding team today? Where do I put my ships today?* Well, you base it on intel-driven scheduling. It's much more productive and it manages risks better. So, that was part of that field level intel network that linked with the higher organizational levels including area intel fusion centers and national intel levels. This all represented a huge transformation of our intel capability and meshed nicely with our other initiatives.

The development of sectors played an important part in our security regime. Increasing operational presence—well, that included Deepwater and increasing our operational presence offshore. Airborne use of force, which we developed, increased our operational presence and capability, as did our Over the Horizon Cutter Boat, our Response Boats, and our Port Security Boat. We delivered over 100 of these in very, very short order—the creation of the Maritime Safety and Security Teams, thirteen of them, and sea marshals. It all helped increase our operational presence in ports for deterrence and protection. Rescue 21, which is our distress and calling and command system for coastal waters of the United States, was developed and implemented. It was great application of technology and enhanced both MDA, security, and our search-and-rescue mission.

JD: Can you talk about expanding the presence with state and local partners?

TC: Yes. I mentioned earlier that one of the transformational items was changing our operational organizational structure for more effective operations and service to our maritime customers. I was convinced that the answer included the creation of sectors. For years, we had two different field command structures—Marine Safety Offices (MSOs) and group small boat commands—in the same area, and that did not enhance unity of command, especially in the new security environment. In the post-9/11 Coast Guard, we didn't need a fragmented command, and control, and intel structure. So, sectors were all about the unity of command, about merging MSOs, and groups. Now, all of the customers and our agency partners had one "belly button" to go to, if you will. Part of the sectors initiative was a parallel effort to establish joint integrated operations centers, so that you would have multiple agencies sitting at the table sharing information. We and DOD call it a common operating picture. Everyone is contributing to, reading, looking at the same intel, and the same information, and the same data about something. And a joint integrated operations center allows you to have that.

Hey, we started one before 9/11 on the west coast in San Diego when I was in PACAREA. I was very impatient to get the field structure thing re-whickered, even in advance of 9/11. And then when 9/11 came, I was convinced this is exactly what we need to do in the wake of 9/11. You know, then everything comes together with unity of command in a port including capabilities like Vessel Traffic Systems (VTS). VTS was always thought of as a safety of navigation system for large vessels. But in post-9/11, it's more than that. VTS is a decision support system for the Sector Commander. It's input to their integrated operations center, in terms of what is going on in the sector because they've got radar sensors, communications, etc.

So, it's part of your all-source intelligence that helps you have a good common operational picture. We now have a number of locations with structured multi-agency involvement at the field level through integrated operation centers. We are not totally there yet and I don't know what the current state of play is on how many sectors now have joint multi-agency integrated operations centers, but I know that was certainly a goal.

Multi-agency integrated operations centers are a powerful concept. When I was in PACAREA in San Diego, California, we had Navy involvement, the State police there, port authority people there, port facility people there, and local police all sitting around the table. I met with them all and I asked, "We all understand this concept, but why are you so interested in sitting at this table?" They said, "It's no other place where we can get such comprehensive information and a systems look at what's going on. Nowhere else can we get it." They were so enthused about it that they were contributing dollars and people into it. In a nutshell, reducing security risk is about integrated operations and MDA. Sectors help you get there.

JD: I don't think the American people realize that the Coast Guard was at one time smaller than the New York Police Department, and it grew 12% during your four years as Commandant. How did they do it?

TC: Some people would say to me, "Well, you've got a 12% increase in people, and your budget went up 60% by the end of your four years as Commandant. You should be fat, dumb, and happy about this." I said, "Wait a minute. If you plot by an arrow vector the amount of budgeting increase, it would be like maybe an inch or something, or whatever the scale is. But, mission growth was three inches. Vector was three." Do you know what I mean? The mission demands just grew out of sight. So, yes, we were fortunate to achieve some growth in people. Yes, we got some growth in budget, but it didn't match the post-9/11 mission growth, and didn't recognize how inadequate our budget was on 9/11 given several decades worth of stagnation in the '80s and '90s.

We also had ships, boats, and planes that were old, tired, and demanding of more and more maintenance dollars. So, those were the kinds of misconnects budget-wise that we had to tackle from the stewardship end of our Commandant's Direction. Okay, we received budget increases. But, wow, we had got a lot of places that it needed to go. Our focus was to put it on the things that gets the biggest bang for the buck. That was part of our challeng—to ensure that it went to those right things. I should note that we have never reached a budget level that has been commensurate with the magnitude of our capital plant—ships, boats, facilities, aircraft—and its needs for recurring capital infusion.

Operationally, we have always tied the budget to our strategic intent. It was tied to those four pillars of our maritime security strategy. That's where the money went to. Oh, by the way, it also went to support search-and-rescue. Everyone, particularly those on the Hill, were concerned about how we were going to maintain all of our other missions given the increased emphasis on security. I frequently stressed that, yes, we had increased the prominence of maritime security amongst all of our missions and it had become a priority one mission, but alongside search-and-rescue as a clear number one. I also stressed that we were not giving up one inch of our SAR response capability and standards in responding to SAR incidents. In effect, maritime security was now sitting alongside SAR as the two priority missions of the United States Coast Guard. Now, that was for the period I was Commandant. It has changed since and, as it should, because priorities change, and your risk environment changes. And so it's a dynamic process of balancing, but we do have operational standards and so forth, and we never gave up on those. They were always met.

JD: Was there any pressure to give up on them, externally?

TC: Look, and this is no slam on the Department of Homeland Security—and they never did anything that wasn't supportive—but their focus was on security. I mean, that's why the Department of Homeland Security was created. So, the Secretary wasn't itching to talk search-and-rescue with you. But, oversight language in the legislation that created the Department of Homeland Security ensured protection of the Coast Guard's non-homeland security missions like search-and-rescue, aids-to-navigation, environmental protection, fisheries enforcement. And a number of members of Congress continued to provide very strong support to our non-homeland security centric missions.

JD: The Coast Guard doesn't pump out volumes of strategy like D)D does. Was the Coast Guard strategy a new thing for some people in the organization?

TC: Strategy development was not new but the scope, volume, and extent of it was. Although, I give credit to both Bob Kramek and Jim Loy who had really put an emphasis on strategic planning and developed overarching strategic plans for the Coast Guard. We are into risk management. We had readiness metrics we developed. We had regional strategic assessments. We had talked about this previously when we talked about my PACAREA assignment and D-14. All of this was part of an overall Coast Guard effort to enhance our strategic planning. But, clearly not on the scale of DOD planning. No one can plan like they can. They plan the planning. Their contingency plans are extensive so, certainly, we were not in their league. But, I think we have gotten better and better at it, with emphasis on advanced planning methodologies, performance-oriented planning, and risk-based planning. It's been all part of the new vocabulary of the last twenty years or so in the Coast Guard, and I think we are a better agency for it. I think that's why we get continually get marks as one of the best run agencies. I remember, we talked offline a little bit about the *Government Executive* magazine's high rating of the CG as a well-run agency.

JD: Can we talk about it online now?

TC: Back when Admiral Loy was Commandant, *Government Executive* magazine rated twenty agencies and we were the only one that got an "A." We were "A"-rated because of a number of dimensions in management, leadership. David Walker (Comptroller General of the United States from 1998 to 2008) said the Coast Guard is about the best run agency in the government. This is the Comptroller General saying it. So, yes, we don't plan maybe on the scale and the magnitude of the DOD, but we are pretty darn good and I'm not going to be bashful about it. I think we've got an excellent record in that regard.

JD: Oh, definitely. I've got a mechanical question. As Commandant, you were only the second Commandant in Coast Guard history with a website, with Admiral Jim Loy being the first. What kind of control did you have over your website or did you leave that to staff?

TC: Well, number one, I was very supportive of the whole objective of making the Coast Guard more IT capable, particularly when it came to the internet, and how to both engage and service our personnel. One of my thrusts, when I chaired the Innovation Council when I was Vice Commandant, was how to build an e-Coast Guard; how to put enabling devices in the hands of our people, like boarding officials and ship inspectors, to make their lives easier given their jobs were so paperwork intensive. So, I clearly felt that the use of a website for the Commandant should continue. I wanted to use the internet as a communications device to let people know what is going on, to generate a general team-building environment. So, things like the Commandant's Directions, high-level strategic documents, and particularly my speeches went on there. I would say every time I gave a speech, it was put on the web. So, it really gave people a catalogue of speeches to read from and, if they wanted to spend the time to review them, it would give them an inside view on what I'm doing and what I'm saying.

JD: Are you glad that social media became a phenomenon after you left?

TC: [Laughs] Oh, yes. Probably. I mean, sometimes it can be dangerous if it is not managed right, and it can be misused as we see in today's world. There are some negative elements to it. So, when you use it, use it with caution and some level of control around it because it can go wild on you if you are not careful. But clearly, as we have seen in today's world, it has become a powerful force in the information world.

JD: Can you talk about your role as Commandant—what role you had in operational issues and things like ordering forces, and compare that to, for example, the CNO, who could not order ships around?

TC: The CNO is not an operational commander. He is leading, administering, training, and equipping the United States Navy, but he's not strictly in the operational chain of command. The Commandant of the US Coast Guard is in the operational chain of command. Theoretically, I was the ultimate operational commander for Hurricane Katrina. I didn't give direct operational direction, but policy oversight and coordination of service-wide supporting resources and assets. Direct/local operations were conducted through Rear Admiral Bob Duncan, who was the commander of the Eighth Coast Guard District, headquartered in New Orleans, Louisiana, and his boss Vice Admiral Vivien Crea, LANTAREA Commander in Portsmouth, Virginia. They worked together on most of the local/regional operational decisions. Now, there were daily briefs to us in Washington, as the ultimate Operational Commander on things, and feedback and direction on a number of issues was provided. I had great confidence in those two Coast Guard leaders and they did an exceptional job.

But, most of my concern is that they had the authorities and resources to effectively execute the mission at hand. Coordination with other agencies was also an important role for myself and the HQ staff, regarding the response efforts. So, that was my priority at the high-end point of the chain of command in Washington, DC. So, in principle, the Commandant is at the top of the operational chain of command. But practically, you act similar to the CNO in many ways.

JD: Prior to 9/11, was there any thought of the Coast Guard going to another cabinet department?

TC: Not that I'm aware of. There might have been some back room-type discussion from time to time. There is always some kind of discussion around the coffee mess about whether or not we should be part of the Navy—a discussion that goes back to the 1790s. In 1914/15, there were major discussions in the administration, and within Congress, regarding legislation proposed to move the Revenue Cutter Service, the predecessor of the Coast Guard, into the Navy and/or to break up the service in a number of separate parts. Commodore Ellsworth Bertholf, head of the Revenue Cutter Service at the time, had to fight that off. He had strong support from several senators that helped him dissuade everyone of that course of action. But instead, and largely due to his efforts, the organization was made stronger by combining additional agencies into the Revenue Cutter Service—Life Saving Service, for example—and forming the modern-day Coast Guard.

And, of course, we have been transferred temporarily, under existing statutes, to move over to the Navy's control during World War I and World War II. But, that was a temporary transfer, as called for in statute, to support the war effort. And then the Coast Guard moved back to its parent department at the wars' end. Through to the current period, the Coast Guard has been in three departments—Treasury, Transportation, and Homeland Security. Moving departments is a major evolution and a great deal of work and disruption. I would hope the Coast Guard has seen its last cabinet move. From my perspective, the Department of Homeland Security is a good fit for the Coast Guard given its wide range of missions-- security, safety, environmental, and law enforcement.

JD: Can you talk about the relationship between the Coast Guard and the Homeland Security Council?

TC: The new Homeland Security Council was created shortly after 9/11 and staffed by Governor Ridge from Pennsylvania. Rich Falkenrath was his Deputy. They had a staff right in the White House and was a counterpart staff to the National Security Council.

By the way, we had a number of Coast Guard personnel in that staff there, including running a small ops center there. Jim Loy went up to Harrisburg, Pennsylvania and visited Tom Ridge well before he got to Washington. It was a trip to inform the governor about the Coast Guard and offer any support that he could extend to him in his new role.

JD: And, they are both from Pennsylvania.

TC: Yes, they are both from Pennsylvania. His visit proved very supportive to the Homeland Security Council and subsequent developments. We ended up staffing many of positions in the new department until they could be filled with permanent individuals. For us, it was a brain drain with everything else that was going on. I had some of my top people in the key slots up there. Now, in retrospect, it was a very, very good thing to do. Number one, it was the right thing to do. It helped the new department in its early stages. Second, it positioned us well with the Secretary, with him recognizing the talent that the Coast Guard brings to the table. And we had a bird's eye view regarding the formulation of the new department.

JD: What was your initial reaction to being informed by Secretary Mineta that the president wanted to transfer the Coast Guard to the newly proposed Department of Homeland Security? Would you have preferred the Coast Guard stay in DOT?

TC: No. I think that if a new department was created for Homeland Security and we were not in it, it would probably be a mistake because that new department needed a maritime dimension to it, given the significance of the maritime transportation infrastructure to this country. To not have a true maritime element agency-type in there would have been a huge mistake.

JD: When was it determined in the process, that the Coast Guard would retain its identity and all of its mission, and not be broken up into pieces?

TC: Well, that's interesting. I have some perspective on that. Not total because I certainly wasn't sitting in the White House day in and day out while they were working this issue. I had a conversation with White House Chief of Staff Andy Card at one point. It was at a reception, or a government-wide award ceremony, or something. We talked about the re-org and he noted that he and the president were really eager to have the Coast Guard as part of this new department because they felt that we had the right culture and work ethic as an organization, and they needed that to bleed over throughout the new department.

I think if you take it from just that comment, the Coast Guard was not about to be split up. Although the legislation was crafted initially in the White House, there was certainly those in Congress that had a very pointed view of what should be in that legislation, including keeping the Coast Guard intact. They ensured legislative language very supportive of the Coast Guard. I know that Alaska Senator Ted Stevens was a strong and influential player relative to that piece of legislation. Coast Guard history and the history of Alaska are inseparable. Ever since we acquired Alaska from Russia in 1867, the Revenue Cutter Service, followed by the US Coast Guard, have been in Alaska providing exceptional service to the state and its public. So, the senator had great respect for our service because of our connection with Alaska, clearly as he should. He was very concerned about our ability to continue to deliver operational excellence across all mission areas with a change in departments. He was an activist in ensuring that we were not split up. Another reason was recognition by Governor Ridge and others that we are an armed service of the United States of America. He wasn't about to mess with that. So, if there was one probably dominant reason, and this is speculation on my part, I think it's that.

As the new Department of Homeland Security was being stood up, one of Ridge's themes was "One team. One fight." [It was] time to bring all of the 22 agencies together, which is a monumental task. Everyone had to now change their uniforms, and have Homeland Security patches on, etc. That was a real shock to other agencies, especially the US Customs Service which had been around a long, long time. In fact, it was a year older than the Coast Guard—1789 vs. 1790. They had their own culture, their own uniforms, their own this, and their own that. They were split in half, and then they had to change many of the trappings—uniforms, etc.—of their organization. It was a culture shock to many in those agencies that moved to the new department. The only agency that didn't have to change anything—flags, uniforms, symbols, patches, etc.—was the United States Coast Guard, in the new department. Again, the reason was, we were an armed force of the United States by statute.

That's one of the continuity things—we are a military organization and we shouldn't ever, ever let that be changed. It positions us in a very strategic and very unique way, to deliver security national security services to this country. The only organization that is both a military organization and a law enforcement agency. At combination is such that there is no other agency that has greater breadth of authorities than the United States Coast Guard.

So, anyway, a long-winded answer to your question, but that is how reorganization played out for the Coast Guard. We were very fortunate for a transition where our service remained very stable, despite all the things in motion.

JD: Was there ever any consideration given to moving the Coast Guard to the Navy Department after 9/11?

TC: I didn't hear of any. Once the president and Congress wanted us in the new department, case closed.

JD: Looking back now, it's been 13 years since DHS was established. Can you talk about how the Coast Guard has positioned itself in DHS?

TC: You know, I think we have positioned very well. We stepped up to serve the new department very early in the process. We committed talented people to the cause. We are one of the key operational agencies in the department with unique capabilities and authorities to which we bring a great deal to the table. We are clearly the maritime experts for the department, and I think we are greatly respected for our leadership and managerial skills. We performed and continue to perform well—well beyond my tenure, we continue to perform and deliver exceptional results for successive secretaries, contributing to the team effort, to the "One team. One fight." mandate. And very importantly, we have continued to perform exceedingly well across all our safety, security, and environmental missions. My understanding is the current DHS Secretary Jeh Johnson is very, very supportive and has great respect for our service. So, these things tell you, well, maybe, we've done right for us, and for the department, and the nation.

JD: Since 1790 the Coast Guard has switched cabinet departments from Treasury, to temporarily to the Navy, twice, and to DOT, and now the DHS. What advice would you give a future Commandant in the event the Coast Guard is transferred, yet again, to another cabinet?

TC: Well, I hope that doesn't happen. But if it does, I guess I would say, "Jump in with both feet. Be pro-active and be part of the solution. You get in early and you help shape and mold some of the basic features, and how that new organization is going to work." That would be my string advice. It is key to contribute to the success of the new organization as best you can, and help shape it. It is critical to positively engage other organizational elements, especially operational agencies within the department. And, build a team atmosphere. Once the president has made a decision, done deal. So, get on board and build it for success.

I know that was Secretary Mineta's approach. When he talked to me very early after my change of command, he noted that he had great respect and admiration for the Coast Guard, hated to see us go, but the decision was made. He is a team player and wanted to make the transition the best possible for us, and for the new department. He was absolutely true to his word.

JD: Did you consider switching cabinet departments a distraction from defending the homeland and preparing for the upcoming war in Iraq?

TC: Clearly, it was yet another thing that was put on our plate—part of the transformational environment that I talked about earlier. There was no use fighting it. Like I said, it was a done deal. So, the question is, *How do you make the transformation the best you can?* Clearly, there was a great deal of effort that was required. But, it's also a positive thing because now you are in an environment where the Secretary's main thrust is maritime security. We had some strong advocates like Secretaries Mineta and Ridge who were very, very supportive and helped us move many initiatives along. So, it was additional work but, in the final analysis, meant greater security for the nation. It was the right thing to do. Not a distraction, but it increased our focus on security initiatives and overall reduced security risks.

JD: Can you talk about the competition for dollars at the Department of Transportation that pitted Coast Guard funding against politically popular programs, like highway funding?

TC: This is no slam on Transportation Secretaries Andy Card and Norman Mineta. Andy Card had great familiarity with us once he was Chief of Staff in the Bush 43 White House, and Mineta, I thought highly of. But, there are very, very strong constituencies for the transportation infrastructure, as part of the Department of Transportation—highways, bridges, and aviation.

There are huge constituencies because there is money at the end of the day for those constituencies and their projects—be it a road or a bridge, etc.

So, budget competition was keen. It's not only the Department of Transportation, it's the constituencies on the Hill, and associated industry groups and their priorities. We were also the most capital intensive of the agencies within the department. In terms of the assets we had—ships, planes, boats, the maintenance they required, and the cost to replace them. So, it was always difficult budget-wise, even though the administration and Congress had great respect and overwhelming support for our programs. It was always a challenge, but I would have to say we were treated very, very fairly by Secretary Mineta all of the time. I have nothing but the greatest admiration and respect for him.

JD: I think history will treat him very well.

TC: Yes. He was a great Secretary.

JD: Admiral Gracey mentioned in his oral history that he almost gave Secretary Mineta a kiss when he referred to himself as Secretary of the Coast Guard because he said, "I've been trying to get transportation secretaries to say that for decades and they wouldn't. And he did. I almost gave him a kiss."

TC: Yes, there was a mutual admiration society between Secretary Mineta and the Coast Guard. He was a wonderful boss. Of course, he made a great decision when he selected me as Commandant. That was one of his great decisions. I'm saying that tongue-in-cheek. I have great respect for him.

JD: Can you talk about when you had been selected to move to DHS, and what transition mechanisms you had to set in place to prepare for the move?

TC: Well, we didn't change physical location until much, much later after my tour, so that eased things a bit. We weren't cut in half or cut in thirds like some agencies were, so that helped. Deputy Secretary of Transportation Michael Jackson was of great help in facilitating the transition. We also met frequently with all of the heads of the operating agencies of the department to ensure that there was interagency coordination. "One team. One fight." That kind of thing. What proved very helpful was the fact that we had engaged early with those preparing the legislation for the new department, and with new department staffs, and had numerous Coast Guard members filling department positions on a temporary basis. I would have to say that latter factor gave us the best view on all things DHS. And, I attended almost daily staff meetings at the secretarial level.

JD: It's March 1st, 2003. The Department of Homeland Security is formally stood up. Can you talk about that change of watch ceremony that occurred on February 25th, 2003 at the DC Stadium-Armory, when Transportation Secretary Norman Mineta handed over the Coast Guard flag to Homeland Security Secretary Tom Ridge?

TC: It was almost like a change of command. We had the Coast Guard band, and the Coast Guard's Presidential Honor Guard were part of the ceremony. Included was the exchanging of flags from the outgoing secretary to the incoming secretary. Very well attended. It was a great ceremony. I gave a short talk and so did the two secretaries. It was a real feel-good event since we had a great outgoing secretary and a terrific incoming secretary. What's not to like?

Governor Ridge was very supportive and he knew us from his experience working with the Coast Guard folks serving the White House. I was very impressed after participating in the whole ceremony and then staying to the very end of the reception—that it was a major change of watch-type of event like that. He made it a point to engage with and shake hands with everyone from seaman apprentice to the most senior people there. He was engaged and impressed everyone. Of course, Secretary Mineta's extremely positive comments, and his emotional reaction to the event, and being associated with the Coast Guard, was very impacting to everyone. We presented him with a Coast Guard leather flight jacket with service patches on it. He really appreciated it. The event was the right thing to do and I think it was done right. It came off very well and I think everyone from all parties appreciated it. It was essential to the transition process.

JD: I'm going to move to Iraq and the war clouds stated appearing, the wardroom started beating the summer of 2002 about Iraq and the weapons of mass destruction. Can you talk about the planning that went into Iraqi Freedom, from a Coast Guard perspective?

TC: There was some discussion at a high level, but after the seeds were planted, we had a dedicated staff—Office of Defense Readiness—that dealt with all of the support to DOD issues, including revised requirements development for Deepwater; what requirements they would like to see in our new cutters, given world events and risks. The staff would provide me preparations for the NAVGUARD Board meetings, but they had a counterpart staff over in the Pentagon and the two staffs were plotting together all of the time. The key was defining what prospective roles we would play, and what resources we would commit, as world events unfolded. There were additional discussions at the higher levels. Increasingly, I attended tank meetings with the Joint Chiefs of Staff.

Another consideration: if we were truly going to have a Navy-Coast Guard National Fleet, and it's going to be complementary and a non-redundant type of systems, and we are going to work together, and train together, and develop common protocols and communications, and whatever, then you've got to actually plan together and operate with each other in real world situations. You've got to exercise the system. Accordingly, I saw our joint efforts as a high priority number one—as the right thing to do, in both Navy-Coast Guard and national interest. Secondly, it oils the Navy-Coast Guard machinery. You have to play in the vineyard. If you are going to be part of the scheme, then play in the vineyard. And I think there was recognition of that on both sides.

I should note that, in the whole scheme of things, we recognized that we were a niche player providing assets and capabilities in selected areas—vessel boardings, port security, embargo enforcement, navigational aids support, patrol boat ops, etc. We ultimately planned for and provided a number of assets—High Endurance Cutters to battle group ops in the Eastern Med, buoy tenders to Iraq waterways, Port Security Units, support folks, etc. A Coast Guard O-6 commanded Patrol Coastal Squadron 1 over there headquartered in Manama, Bahrain, that was responsible for the protection of offshore platforms. We were there to enforce the embargo against ships coming back and forth, ensuring that they weren't carrying war materials.

You know, I am convinced to this day that all our efforts were the right things to do and, if it happened again, we should do that—helping to leverage all our nation's armed service capabilities in our country's interests. Just like we participate in mil-to-mil engagement around the world and support the CINCs, the combatant commanders, and provide in our little niche areas. *Are they significant things to them?* Yes. *Are we a player?* Yes. So, all in all, I think it was the right thing to do and I think our people benefited from it. Our nation benefited from it.

Unfortunately, we lost Petty Officer Nathan Bruckenthal, along with two Navy sailors who were blown up by a suicide boat attack on an offshore oil terminal in the northern Persian Gulf on April 24th, 2004. That was a tragedy and, clearly, we mourn his loss. He is from a great family on Long Island. His father was the police chief of the Northport Police Department. I participated in the interment ceremony at Arlington National Cemetery where we mourned his loss, but we honored his service and those Navy people that also lost their lives. But, we were there as we should have been and served our nation with distinction.

JD: How much time did it take on your schedule in preparing for Iraq, and going to the Pentagon for the briefings and meetings?

TC: You know, they were always well-staffed issues. I give hats off to our operational defense readiness staff. They were always well prepared. I would discuss related policy, planning, and resource issues frequently with the respective staffs in HQ. So, it was continuous involvement. If I had a tank session, there was usually a little three-ring binder with background material on the issues that you are going to hear, and that's typical of how tank sessions are run. I mean, it's not fly by night. They are usually issue specific. They are not just general ops briefs and things.

As Commandant, I went to every combatant commanders' conference. My spouse also attended because they had a spouse program dimension to each conference. I was included in the entire agenda, even when there was the annual session between the president and all of the combatant commanders at the White House Cabinet Room. Each combatant commander would give a short brief to the president on what's the latest going on in their AOR. Usually, the president would host a dinner for all of the service chiefs and combatant commanders, and their spouses up in his quarters. President George W. Bush had great, great respect for our armed forces and the values that they represent.

So, I saw DOD and National Security leaders a great deal—all of the members of the Joint Chiefs of Staff, the combatant commanders. In a way, it was a continuum of involvement with DOD leadership that I had been involved with in the 14th District and the PACAREA.

JD: And your previous background had to come in handy for these additional responsibilities you had as Commandant.

TC: It was. It kind of came all together. There are some very, very talented people in the Department of Defense. They have awesome capability in terms of assets. There is no national security organization on the planet that has the leadership and scale of DOD, as an organization and/or [in terms of] their capabilities. They are smart, smart people and represent our nation's highest values. So, I have great respect for all of the DOD services and honored to have the opportunity to engage with them. That relationship served me well in my role as Coast Guard Commandant.

JD: Operation Iraqi Freedom started on March 19th, 2003. Do you remember much from that day that you can share?

TC: Like all Americans, I was obviously very interested and concerned in watching the issue unfold. There were some difficult moments, at first, and questions about having it move along in a way that we would like it to end. There was no question about the dominance of our armed forces there. But, you've got to win, and then the hard part is, *What do you do when you win?* Defining and managing the end game has frequently been a challenge in the history of our armed conflicts. In the early stages of March 2003, I was impressed with the might and professionalism of our armed forces, but concerned about the end game. I also knew that, from that day forward, the USCG must be prepared to do our niche part to support the overall effort—and we did where and when appropriate.

JD: Can you talk about the preparations of the Coast Guard leading up to the start of Iraqi Freedom, like protecting the outload of ships ferrying war supplies?

TC: Yes. Fortunately, we had created Maritime Safety and Security Teams (MSSTs) and deployed them, along with our Port Security Units (PSUs) to places like Wilmington, North Carolina, which was a huge shipping point for a lot of war supplies. And fortunately, we had called up and actively trained/utilized our Reserve forces in the aftermath of 9/11. Our Reserves were very active in outload port security.

JD: I actually visited Wilmington, North Carolina, to see the outload of ships preparing for Iraq. Again, the Coast Guard was actively engaged there, including CG Reserves.

TC: The MSST deployed to Wilmington had prepared appropriately for this important mission. We also had provided MSST to the Arabian Gulf. Nationwide, we ultimately had 13 MSSTs of up to 100 people each. They had skills in the areas of port operations, small boat operations, defense operations, setting a security zone, boarding, providing escort, etc. All of these skillsets played out during this effort.

JD: Can you talk about the role of reservists during this period?

TC: Well, the Reserve effort was nothing short of spectacular, both overseas and domestically, providing support all the way around. As I recall, we mobilized something like 72% of our Reserve force. They were invaluable, leading the senior leadership council to re-whicker our whole selected Reserve in terms of numbers, programs, and ceiling. We commissioned a Reserve employment study to define how large the Reserve should be. A component of the study was to identify what skillsets and qualifications needed to be in the Reserve component, and how to develop them. It wasn't concluded by the time I retired, but findings were utilized along the way even before the study was finalized.

The basic indisputable fact is that the Coast Guard Reserve is an indispensable surge force for the United States Coast Guard, and they performed extremely, extremely well. This goes for the CG Auxiliary as well. They have, obviously, a different role but they made significant contributions, delivering millions and millions of man-hour support to us during those years, filling in administratively and backfilling us in the SAR mission.

JD: You had an opportunity in your last few years of your career, as Vice Commandant and Commandant, to work with this nation's most senior leaders—like four or five different cabinet secretaries, President Clinton, President Bush. What was it like working with senior leaders?

TC: Well, I was honored to deal with/work for these distinguished individuals. I felt honored to be able to engage with them on selected occasions. It wasn't a day-in and day-out [relationship], but on selected occasions.

As PACAREA Commander, I had the opportunity several times to deal with Transportation Secretary Rodney Slater including on January 31st, 2000 during the Alaskan 261 plane crash off the California coast. We ultimately had a memorial ceremony and Secretary Slater came to represent President Clinton. Secretary Mineta, Secretary Ridge, Secretary Chertoff were the secretaries that I dealt with closely regarding CG operations, policy/planning, and budgets, and they were all very, very accomplished—very quick and decisive leaders. Both Secretary Ridge and Mineta are extremely people-oriented leaders and managers. Secretary Chertoff, a very intelligent professional, was very detailed and a quick study on things—a very focused, results-oriented secretary. So, they all had different styles and different personalities, but they were all very competent. They were very open to CG input on all issues being worked on within the department. They all treated the Coast Guard well, and it was an honor to work for them. I had a number of occasions to meet with and work with President George W. Bush, including White House receptions, the Coast Guard Academy graduation ceremony, combatant commander-president sessions, and the like. I had frequent engagement with departmental and White House staff on key CG budget and policy matters. In all regards, it was clear that the US Coast Guard was held in high regard within the administration—although winning in the budget battles was always a challenge.

In March 2003, President Bush visited the Port of Philadelphia for a town hall-type meeting on maritime port security with shipping containers in the background. The President was briefed by local Coast Guard commanders, and then delivered a speech to hundreds of Coast Guard personnel. I had the wonderful opportunity to fly up on Air Force One with him, and then onto the local CG Captain of the Port facility with him, one-on-one, in the presidential limo. I can remember saying to myself, "What am I going to talk to the President of the United States about here, one-on-one, in this limo? How am I going to break the ice here?" The first thing I thought of was that it happened to be the opening day of the baseball season, and that the president had been a prior owner of the Texas Rangers, so our conversation started easily with baseball and then moved on to business matters of the day. But clearly, it was an honor to have been invited to ride with him.

On other occasions when the combatant commanders met with the president, he was always very gracious to the Coast Guard. We were a little bit odd man out during those sessions. It included all of the other combatant commanders and the Secretary of Defense. The CG was the only non-Department of Defense element there, and always last to speak. But, the president was always so supportive and knowledgeable about what we were doing, and appreciative of our work in front of the other combatant commanders. I had great respect for him doing that because I think he realized we were the one "outsider." We are the small guy, yet he gave us airtime and appreciation. So, I thought that was a terrific thing for him to do, and a very sensitive thing to do.

We also had the opportunity to go up to New London on May 21st, 2003, when President Bush delivered the commencement address for the Coast Guard Academy's Class of 2003. I flew up on the Gulfstream V (GV), while Governor Ridge and President Bush flew up on Air Force One. We spent some time at the Academy and he participated in the ceremony, and then travelled to the old Trumbull Airport in Groton, Connecticut to fly back to Washington, DC. President Bush was in his limo. The rest of us were transported in a van. I tripped coming out of the van. There was a coil wire in the bottom of this van that I didn't see. My foot got caught in it, and I did a head dive off of the van and broke my fall with my hand, and I broke my finger. My finger was at a 45-degree and it was bleeding, and I had blood all over my service dress white. Governor Ridge was also travelling in the party. We all flew into Andrews AFB, and I went right over to the clinic and got worked on. Overall, it was quite a scene.

I happened to attend a reception the following week at the White House. Typically, at these receptions you go through a presidential receiving line. As I recall my, my daughter was with me that day. As a result of the earlier accident in Groton, I was sporting a large bandage/dressing on my finger. The president didn't cut me any slack. When I approached him in the receiving line, he said, "Tom, can't take you anywhere. You get in trouble everywhere I bring you." We both had a good laugh. But, he was terrific that way. He was a very supportive, indirect boss to me. I didn't have to deal with him on a day-to-day basis, but I had selected opportunity to deal with him, and he always treated the Coast Guard very, very graciously. And, of course, on July 10th, 2002, President Bush met with me and all the former Coast Guard commandants in the Oval Office, to get their support for the new Department of Homeland Security legislation that was going through Congress. He wanted all of the commandants to endorse this, but before doing so, he wanted to make sure that they were comfortable doing it. So, that was the reason. We all voiced out support to the CG being in the new department. It was a short session, but it was nice of him to do that. The retired commandants that attended were Admiral Jim Gracey, Admiral Paul Yost, Admiral Bill Kime, Admiral Kramek, Admiral Jim Loy, and myself.

It was a nice thing for him to do and a right thing for him to do. Effective coalition building. But, anyway, those were the senior leader engagement opportunities that presented themselves, and I have very good recollections/feelings about the senior leaders that I had to work for. Not to say that everyone made the right decision at the right time. No one does that. But, as bosses, we received pretty good support across the board.

JD: Can you talk about what it was like to be on the House floor for the State of the Union addresses?

TC: I enjoyed going to that because there was a great deal of pomp and circumstance associated with that address and, you know, everyone in a leadership position in Washington is there. You gather with the other service chiefs ahead of time in a designated spot. All of our handlers made sure we got to the right place at the right time. You meet with all of the other service chiefs and you chat a little bit on how are we going to act and react during the address. There were always things that we were not supposed to clap for, so as to remain apolitical. The service chiefs are expected to be apolitical, similar to the Supreme Court Justices. We frequently found ourselves clapping for military-related issues that were being addressed but, otherwise, remained silent. But, I found it fascinating to be part of that spectacle, and I enjoyed going, and I enjoyed that fellowship with the Chairman and the other service chiefs. My wife also attended the session, along with the other service wives.

JD: Did you ever think when you were teaching American Government at the Coast Guard Academy, that you would get to see it up close and personal?

TC: Not at all. Frequently, my wife Nancy and I look back in wonder at the road we've travelled, and the people we've met, and the things we've seen. We've travelled a pretty fascinating road and both feel very, very honored to have had the opportunity to have made the journey.

JD: Were you able to attend any of the Memorial Day concerts on the West Front of the US Capitol to represent the Coast Guard? And what was that like?

TC: Yes. If I was in town, I was there. If I wasn't there, then the Vice Commandant went. Same thing when I was Vice Commandant. If Jim Loy wasn't in DC, I went. I don't recall how many I went to, but I went to a bunch, and it is always a great feel-good event. It is another important representational aspect of the job where the CG, as an armed service, needs to be included along with the others. We also have the Presidential Honor Guard to show the flag on numerous ceremonial national events.

Oh, by the way, they are absolutely the best. They are the hardest working of them all because the other services have a much larger Honor Guard to share the load. There is larger depth on the other services' benches. Our folks are like one deep, so they do everything. They are almost all over six-feet and are all impeccable, attractive people that are squared away. They represent us well. But, it's one of those things that, if you are going to be an armed force of the United States of America, then you have a Presidential Honor Guard and, oh by the way, you have a band. At one time, when we were doing streamlining, there was a move to do away with the band. I responded with a strong negative to that. We were just not going to do it. Case closed. I didn't want to lose the band. That's part of who we are—one of the representational trappings of being an armed force.

JD: Speaking of one more representational event, can you talk about the 2005 Presidential Inaugural Parade? And how different it was from the 1965 Presidential Inaugural Parade, when you marched?

TC: It was a lot different. I marched in the 1965 Inaugural Parade during LBJ's Inaugural as a cadet. It was a very cold winter's day. My experience as a service chief for President Bush's 2005 Inaugural Parade was very different. All of the service chiefs sit together during the swearing-in ceremony. After the ceremony, there was a break prior to the start of the inaugural parade because the president was having lunch on Capitol Hill. We would have all the service chiefs and the Chairman and Vice Chairman of the Joint Chiefs of Staff over for lunch at the flag mess at Coast Guard Headquarters because it was the closest service facility to the parade. After lunch, we would all head to the parade viewing area. When your service contingent marched by, you would go stand next to the president. The Coast Guard was the last to go through because of service rank order. We assigned a captain as the Inaugural project officer. It was a full-time job, commencing almost a year ahead of the event.

JD: And this was the first inauguration since 9/11 too.

TC: That's right. And we had MSSTs involved in the event as well. They were involved in a number of national ceremonial events in the post-9/11 era.

JD: I want to talk about the National Fleet concept. Can you talk about your relationship with the CNOs and the impact it had on the National Fleet concept?

TC: The National Fleet concept had an extended gestation period, if I can describe it that way. The dialogue was started amongst our defense ops staff and the Pentagon Navy staff, and then it was discussed at the NAVGUARD Board. It evolved and it received greater emphasis after 9/11, especially in trying to define where Homeland Security ends and where national defense begins. Ultimately, its final form and substance resulted from Commandant-CNO/VCNO discussions we had, with CNO Vern Clark, VCNO Fox Fallon, and, ultimately, with CNO Mike Mullen. I can recall an executive session of the NAVGUARD Board, when Mike Mullen and I discussed the latest version of the National Fleet concept. We both agreed the concept, and its terms and conditions. It was ultimately signed by Admiral Mullen and myself.

JD: Were you surprised after you left, that Admiral Mullen was tapped to become the 17th Chairman of the Joint Chiefs of Staff?

TC: No. All of the service chiefs are extremely capable professionals and leaders, and certainly he fit that bill—had a great record. I thought he was a great fit.

JD: Did you have much of dealings with the Marine Corps commandants?

TC: Yes. I had a number of dealings with General Mike Hagee and his predecessor, General Jim Jones. We created the Special Missions Training Center (SMTC), located in Courthouse Bay down in Camp Lejeune in 2003. It was a training complex we created for the MSSTs, and for their counterpart Marine Corps special operation forces doing the same thing. It was about offensive and defense small boat ops, both in a bay environment, river environment, and an offshore environment. Camp Lejeune had all of these different environments. So, it was a great training area. The Training Center had both Coast Guard and Marine Corps instructors. General Jim Jones and I went down and cut the ribbon on that facility together. It's just one example of the Coast Guard and Marine Corps working together. The Marine Corps was also instrumental in helping us develop the doctrine associated with the airborne use of force from helicopters. We did extensive prep work down at NAS Pax [Patuxent] River, including selecting the particular hardware to go with the doctrine which was developed there. Overall, we had a fairly close relationship at all levels, with the Marine Corps.

JD: Also, during your time as Commandant, the US Northern Command (NORTHCOM) was stood up as a new combatant command at Peterson AFB, Colorado on October 1st, 2002. Can you talk about the Coast Guard's role in Northern Command and your relationship with first Commander and General Ed Eberhart?

TC: I have the greatest respect for Ed Eberhart. A very professional and very successful USAF leader, and a terrific person. I have a close personal relationship with him to this day. I first met him when he was US Forces Japan (USFJ), and I was a district commander in Hawaii. We had a small marine inspection staff out there on his base. And during visits out there, I would engage with Ed and extend my gratitude for the tremendous support he extended to our small staff. We were both graduated from our respective academies the same year, so we referred to each other as classmates. I was very pleased to see him become the first commander of NORTHCOM. We had senior CG personnel on NORTHCOM's staff, from the very formative stages of NORTHCOM. The J3 was a Coast Guard officer, and that was particularly helpful when we were developing the concept of the common operating picture for homeland security applications. I talked about that earlier in the context of maritime domain awareness, and how important the common operating picture concept is to getting domain awareness, and all of the associated processes and systems, and the doctrine associated with the CONOPs. We worked closely with NORTHCOM on that and they were very, very helpful.

JD: Did NORTHCOM ask for more resources from the Coast Guard than you could provide? Was your inbox overflowing?

TC: I don't think so. We tried to answer the mail, and we did answer the mail on every request. We saw the importance of being connected, let me say that. sS we were sympatico in what we were doing in the homeland.

JD: Can you talk about the US Coast Guard and its relationship with US Southern Command?

TC: JIATF South reports to SOUTHCOM and has always been commanded by a Coast Guard flag officer. It is jointly staffed by the Coast Guard, Customs & Border Protection, DEA, Navy, etc. It has a dotted line up to the US Interdiction Coordinator (USIC), who is the Commandant of the United States Coast Guard. It's another hat that the Commandant wears and because of that there is a close policy/planning/doctrinal/operational relationship between JIATF South and the USCG, and to a lesser degree SOUTHCOM.

The same thing with JIATF West. The commander of JIATF West was my next door neighbor, on Coast Guard Yerba Buena Island in San Francisco, when I was commander of PACAREA. There is a very close affiliation with those two joints staff just because of the nature of the business, and it's a joint business. The United States Navy and Coast Guard combats illegal drugs through the maritime zones. During the time I was PACAREA, the Navy allocated something like 44% or 45% of the ship days devoted to anti-drug patrols. Since they aren't a law enforcement authority, we place Coast Guard law enforcement detachments (LEDETs) onboard their ships to do the boarding and the arrests, as necessary. Counterdrug ops involves a very, very joint effort between the DOD, Navy, and Coast Guard.

JD: Can you talk about your role as US Interdiction Coordinator and what did that entail?

TC: It involved working with the drug czar and his staff, and supporting the war on drugs by developing the policy, the overarching strategies, and the coordination between Customs, DEA, Coast Guard, and Navy. Those were the principle agencies involved. We had periodic coordination meetings with those players to assure they were all on the same page, to ensure coordinated ops in keeping with national policy and strategy. It had a great deal to do with what kind of resources an agency could allocate to the effort.

JD: How much time did that role take?

TC: It was a sporadic thing. It would spike. It was a recurring, episodic-type of workload.

JD: How often did you visit the Academy in New London, and what were some of the things you talked about?

TC: I'm a creature of the Academy in New London and the state of Connecticut. I graduated from the Coast Guard Academy. I married a local girl. My post graduate school was in Connecticut. I taught at the Academy. My youngest daughter, Kate, was born in New London. I had a command assignment in Connecticut. I have fond memories and great respect for the Academy as an institution of higher learning. As Commandant, I would travel to the Academy at least once a year to speak on the subject of leadership to a gathering of all of the cadets, and attempt to connect their Academy experience to real world CG ops. I did that speech every year, followed by lunch or dinner with a table full of cadets. I just kind of pick their brain and engaged in a free-wheeling discussion on what it's like to be a cadet these days. I will tell you I came away incredibly impressed with the talent, the poise, and the insight that these young men and women had.

JD: Another New London question. Can you talk about the decision to locate the National Coast Guard Museum in New London?

TC: I was interested in getting the maximum exposure to the Coast Guard because the national museum is all about telling the Coast Guard's story to our customers and taxpayers about their Coast Guard. My preference was to locate it in a three-story Coast Guard building located at the tip of Manhattan. The building was a prior Captain of the Port/MSO building that is adjacent to the Staten Island Ferry terminal. Ten million people go through that ferry terminal and Battery Park each year, giving us maximum exposure. The plan would have been to redesign/renovate our building along with the waterway facilities. The bulkhead had deteriorated but would be restored, and a pier added to occasionally allow berthing the *Eagle* there as an added museum attraction. That would be quite a draw. So, that was the early, very preliminary concept. I had approached New York City Mayor Michael Bloomberg about it because the city planners had their eye on that property. I gained his tentative support if we went ahead with the project at the Battery. The museum project hadn't been funded yet, but we were in the early stages of creating the National Coast Guard Museum Association, an offshoot of the Coast Guard Foundation.

Jimmy Coleman from the Coast Guard Foundation and New Orleans was a key driver of the new museum foundation initiative.

Unfortunately, the New York option for the museum ran into the Connecticut Congressional delegation, which was opposed to any museum initiative that was not located in Connecticut, with a very high priority to collocate it in New London, near the USCG Academy. They, collectively, made those points quite clear to me in a meeting in Senator Dodd's office.

Ultimately, language sponsored by Representative Rob Simmons, a member of our Authorization Committee in the House, was included in the Coast Guard and Maritime Transportation Act of 2004, and it mandated that the new National Coast Guard museum be built in New London. When that happened, Connecticut became the state for the museum and New London the favorite site within the state. From my view, I still think it's very unfortunate because the tip of Battery Park would have provided the greatest exposure. But, I understand local politics and how they play out. And fortunately, the National Coast Guard Museum Association is doing wonderful work. They are raising money. They have gained some federal funding support. They've got design plans. They worked very closely with Admiral Bob Papp, Admiral Loy, and New London city officials. It's going to be on the New London city waterfront, up near the Union Station which is a historic train station. And, it will have a dedicated berth for the *Eagle*. So, it's moving along smartly. We will have an impressive museum and I think that is important for the service.

JD: Next category of questions is going to be about your trips as Commandant.

TC: I had a feeling we were going to cover this, so I found my trip report binder in the deep recesses of my attic. In 2003, I took five OCONUS trips. In 2004, I took three. In 2005, I took three. In 2006, I took two. When I was Vice, I just took two each year and the one report that is not in here was the trip I took to the Middle East. It's not in here because it's classified. Each of the trip reports identified the nature and reason for the trip, identified those in the party, and summarized trip events and accomplishments. There are some specific programmatic and policy issues for every trip I took.

I went to Qatar, Kuwait, and finally to Naval Support Activity Bahrain to visit the Coast Guard Patrol Forces Southwest Asia (PATFORSWA) squadron, which was commanded by a Coast Guard O-6, and consisted of the 110s and 179s. The squadron was responsible to NAVCENT for protecting all of the gulf's offshore platforms. They had a maintenance support team associated with them. The boats were maintained in pristine condition. It was a great trip for me to go and to see our folks in action, see how they are performing their job, and giving them the support and the visibility they needed. I visited Qatar because we had port security issues associated with Qatar, and their LNG ships pulling in and out of Kuwait as part of the International Ship and Port Security Code (ISPSC) initiative. I also, on the rebound, went to Naples, Italy and visited with the Commander of US Naval Forces (NAVEUR) because we do provide support to NAVEUR through the Med, and I wanted to make sure that we were on the same page. So, it was a very productive trip.

Another trip was to Greece to meet with international shipping interests to discuss the safety and security initiative underway within the International Maritime Organization (IMO). The goal was to underscore the importance of the ISPSC efforts and gain support for them.

One very interesting trip I had as Vice Commandant in 2001 involved a trip to Trinidad and Tobago, Chile, Guyana, Argentina, Panama, and Key West, Florida. There was a reason for going to each one of those countries. For Guyana and Panama, it had to do with us transferring patrol boats to them and gaining a maritime agreement which facilitate counterdrug operations. And there was usually a ceremony associated with the transfer of the patrol boats.

Guyana was fascinating. It's a very, very poor country. It fell in the same category as Haiti because they were the two debtor nations in the western hemisphere that were supported by the World Bank. Because they were a debtor nation with special loans, they had certain restrictions, given the need to service the loans, on what they use their funds on. They did have a coast guard, but in name only—just people with uniforms, no boats. One of the restrictions of their status as a debtor nation was they couldn't spend any money on capital equipment. They had no boats and they had disputes with neighboring countries, Suriname and Venezuela, to their east and west. They both had claims on Guyana territory including their offshore oil. Guyana wanted to develop their oil industry to get out of their debtor status. They had difficulty doing so because they couldn't maintain an operational presence offshore to defend their territory against the claims made by their neighbors. Bottom line—they needed an effective coast guard and we needed something from them which we weren't getting. We needed a maritime agreement to facilitate law enforcement (LE) efforts in the lower Caribbean. I think when I left, we had 23 maritime agreements with nations through Central America, South America, and the Caribbean, which allowed us to facilitate our hot pursuit after a smuggler, and to allow us to go into territory waters of a country without advanced permission. The State Department was very supportive and collaborative with our work in this area.

We were having difficulty in gaining a LE maritime agreement with Guyana for a number of reasons, including their lack of legal expertise in this area. We were able to strike an arrangement where we would provide excess/retired CG boats in exchange for a formal maritime agreement with them. The boats were excess small utility boats with maintenance support included. To facilitate the transaction, I arranged for two of our best LE lawyers from Washington to fly down to Georgetown, and help craft the agreement document. So, the trip resulted in a maritime agreement—that alone justifying the time and effort for my trip.

JD: Definitely.

TC: That OCONUS trip also included Argentina. We have a great relationship with Argentina. They've crafted their Coast Guard along the lines of the United States Coast Guard. They are a huge supporter in IMO. I visited them to cement those relationships and, in large measure, to give us support in IMO, as we were working the ISPSC. We needed advocacy. We needed strong support. So, many of the places I visited were to build that ground support, so they would be with us when we were pushing issues that were key to the security of the global maritime system. We are only as risk free in the maritime as is the global maritime transportation system. And, in addition, the Maritime Transportation Security Act required us to inspect all of our trading partners—the ports and the port facilities of all of our trading partner—to ensure that they were meeting international security standards. So, we had to create a foreign inspection program and an associated staff/teams. We had a detachment in Rotterdam, Netherlands to cover inspection requirements in Europe.

Our port inspection requirements also included China, a major trading partner. The challenge was how to pull off our inspection responsibilities with China, given the historical/political sensitivities involved. We had to turn up the pace and intensity of dialogue with China to pull this off. My trips to China after 9/11 included engagements on a number of fronts, including the ship rider program, fisheries enforcement, high-seas drift net fishing, and ISPSC.

My proposal to them regarding our port inspection responsibilities was to share our best practices—and, ultimately, it was successful. I spoke to their security folks and the maritime authorities, and stressed that our bilateral trade is very valuable trade for both parties and we, jointly, need to make sure it's both safe and secure. Both of us have interests in that, and there are things that we are each doing in our respective ports to ensure that they are safe and secure. And, we had such a large stake in this together. I urged that we share best practices. The arrangement that resulted was to invite them to our port/port facilities to examine best security practices, and then we in turn will come and see their ports through the establishment of sister ports. For example, Shanghai was linked with Seattle and used as a prototype for the arrangement. So, the marine inspectors from Seattle went to Shanghai, and Chinese marine inspectors went to Seattle. The reason that I picked Seattle is because the Captain of the Port was ethnically Chinese, and his family descended from Shanghai. So, it worked—It was a two-way street-type of concept that was acceptable to all.

JD: For the record, do you want to talk about other trips?

TC: I will make some comments about a trip to Moscow in the middle of the winter, to meet with my Russian counterpart from the Russian Border Guard to discuss their possible participation in North Pacific Coast Guard Forum. That was so successful for us. We wanted to get them involved. They are a player in the Bering Sea. We are in the Bering Sea. We needed to talk and work together on things. We've had to facilitate operational communications, especially in crisis situations.

JD: What was that like?

TC: Oh, it was fascinating because the meeting was held in the Lubyanka Building, which was the previous headquarters and prison of the Soviet KGB. As you know, the Russian Border

Guard (RBG) had been part of the KGB. They hosted an elegant dinner with spouses, as my wife was with me on the trip. I whispered to my wife, "I just hope there is not any one-way doors here in this place." Seriously, they were very good hosts and a spirit of cooperation prevailed. We attained their commitment to the North Pacific Coast Guard Forum. We established lines of communication. The trip met its objectives. In fact, most of these trips I went on, I would give at least a B+ in terms of meeting the trip objectives that we had wanted to accomplish.

The several trips to China were most memorable. We have already talked about inspecting the ports, but it was also about the ship rider program and a number of other issues. They were very gracious hosts. Along with business engagement, they included cultural activities to give us a sense of who they are as a country and people. They took us everywhere. They took us to the Great Wall and other historical sites. Of course, the agenda was coordinated with our embassy in Beijing, and I had an opportunity to meet with our Deputy Chief of Mission at the US Embassy.

Engagement with high-level Chinese officials was also part of the agenda, including a meeting with the head of the Ministry of State Security, one of the twelve members of the Politburo Standing Committee of the Communist Party of China. Every police/LE function from the local to the national level, as well as the intelligence services, is under the Ministry of State Security. I thought it would probably be just a 15-minute "grip and grin," but it went on for about an hour and a half, with discussions focusing on the structure of their fragmented, inefficient set of maritime related missions. They were in the process of redefining and reorganizing them. Unlike the United Sates Coast Guard, which is one agency in one department, their maritime responsibilities and functions are fragmented across many departments, leading to greater costs where several of the organizations were building out similar capital assets—i.e., ships, boats, aircraft. I recall that I asked the Minister, "What is your objective?" He said, "For our maritime services, we would like to be structured and organized similar the United States Coast Guard." It was a very interesting discussion.

What smoothed the way for a positive exchange was the fact that several months earlier, I had hosted a Chinese delegation led by his Vice Minister, in my quarters in Washington. During that reception for him at my quarters, we had rolled out the red carpet, pun intended. That was very,

very much appreciated by them and so they reciprocated. Overall, it was a very productive trip, with a number of different issues on the agenda with several different ministries.

Again, I had my spouse with me, and she was very impressed with everything, and materially added to the team. During that trip, we met with senior fisheries enforcement officials aboard one of their ships in Shanghai. We got a commitment from their fisheries agency, which is in their Ministry of Agriculture, to commit ships to high seas drift net enforcement. We attained this commitment largely because of their positive participation and experience in our ship rider program run by PACAREA.

Anyway, that's just a sampling of some of the trips, why they were made, and what was achieved.

JD: What was it like traveling on CG-1?

TC: Well, I thought I had died and gone to heaven. We talked about the GV aircraft in a previous session, but the Coast Guard acquired this aircraft because of former House Appropriations Committee Chairman Bill Young of Florida. His house district included St. Petersburg and Clearwater, and knew how important the United States Coast Guard was to the state of Florida. He's passed on now, but he was a great supporter of the Coast Guard. He and his wife Beverly had travelled on the old rickety GI Gulfstream plane that Admiral Loy had flown around in as Commandant. He and his wife traveled on that plane with Jim on occasion, and they didn't like it. They felt it was not appropriate or productive for the Coast Guard, and we needed to do better. So, he directed that the next GV off the DOD line be diverted to the Coast Guard. Jim, to his credit, stressed that the CG needed other capital assets—operational assets, that were of higher priority. But Young was convinced that the GV was appropriate at that point in time, and made the transaction happen. So, it was a done deal and that's how we got that GV.

The aircraft has long legs, has the ability to fly at very high altitudes above commercial traffic, and provides continuous secure communications capability. So, all in all, it provides great productivity and comfort for the Commandant or the Secretary. It is an awesome aircraft supported by an exceptional CG aircrew at CGAS Washington, DC, which is located at Reagan National Airport alongside several CG HH-65s. The CG also has air space security responsibility for the Washington, DC area. For low and slow aircraft, not the big jets. So, we have armed helicopters that can respond to any acts of air terrorism in and around the national capital region, and they are stationed there, as well, at CGAS Washington, DC. That's another thing that we haven't gotten into yet, but use of force from our helicopters has been part of our capability buildout since the late '90s. And part of our post-9/11 strategy is increasing operational presence, and that includes capability and presence. And, use of force from helicopters was one of the things that we developed that could support MSSTs, in addition to facilitating out counter drug missions. It also includes the capability of repelling down from helicopters for insertion onto vessels or elsewhere when and where appropriate.

JD: Do you want to talk about the decision to use them to patrol our ports, and putting guns on the HH-60s and the 65s? And letting the MH-68A Stingray's lease expire, and the change of the culture in the aviation community?

TC: Yes, it was certainly a culture change for a selected few in the aviation community who asked, "When did we sign up to be warfighters? We are lifesavers. We fly our helicopters to save lives." Change is hard sometimes, but as new policy is developed, you have to look at the various impacts, mitigate safety risks, and develop the associated doctrine. But, in the end, we put the needed capabilities in the hands of CG men and women to meet the operational challenges facing our nation and our service. And you try to communicate the reasons for the change, and you try to implement it effectively. You must ensure they are safe, well supported and prepared, and trained as part of the post-9/11 environment. I think we did all those things. We still fly helicopters to save lives. It is our highest priority and will remain so. But arming our helicopters was the right thing to do.

One example of the benefit in the use of armed helicopters is our Helicopter Interdiction Tactical Squadron (HITRON) that specialized in the airborne use of force to stop go-fasts by shooting out their engines. Jim Loy was aggressive in recognizing the need for that capability. That program is batting 1000%. I mean, any baseball player would love to have HITRON's batting average. We've been successful in every instance using it and, so much so, that it is a transformational change to our capabilities.

In dealing with the post-9/11 environment in the 2002 to 2006 timeframe, I can't overuse the word transformational enough. Use of force from helos was but one element of a number of transformational initiatives dealing with strategy, capabilities, and capacity. We changed capability. We increased our capacity to deal with crisis and emergency. We enhanced partnerships and maximized/leveraged existing and expanded authorities to advance our maritime homeland security strategy and associated policy. There are people implications, training implications, logistics implications, for all of the parts of our strategy. 9/11 is the genesis of a clearly transformational era for the United States Coast Guard. We have a greater breadth of capability and competencies than we have ever had. Our organizational structure is more efficient and customer-focused. And since 2006, additional mission adjustments have taken place. *Has the balance between programs changed a bit? Have some of the imperatives and the priorities changed a bit?* Absolutely. *Should they?* Absolutely. Change and adjustment—that's the story of the United States Coast Guard since 1790. Being adaptable, and to change to the threat or mission environment over time. That's who we are. That's what we've done. It's the history of our organization and its continuing, as we speak. So, during my tenure, maritime security and post-9/11 dominated the scene. *What's today?* Cyber security. Energy in the Arctic. *Are they the right priorities?* Absolutely. *Has the CG abandoned maritime security?* No. But, the priorities have shifted a bit and, when priorities change strategically, your resource base gets changed a little bit to meet that. Budget to strategic intent. So, I'm pleased that the CG remains a dynamic organization, and the current leadership is adapting the service to the imperatives of the day. Hallelujah!

JD: You have to feel good that you had four years of change, and you left the Coast Guard a better organization so that your predecessors can worry about new missions like cyber and the Arctic, instead of worrying about old business because you cleared the deck for them.

TC: I hope that was the case. If you were to ask me what I think the most impacting things we've done were, I might suggest that there may be three things. One is the Deepwater, recapitalizing our fleet. That really, really gives us the readiness that we need, and it gives us the MDA we need because, as I mentioned, this is a very network-centric information gathering type of system of systems. So, you get a two-for with that. You get at-sea capability, flexibility, and presence, all adapted to current-day challenges. You get intelligence and MDA. So, that's huge. I'm very proud of the road we have traveled here. *Were there some bumps and hiccups in that program?* Yes. *Unexpected?* No, especially with a program of that scope and that complexity. The biggest one ever with the smallest staff ever, and underfunded and stretched out way too far due to budget constraints. So nevertheless, a program of positive transformational impact on the CG.

The intel transformation we undertook, I think, is another one I would put up near the top, in terms of infrastructure, policy and process, and overall capability. It was not only our new membership in the intelligence community, but our new 30 Field Intelligence Support Teams (FIST), our extensive collaboration with the DOD intel community, and our Maritime Intelligence Fusion Centers. It was the competencies that we were worried about, i.e., how you develop and grow intel competencies. The CG has come a long, long way regarding competencies and capabilities in the intel aspects of maritime security, to the benefit of all our missions.

And the third most impacting thing was the change to our operational infrastructure, with the priority starting at the field level—the integration of CG groups and MSOs, the attainment of integrated operations, the development and implementation of the sector concept. We sought to optimize the service delivery point involving groups and the MSOs/Captain of the Port, so there is a unity of command with integrated operation centers supported by intelligence. One belly button. Long overdue in my mind. Absolutely a necessity in the post-9/11 environment. Had trouble getting it done in prior assignments and made it an imperative when I became Commandant. For this unity of command to happen, you had to integrate marine safety and marine inspection with surface operations. It definitely changes how you re-whicker the chain of command going upward.

To optimize the field, you had to change the Headquarters to match the field. So, the field on the sectors, instead of being programmatically structured and organized at the sector, were functionally structured. It's structured around response and prevention, instead of "Here's aids-to-navigation, here's search-and-rescue, here's marine inspection." So, subsequently, the organization of the districts changed accordingly through the dynamics of response and prevention. The area commands changed and Headquarters changed. It forced the change all the way up. I have since talked to a great deal of people involved in the organizational change that was undertaken and it has all been very, very positive feedback. *Were there some people against it, initially?* Yes. It was those that were closest to the command positions in the old command structure. They were about to be new Captain of the Port or head of Marine Safety Office (MSO), under the old command structure. They didn't like it at all because that was their next stop, and now their stop was gone. But, I think the detailers were careful about putting the right peg in the right hole under the new command structure, and those people still had an opportunity for command. Again, to me, I look back at sectors as one of the real high, high impacting transformational things for the service—among many, but, that one I feel to this day was absolutely overdue and was the right thing to do. We had to break some dishes in order to get everyone onboard. But, I think it clearly has, and is going to continue to have, great benefits for our CG, and for the public and nation we serve.

JD: If somebody would have told you on 9/11, that there would not be a maritime attack anytime soon, would you have believed them?

TC: No. Our inclination was that they had targeted just one element of the transportation system for use against us. I mean, that's what they did when they used the aviation part of our transportation system against us, and that was the vehicle by which they did their dastardly deed. What was to stop them from using the maritime part of our transportation system against us? Our thoughts were, *Why wouldn't it be the maritime?* I mean, you could probably wreak even greater havoc by taking down a waterside chemical plant or refinery, a bridge, or any number of our maritime-related transportation facilities. Take down the I-10 bridge that goes across the Mississippi River and see what happens.

So, risks and vulnerabilities in the maritime was on our mind. Immediately post-9/11, your mind runs in all kinds of different directions on what the potential threats could be. We knew there were absolutely fundamental security vulnerabilities/gaps in the maritime part of our transportation system. At that time, there was no national maritime security structure per se, other than for large capacity cruise ships. There was access control and screening of passengers and so forth for large capacity cruise ships because of legislation passed after the October 7th, 1985 hijacking of the cruise ship *Achille Lauro*. But, other than that, there weren't those kinds of structures in place. So, that needed to be closed and that's why we pursued it both domestically and internationall—to close those gaps as soon as we could.

There was a sense of urgency and the speed by which that happened that passed my wildest expectations. We were successful in developing both a domestic and international maritime security regime in a little over a year. But, it's not to say that a terrorist incident can't happen. We must pursue eternal vigilance here.

JD: I want to talk about when you were traveling overseas. How did you keep in touch with Headquarters?

TC: Well, another great thing about the GV was that you didn't have to go through standard ticket counters, and go through TSA lines, and all of those other kinds of things. Everything is done to make your time more productive, as well as convenient. The other thing is that the GV has secure communications, so you are really never out of contact. That's why the secretaries—Mineta, Ridge, and Chertoff—liked it so much. So, you could work issues in an all-secure environment. That was a great force multiplier, in terms of your time. The plane could seat 12, as I recall. I would typically bring my aide. I would also bring a subject matter expert if the issue was technical. My security team would also go with me. Sometimes my spouse would go with me when there was a spouse-to-spouse engagement included in the trip agenda—but not on all of trips.

JD: I want to talk about your domestic trips. Can you talk about the importance of your all-hands visits?

TC: Oh, they were terrific. I got as much, or more, out of them than anybody. I mean, to me, it was a great experience. Number one, it was a feel-good experience. I got energized by going out there. Our personnel throughout the service needed to know why we were doing certain things; where their organization was going. They needed to know that because they were major contributors to the various efforts underway. They needed to know what my expectations of them were; what were my standing orders in terms of how I would like you to behave as a Coast Guard member. I would give them that pitch. I stressed things like being agents of change; embracing innovation; leaning forward; being willing to take necessary measures and reasonable risks to undertake change; being humble enough to put your subordinates ahead of your interests; focusing on building the team; being effective in partnering with others; being careful to be aligned, so as to understand all the way up and down the chain of command, why we are doing something, and how you can contribute to it and be in line with it. Those are kind of the soft messages that I would give. In turn, I received invaluable feedback in Q&A sessions that were helpful in working the issues of the day, when I returned to HQ.

During all-hands sessions, I would also give an update on what specific things we were doing policy-wise, and why we were doing it—like what we were doing on the HR front to improve our workforce. I have to give my hat off to Rear Admirals Fred Ames and Ken Venuto for all of the amazing things that they did for our workforce when they served as Assistant Commandant for Human Resources. Things like offering expanded leadership training for Coast Guard NCOs, and leadership development programs for non-rates where you had to sit down and you would be mentored, and you had to have a written plan on how you are going to develop this guy or gal. Pay comparability with DOD. Increased sea pay. We were behind the DOD in terms of sea pay. Well, we closed that. Tripled tuition assistance.

JD: I want to thank you for that because I personally benefited from tuition assistance.

TC: It was a very positive thing for our workforce. Good for the workforce and good for the organization. It demonstrated a commitment to our personnel. Commit to our people so that they are committed to the Coast Guard. It's a two-way street and these types of initiatives become very, very strong signals. There were other initiatives as well. Joint ratings review was an initiative. The goal, given all of these new capabilities and competencies we are undertaking, such as the use of force from helicopters and MSSTs, was to review our ratings and see where they are going. Where appropriate, we changed rating structures and the qualifications needed, to the benefit of both service members and the overall CG.

JD: How was that received?

TC: Positively. We ensured ample input from the enlisted community, led by our master chiefs. Creation of a new maritime law enforcement (LE) specialist rating was one of the higher priorities. It was supported throughout the service given the prominence and importance of our

LE related missions, particularly the extensive vessel/boat boardings that our LE personnel do. Again, it was a fourth-quarter agenda item completed in my last year. The goal was to examine and treat boarding as a system. Boarding has now become a huge core capability for us because it is such a key function in executing the LE missions. It is such a central part of how we do our business. We are inserting from helicopters. We've got rescue swimmers. We are boarding container ships with Maritime Safety and Security Teams (MSSTs), etc., and we've never taken a holistic view of our doctrine, qualification set, and training for it. We needed to look at it very holistically—see how we are doing and ensure the necessary competencies had been identified and accounted for in our training and qualification processes.

JD: You had no shortage of things to keep you busy. In FY2002, more than 150,000 pounds of illegal drugs were seized by the Coast Guard and this was right after 9/11. There was reduced counter drug patrols in favor of Homeland Security missions. And just two years later over 242,000 pounds.

TC: The next year we got over 300,000.

JD: Yes, and just kept on going. Can you explain?

TC: Yes. I received many pointed and legitimate questions in hearings on the Hill about being able to service all of our missions, given the up-ramp in the maritime security mission questions that they made. My point back to them was that we were still attentive to our other missions, and we were not backing off on our performance standards for SAR and other missions. We never missed a beat on SAR. We met all of our SAR standards. We achieved very productive boarding and related outcomes—we boarded more fishing vessels than we ever did. For example, we handled more high seas drift net fishing violations. We had record-breaking drug seizures. The USCGC *Midgett* [WHEC-726] had a record-breaking drug seizure that was about mid-time in my tour. In the third year of my tour, we broke the annual record at the time by seizing 300,000 pounds.

People asked, "How are you doing this?" My response was, it was because we were developing increasing levels of maritime domain awareness (MDA), so we were getting more productivity from less resources. We had better MDA through better intel capability and capacity. And we used technology to the maximum extent. We were putting metal on target. When you have greater visibility of the threat in your AOR, you can position your assets to do the best in terms of the mitigating risk or accomplishing the mission, and that's what was happening here. We were more effective on the boundary line enforcing fisheries laws. We were more effective in tracking down the high seas drift net offenders. We had ELINT. We had a special ELINT rig from the DOD that we developed to be carried by pallets on our C-130s. Our fusion centers and, subsequently, our operational commanders had an improved picture of the western Pacific.

We had success across all our missions during my four years as Commandant, even though we diverted a number of resources to homeland security in the aftermath of 9/11. Although resource/asset allocation to homeland security did taper off, given recurring threat assessment dictating resource adjustments—it tailed off from a high of 53% of our resource base immediately after 9/11, down to about 20% by the 2005/2006 timeframe.

It was a dynamic process which involved a risked-based allocation of resources. And our assets/platforms/personnel are multi-mission. It's not like we have our major platforms solely dedicated to SAR platform, or drug enforcement, or port security, etc. Our ships, boats, and aircraft are multi-mission assets. That is the strength of the United States Coast Guard. Military, multi-mission, and maritime. That's the characteristics of our organization. Those characteristics give us extended capability, flexibility, and responsiveness. It involves leveraging our assets for the benefit of the American people across a number of maritime missions, resulting in good return on investment. That's called good stewardship. An example—our new seagoing buoy tenders. They were designed with multiple capabilities, not just those needed to work aids-to-navigation. They have ice-strengthened hulls providing icebreaking capabilities for our ports and waterways. The crew is also trained to conduct search-and-rescue or oversee boating safety events, when needed. It can provide escort services or enforce security zones. It can set up security zones. So, our assets are not one-dimensional. Our people are not one-dimensional. That's the strength of our organization and a major factor in being able to meet all our mission requirements, even while allocating additional assets and hours to homeland security.

JD: In 2003, your first full year as Commandant, Coast Guard High Endurance Cutters lost 676 operating days because of unscheduled maintenance, which is the equivalent of losing four cutters a year. Can you explain this from a readiness perspective?

TC: Yes, it was huge adverse impact on our readiness. Remember when we talked about my previous assignment in PACAREA, you asked me, "What were some of the challenges you had?" I said, "PACAREA was a large AOR and the challenges were the tyranny of distance, plus the readiness challenges, in terms of the age of our old, tired platforms." Unfortunately, it took us a long time and great effort to get through the budget gauntlet to get the policy, political, and budget support to design and build new ships, boats, and aircraft.

It's a challenge to our ability to do our mission when you lose four cutters worth of annual cutter days. When you lose that, you lose capability and performance to serve the American people, to mitigate risks, to rescue people, to preserve our fish stocks—all of that. That was the greatest challenge when I was the senior operational commander in PACAREA. It was one of the greatest challenges when I was Vice Commandant and Commandant. It's one of the greatest challenges today for the present Commandant, Admiral Paul Zukunft.

JD: Can you talk about the engine problems with the HH-65 helicopters?

TC: As we have discussed, we had experienced years and years of chronic underfunding. Maintenance accounts were going down, parts inventories were not what they should have been—all at a time when our maintenance needs were going up because our platforms were getting older. Our aircraft were not exempt from this problem. The original HH-65 engines, required to be in the original acquisition by Congress, were not optimally mated to the aircraft. They were under powered, among other problems. The engines in our HH-65 helicopters were experiencing power failures to the point that we had to restrict operations for that helicopter. We changed out all of those with new, more appropriately configured engines matched to the needs of the platform. Cost us a bunch of money as part of the Deepwater program. It took a great deal of effort to convince Congress on the immediate need to replace the engines. Secretary Ridge was indispensable in working the issue with the Hill.

I should note that Deepwater was not only about buying new capital assets, it was also managing the associated legacy systems at the same time. Deepwater looks at our assets—ships, boats, aircraft, sensors—as a system. It was a combination of legacy systems, existing old systems, and the new assets that would replace them in a staggered, measured way over time. The challenge was how to keep the legacy assets alive because Deepwater was stretched out as a 25-year program. Not by desire, but by budget constraints. At that timeframe, it was a $24 billion, 25-year program.

Trying to recapitalize over a 25-year period is a substantial challenge. You are faced with shifting variables you must deal with. The missions can change. The technology can change. The political environment can change and the budget support can change. Accordingly, there's huge risks to an acquisition program on the scale of Deepwater. The longer you stretch it out, the risk of cost growth increases because, among other things, there is uncertainty to the supplier. Uncertainty equates to increased risk of cost growth. This is why year-by-year budgets are also problematic, because there is uncertainty to the contractor and they have to price that into their contract.

Our current Commandant, Admiral Zukunft, did receive a modestly increased capital budget with the FY17 budget. I'm pleased that the relatively small uptick will allow getting on with building the Offshore Patrol Cutter (OPC), as well as the design of a new icebreaker. Making progress in acquiring a new icebreaker was another one of the agenda items that I had coming into the job. One of the priority agenda items was clearly Deepwater, another was the creation of sectors, and the third was teeing up the icebreaker issue. We teed up the icebreaker issue by having the National Academy of Science do a study for us to validate the need for icebreakers, from both a scientific rationale and also from a national security strategy rationale. I participated in various forums to get support for new icebreakers, but it was treated like a disease. No one in the interagency provided strong support because signing up for it might mean it might come out of your budget. There was no way for it to come out of the Coast Guard budget since the cost of one dwarfs the Coast Guard's acquisition budget. I should stress that this is not a Coast Guard issue alone. This is a national issue and a national security issue. Fortunately, it appears it has finally been recognized as such. President Obama, Secretary Johnson, and now the Congress has recognized it as such. Well, that has finally "broken the ice." Very appropriate!

JD: What would you say were the obstacles to funding a new icebreaker fleet for the United States Coast Guard?

TC: Building new icebreakers is a very, very expensive proposition. Acquiring the proper budget for it and attaining strong, sharply-focused advocacy groups for it are essential. And with the threat and realities of Arctic warming, Arctic issues have become more visible and a higher national priority. So, that's why there is an Arctic Council. That's why there is an Arctic Forum. That's why it is high on the agenda of the existing Commandant. So, the environment has changed significantly. That's why the Coast Guard has to adapt to a new mission profile and a new set of priorities. Because the landscape has changed. It is a moving target. The current Commandant and Secretary Johnson have made the Arctic and the need for icebreakers a high priority, as they should. I think they are doing absolutely the right thing.

JD: And they were able to do that because you cleared the decks by getting a lot of things set in motion, like recapitalization.

TC: Yes, the biggest elements of recapitalization are underway. But I wouldn't say that the decks are cleared. There will continue to be great competition for capital dollars and much of Deepwater remains to be built out, especially the OPCs. I am sure there will be a budget balancing act that will take place within the CG. You make the adjustment you need. You assess capital programs that may be less critical for a given new environment and then make the necessary adjustments. That's the job of each respective leadership team, and the good news is that is the way the Coast Guard is structured.

JD: I was looking back at your first full year as Commandant, and your inbox for requests from your international partners had to be overflowing. Can you just talk about?

TC: We have been continually and actively engaged with our international partners. Many would seek CG support in selected areas, from the combatant commands and the US embassies, and from other countries. We have CG personnel on combatant commanders' staffs and in US embassies around the world. The International Affairs staff at Coast Guard Headquarters would orchestrate and prioritize these support requirements and consider the input from the Commandant, commanders, and the country teams. With program manager input, they would make judgments on the importance of the requests, and we would field what we could field given our limited resources.

Unfortunately, we didn't have the resources to support all needs, but I was amazed how much in-demand CG personnel were and continue to be. I think the recognition is that there is one agency on the planet that does maritime mission-related requirements pretty well and are very professional at it—that is, the United States Coast Guard. I'm not totally objective here, but I think we are one of the model structures in the world on how you do this non-DOD maritime mission business. And, we are very much sought after, accordingly. In addition, we had a number of different all-CG teams working issues around the globe—ISPS inspection teams, liaison personnel, marine inspection staff, etc.

JD: You may not remember this, but I had to do a trip report on Belize one drill weekend for the ISPS teams visiting the ports of Belize. I was amazed to learn that the Prime Minister of Belize requested that US Coast Guard create a station in Belize for forward deployed Coast Guard personnel. I mean that's a tribute to the professionalism of the men and women of the US Coast Guard.

TC: It is a tribute, and you see that kind of respect when you work with an institution like the International Maritime Organization. You see it at the North Pacific Coast Guard Forum. The international community defers to your comments and your inputs, and I think it's a reflection of the fact that we have such a proven track record. I am being very objective when I say that the USCG is considered the premier Coast Guard in the world.

JD: I was reading the May 2003 *Naval Review* issue of *Proceedings* and retired Vice Admiral Howard Thorsen quoted you as saying, "I have the best job in the world because the men and women wearing the Coast Guard uniform are the finest anywhere."

TC: Well, again, I thought it then. I think it now. And I would extend that thought to those men and women in uniform of the other armed services—all are about selfless service and professionalism. They represent the best values of our nation. So, well, yes, I sign up to that comment.

JD: He mentions several of your accomplishments in the eyes of the enlisted forces, just in your first year alone. We discussed some of them and one we haven't discussed was your expedited approval of the battle dress uniform changes, which was very popular.

TC: When I went around for the all-hands sessions, I got a standing "o" for that. It was long overdue and there was always a reason why we couldn't do it. "Oh, it will cost money. Transitioning to a new uniform presents this or that difficulty." I said, "Time out. My default setting on the issue is to approve it, but send me a decision paper and lay out the case for it." From my perspective, it was not a difficult decision to make. It means a lot to our folks.

How do we make their workplace more conducive to performance? Maybe you give them an iPad and develop apps that allow them to do their job more efficiently. You provide better uniforms. You pay them appropriately, etc. So, all those things have huge dividends and I'm glad that we were able to do battle dress uniform.

JD: Another one you mentioned in 2003 was providing relief to small boat forces with more people and new boats; and that it was the largest procurement of small boats in Coast Guard history, occurred under your watch.

TC: That's another initiative that fit one of our four strategic objectives—Increase operational presence in our ports and waterways. That meant more people on more boats. It also meant use of force on helicopters, etc. It was part of how we used our increased budgets over the next few years. We increased SAR stations by 1,000 people. So, it wasn't just maritime security that got the headcount increase. We recognized deficiencies in our SAR stations, and the amount of overtime, and extra work, and so forth at SAR stations. And so, we put 1,000 people into SAR.

JD: Speaking of SAR, we talked a little bit about Rescue 21. Can you talk about why the need to replace the National Distress and Response System?

TC: The CG had an antiquated distress and calling system that was long overdue for replacement. The quicker you get on the scene of a SAR requirement, the more you eliminate the risk of having injury, or death, or property damage. So, we replaced our antiquated system for handling distress calls with one that could vector response resources into the exact position of the distress call. Talk about putting metal on target. It's very MDA-ish and provides improved response outcomes. It is something that we pushed very, very strongly, and received fairly strong support for on the Hill. It's part of our recap program and it's been instituted, so I'm pleased.

JD: Can you talk about the patrol boats the Navy wanted to get rid of one time and give them to the Coast Guard, and now the Navy has them back?

TC: The Navy transferred five of their 179-foot patrol boats after 9/11 with no questions asked. CNO Vern Clark and Secretary of the Navy Gordon England asked, "What do you need?" We were short patrol boat hours so Jim Loy and I responded that additional patrol boats would be most welcomed. They extended a commitment for five. They were in the midst of trying to define how they wanted to use their patrol boats. So, there was a time when it was unsettled a bit. Ultimately, it played out, I think, to everyone's satisfaction.

JD: In early 2004, there was concerns about a mass exodus from Haiti, given the latest round of chaos, and President Bush ordered the positioning of assets to discourage a mass exodus of Haitians. Can you talk about the Coast Guard's role in this potential migration crisis?

TC: We deployed a number of High Endurance Cutters and several buoy tenders as part of the first-ever Joint Task Force under the Department of Homeland Security. The JTF consisted of Customs, ICE, NS, and the Coast Guard; and, as I recall, we might have had Navy and SOUTHCOM participation, as well. But, it was DHS's first joint task force and we performed well providing the deterrence needed.

JD: Can we talk about the Coast Guard's shore infrastructure and how it was chronically underfunded?

TC: The CG has an extensive and nationally distributed facilities that are essential to the support of our assets and personnel. Unfortunately, in terms of the capital budget, it was the budget component with a big sucking sound. When competing for scarce dollars, it always loses because it is appropriately deemed a lower priority than operational assets—a new aircraft or cutter. Of course, shore plant does get some funding, but clearly not enough, given necessary service life considerations of the facilities involved, and associated recapitalization rates. We were always playing catch up with these assets. And unfortunately, I don't see that changing much now and into the future.

JD: Did you ever feel that the Coast Guard needed a Base Realignment and Closure (BRAC) Commission like the Department of Defense?

TC: Something like it may have been a good tool. On one occasion, while Admiral Kramek was Commandant, we proposed closing ten SAR stations. That got nowhere. We included ten station closures in our budget to realize budget savings. Unfortunately, Congress took the funding reduction while mandating that we keep the SAR stations open. So, basically, it was a double-whammy. We had to keep them open, plus we had fund them out of our hide. So, that was a bad experience. Closing stations are politically sensitive. So, some kind of mechanism that would have prevented that would have been welcomed.

JD: Can you talk about the decision to create Maritime Safety & Security Teams (MSSTs)?

TC: Very quickly after 9/11, we recognized that we needed a focused, well-trained, highly qualified SWAT-like team to deal with maritime security risk/threats, especially in the boarding of high security risk vessels ashore and at sea. MSSTs were one of the first concepts that we came up with. And it was important that, like all our operational assets, they possess multi-mission capabilities. They were developed and implemented as multi-mission so as to be able to respond to a whole panorama of Coast Guard missions. They can do a safety mission. They can enforce security zones that we need for regattas or other marine events. The MSSTs were one of the first initiatives under our strategy of increasing operational presence for deterrent and prevention purposes, and we had 13 of them at the end of my tenure in 2006.

JD: Can you talk about the role of the Coast Guard in providing security for events designated as National Security Significant Events (NSSE), like the 2004 political conventions in New York City and Boston, especially since they were the first conventions since 9/11?

TC: There was no shortage of NSSEs designated by the Secretary of Homeland Security. There were the Super Bowls, the two major political party conventions in 2004, the 2005 Presidential Inaugural, and President Reagan's June 2005 state funeral. The Department of Homeland Security was responsible, with support of local law enforcement, to make sure the event was secure. And, thus, the special title that they put on these events.

Some of the resources that the Secretary of Homeland Security had in their quiver were Coast Guard MSSTs for events that had a waterside component that needed a security zone around the event, with patrols to ensure there were no intrusions in it and those kinds of things. So, all of the skillsets of those MSSTs were brought to bear. It was coordinated, clearly, with the Secret Service and FBI. So, it's a joint-coordinated operation among agencies within the department and, when appropriate, those outside the department.

JD: On December 8th, 2004, the Malaysian-flagged freighter M/V *Selendang Ayu*, carrying 66,000 tons of soybeans and more than 500,000 gallons of fuel, grounded and split in two off of Unalaska Island, a remote wildlife-rich area in Alaska's Aleutian Islands. More than 300,000 gallons of heavy bulk fuel leaked from the M/V *Selendang Ayu*, much of it washing ashore on beaches of Skan Bay and Makushin Bay—areas that provide recreational, subsistence, and commercial fishing resources for residents of the Dutch Harbor/Unalaska community. Can you talk about this incident?

TC: I remember, this was one of the calls I got about quarter to midnight that started with, "Boss, we've got this thing going on with the M/V *Selendang Ayu*." It was bound for China and was sailing the great circle route when it lost its propulsion in a heavy winter storm. Twenty- to twenty-five-foot seas, and 45-knot arctic gales, near freezing water temperatures, in fog and snow, and drifting down on Unalaska Island.

In response, a HH-60 CG-6020 was dispatched from Kodiak. It had hoisted a number of crew off the ship. While hoisting the remaining crew, mostly Captain and remaining ship's officers, a rogue wave hit the side of the vessel and thrust upward engulfing the helicopter. The helicopter lost power and fell out of the sky, hitting the vessel, and entered the icy waters inverted and quickly submerged. Fortunately, USCGC *Alex Haley* [WMEC- 39] was also on scene a couple of miles away and had an HH-65 aboard helo, CG-6513. CG-6513 was technically not supposed to launch. The blizzard, sea conditions, the wind, and the condition of the vessel was such that it exceeded the operational envelope for launching. It launched anyway and preceded to the scene of the distress. It went into the trough of the seas adjacent to the stricken vessel, and rescued all three crew members from the downed helicopter, and one member of the *Selendang Ayu*'s crew.

The rescue was performed in unbelievable conditions—at night, in the fog, snowing, high seas, and wind. Unbelievable!

Concurrently, a second HH-60 was launched and deployed to the scene from Kodiak base. At that point, the master and the CG rescue swimmer were still onboard the distressed vessel that was aground and breaking in half with the bow pointing upward. They were up on the bow clinging to the life rails. The HH-60 from Kodiak hoisted the master and rescue swimmer when they arrived on scene. The crew from the downed HH-60 survived because they were trained to evacuate from a submerged helicopter, inverted or whatever. They are trained in the dunk tank with other nasty conditions that can be simulated. Plus, they had the proper suits on. They had the dry suits on for extreme cold water immersion. So, they had the required equipment and they had the right training. The Coast Guard air crew all survived. The *Selendang Ayu* didn't have the proper equipment onboard. If they were a US flag vessel, they would have the right equipment onboard because it was mandated. Instead, their flag state didn't mandate it and they were in international waters. They didn't have the training to get out. Unfortunately, they perished under those conditions, but it was unbelievable work by everyone in that case under extraordinarily difficult conditions.

The air crew of CG-6513 were awarded the Distinguished Flying Cross for their heroic actions that day. I had made sure that their award ceremony would occur expeditiously because I found out that Senator Ted Stevens was going to take a trip up to Alaska. I called him to inform him of the rescue and ask if he would mind participating in an award ceremony for the crew. He was amazed with the case. Of course, he was a World War II pilot flying over the hump in the China theater in World War II. So, in general, he was very interested and supportive of air operations, and of this case in particular. So, we had a luncheon for the surviving HH-60 crew and the rescuing HH-65 crew at the Captain Cook Hotel in Anchorage. Senator Ted Stevens attended and presented them with the Distinguished Flying Cross. I was not going to miss that event, so I was there as well.

There was a cartoonist from the *Anchorage* paper, Dunlap-Shohl, who sent me a personal copy of a cartoon that had appeared in the local newspaper and had caught the spirit of the rescue very well. The cartoon was all black and dotted by accentuated seas, with a CG helicopter flying over those high seas. In a caption at the bottom of the cartoon, it read: "WATER TEMPERATURE = 43 degrees, WAVES = over 20 feet, COURAGE = ABOVE AND BEYOND." He inscribed the cartoon saying, "To the Coast Guard Rescue team, with awe and admiration." That said it all! I have the cartoon displayed prominently on the bulkhead in my study. Another one I have displayed is a cartoon from a New Orleans paper of a Coast Guard helicopter in action at night doing hoists, and there is a big halo over the helicopter and the caption reads "The Real New Orleans Saints." The cartoon was done in recognition of the incredible performance of our air crews during the aftermath of the passing of Hurricane Katrina.

JD: Both of them had to make you really proud as service chief.

TC: Yes. You know, it's almost better than a paycheck. Probably better than a paycheck. Such performance makes one proud to wear the uniform, and to have a small part in an organization that does things like that. But, it's the guys and gals on the service delivery point that make everything happen for our service and for the American people. Those senior folks at the top are just the enablers that help provide some direction, ensure our personnel are properly supported. But, it's the pointy end of the spear that counts in our organization. That's what counts and that's why I was so fixated on developing and implementing the sectors concept—fixing the organization at the pointy end of the spear so it was optimized for the men and women performing their incredible, selfless work.

JD: Talking about doing good stuff in the midst of a tragedy, can you talk about the Coast Guard's response to the December 2004 tsunami in Southeast Asia, in which two C-130 aircraft flew around the clock?

TC: Humanitarian Assistance and Disaster Response is a central part of PACAREA's mission. The December 2004 tsunami was just the latest example. I was at D-14 when Typhoon Paka struck Guam at wind speeds of 145 miles per hour. *Who was the very first on scene?* It wasn't the Department of Defense—no hit on the Department of Defense. But, as I mentioned earlier in terms of our readiness posture, we have the most incredible firehouse-type of readiness posture of any organization. Coast Guard C-130s were the first on scene to deliver water supplies, generators, etc., needed in the aftermath of a natural disaster. The C-130 is a workhorse out there. It can land on short runways. It's built into a lot of the DOD's contingency plans, and we work very, very closely with the Department of Defense. So, this is no slam on the Department of Defense. They are wonderful, wonderful partners, but it's just the way that we are well-positioned in terms of our rapid response capabilities. We are a first responder. That's what we do. So, clearly, I'm not surprised because all of these things are just the next addition of how we do our business.

JD: Can you talk about the relationship between the Pacific Islanders and the United States Coast Guard?

TC: The islanders love the Coast Guard. We are there for all kinds of things all the time, whether it's a disaster or something else. The islanders know they can depend on the United States Coast Guard and we are welcomed wherever we go. When I was at D-14, I had a Coast Guard buoy tender and a 110-foot sail a 5,000-mile support mission to the islands. They were outfitted to bring medical supplies, dental supplies, books, and other things to the various islands. It was a long journey for a 110-footer but the buoy tender was close enough at hand to render support, if and when needed. I remember the commanding officer of the 110-footer out-briefing me on his return to Honolulu. He said, "Boss, I can't thank you enough. This is the most incredible adventure I've ever had in my whole life. Going to the outer islands, sitting on the thatched buildings with the islanders, and extending a hand to them on all types of things."

JD: Admiral Thorsen writing in a May 2006 *Naval Review* issue of *Proceedings* said that, in the history of the peace time Coast Guard, one word will forever conjure up images and reflections of the men and women who responded to one of our nation's most horrific natural disasters—Katrina. Can you talk about?

TC: Of course, Katrina was front and center for the CG in many ways, for an extended timeframe. There are several sides to that response. There is the interagency/federal response to Katrina, followed by the local response. And then there is the Coast Guard response to Katrina. The local and the federal response go together, but are really two different components of the response. The federal response was first led by FEMA, while the local governments were trying to execute their own contingency plans. The CG mission is saving lives and property in the maritime domain. We don't need any new enabling authorities. We don't need direction from Washington to say, "Go do this." It's part of our statutory responsibilities and outlined in existing contingency plans for natural disasters and hurricanes. When it happens we implement the plan. We train to the plan. We resource to the plan. We make it happen, and that's what we did.

In New Orleans, the key challenges occurred in aftermath of the storm passage as the levies broke and extreme flooding problems followed. Mississippi is the one that got hit with the wind and water surge elements of the storm. You could walk the first quarter- or half-mile from the beach inland, and it was just absolutely destroyed. I mean, houses were rendered to splinters and I'm not over exaggerating. They were absolutely splinters. There were casino boats moved one-half a mile.

Prior to the arrival of Katrina, the CG evacuated its resources to get them out of the path of the storm. They are no good in the middle of the storm anyway. Get them out of the storm's damaging effects so they can be of use in the aftermath of the storm's passage. That's really a central feature for all of our hurricane plans. You disperse, then you reconfigure for response purposes. We were right on the backside of the storm, rescuing people. Within minutes of Katrina's eye passing, we were hoisting people. We rescued and/or evacuated, by boat or by plane, half of them by helicopter, 33,000 people within the first week to ten days. Within days, we had relocated a substantial part of entire CG air assets to the Gulf Coast, with the bulk of our aviation assets deployed to Louisiana and Mississippi. That's how fast we responded to that.

Support bases were designated at our air facilities in Mobile and Houston. They supported maintenance needs or whatever they had to do to service our helicopters, so as to put a new crew back in the game ASAP. We operated around the clock, 24/7, at night, in all kinds of conditions. Hoisted those in distress from every kind of place that you could imagine—busted through roofs with axes; people hanging off the rafters in attics, with the water up to their necks; rescue swimmers busting through and pulling them out through roofs. We had configured all of our helicopter hoists with cameras. So, there is a camera on each hoist, where the cameras could look and record what was happening down the hoist. Plus, we did put a lot of members of the media in our helicopters so that they could see what we were doing. That was a great communications tool. So, people saw the Coast Guard in action.

After rescuing people, we cared for them until they could be relocated to longer term care. Rear Admiral Duncan, the local District Commander, said, "Once we touch them, they are ours. If we touch them, they are ours, and we care for them with water and other forms of assistance." Incredible performance. The 8th District staff was relocated out of New Orleans, up to Alexandria, which is a municipality halfway between New Orleans and Baton Rouge. We took over a motel which became a temporary new District Headquarters. I remember visiting and observing a little cubby hole that had yellow sticky post-it notes all over the bulkhead. People on telephones coordinating rescue missions, working with other agencies, local and federal, regarding maritime issues. It was impressive.

The mission priorities were saving people and property, responding to oil spills, and restoring the critical waterways. There were over 540 individual oil spills that spilled an estimated 11 million gallons of oil because of ruptured pipelines and tank farms. Those were the three things that we did, and it was a joint operation center set up there. They had the tugboat folks in there. They had private companies in there. They had everybody where extensive coordination was deemed necessary. In a nutshell, it was joint, integrated approach to Katrina.

The role of LANTAREA and Headquarters was to ensure that the operations were resourced properly, and to work interagency issues in DC. Augmenting air assets came from as far away as Coast Guard Air Station Cape Cod, and Sitka and Kodiak, Alaska. We had aircrews and planes from all over the Coast Guard down there within a few days. As I recall, at one point over 45% of our air assets were deployed there. Small boat and crews along with our cutters were also part of the action.

The immediate questions I got from some on Capitol Hill and others was, "Well, what about our response in areas where CG resource had been relocated to Katrina? What about all of those assets you've removed? Are we going to be covered?" Well, the solution to that involves partnering. In New England, we had always trained jointly with Canada agencies, so Canada personnel stepped forward to backfill some of our SAR responsibility for New England. The Auxiliary stepped to the plate. The Reserves stepped to the plate. So, we didn't leave many holes. That shows you the flexibility of the Coast Guard.

But, the other side of the equation was that the federal response and the local response didn't initially jive well within the disaster areas. Communication and coordination issues abounded. Many of those federal coordination difficulties were mitigated when my Chief of Staff, Vice Admiral Thad Allen, was designated by Secretary Chertoff and the president as the principle federal official for the disaster. He deployed down to the Joint Field Office in LA and immediately and positively impacted federal response/disaster operations. He did a bang-up job running the whole federal response. He was acting as the principle federal official coordinating the overall federal response. CG operations remained within the CG chain of command. By the time Thad had arrived, DOD had set up a Joint Task Force-Katrina under the command of Lieutenant General Russel Honorè, US Army. To his credit, Thad worked very closely with the JTF, which was a very smart thing. The principle federal official and the joint task force commander became joined at the hip. Everything improved considerably from that point, partly because of Thad's leadership, but also because the Department of Defense had begun to execute their contingency plans, bringing the scale and capabilities of DOD to bear. I know the Secretary and the president appreciated the work of Vice Admiral Allen. I know the president really appreciated the work of the Coast Guard there, as well. He should have. He awarded us the Presidential Unit Citation because of the CG's contributions.

JD: Can you talk about the Presidential Unit Citation?

TC: Getting one is something that does not happen every day. It was presented at my change of command. Number one, for the president to show at the change of command and then award the Coast Guard, not just me, the Presidential Unit Citation was awesome and richly deserved by our folks. Their performance was spectacular. I visited down there several times after Hurricane Katrina. One time, within the first three or four days, I flew down with Senator Olympia Snowe from Maine and accompanied her to the Mississippi coast, and met with the crew at Coast Guard Station Gulfport, Mississippi. They were operating out of makeshift trailers, but there was a hubbub of activity. CG personnel had lost their homes, along with many of the local population. They were impacted personally by the storm, yet they were in the trenches doing the king's business. I remember going to Coast Guard Air Station New Orleans in Belle Chasse, Louisiana. Augmenting personnel were sleeping on mattresses in the corridor, and then deploying when called upon, which was frequently. An amazing response. At Gulfport, we had an all-hands town hall meeting with Senator Snowe to discuss what they did, how they did it. You could just feel the positive energy in the Coast Guard crowd. I think it brought a little tear the Senator's eye, hearing all of this stuff, especially when I said to them, "Well, you know Katrina has been a high tempo response, but don't unpack your sea bag yet because Hurricane Rita is coming right behind." In response to that, we heard a big, in unison, "Hooray!" from everyone. It was like the CG crowd was saying, "Hey coach, it is game day. Put me in!"

We then visited Coast Guard Air Station Mobile, Alabama, where all the aviation rescues were staged out of, and chatted with some of the rescue swimmer/survival guys that were there, they presented me with one of the axes they used to bust through roofs, and it was all signed by everyone that participated. So, I got that too, hanging on my bulkhead.

Even Station Lake Pontchartrain, a relatively new station, had been evacuated. It's on Lake Charles and they evacuated it in the face of the storm. Unfortunately, all of the local homeless took over the station, and they had an assortment of weapons. The CG personnel had to take back the station by force. Locals had ripped the urinals out of the restrooms; they had put feces all over the walls. It was not a pleasant thing. But, Coast Guard station personnel, when they returned, restored law and order in the facility, apprehended all of the guilty parties that had invaded the station, and then clothed them, and fed them, and housed them, and then let them go. Taking care of people is what CG personnel do.

We had team from a 210-foot Medium Endurance Cutter brought into New Orleans. Several of the response and assistance teams from the 210 were up in town providing aid to indigenous people in town and in hospitals. The entire disaster response has stories after stories of the good work of CG personnel. And, I know Senator Olympia Snowe from Maine, in particular, was impacted by it. A few days later, she made an impassioned speech on the floor of the United States Senate about what she saw and what a model agency the CG was, in terms of responding to disasters.

There are a lot of things that didn't go right in the overall Katrina response effort and I think the interagency coordination part is always an issue. There were some comments that maybe DOD needs more authorities, and not be restricted by the Posse Comitatus Act that restricts DOD from law enforcement actions. I think my conclusion, as well as the local District Commander's, was there were no questions about the Coast Guard's authorities. We had plenty of authority. It was a matter of coordination between and among the agencies involved, and in the local, state, and federal levels of government. It was a question of federalism—federalism not working well and delayed decision-making. You know, they had a significant number of buses to transport people that didn't have the wherewithal to evacuate themselves. That's got to be part of your plan. But the buses were not mobilized in a timely way by local authorities. They were left in a parking lot underwater.

There were some early interagency coordination and levels of government issues that may have caused delayed decision-making. From my perspective, a disaster of Katrina's magnitude requires great capabilities with scale, and the ability to support operations independently—to be self-sufficient. We all know there is one agency that has the capability to conduct expeditionary operations better than anybody, and that's the Department of Defense. When you go to a natural disaster like a hurricane that destroys communication, water supplies, electricity, etc., etc., you have to be self-sufficient. You have to be self-sustaining. DOD can do that. There are not too many organizations that can do it as well as they, which raises the question of when you pull the trigger to bring their capability into bear on a disaster. The CG does not have the sustaining, big-scale capabilities of the DOD. We have very quick and very skilled targeted short-term response capabilities that met and exceeded all expectation during Katrina. I'm very, very proud of the Coast Guard men and women in our disaster response efforts. However, we can always improve in terms of interagency coordination and communication systems capability. But, I was proud of our men and women. No one worked longer and harder.

Did well on Hurricane Rita too. Rita hit Texas and Louisiana after Katrina on September 24th, 2005. Again, I'm very, very proud of those involved in the CG's response, and it was a really great honor to have President Bush recognize their performance and award us with a Presidential Unit Citation.

JD: When did you know President George W. Bush was going to award the US Coast Guard a Presidential Unit Citation at your retirement ceremony?

TC: I knew a couple of days before the ceremony. There were some questions as to whether the president was going to be there or not because of the demands of his schedule. In fact, the president's attendance is always subject to what the crisis of the day is. But, it worked out that his schedule allowed his participation. In fact, I had one speech that was a little longer than the other, in terms of my comments. If the president was going to be there, I was using the short one. If he wasn't going to be there, I would use the longer one. It was an honor to have him there and I know Admiral Allen felt the same way because it was an honor for him, as well.

JD: Is there anything else you would like to add about Katrina?

TC: No, just that it was an outstanding performance across the board. I was very pleased about how we were able to shift resources to the requirement, as well as manage the interoperability of our crews and assets, with assets and personnel from different areas of the country. It showed the quality and uniformity of our doctrine, training, and maintenance protocols. So, very proud of our folks and, again, it is just testimony to the fact that we remain multi-mission, despite the immediate demands of post-9/11, and the uptick in the maritime homeland security. That characteristic is a powerful concept. We remained "Johnny-on-the-spot" for these kinds of things. That's what we do.

JD: You might have been surprised by the scale of the disaster, but I doubt you were surprised by the Coast Guard's response.

TC: No, I wasn't surprised by our response. It was just on a bigger scale. But, it's the blueprint of how we do operations. If you go to one command and then go to another command, you look at the hurricane plan, it is very similar. I think where we need to continue to work on—and it's a never-ending thing—is on the interagency coordination part. You've got to keep working at that and working that hard. It's terribly important. The other thing is communication. Effective communication with all of the parties involved and that is something that is always the major hot wash-up issue in training exercises or real world events.

JD: Did you ever have any interest in serving more than four years as Commandant?

TC: No. It was never a part of my mindset because the standard procedure was four years and out. I figured, I'm retiring after four years, so I'm going to go 110% or more for four years and then I'm out the door. In addition, I have such continuing admiration for the quality of CG leadership, and for those ready to be the next leadership team. It's the "long blue line" concept.

JD: What do recall the process in which Admiral Thad Allen was chosen as your successor?

TC: It was very similar to previous ones. Résumé packages were prepared; the packages of two-stars and above who wanted to compete were included. The process was outlined for the Secretary noting that an initial list of flag officers, two-stars and above, along with their packages would be provided. And, if he is not uncomfortable with the number and/or quality of the list, then we can go down deeper with it. Then the packages went forward and interviews were conducted. The retiring Commandant is not actively involved in picking his successor because that's between the candidates and the Secretary. The Secretary ended up selecting Admiral Allen. He has a great record. He's an accomplished professional and leader. His performance during Hurricane Katrina didn't hurt his standing either. But, a good decision and he served a quality tour as Commandant.

JD: And, this wasn't the first time you and Allen had worked closely together. Wasn't he one of your deputies earlier on in your career?

TC: When I was Chief of the Programs Division, he was my deputy. We worked very closely together and so I know him very, very well. And, again, he served as Coast Guard Chief of Staff for four years from 2002 to 2006, while I was Vice Commandant and Commandant. That's a long time for a Chief of Staff.

JD: What did you do during Allen's absence, while he was the principal federal official for Hurricane Katrina? You pretty much lost a Chief of Staff for a while.

TC: We did, but the good thing is that it's amazing how many quality people we have in our organization. They stepped up to the plate and performed. It's always hard to lose that kind of competence, but, we clearly were able to backfill.

JD: You mentioned President Bush attended your retirement ceremony. Is there anything else you would like to add about that ceremony?

TC: It's just that those are the kind of days and events that are special. I mean, your organization is recognized at the highest levels of government. And, in a way, it was an opportunity to let out a big sigh on what a four-year whirlwind my wife and I had been involved in, and speculate what was ahead for us. And, at the same time, we recognized that it was a privilege and an honor to have travelled the road we did, and to have had this opportunity to work alongside such quality people throughout the service. To have the president attend the ceremony was the icing on the cake.

JD: You had to breathe a sigh of relief that no acts of terrorism occurred during your watch.

TC: Yes. It was amazing that we haven't had such an act in the maritime. I would hope that, in no small measure, it was the result of the hard work and preparations put into creating a comprehensive maritime security regime not only for our nation, but one that extends globally. We certainly had our mix of challenges and successes in other mission areas—migrant issues, hurricane issues, search-and-rescue cases, ship disasters, drug interdiction, and the like. We didn't experience a terrorist act and I hope we never do. But, eternal vigilance is the key.

I would like to think a contributing factor in risk/threat reduction is the fact that we have increased maritime domain awareness. We built both domestic and international security regimes and build out an enhanced intelligence capability. We increased our operational presence and we are even better at response and recovery than we have ever been. I think the gains that we made on those things during those four years and after has served a little bit as a deterrent to bad things happening in the maritime. It definitely reduced the risk. You must manage risk, not necessarily eliminate risk. If you want to eliminate the risk, you can stop ships from entering the United States of America, which we did for a couple of days after 9/11 because we didn't know exactly what we were going to have. But, that's not what you want to do given its negative impacts. The whole thrust of the effort is, *How do you manage and reduce the risk at the same time keeping commerce that is vital to the United States, and other traffic within our ports going? How do you facilitate that as well as reduce risk?* That's the conundrum.

JD: What was it like hanging up the uniform for the final time?

TC: It was a challenge! Jim, I have to decide what to wear every day! I mean, big decisions. I mentioned to you earlier offline here, that I had gone down to Sector Key West over the spring, to give an address at their annual ball. It was a formal event and I wore my dinner dress whites. The uniform fit by the way, so I was amazed. It was the first time I had that uniform on since

2006. But, what I didn't find in reconstructing my uniform, Jim, was my shoulder boards. I couldn't find my four-star Admiral shoulder boards. I found all of my miniature medals and all of those things that go with that uniform, like bow tie, shoes, etc. After all of these years, I couldn't find my shoulder boards, so I was in a little bit of a panic, with the Key West event close at hand. But, I went on eBay and I found a brand new pair that they could get to me within three days. So, I did hang up my uniform, but I found some of them again, and they fit. By the way, the Sector Key West Ball was a great deal of fun for both my wife and I.

JD: That's great. Looking back at your career, some people would say that you were groomed for Commandant because you had important commands throughout your career. Do you feel that it is important to identify officers early in their career that would be excellent flag officers?

TC: I think the system does that, in a way. I think I mentioned it before to you, that I've always been very impressed with the Office of Personnel throughout my career. I've always been impressed on how professional and well-thought out they are, in terms of who they place, and where, and when, and what capabilities to look for.

You can't go into any job and say, "Okay, in ten years, I want to be in such in such a position." I don't think that is the approach you take. My approach was, and I think it would serve anyone well, that you go after the best job you can at the time. "Best" meaning the one that can be most exciting for you, one where you can contribute the most, the most impacting job you can find. Then go after it. It could be a command assignment or not, but go after that one, and then make the most of it. Enjoy it, be aggressive, build a team, work well with others, get results, and that all counts and sets you up well for the next assignment opportunity. I think this kind of approach is the one that gets people success at the end of the day. There is no foregone conclusion that anyone, including myself, is going to get to flag rank. You can't bank on that, and if you make day-to-day decisions based upon where you want to be in ten years or so, that's not the right way to do it.

Personal success is about making the team successful; making the boss successful; making the department, unit, organization successful. I think that is a recipe for success, and I think the detailers, again, recognize that and do their job targeting the individuals, vis-à-vis senior training opportunities and assignments that excel in those areas. They also consider the type and sequence of assignments and experiences you have had. I clearly have no complaints about my assignments because I've had interesting job after interesting job, but it was because I paid attention to the job I'm in. I didn't worry about the job that's three jobs away.

JD: If I could interview your wife, what advice would she give about being a Coast Guard spouse, and also being the spouse of a Commandant?

TC: I think she would say keep flexible and maintain a balance between work and family life. Make sure family stays the highest priority. Also, do not to be afraid to speak one's mind about work-life issues when and where appropriate. A Commandant's spouse is very important in and during the social engagement roles the Commandant is involved in. She understands service life impacts the family, and can be a great source of sound advice when the active duty member is dealing with those types of issues. She is involved in high level governmental circles, and in international visits, and must possess all the associated and necessary social graces. Nancy was super in that regard—kept me out of trouble all the time. She also added value to me as a sounding board regarding what I was up to at any given time. She was a great support for me. She managed the household when I was away and working long hours. In many ways, as a CG spouse, you are as part of the organization as well the principal. And, probably most importantly, she would give advice to be yourself and above all, make room for fun as a CG spouse, while not taking everything too, too seriously. Of course, Nancy is also my lifelong partner, and any success I have achieved was due in no small measure to her love, support, and positive contributions. By the way, we are close to celebrating our 50th wedding anniversary—a solid loving fifty-year partnership.

JD: You mentioned that you moved 15 times during your Coast Guard career. Any advice or secrets that you would like to share?

TC: Retain your flexibility, and hopefully your kids are flexible enough to deal with the change associated with reassignments. There is significant impact on the kids in conjunction with moves—having to make new friends and the social impact, particularly when they get to junior high and high school. My younger daughter went to three different high schools in three different geographic locations, including Hawaii. I had a little bit of a guilt trip sometimes and tried to manage around that, but that's the challenge of moving so many times. I would also offer, when moving to a new location, get your children engaged in community and school activities right away, so as to build new friends and relationships.

JD: Please bring us up to date on your children and grandchildren.

TC: Well, let's see. I have one daughter, Christine, who lives here in DC area. She just changed jobs. She now works for Sea Scouts of all organizations—keeping in the maritime venue! My youngest daughter, Kate, works in marketing for SAP, the German IT company. She works out of her house in Charlotte, but travels a little bit. She and her husband, Richard, have two children. Just bought a new home. They live about a mile and a half from us, and have a six-year-old daughter, Hadley—the sweetest thing on the planet. Every grandfather has that kind of opinion. And, also a three-year old red-headed son named Jack. It's very nice to have them close at hand. The grandfather gig is a great one. And given the grandchildren, I couldn't get Nancy to move with a stick of dynamite!

JD: How is retirement treating you and is it something you recommend to others?

TC: Well, I miss the Coast Guard terribly. I miss the people in the Coast Guard. Now, I don't miss some of the other things about the job, like going up to Capitol Hill. I understood going up on the Hill—doing hearings and all of that—was part of the job, and very important, but I didn't terribly enjoy that part. So, some things I'm glad I'm not doing, but I miss the people. I don't think there is any better combination of dedicated servants, selfless service, and professionals anywhere. I haven't run into them elsewhere. So, I miss that.

But, retirement is good. Some service folks retire and they want to jump into a full time private sector job. I didn't want to do that. So, I'm engaged with four companies in terms of board of directors, and I do a little consulting in and around those director positions, and that's just about right for me. It gets me out of the house several times a month and, of course, there is compensation related to it. It keeps you active and your brain cells engaged, and I think it is good for me. Charlotte, North Carolina is a nice location—easy to get in and out of because it is a hub for American Airlines. It has a lot of the benefits of city life, but leaves some of the ills behind. So, I think it's a pretty good setup.

JD: Admiral, one final question. Would you do it all over again, if you could?

TC: Wow, quite frankly, I wouldn't know how to do anything else but what I did. From the time I was 18 years old and stepped into the Coast Guard, it was a terrific experience and a great honor, and I'm thrilled that I had the opportunity to do it. I would very likely do it all over again.

Before I got accepted into the Coast Guard Academy, I wanted to be a dentist of all things—a very different career path from the one I ended up in. I was going to be a dentist, going to Bowling Green in Ohio because they had a very, very good pre-dental program. I had been accepted. I had my deposit down. But when accepted into the Academy, I jumped at it and haven't looked back. So, it's funny how one decision can impact so much of your life. But, I think it was the right decision. I feel privileged to have the opportunity to participate in such a positively impacting organization and, hopefully, I added a little value along the way. I worked hard, but had a lot of fun doing it at the same time. The United States Coast Guard is a national treasure.

JD: I have to say it's truly been an honor for me to interview you for the United States Naval Institute. Your oral history will make a great contribution to [our collective] knowledge, and be a treasure trove for researchers for decades to come, especially your years as Commandant.

TC: Thank you, and hats off to all of the great men and women of our service.

End audio file Collins6.2.Dolbow.USNI.4.18.16

Launched in 1969, the U.S. Naval Institute's award-winning oral history program is among the oldest in the country. Used in combination with documentary sources, oral histories offer a richer understanding of naval history through candid recollections and explanations rarely entered into contemporary records. In addition, they help depict the atmosphere of a particular event or era in a manner not available in official documents.

The nonprofit Naval Institute accomplishes its history projects through contributed funds and gratefully accepts tax-deductible gifts of all sizes for this purpose. This support allows the Institute to preserve the life experiences of today's service men and women so they may enlighten and inspire future generations.

For information about opportunities to underwrite Naval Institute oral history projects, please contact the Naval Institute Foundation at 291 Wood Road, Annapolis, Maryland 21402; by phone at (410) 295-1054; or by e-mail at foundation@usni.org.

Academy Introductory Mission (AIM) Program, 24

Acushnet, 103

admiral, Collins' promotion to, 120, 136–38; and Capstone course, 138; three star promotion, 184

aides to flag officers, desirable qualities in, 263

aids-to navigation (ATON): as Coast Guard responsibility, 80; Collins as Group Commander Long Island Sound and, 109; push to privatize, 99–100

AIM (Academy Introductory Mission) Program, 24

aircraft, and operational presence, increase in, 273. *See also* C-130 aircraft; helicopters

Alaska: lack of good liberty port in, 220; long Coast Guard history in, 281; *Selendang Ayu* wreck and fuel leak, 319–21. *See also* Kodiak, Alaska

Alaska Airlines Flight 261 crash, 192–95, 222, 290

Alex Haley, 319

Allen, Thad: as Chief of Staff, 267; and Coast Guard budget cuts, 125; Collins' work with, 120, 329; as Commandant, 156, 188, 221, 230; Commandant change of command ceremony, 252–53, 328; George W. Bush's respect for, 252–53; as Group Commander Long Island Sound, 106; and Hurricane Katrina response, 252–53, 325, 329; selection as Commandant, 329; and September 11th attacks, 241; time at CPA, 104

Allotment Fund Control Codes (AFC), 84

Alumni Association, Vice Commandant Collins as liaison to, 233

American Samoa, Marine Environmental Protection in, 181

America's Shield, 271

Ames, Fred, 221, 309

AMVER. *See* Automated Mutual Assistance Vessel Rescue System

Antarctica: Collins' visit to, 215; PACAREA operations in, 186, 187; as scientific resource, 215–16

Arctic, PACAREA operations in, 186

Arctic Coast Guard Forum, 211

Arctic energy, as current Coast Guard issue, 305

area commanders, advice for, 224

area of operation (AOR), importance of knowing, 224

Argentina, Collins' visit as Commandant, 300–301

Asaro, Rich, 55

Aspen, 145

Automated Mutual Assistance Vessel Rescue System (AMVER), 176

Auxiliary, Coast Guard: and 14th District, 181–82; and Group Long Island Sound (GLIS), 114–15; and Group St. Petersburg, 87–88

Balanced Budget and Emergency Deficit Control Act of 1985 (Gramm-Rudman-Hollings Act), 103. *See also* budget cuts

Barque Eagle: berth for, at National Coast Guard Museum, 297; Collins' Academy cruises on, 6, 9, 16–17, 18; at Collins' induction as Commandant, 251, 252; domestic *vs.* foreign ports of call, 16–17; improvements to, 17–18, 68; living conditions on, 68; as public relations asset, 17; sister ships, 18; value of cruises on, 17, 68; as war reparation from Germany, 18

Barrett, Ed, 98

Barrett, Thomas, 261–62, 267

Base Realignment and Closure Commission (BRAC): and closing of Barbers Point air station (Hawaii), 165; and DOD cover for base closures, 131; and DOD departure from San Francisco, 204, 208

Basswood, 163, 172, 180

battle dress uniforms, change of, 316

Belz, David S., 162, 189, 208

Bering Sea: concentration of High Endurance Cutters in, 172, 187; fisheries law enforcement in, 158, 188, 199, 213, 224; need for large, sturdy vessels in, 149; as PACAREA jurisdiction, 186; pursuit of Russian cooperation in, 301; stress on crews in, 220

Bertholf, 146

Bertholf, Ellsworth P., 146, 279

Biscayne Bay acquisition, Collins' review of, as Program Analyst, 96

Blackthorn, collision with tanker *Capricorn*, 86–87, 195

Bloomberg, Michael, 297–98

Blore, Gary, 63–64, 104, 112

Bluenose II, 25–26

Bremerton, 198

Bruckenthal, Nathan, 287

budget, Coast Guard: budgeting process, 260; and deferred maintenance, 97, 103; *vs.* DOD budget, 131; in FY2017, 313; ongoing competition for funds, 314; political drivers of, 243; risk-based allocation of resources, 311; and search-and-rescue *vs.* post-9/11 security responsibilities, 276; sequestration and, 134; and ships, age of, 29, 103. *See also* shore facilities

budget cuts: advice on approach to, 132; and aging assets, cost of maintaining, 122, 129, 140, 150, 151, 153, 235, 275; Balanced Budget Act of 1985 and, 100, 103; and base closings, political resistance to, 100, 102–3, 318; Coast Guard Band and, 293; Collins' work to accommodate, 100–102; and consumption of assets, 103, 131–32, 150, 160, 178, 227, 235; and "curse of the can-do," 133; and dual-hatting of commanders, 191–92; flag study groups on, 101; and 14th District asset shortages, 159–60; Gilbert Study on, 101; leadership meetings on, 155; and morale, 139; and mothballing of ships and planes, 126–27, 133–34, 235; persistence through 1980s–90s, 122; preservation of service-delivery assets as priority in, 102–3, 122, 123, 125, 128, 132, 133; and readiness, decline of, 133–34, 178–79, 209, 234, 235, 312; and staff cuts, 118, 126, 147–48, 149, 165; and streamlining efforts, 122, 123; and support services consolidation, 101. *See also* Programs Division, Collins as Chief of, and budget cuts

budget increase after 9/11 attacks, 127, 237, 242, 246–47, 275; as much-needed funds, 246; and need for smart growth, 134, 242–43, 267; and spending on intelligence capabilities, 245; as still inadequate to mission, 275–76

budgeting and planning: and Coast Guard as non-DOD agency, 73–74, 99; and Collins as Chief of Administrative Division, 14th District, 117; and Collins as Deputy Group Commander St. Petersburg, 90; Collins' assignment to, as opportunity, 70, 77; and competition for Department of Transportation funds, 74, 99; defending of budget in budget food chain, 73–74; and Secretary of Transportation, benefits of support from, 74. *See also* Office of Acquisition; Office of Research and Development; Programs Division; Research, Development, Test and Evaluation (RDT&E) appropriation buoy tenders: as multi-function platforms, 100, 172; new, capabilities of, 143, 311; new, Collins' role in development of, 141, 142, 144, 145

Buoy Utility Stern Loading Boat (BUSL), replacement for, 141, 142, 147

Burnley, James H. IV, 111

Burns, Dave, 205

Bush, George W.: at change of command ceremony for departing Commandant Collins, 252–53, 327–28; Coast Guard Academy commencement address (2003), 291; and Coast Guard joining of intelligence community, 245–46; Collins' work with, 290–92; and Department of Homeland Security, creation of, 264, 291–92; and Haiti refugee crisis (2004), 317; and Hurricane Katrina, 325, 327–28; Inaugural Parade (2005), 293–94; and Iraq War combatant commanders' conferences, 287; Philadelphia speech (2003), 290; and post-9/11 security policy, 239; respect for armed forces, 287; respect for Coast Guard, 252–53, 290–91

BUSL. *See* Buoy Utility Stern Loading Boat

C-130 aircraft: and airborne surveillance in 14th District, 170, 171; basing agreement with Guatemala, 212; budget-related maintenance issues, 133–34, 235; and fisheries law enforcement, 210; and Group St. Petersburg facilities, 82; in PACAREA, 182, 187; and search-and-rescue in Southeast Asia tsunami (2004), 321–22; and Super Typhoon Paka response, 178

Canada: and fisheries law enforcement, 171, 210; and Hurricane Katrina, 324; and Maritime Transportation Security Act, 270; and North Pacific Coast Guard Forum, 199

Cao Yu 6025 incident, 171–73, 189

Cape Morgan: Charleston as home port of, 44, 46; described, 36; food and mess staff aboard, 41–42; mission of, 37, 38; retirement of, 54; weaponry, 38; Wilkins as CO of, 33

Cape Morgan, Collins as CO of: apartment in Charleston, 33, 45; and Captain of the Port support, 43; change of command ceremony, 35; change of command process, 35–36, 39; and classified information, 51–52; and connectivity to families, lack of, 41; cooperation with Charleston police, 48; duties, 51–52; and Hurricane Camille, 40–41; interactions with Navy, 43, 46; lessons learned in, 37, 40; logistical support, 42–43; memorable incidents, 48–50; and missions, satisfaction gained from, 53; on-call status, 43; patrol areas, 43; patrols in Florida Straits, 38–39, 43, 52; pay, 53; preparations for command, 34–35; and radio traffic, 44; and responsibility given to young Coast Guard officers, 28; sadness at leaving, 54; SAR work, 38, 39–40, 43–44, 47–50; selection for, 32–34; typical day, 52; and weather forecasts, 44

Cape Morgan crew, 36–37; building of teamwork in, 37–38, 39; Collins' mentoring of, 53; entertainment for, 52–53; experience and knowledge of, 36, 55; size of, 36

Capricorn, collision with *Blackthorn*, 86–87, 195

Capstone course, Collins in, 138

captain, Collins' promotion to, 113

Captain of the Port (COPT): Collins's responsibilities as, while Group Long Island Sound Commander, 104–5, 106, 108, 109, 110–11, 115–16; and post-9/11 security, 269, 271–72; sector reorganization of Coast Guard and, 198, 306; as Security Coordinator, under MTSA, 271–72; and September 11th attacks, 236; value of Collins' familiarity with duties of, 115–16

CARAT. *See* Cooperation Afloat Readiness and Training

Card, Andrew, 98–99, 124, 134, 264, 281, 283–84

Card, Jim, 158, 176–77, 185, 186, 207, 223

career of Collins: and budgeting and planning assignments as opportunity, 70, 77; Collins' approach to, 20, 93, 113, 119, 136–37, 331; Collins' pleasure in, 334; Collins' surprise at success of, 292; and flag rank, Collins' views on possibility of attaining, 113; and grooming as promising officer, 331; importance of Headquarters assignment to, 69, 70; and losses in housing market, 105, 139; luck in getting good assignments, 92–93; path to Commandant's post, components in, 70; principles emphasized in, 183; and Program Analyst position, benefits of, 119–20; promotion to admiral, 120, 136–38; promotion to captain, 113; promotion to commander, 93, 101; promotion to three-star admiral, 184; selection as Commandant, 120

Casto, Roy, 104

Cayetano, Ben, 161, 180

challenges, Collins' love of, 20

Chambers, John, 250

change. *See* innovation

chaplains, Navy, value to Coast Guard, 263–64

Character in Action (Loy and Phillips), 227

Charleston, South Carolina: birth of first child (Christine) in, 34, 45; Coast Guard base in, 46; Collins apartment in, 33, 45; described, 44–45; heavy military presence in, 46–47; Nancy Collins' enjoyment of, 34; sadness at leaving, 54

Charleston police, cooperation with Coast Guard, 48

Chase, 171

chemical, biological, radiological detection and protection capabilities, addition to Coast Guard ships after 9/11, 151, 241

Chertoff, Michael, 290, 325

Chief of Staff CPA: distinguished former staff of, 104; as hard-working group, 104; importance of work done at, 119; leadership of, 103. *See also* Programs Division

childhood of Collins, 1–4; career plans, 5–6, 334; and Coast Guard, early exposure to, 5; jobs, 4, 8; reading, 5; religious training, 4–5; schooling, 2–3, 4; sports and activities, 3–4; summer away from home, 8; wide-ranging experiences of, 4

children of Collins: adult lives of, 333; births of, 33, 45, 64, 66–67; at Collins' induction as Commandant, 252; and frequent moves, 332–33; and life in Hawaii, 118–19; and life in St. Petersburg, 78, 92. *See also* Collins, Christine; Collins, Kate

China: Collins' visits to, 212, 222, 301, 302; delegation to Collins as Commandant, 302–3; development of cooperative relationship with, 200–201, 212, 214, 218, 222; and fisheries law enforcement, 173, 175, 199–200, 210, 212, 302, 303; fragmented maritime responsibilities in, 302; illegal migrants from, 167–68, 199, 218, 222; and North Pacific Coast Guard Forum, 199, 213–14; and port security after 9/11, 301; and ship-rider program, 175, 200, 210, 212, 302

CINCPAC Fleet: and Coast Guard ship in Persian Gulf, 186–87; cooperation with Coast Guard, 161–62, 176, 206; and fisheries law enforcement, 171; and Pacific Maritime Defense Zone, 206

CISCO managerial workshop, 250

Clark, Vern, 237, 246, 294, 317

Clemins, Archie R., 161, 162–63

Coast Guard: appeal of life in, 21; as both law enforcement and military agency, 214, 281–82; Collins' early exposure to, 5; early history of, 146, 279; early opportunities for responsibility in, 28; flexibility and adaptability of, 305, 311; George W. Bush's respect for, 252–53, 290–91; high value relative to cost, 100, 126; international affairs staff, 201, 314; international respect for, 214, 315; as model for other nations, 176, 214–15, 246, 302, 315; move to Department of Homeland Security, 264, 279, 280–85; moves between US departments, 264, 279, 282; moves between US departments, advice for management of, 282–83; as multi-mission force, 100, 196, 311, 328; and political appointees, lack of, 98; ranking as best-run federal agency, 277; three "M"s of (multi-mission, maritime, military), 100. *See also* budget, Coast Guard; personnel, Coast Guard; *other specific topics*

Coast Guard Academy: academic tracks, increase in, 60; and active duty instructors, value of, 13, 55; admission of women, 68–69; admissions criteria, 4, 24; advice for applicants to, 24; cadets, as increasing talented, 23, 63, 256; changes since Collins' cadet years, 60, 68–69; Collins' fondness for, 10–11, 15, 297; Collins' visits to, as Commandant, 23, 63, 67, 256, 297; faculty, composition of, 25, 55; faculty, new, advice for, 63; success as educational institution, 23; and teamwork, development of, 9, 11–12, 17; values instilled at, 22–23

Coast Guard Academy, Collins as cadet at: academic award, 14; academic load, 12; acceptance, 6; arrival, 7; assignment night, 20; barracks life, 11; calls and visits to family, 14; class year of, 9; classmates, 23; comradery with classmates, 11–12, 18, 23; course of study, 13–14; dating of future wife, 14–16; drills and ceremonies, 11; *Eagle* cruises, 6, 9, 16–17, 18, 68; entrance exam and physical, 5–6; faculty, 13; first assignment following, 15; as fourth classman, 12, 15; and future career, difficulty of envisioning, 19–20; graduation, 15, 21; graduation speaker, 20–21; hazing and, 9; isolation from unrest of 1960s, 19; limited engagement with regimental structure or administration, 15; mediocre academic work in first years, 13; as positive experience, 8, 10–11; pre-matriculation preparations, 7; as second classman, 18–19; summer leaves, 14, 15; and teamwork, development of, 9, 11–12, 23; as third classman, 12. *See also* Swab Summer; Zulu Company

Coast Guard Academy, Collins as professor at, 13; academic preparation for, 55, 58; birth of second daughter, 66–67; and cadet cruises, 16, 67–68; challenges of first semester, 58,

62; class preparation, 61–62; courses including women from Connecticut College, 60; courses taught, 56, 60–62; departure, mixed feelings about, 66; effect on career, 67–68; high quality of colleagues, 59; house in New London, 58, 66; multifaceted role of, 59–60; notable students, 63–64; as positive experience, 59, 67; as preparation for real-world political arena, 62; teaching strategies, 61, 62

Coast Guard Activities Far East (FEACT), 163

Coast Guard and Maritime Transportation Act of 2004, 297

Coast Guard Band, Collin's protection from budget cuts, 293

Coast Guard Foundation, 233, 257, 297–98

Coast Guard Headquarters: atmosphere after 9/11, 240–41; and budget cuts, reorganization due to, 101; buildings used for, 155–56; Collins's first assignment at, 70–71; Commandant and flags meetings at, 155; flag officers' offices and amenities, 155; and procurement decisions, 147

Coast Guard missions: changes in, in post-9/11 environment, 265–66; global warming and, 314; justification of, 100; as multiple, 100, 196, 311, 328; post-9/11 appreciation for, 127, 163, 238–39, 241; revalidation of, in Deepwater review process, 142. *See also* drug law enforcement; fisheries law enforcement; Marine Environmental Protection (MEP) duties; port security after 9/11; search-and-rescue (SAR)

Coast Guard organizational structure: as confusing to public, 88; inefficiency of, in Collins' early career, 88–89; systems approach, need for, 89. *See also* sectors, reorganization of commands into

Coast Guard Patrol Forces Southwest Asia (PATFORSWA), 299

Coast Guard Systems Acquisitions Manual (SAM), 142, 144, 145

Coccia, Joe, 113

Coleman, Jimmy, 297

Collins, Christine (daughter): adult life of, 333; birth of, 34, 45; career of, 138–39; in high school, 123. *See also* children of Collins

Collins, Harley (father), 1

Collins, Inger (mother), 1

Collins, Kate (daughter): adult life of, 67, 333; birth of, 64, 66–67; in college, 138; and Collins' application for Commandant's post, 247, 252; in high school, 138, 184. *See also* children of Collins

Collins, Nancy Monahan (wife): advice for Coast Guard spouses, 332; as *Aspen* sponsor, 145; birth of first daughter, 45; birth of second daughter, 66–67; celebration of Collins' promotion to Commandant, 248; and Collins' career, success of, 292; and Collins' promotion to admiral, 136; and Collins' promotion to PACAREA Commander, 184–85; courtship of, 14–16; first meeting of, 8, 15; and frequent moves, 30; and grandchildren, 333; honeymoon, 22; and Iraq War combatant commanders' conferences, 287; life, after retirement, 255; life, with Collins aboard *Cape Morgan*, 34; life, with Collins aboard *Vigilant*, 30, 34; life, with Collins as Academy instructor, 66; life, with Collins as Commandant, 255, 258, 302, 303, 308, 332; life, with Collins as PACAREA Commander, 204, 226; life, with Collins as post-graduate student, 55–56, 58; life, with Collins as Vice Commandant, 227; life, with Collins in Hawaii, 118, 158, 184; life, with Collins in St. Petersburg, 78; parents of, 15, 23; proposal of marriage, 31; at State of the Union Addresses, 292; wedding, 15, 21, 22

Collins, Thomas H.: birth of, 1; grandchildren, 8, 333; grandparents, 5–6, 17; siblings of, 1–2, 3, 4, 5, 8, 21. *See also* career of Collins; childhood of Collins; children of Collins; education of Collins; honors and awards for Collins; parents of Collins; *other specific topics*

Colombia: Collins' visit to, 191; and drug law enforcement, 190–91

Commandant: Executive Assistant of, 228; as flag detailer, 137–38; importance of spouse's role, 332; quarters. move to Bolling AFB, 230–31, 258; as US Interdiction Coordinator (USIC), 296

Commandant, Collins as: accomplishments, 265–66, 305–6, 311; and advice from past Commandants, 257; agenda priorities of, 251, 262, 267, 313–14; application essay on priorities, 247–48, 265; and area commanders, 262, 267; and avoidance of ivory tower problem, 261; and battle dress uniforms, 316; budget responsibilities, 259–60; and change, strategies for creating, 250–51, 255–56; change of command ceremony, 251–52; changes overseen by, 265–66; chauffeured car assigned to, 253; and Chinese delegation visit, 302–3; and Coast Guard benefits, efforts to improve, 220, 309; and Coast Guard move to DHS, 264, 279, 280–85; and Coast Guard Museum location, 297–98;

Commandant Direction of, 267–68, 275; and Commandant website, 277–78; confirmation hearing, 248–49; and congressional hearings, preparations for, 260; and Deepwater program, 266, 305–6, 313; division of labor with Vice Commandant, 262; efficiency of service delivery as goal of, 266; end-of-tour change of command ceremony, 252–53, 327–28, 329–30; and events in Washington DC, 292–93; expansion of graduate education opportunities, 59; and experience gained in career, 135, 239, 248, 249, 260, 287–88; family celebration of promotion, 248; final push to complete agenda, 263; flag conferences, 262–63; and global monitoring system for shipping, development of, 269–70; growth of Coast Guard under, 275; and Haiti refugee crisis (2004), 317; and High Endurance Cutter maintenance issues, 312; and Hurricane Katrina, 252–53, 255, 278–79, 322–28; and Hurricane Rita, 255; and icebreaker, efforts to fund, 313–14; and importance of listening, 257; and intelligence capacity, development of, 306; interaction with Marine Corps, 294–95; and international partnerships, 266, 314–15; and international visits, protocol for, 201; and Iraq War, Coast Guard participation in, 237, 266, 285–89; issues faced by, 250; and joint ratings review, 220, 309; and lack of work/life separation, 254–55; leadership style, 255, 257; living quarters, 248, 257–58; and Maritime Transportation Security Act, 266, 268–69, 270, 271; and Master Chief Petty Officer selection, 261; and Mineta as Transportation Secretary, 249–50; Mineta's guidance for, 264, 265, 268; and modernization program, justification of, 266; more-efficient field structure as goal, 251; and naming of Coast Guard ships, 146; and National Fleet concept, 233–34, 294; and national maritime security strategy, 270–71, 272; and nations' senior leaders, work with, 289–92; off-duty activities, 255; as operational commander, 278–79; and port security after 9/11, 238, 242, 265–66, 268–73; and post-9/11 changes in Coast Guard, 265–67; preferences for presentations by subordinates, 261; and pride in Coast Guard, 321; principles emphasized in, 183, 220, 267–68; private jet available to, 253, 303–4, 308; projects inherited from predecessor, 251; and quality of life issues for Coast Guard personnel, 220; readiness as key focus of, 183, 220, 266, 267; reluctance to apply for post, 247–48; Rescue 21 program, 266, 273–74, 316–17; and Reserve callups, 266; and retention efforts, 221; and second tour, thoughts on, 328; and sector-based reorganization of Coast Guard, 266, 273, 274, 306–7; security detail for, 253–54; and selection boards, 259; selection for post, 239, 247–48, 265; and Special

Missions Training Center, creation of, 294–95; speeches as, 254, 258–59, 278; staff of, 254, 259, 261; and staff excellence, 266–67; and staff performance metrics, 271; and State of the Union Addresses, 292; and terrorist attacks, lack of, 330; and training and qualification reform, 310; travel overseas, 253, 297–98, 300–304, 308; typical day schedule, 254; and US Interdiction Coordinator role, 296–97; and US Northern Command, 295–96; and Vice Commandants, selection of, 261–62; visits to Coast Guard Academy, 23, 63, 67, 256, 297; visits to Coast Guard personnel (all-hands sessions), 308–9; work-related entertaining, 257–58

commander, Collins' promotion to, 93, 101

commanding officers, new: Collins' advice for, 53–54; lack of school for, in Collins' early career, 34

commercial off-the-shelf (COTS) purchasing, Collins' support for, as Chief of Office of Acquisition, 140, 141, 142, 143, 144, 156

Constellation Carrier Battle Group, deployment of Coast Guard ship with, 186–87, 216–17

Cooperation Afloat Readiness and Training (CARAT), 206

Costello, John D., 70, 233

COTP. *See* Captain of the Port

CPA. *See* Chief of Staff CPA

Crawford, Dave, 86

Crea, Vivien, 267, 278

crisis management: advice for, 239; Collins' development of procedures for, in 14th District and PACAREA, 197; Collins' interest in, 87; and information, demands for, 195; training for, through experience, 195

Cross, Terry, 98, 261–62, 267

culture of Coast Guard, Collins' efforts to preserve, 134, 162, 242, 247–48, 265

cutters, naming of, 146

Cyber security, as current Coast Guard issue, 305

Dallas, 212

Danmark, 18

David R. Ray, 198

Deck Watch Officer Guide, 34

Deepwater Major Systems Acquisition: assets targeted for replacement in, 142, 149; awarding of contract, 151, 232; budget constraints on, 151–52, 153, 232, 313; Collins' long engagement with, 143; Collins' work on, 142, 147–52, 156, 227, 231–33, 266, 305–6, 313; cost-effective procurement process in, 143, 148; design phase of, 148; and HH-65 helicopters, replacement of engines in, 312; increased funding after 9/11, 243; lengthy approval process for, 142, 148; long timeframe of, 150, 153, 313; maintenance costs of old systems as drag on, 152, 153; and management of aging systems, 313; and maritime domain awareness, 189, 273, 305; as most complex Coast Guard project ever, 156; naming of, 149, 231; and National Fleet concept, 233–34; need for asset modernization, 149–50; and 123-foot patrol boat project, 148, 151–52; operational requirements for, 232–33; performance-based contracting in, 231–32; and post-9/11 ship design changes, 151–52, 241; project management issues in, 148; and staff cuts, effect of, 147–48, 149; system of systems approach to, 148, 231–32; and systems integration, as issue, 232; types of assets included in, 232–33; unfinished projects in, 314; unforeseen cost increases in, 152; use of commercial systems integrator, 148, 232

Defense, Department of (DOD): BRAC and, 131, 165, 204, 208; budgets *vs.* Coast Guard, 131; cooperation with Coast Guard, 206, 306, 321–22; and drug law enforcement, 296; and Hurricane Katrina response, 325, 326, 327; impressive capabilities of, 288; increased cooperation with, after 9/11, 237; value in disaster response, 327

defense in depth, in port security after 9/11, 271

detailers. *See* Office of Personnel detailers

DHS. *See* Homeland Security, Department of

Dickey, Bruce, 106

Dimmick, Ray, 15

Dimon, Jamie, 250–51

district commanders, new, advice for, 183

district staff reductions, in budget cuts of 1980s–90s, 123–24

DOD. *See* Defense, Department of

Dole, Elizabeth, 98

Donnell, William C., 118, 158

Donohoe, Kathleen, 121

Douglas Munro Coast Guard Headquarters Building, 156

Downey, Mort, 142

drift nets: destructiveness of, 159; fisheries law enforcement and, 159, 171–73, 175, 199–200, 210; as UN-banned fishing method, 159, 171, 199

drug law enforcement: and armed Coast Guard helicopters, 173–74, 219, 304; and Collins as PACAREA Commander, 171, 189–91; DOD and, 296; Group St. Petersburg's role in, 83, 85–86, 87; intelligence as tool for efficient use of assets in, 189–91; international partnerships and, 212; Navy and, 189, 296; volume of drugs seized, 310

drug law enforcement, and go-fast boats: armed Coast Guard helicopters as tool against, 173–74, 304; targeting of refueling ships for, 190–91, 218–19

Duca, Steve, 94, 103

Duncan, Bob, 278, 324

East Asia: Collins' course on, at Coast Guard Academy, 60–61; in 14th District AOR, 159. *See also individual nations*

Eberhart, Ed., 295

Ebersole, John, 35, 47

e-Coast Guard, Collins' work to create, 256, 277

education of Collins: career plans, 5–6; primary and secondary, 2–3, 4; religious training, 4–5; University of New Haven MBA, 64. *See also* Coast Guard Academy, Collins as cadet at; Weslayan University, Collins' post-graduate work at

EEZ. *See* Exclusive Economic Zones

efficiency of service delivery: as Collins' goal as commandant, 266; as Collins' goal as PACAREA Commander, 202, 209, 223, 224; as Collins' goal in 14th District, 160, 162, 169, 170, 174, 178; as goal of reorganizing commands into sectors, 266, 274, 306; and increased MDA through technology, 170, 176, 179, 310–11; and Innovation Councils, introduction of, 255–56; intelligence as tool for, 162, 168, 171, 189–91, 199, 210, 218–19, 223; introduction of computer-based systems and, 256, 277, 316

Electronics Technician School, Collins' review of, as Program Analyst, 97

ELINT, in fisheries law enforcement, 311

embassies, US, and international visits, 201, 221

England, Gordon, 237, 317

ensign, Collins as. *See Vigilant*, Collins aboard

ensigns: advice for, 32; Swab Summer duty by, 32

environmental law enforcement. *See* Marine Environmental Protection (MEP) duties

ESSO Christina, 25

ethics rules, on acceptance of gifts, 92

Evans, Ray, 164

Exclusive Economic Zones (EEZ), enforcement of, in 14th District (Hawaii), 159, 169–70

Falkenrath, Richard, 264, 280

Fallon, Fox, 294

Fast Response Cutter, delays in purchase of, 152

FBI, Collins' work with, as 14th District (Hawaii) commander, 167

FEACT. *See* Coast Guard Activities Far East

Field Intelligence Support Teams (FIST), 273, 306

Fiona, explosion aboard, 110–11

Fiorina, Carly, 250

fisheries law enforcement: aboard *Vigilant*, 26–27; as Coast Guard mission, 24–25; and Collins as Commander of 14th District, 171, 177; and Collins as Group Commander Long Island Sound, 109; and Collins as PACAREA Commander, 171, 224; cooperation with China on, 173, 175, 199–200, 210, 212, 302, 303; cooperation with Russia on, 199, 213; and EEZ enforcement, 159; in 14th District (Hawaii), 159, 169–70; illegal drift nets and, 159, 171–73, 175, 199–200, 210; international partnerships and, 210; results in, as morale booster, 173–74; and Vessel Monitoring System (VMS), 169–70

FIST. *See* Field Intelligence Support Teams

flag officer(s): Collins on selection criteria for, 259; Collins' promotion to, 120, 136–38; evaluations of, Collins as Vice Commandant and, 259

Fleet Logistics System (FLS), development of, 141–42

Fleet Renovation and Modernization (FRAM) program, 150

Florida Marine Patrol, cooperation between Coast Guard and, 85

FLS. *See* Fleet Logistics System

14th District: area of responsibility of, 159; commander prior to Collins, 158

14th District, Collins as Administrative Division Chief of: benefits of, 119; and difficulty selling house in Connecticut, 116–17; emphasis on change, 117; housing shortage, alleviation of, 117, 121; off-duty activities, 118; and planning and budgeting reform, 121; quarters at Wailupe, 117, 121; staff, high quality of, 121; staff cutbacks and, 118; and Total Quality Management, 118, 121; travel to Hawaii, 117; work with Navy, 119

14th District, Collins as Commander of: and aid to Pacific Islanders, 322; and airborne surveillance, 169–70, 171–72; appointment to, 157–58; and Barbers Point air station, closing of, 165; challenges faced by, 180–81; and Chinese illegal migrants, 167–68, 199; and Coast Guard Ball, establishment of, 162–63; communication of vision for district, 183; and crisis management procedures, 197; and Deepwater program, 158; efficient use of limited assets as goal, 160, 162, 169, 170, 174, 178; as enjoyable job, 184; entertaining of military visitors, 176–77; experience gained in, 184; facilities improvements under, 164; and FBI, collaboration with, 167–68; fisheries law enforcement, 159, 169–70, 171–73, 177; and fishing industry, relations with, 177; focus on readiness, 158, 178, 179; and foreign visitors from region, 176; good relations with Hawaiian officials, 161, 165, 166, 167, 180; headquarters offices, 164; independence, 158; and intelligence as tool for efficient deployment of assets, 162, 168, 199; and intelligence assets, development of, 162, 168, 171; interaction with PACAREA Commander, 158–59; and interservice contacts, development of, 160–61; and Korean Air Flight 801 recovery efforts, 178; late-night crises, 180; leadership style of, 165–66; and legal advisers, importance of, 197; living quarters on Diamond Head Road, 158, 176–77; and Marine Environmental Protection duties, 180–81; and maritime domain awareness, 199; and MDZ responsibilities, 168, 182; objectives of, 178–80; and Omega Station (Haiku Valley), closing of, 166–67; and Pacific, importance to Coast Guard's future, 184; and partnerships, value of, 173, 179; partnerships with Hawaii National Guard, 168; partnerships with local agencies, 166, 168, 180; partnerships with Pacific countries, 174–76; partnerships with US military, 161–63, 174–76; and pleasures of living in Hawaii, 176–77; and previous experience in 14th District, 119, 157–58, 169; and Reserve and Auxiliary roles, 181–82; and Sand Island Base, local efforts to close, 165–66; search-

and-rescue efforts, 180; shortage of assets to cover AOR, 158, 159–60, 165, 168; staff cuts and, 165; staff excellence, 170; staff size, 159, 165; stations and assets, 163–65; and strategic assessments, introduction of, 168–69; and strategic view of AOR, 168–69, 179; and Super Typhoon Paka on Guam, 178; support of Coast Guard objectives as goal, 179–80; technology to increase Coast Guard effectiveness, 170, 176, 179; and TQM principles, 169; and value of previous experiences, 182, 183; work with Allen, 120

Foye, Paul, 13, 23

FRAM. *See* Fleet Renovation and Modernization (FRAM) program

Future Force 21, 221

Future View 2010, 169

G-A. *See* Office of Acquisition

Gallatin, 173–74

Garrett, Jeff, 104

George Washington, 43

Gilbert, Ed, 65, 79, 86, 87, 101, 195

Gilbert, Marshall E., 112

Gilbert Study, 101

global warming, and Coast Guard mission, 314

golden rule, as value learned from family, 1

Gore, Al, 144

Government Executive magazine ranking of Coast Guard management, 277

Governor's Island, Coast Guard move from, in budget cuts of 1980s–90s, 124, 128

Gracey, Jim: and budget process regularization, 98, 292; career of, 119–20; as Chief of Program Division, 131; as Chief of Staff, 70, 104; and Coast Guard budget cuts, 100; as Commandant, 79, 93–94, 99, 103, 255, 257; CPA experience, 103–4; innovative thinking of, 104; oral history of, 99, 284; and RCP process, 73

graduate education: Coast Guard as leader in, 59; Collins as advocate for, 58–59; Collins' University of New Haven MBA, 64. *See also* Weslayan University, Collins' post-graduate work at

Gramm-Rudman-Hollings Act. *See* Balanced Budget and Emergency Deficit Control Act of 1985

grandchildren of Collins, 8, 333

grandparents of Collins, 5–6, 17

Greece, Collins' visit to, as Commandant, 299

Greenpeace, and *Pennsylvania* commissioning, 108–9

Griebel, Phil, 27, 31, 50

grooming of promising officers, Collins on, 331

Group Long Island Sound (GLIS): area of responsibility, 106–7; Commander of, as sought-after position, 104–5, 106; commanders before and after Collins, 106; and fisheries law enforcement, 109; headquarters of, 105; heavy commercial traffic in, 107, 109, 114; large civilian boating population in, 107, 114; lighthouses in, 107; stations and assets, 107

Group Long Island Sound (GLIS), Collins as Commander of: and ATON responsibilities, 109; Captain of the Port functions, 104–5, 106, 108, 109, 110–11, 115–16; change of command ceremony, 106; Coast Guard leadership during, 111–12; Earth Day event, former students at, 65; experience gained in, 182; and *Fiona*, explosion aboard, 110–11; house in Westbrook, Connecticut, 105, 116–17; and inbox management, 114; as interesting and educational job, 115–16; Marine Environmental Protection (MEP) duties, 109, 115; Maritime Defense Zone Commander function, 105, 107–8; and overlapping jurisdictions, 109; and *Pennsylvania* commissioning, 108–9; preparation for, 110; and Reserves and Auxiliary role, 114–15; responsibilities, 105, 113; and return to Connecticut, 104, 105; and Sailfest event, 113; and SAR duties, 109, 110; and submarine escorts, 108; supervisory style, 113; 24/7 on-call status, 115

Group St. Petersburg: area of responsibility (AOR), 79; and *Blackthorn-Capricorn* collision, 86–87, 195; Collins' visits in later career, 91; cooperation with Florida Marine Patrol, 85; headquarters facilities in St. Petersburg, 82; maintenance-assist team (MAT) support building, acquisition of, 83–84; missions of, 80; and Reserve and Auxiliary support, 87–88; stations and assets in, 79–80, 82–83

Group St. Petersburg, Collins as Deputy Commander: appointment to position, 78; average day, 90; Coast Guard leadership during, 78–79; and complimentary membership to St. Petersburg Yacht Club, 92; and disaster planning, 85; and district inspections, 80–81; and drug law enforcement, 85–86, 87; experience gained in, 86, 182; facilities improvement efforts, 82–85; focus on safety and readiness, 80; and Group leadership, 79, 90; and hurricane/tropical storm planning, 78–79; Mariel boatlift and, 78–79; and move away from extended family, 78; off-duty activities with family, 92; and on-base drug use, 87; and operational casualties, lack of, 91; and responsibilities as CO of Station St. Petersburg, 78, 81, 90; responsibilities of, 80, 90–91; as rewarding position, 92–93; staff under, 80

Group St. Petersburg facilities improvements: after Collins' departure, 91; Collins' work on, 82–85; funding of, 84; preservation of wardroom Coast Guard mural, 91–92; self-help projects in, 84–85

Guam, and Super Typhoon Paka, 178

Guatemala, US partnerships with, 212

Guyana, Collins' arrangement of LE agreement with, 299–300

Hagee, Mike, 294

Haiti refugee crisis (2004), 317

Hamilton, Fred, 94, 101–2, 111–12

Hammer Award, 103, 144

Hathaway, Jeff, 236

Hawaii: high concentration of military in, 160–61; Honolulu Coast Guard station, 164; Omega Station (Haiku Valley), closing of, 166–67; pet quarantine laws, as hardship for military families, 177. *See also* 14th District

Hawaiian National Guard, 168

Hayes, John B., 70, 79

Healy: acquisition of, 153–54; and Arctic research, 186; Collins' review of acquisition, as Program Analyst, 96

Healy, Michael A. "Hell Roaring Mike," 153

Hebert, John, 36, 37, 41–42

HECs. *See* High Endurance Cutters

Helicopter Interdiction Tactical Squadron (HITRON), 304

helicopters: crews, training of, 320; in Hurricane Katrina response, 323. *See also* HH-60 helicopters; HH-65 helicopters

helicopters, armed: controversy surrounding, 219, 304; as correct course, 304; drug law enforcement and, 173–74, 219, 304; and MSST support, 304; and port security after 9/11, 304; as transformational change, 305

Henn, Gene, 139

Herr, Richard D. "Dick": career of, 104; and Coast Guard budget cuts, 123, 125; as Collins mentor and friend, 66, 94; as Vice Commandant, 139; visit to Collins in 14th District, 176–77

Hessler, Tom, 52

HH-60 helicopters: arming of, 304; Collins' review of acquisition, as Program Analyst, 96; Navy-Coast Guard collaboration in acquisition of, 154; rescue operation accident involving, 319–21

HH-65 helicopters: arming of, 304; budget-related maintenance issues, 235; Collins' review of acquisition, as Program Analyst, 96; in Persian Gulf, 186–87, 217; replacement of engines, 217, 312; in rescue operation, 319; under-powered engine in, 96–97, 187, 217, 312

High Endurance Cutters (HECs): alcohol abuse by crews of, 203–4; Fleet Renovation and Modernization (FRAM) program for, 150; maintenance issues in, 312; in PACAREA, 187; shortages of, in 14th District, 158

HITRON. *See* Helicopter Interdiction Tactical Squadron

Hollings, Fritz, 248

Homeland Presidential Directive 14, 196

Homeland Security, Department of (DHS): and Coast Guard search-and-rescue function, 276; creation of, 264; culture shock in agencies transferred to, 281; headquarters facilities for, 156; move of Coast Guard to, 264, 279, 280–85

Homeland Security Council (White House), 264, 279–80

Homeland Security Presidential Directive 13 (HSPD 13), 238

honesty, as value learned from family, 1

Hong Kong: airport in, 175; annual international SAR exercise in, 174–75, 211; relationship with US Coast Guard, 174–75

Honorè, Russel, 325

honors and awards for Collins: academic award from Coast Guard Academy, 14; Hammer Award, 144; Legion of Merit award, 136; president of class in high school, 2; Stoughton High School Hall of Fame, 2

Hull, Jimmy, 267

Hurricane Camille, Collins' experiences in, 40–41

Hurricane Katrina: Allen as federal official in charge of response to, 252–53, 325, 329; Coast Guard personnel's exceptional efforts in, 325–26; Coast Guard response to, 322–28; and Collins as Commandant, 252–53, 278–79; coordination of Coast Guard local efforts, 278–79; early issues in coordination of aid, 325, 326–27; and environmental protection duties, 324; vandalism of Coast Guard facilities in, 326

Hurricane Rita, Coast Guard response in, 326, 327

hurricanes: Coast Guard planning for, 78–79, 81–82, 328; damage to National Security Cutter shipyard, 152

IC. *See* Intelligence Community

icebreakers: in Antarctic, 186, 215; budget-related delays in acquiring, 150; high cost of, 313–14; new, plans for, 313–14; new buoy tenders' function as, 143, 311; in PACAREA command, 187

ICS. *See* Incident Command System

IMO. *See* International Maritime Organization

Incident Command System (ICS), 197–98

Industrial College of the Armed Forces (ICAF), Collins' decline of tour at, 116, 119

innovation: advice for winning approval for, 112–13; Collins' emphasis on, as 14th District Administrative Division Chief, 117; Collins' emphasis on, as Vice Commandant, 255–56; Collins' strategies for creating, 250–51, 255–56

Innovation Councils, Collins' establishment of, 256

Innovation Expo, Collins' introduction of, 256

Inouye, Daniel, 128, 146–47, 165, 166, 180, 249

integrity, as value learned from family, 1

Intel Coordination Center, 272

intelligence: Coast Guard improvements in, 162, 306; Collins' development of, in 14th District, 162, 168, 171; Collins' emphasis on, as Commandant, 306; increased spending on, after 9/11, 245; and terrorist threat, 330; as tool for efficient service delivery, 162, 168, 171, 189–91, 199, 210, 218–19, 223. *See also* maritime domain awareness (MDA)

Intelligence Authorization Act of 2000, 245–46

Intelligence Community (IC), Coast Guard joining of, 171, 245–46, 271, 306

Interagency Task Force on US Coast Guard Roles and Missions, 142, 232–33

international incidents: development of protocols for, 50. *See also* Simas Kudirka incident

International Maritime Organization (IMO): Collins efforts to shore up international support for, 300–301; and port security after 9/11, 238, 240, 269–70; and respect for US Coast Guard, 214, 315; Singapore support for US Coast Guard in, 174

international partnerships. *See* partnerships, international

International Sea Power Symposium (ISS), 246

International Ship and Port Security Code (ISPS Code), 240, 269–70, 271, 299

international visits, protocol for, 201, 221

internet: Collins' efforts to increase Coast Guard use of, 256, 277–78; and e-Coast Guard, Collins' work to create, 256, 277

internet connectivity aboard cutters: Collins' introduction of, 201–2, 256; as quality of life improvements for personnel, 220

Iraq War (Iraqi Freedom): Coast Guard as niche player in, 286; Coast Guard casualties in, 287; and Coast Guard involvement in combatant commanders' conferences, 287; Coast Guard participation in, 237, 266, 285–89; Coast Guard planning for, 285–86, 287; Coast Guard protection of supply ships, 288–89; Coast Guard Reserves and, 288, 289; end game in, as concern, 288

Irwin, Jim, 94

ISPS Code. *See* International Ship and Port Security Code

ISS. *See* International Sea Power Symposium

Jackson, Michael, 247, 249, 284

Japan: Coast Guard staff in, 206; and fisheries law enforcement, 171, 172, 210; and North Pacific Coast Guard Forum, 199, 212, 213–14

Japanese Maritime Safety Agency (JMSA): Coast Guard as model for, 176, 214–15; cooperation with Coast Guard, 176; name change to Japan Coast Guard, 214

Jarvic, 164

JIATF East. *See* Joint Interagency Task Force East

JIATF South. *See* Joint Interagency Task Force South

JIATF West. *See* Joint Interagency Task Force West

JICPAC. *See* Joint Intelligence Center Pacific

Johnson, Harvey, 267

Johnson, Jeb, 282, 313, 314

Joint Chiefs of Staff, Collins' meetings with, as Vice Commandant, 229–30

Joint Intelligence Center Pacific (JICPAC), Coast Guard partnering with, 162, 168, 171, 189

Joint Interagency Task Force East (JIATF East), 162

Joint Interagency Task Force South (JJATF South), 296

Joint Interagency Task Force West (JIATF West): and drug law enforcement, 162, 189, 190, 219; headquarters in San Francisco, 208, 296

joint ratings review, 309–10

Jones, Jim, 294, 295

junior officers, importance of mentoring, 65–66

Key West Command, and Mariel boatlift, 78–79

Kime, Bill: and Coast Guard budget cuts, 123, 125, 126; and DHS creation, 292; as District 7 Commander, 79; style and personality of, 135–36

King, Irv, 59

Kodiak, Alaska, Coast Guard base in: aircraft stationed at, 171, 172, 187, 200; base improvements, 97, 109, 153, 186, 220; as major base, 186

Korean Air Flight 801 recovery efforts, 178

Kramek, Robert E. "Bob": advice to Collins as Commandant, 257; character of, 136; as Chief of staff, 123; and Coast Guard budget cuts, 125, 126, 134, 160; as Commandant, 136, 139, 146, 157, 178; and leadership council, 207; and national maritime security strategy, 276–77

Kudirka, Simas, 26–27, 50–51

Kukui, 146–47

Kuwait, Commandant Collins' visit to, 299

LANTAREA: and Arctic Forum, 199; commanders, Collins' advice for, 224; and Hurricane Katrina, 324; and North Atlantic Coast Guard Forum, 199

lawyers, importance to Coast Guard operations, 197

leadership, Collins on, 182, 183, 202; and accountability for misbehavior of crew, 202–3; at area commander level, 224; and communication of vision, importance of, 183; and listening, importance of, 165, 202, 257

leadership council, 207–8

Lee, Dean, 80

Letterer, Cindy, 254

Liotta, Joe, 130

Lockheed Martin, and Deepwater project, 148, 232

Long Island Lighting Company, and *Fiona*, explosion aboard, 110–11

Loy, Jim: and arming of helicopters, 173, 304; book on leadership by, 227; on budget cuts, 126, 133–34, 160, 178–79, 209, 234, 235; character and background, 227–28; and Coast Guard relations with Department of Homeland Security, 280; as Commandant, 157, 160, 184, 185, 227, 234, 277, 303, 317; and DHS creation, 292; focus on readiness, 227, 234; and Future Force 21 program, 221; and leadership council, 207; and National Coast Guard Museum, 297; and national maritime security strategy, 276–77; and North Pacific Coast Guard Forum, 200; and port security after 9/11, 317; selection of Collins as Vice Commandant, 224–25; selection of Collins for PACAREA command, 185; and September 11th attacks, 236, 237, 238, 239; at TSA, 226, 253, 264; on unique role of Coast Guard, 214; as Vice Commandant, 185

Lum, Maxine, 121

Lusk, Clyde, 94, 111

Lyons, Dave, 106

Maintenance and Logistics Commands (MLCs), 123–24; lack of, in Collins' early career, 42

Manning, Al, 70

MARDEZPAC. *See* Maritime Defense Zone Pacific

Mariel boatlift, 78–79

Marine Corps: Collins' interaction with as Commandant, 294–95; and Cooperation Afloat Readiness and Training, 206; and development of Coast Guard doctrine on armed helicopters, 295

Marine Environmental Protection (MEP) duties: Collins as Commander of 14th District and, 180–81; Collins as Commander of PACAREA and, 196–99, 222–23; Collins as Group Commander Long Island Sound and, 109, 115; in Hurricane Katrina, 324; maritime domain awareness and, 196; Navy cooperation in, 198; need for Coast Guard expertise in pollution response, 75; and *New Carissa* oil spill, 197–98, 222; oil fingerprinting and, 75, 109; procedures for addressing, 197–98; value of partnerships in, 196

Marine Information for Safety and Law Enforcement (MISLE) database system, 141

Marine Safety Offices (MSOs): and confusing structure of Coast Guard, 88–89; merging of, in sector reorganization, 274

Marinette Marine, 143, 145

Maritime Defense Zone Pacific (MARDEZPAC), Navy and Coast Guard cooperation in, 161–62

Maritime Defense Zones (MDZs): and Collins as Commander of 14th District, 168; and Collins as GLIS Commander, 105, 107–8; functions of, 161; reservists and, 182

maritime domain awareness (MDA): Coast Guard's joining of Intelligence Community and, 245; components of, 271; Deepwater program and, 189, 273, 305; in 14th District, 199; and intelligence as tool for efficient use of resources, 273, 310–11; Marine Environmental Protection and, 196; as multi-agency effort, 273; in national maritime security strategy, 271; of officers, regarding events aboard ship, 203; in PACAREA, 188–91, 210; and port security after 9/11, 271, 273; and terrorist threat, 330; universal awareness of need for, 245–46; Vessel Traffic Service and, 140–41, 274

Maritime Intelligence Fusion Centers, 306

maritime law enforcement (LE) specialist rating, introduction of, 309–10

Maritime Operational Threat Response Plan, creation of, 196

Maritime Safety and Security Teams (MSSTs): armed Coast Guard helicopters and, 304; and boarding as core Coast Guard capacity, 310; Bush Inauguration and, 273; development of, 273, 318; Iraq War and, 288–89; multi-mission capabilities of, 318; and National Security Significant Events, security for, 319

maritime sector: expectations for September 11th attacks in, 240; high value targets in, 237, 268, 307

maritime sector security: Coast Guard designation as lead federal agency for, 271; Coast Guard's ability to provide, while continuing traditional duties, 310; declining emphasis on, over time, 305, 311; efforts to secure after 9/11, 236–38, 268–69, 307; lack of national structures for, before 9/11, 307–8; speedy implementation of, 308. *See also* port security after 9/11

Maritime Transportation Security Act (MTSA), 240, 266, 268–69, 270, 271, 300–301

Master Chief Petty Officer of the Coast Guard (MCPOCG), 261

Matsudo, Susan, 121

MBA degree of Collins, 64

McGinn, Denny, 192–93

McKinley, Dan, 55

MCPOCG. *See* Master Chief Petty Officer of the Coast Guard

MDA. *See* maritime domain awareness

media contact during crises, training for, through experience, 195

Memorial Day concerts (US Capitol), Collins' attendance at, 292–93

MEP. *See* Marine Environmental Protection (MEP) duties

Mexico, Coast Guard partnership with, 211–12

MH-68A Stingray, 304

Midgett, 186–87, 216–17, 310

Mierzwa, Mike, 170

military, US: Collins' good relationship with, 230; coordination with Coast Guard, in 14th District (Hawaii), 161–63, 176; high concentration in Hawaii, 160–61; service chiefs' cordial relations with Coast Guard, 161, 230. *See also* Defense, Department of (DOD)

Millinger, John, 57

Mineta, Norm: and Coast Guard funding, 283–84; and Coast Guard move to DHS, 283, 285; and Collins as Commandant, 249–50, 264, 265, 268; as Collins' change of command ceremony, 251–52; Collins' frequent dealings with, 290; and Collins' interview for

Commandant, 248; as great Secretary of Transportation, 284; and September 11th attacks, 236; valuing of Coast Guard, 134, 284

MISLE. *See* Marine Information for Safety and Law Enforcement (MISLE) database system

Mobil Gas, Cape Morgan rescue of, 40, 47

motor lifeboats (MLB), and early opportunities for responsibility in Coast Guard, 28

MSO. *See* Marine Safety Offices

MSSTs. *See* Maritime Safety and Security Teams

MTSA. *See* Maritime Transportation Security Act

Mullen, Mike, 234, 294

Munro, Douglas, 164

murder boards, 260

Myers, Richard, 251

National Coast Guard Museum, location of, 297–98

National Coast Guard Museum Association, 297–98

National Distress and Response System, replacement of, 316–17

National Fleet concept: Collins' work on, 233–34, 294; and Iraq War, 286; September 11th attacks and, 294

National Maritime Intelligence Center, 244

national maritime security strategy: Coast Guard experience in strategic planning and, 276–77; development of, 270–71

National Military Command Center, Collins at, as Vice Commandant, 229–30

National Security Cutter (NSC): design, criticisms of, 152; as highly capable ship, 152; hurricane damage during construction of, 152; in PACAREA, 187; post-911 changes to design of, 151–52

National Security Significant Events (NSSE), Coast Guard security role in, 318–19

national strike force, 188

National Vessel Movement Center (NVMC), 245, 271

Naval-Coast Guard Board (NAVGUARD Board), 233–34, 286, 294

Navy, US: and Alaska Airlines Flight 261 crash, 192–93; Collins' work with, as Chief of Administrative Division, 14th District, 119; and Cooperation Afloat Readiness and

Training, 206; and drug law enforcement, 189, 296; and global monitoring of shipping after 9/11, 244; history of coordination with Coast Guard, 163, 193, 206, 279, 296; and Marine Environmental Protection, 198; and National Fleet concept, 233–34, 294; patrol boats loaned to Coast Guard after 9/11, 317; ship building for Coast Guard, 153–54; talk of absorbing Coast Guard into, 147, 279, 282

Navy League, San Francisco, 204

Navy Reserves, and MDZ responsibilities, 161

Nelson, Bob, 123, 125

New Carissa, wreck of, 197–98, 222

New York, move of Coast Guard operations from, in budget cuts of 1980s–90s, 124

Nichols, Bob, 79

North, Bob, 111, 112

North Atlantic Coast Guard Forum, 211

North Pacific Coast Guard Forum (NPCGF), 199–201, 210–14, 301–2, 315; Singapore support for US Coast Guard in, 174

Northern Command (NORTHCOM), Coast Guard and, 295–96

Northrop Grumman, and Deepwater project, 148, 232

notices of arrival and departure (NOADs), in port security after 9/11, 272

NPCGF. *See* North Pacific Coast Guard Forum

Nuclear power plant protection, in Group Long Island Sound, 108

NVMC. *See* National Vessel Movement Center

Obama, Barack, 313

O'Connor, John, 254, 261

Office of Acquisition (G-A), Collins as Chief of: accomplishment, 156; and Acquisitions Manual, rewriting of, 142, 145; budget constraints and, 152–53; and Buoy Utility Stern Loading Boat (BUSL) replacement, 141, 142, 144, 145, 147; Coast Guard leadership during, 139; Collins' background in procurement and, 143; Collins' background in TQM and, 143; Collins' familiarity with Coast Guard programs and, 137, 139; and Collins family continuity in Washington DC, 137; Collins' leadership approach in, 154; and commercial off-the-shelf (COTS) purchasing, 140, 141, 142, 143, 144, 156; and contractor protests of contract awards, 156–57; critical issues to be addressed, 139–40; and Deepwater program, 142, 147–52, 156; and Fleet Logistics System development, 141–42; and IT system reforms, 154–55; and life-cycle costs, focus on, 140, 142, 143; and morale, 154; office and office staff, 155; as opportunity to have impact, 144; and performance-based contracting, 140, 141, 156; and port security, 140–41; prioritization of projects, 147; and procurement coordination with Navy, 153–54; and procurement reforms, 140, 142, 143, 144–45, 156; and quality action teams, 144, 147, 179; as satisfying assignment, 146; and staff, excellence of, 143–44; and staff cuts, effects of, 147–48, 149; staff size, 147, 153

Office of Defense Readiness, 286

Office of Management and Budget (OMB): Circular A-76 on privatization, 99; and Coast Guard budgeting process, 259–60; continuity of staff across administrations, 133; and Deepwater program, 148, 231; and Program Division budget review, 95, 99, 129; RDT&E budget review by, 72–74; requirements for acquisition programs to have mission analysis (A109 circular), 232–33

Office of Naval Research, work with Coast Guard, 75–76

Office of Personnel detailers: knowledge of personnel and positions, 33–34, 36; as source of information on units, 53; talent of, 55, 78, 119, 130, 331–32

Office of Research and Development: budget process in, 72–73; staff of, 71

Office of Research and Development, Collins in: average day schedule, 70–71; carpool from Fairfax, Virginia, 69, 76, 77; Coast Guard leadership during, 70; effort to standardize procedures, 72, 73; as first staff job at headquarters, 70; as good position for learning about Coast Guard operations, 71, 72, 77; house in Fairfax, Virginia, 69, 76; importance to career path, 69, 70, 72, 93; and IT system improvements, 74; and life in Washington, DC, 76–77; mentors, 65–66; notable projects, 75; selection for, 69, 70–71; work with Naval Research Office, 75–76

Officer Candidate School, co-location with Academy, 23, 69

officer in charge of marine inspections (OCMI), in New York and Connecticut, 109

Offshore Patrol Cutter (OPC), funding for, 313, 314

oil fingerprinting, 75, 109

Omega Station (Haiku, Hawaii), closing of, 166–67

123-foot patrol boat: design problems in, 148; as stop-gap measure, 151–52

O'Neill, Jerry, 22

OPC. *See* Offshore Patrol Cutter

operational assignments, rotation between non-operational assignments and, 93

Operations System Center, IT upgrades for, 141

P-3 Orion aircraft, and surveillance in 14th District, 172

PACAREA: area of responsibility, 186, 188; commanders before and after Collins, 158, 185, 223, 225; districts included in, 186; headquarters of, 186, 208; and housing costs in San Francisco, 208–9; restructuring of, under Allen, 188

PACAREA, Collins as Commander of: accomplishments, 222–24; and Alaska Airlines Flight 261 crash, 192–95, 222, 290; and alcohol abuse, efforts to address, 202, 203; assets available to, 186, 187–88; challenges faced by, 188; Coast Guard leadership during, 185–86; and Commandant and Vice Commandant, interaction with, 207–8; and communication across time zones, 201; and cooperation across US agencies, 196, 206, 222; and District Commanders, relationship with, 207; and drug law enforcement, 171, 189–91, 218–19; efficient use of resources as goal, 202, 209, 223, 224; as enjoyable and rewarding assignment, 204, 205, 225; and fisheries law enforcement, 159, 171; and flag conferences, 201, 207; and flag evaluations, 259; and housing improvements, 220; and illegal Chinese migrants, 167–68, 199, 218, 222; and intelligence as tool for efficient deployment of assets, 171, 189–91, 210, 218–19, 223; intelligence assets available to, 162; and international partnerships, value of, 209–13, 224; and international visits, protocol for, 201; and internet connectivity aboard cutters, 201–2; JIATF West and, 296; and *Kukui* commissioning, 146–47; and leadership council, 207–8; leadership style in, 202, 255; and Marine Environmental Protection duties, 196–99. 222–223; and maritime domain awareness, 188–91, 210; and MDZ responsibilities, 161, 205–6; and nations' senior leaders, work with, 290; and *New Carissa* oil spill, 197–98, 222; and North Pacific Coast Guard Forum, 199–201, 210; notification of appointment to, 184–85; number of personnel, 188; and professional development, emphasis on, 202; and promotion to three-star admiral, 184; and quality-of-life improvements for personnel, 220; and quarters on Yerba Buena Island, 184, 208; and responsibilities as 11th District Commander, 186,

191–92; and retention, focus on, 221; search-and-rescue duties, 192–95; and sector organizational structure, 274; and sexual harassment problems, 202–3; shortage of assets to cover AOR, 171; and staff, excellence of, 204–5; and strategic assessment and planning, introduction of, 169, 188–89, 202, 209, 218, 222–24; and technology to increase Coast Guard effectiveness, 188–89, 210; and value of experience gained in past commands, 184, 185; and Y2K preparations, 216

Pace, Peter, 253

Pacific Islanders, love for Coast Guard, 322

Pacific Maritime Defense Zone, Collins as Commander of, 205–6

PACOM, Coast Guard cooperation with, 206

Papp, Bob, 155, 297

parents of Collins, 1; and arrival at Academy, 7; car purchased for Collins' use, 14; at Collins' Academy graduation, 21; Collins' calls and visits while at Academy, 14; deaths of, 252; pride in Collins' acceptance to Coast Guard Academy, 6; values learned from, 1, 20

Parker, John, 208

partnerships, international: annual SAR exercise in Hong Kong, 174–75, 211; CARAT program and, 206; and Coast Guard as less threatening than DOD military, 214; Collins as Commandant and, 266, 314–15; Collins as Commander of 14th District and, 174–76; and development of trust, 200–201, 212, 214; and fisheries law enforcement, 173, 175, 199–200, 210, 212, 213, 302, 303; with Guatemala, 212; and Hurricane Katrina, 324; management of, 314–15; with Mexico, 211–12; North Pacific Coast Guard Forum and, 174, 199–201, 210–11, 212–14; and port security after 9/11, 269–70, 305; for search-and-rescue, 175, 176, 199; value of, 209–13

patrol boats, new, capabilities of, 54

Pekoske, Dave, 104, 106, 125

Peña, Federico, 124–25

Pentagon, September 11th terrorist attack on, 236

performance-based contracting: in Deepwater Major Systems Acquisition, 231–32; in Office of Acquisition under Collins, 140, 141, 156

Perreault, George, 55

Perry, Ellis, 70

Persian Gulf, Coast Guard ship with *Constellation* CBG in, 186–87, 216–17

personnel, Coast Guard: and attractiveness of Coast Guard mission, 220–21; and budget cuts, adjustments required by, 125–26; Coast Guard investment in education of, 59; Collins' high regard for, 315; Collins' insistence on professional development planning for, 182–83, 202; concern for, as hallmark of good leadership, 182, 183; as focus under Collins as Commandant, 183, 220, 268, 309; frequent moves, Collins' advice on, 332–33; high skill levels of, 84–85; improving workplace for, 316; interest in Coast Guard heroes, 164–65; and joint ratings review, 309–10; and morale during budget cuts, 139; as multi-mission trained, 100, 311; pay and benefits *vs.* DOD, Collins' efforts to improve, 220, 309; results as best morale booster for, 173–74, 190–91

Phillips, Don, 227

plane crashes. *See* Alaska Airlines Flight 261 crash; Korean Air Flight 801 recovery efforts; TWA Flight 800 crash

Platt, Bob, 65, 71

Polar Star, 186, 215

pollution. *See* Marine Environmental Protection (MEP) duties

port security after 9/11: and America's Shield, 271; armed Coast Guard helicopters and, 304; under Collins as Commandant, 238, 242, 265–66, 268–73; and defense in depth, 271; delays in implementation of, 271–72; and field intelligence support teams, 273; and global monitoring system for shipping, development of, 244–45, 269–70, 272–73; graduated response to suspicions vessels, 244, 272–73; IMO and, 238; increase in, 240; increased Coast Guard budgets and, 237; increased small boat forces and, 316; initial efforts to secure, 236–38; and inspections of foreign ports, 238, 300–301; and intelligence as tool for efficient use of resources, 244, 273; International Maritime Organization and, 238, 240, 269–70; international partnerships and, 269–70, 305; International Ship and Port Security Code and, 240, 269–70; Iraq War and, 288–89; Maritime Defense Zones and, 161; maritime domain awareness and, 271, 273; and Maritime Safety and Security Teams, 273; Maritime Transportation Security Act and, 240, 266, 268–69; measures to improve, 238; and national maritime security strategy, 270–71; Navy patrol boats loaned to Coast Guard, 317; and operational presence, increase in, 273–74; and Pacific Maritime Defense Zone, 206; risk assessment and security planning in, 244; and sectors, reorganization of commands into, 273, 274–75; Vessel Traffic Service and, 140–41, 274

Port Security Units (PSUs), 206; Iraq War and, 288

post-9/11 environment: atmosphere at Coast Guard Headquarters, 240–41; and Coast Guard mission, changes in, 265–66; and Coast Guard mission, increased appreciation of, 127, 163, 238–39, 241; declining urgency over time, 239; and Deepwater design changes, 151–52, 241; development of necessary authorities and capabilities for, 243; efforts to secure maritime sector, 236–38; and intelligence gathering, emphasis on, 171; and National Security Cutter, changes to design of, 151–52; and national security plan development, 238; and National Security Significant Events security, 318–19; and national strike force, creation of, 188; and Navy-Coast Guard coordination, 234; port security focus in, 115–16; retention in, 221; risk assessment and security planning in, 244; and transformational change, 305. *See also* budget increase after 9/11 attacks; port security after 9/11

Presidential Directive 27 (PD-27), 196, 222

Presidential Honor Guard, Coast Guard, 293

Presidential Inauguration (2005), Collins at, 19–20, 293–94

Presidential Inauguration Parade (1965), Collins in, 19

Presidential Unit Citation, for Coast Guard Hurricane Katrina response, 325, 327

privatization proposals for Coast Guard functions, 99–100

Proceedings magazine, 315, 322

professional development planning for Coast Guard personnel, Collins' insistence on, 182–83, 202

Programs Division, Collins as Chief of: and Allen, work with, 329; average day, 129; changes of administration and, 132–33; family's happiness in DC area, 138–39; home in Chantilly, 123, 139; interaction with senior leadership, 129, 136; responsibilities of, 129, 131; as return to familiar territory, 120, 122; and Round Room meetings, 129; staff of, 129–30; travel, 135; valuable experience gained in, 135; and value of past Programs Division experience, 130

Programs Division, Collins as Chief of, and budget cuts: across-the-board, as unwise practice, 126–27, 134; adjustments required of Coast Guard personnel, 125–26; challenges presented by, 122; Coast Guard leadership and, 125; Collins' desire to address, 125; consolidation and reduction of staff, 123–24; and continuous improvement imperative, 135; and costs of facilities mothballing, 126; and costs of staff cuts, 126; and cutting into muscle, 124; effect on operational readiness, 133; end of, with 9/11 attacks, 127; impact on Reserve, 130; multi-year plan for, 123, 129; preservation of service-delivery assets as priority in, 125, 128; savings efforts at all levels, 135; and search-and-rescue station closures, 125, 126; senior leadership input on, 123; ships and planes mothballed during, 126–27, 133–34; staff reductions, 128; streamlining efforts in response to, 122, 123, 128, 130; and supplemental appropriations, 124–25, 127, 242; as well-managed, 128. *See also* budget cuts

Programs Division, Collins as Program Analyst in: aircraft sensor acquisitions, 97; appointment to position, 93; and aviation programs, 97–98; and Balanced Budget Act budget cuts, 100–102; and budget documents, 98; career benefits of, 119–20; Coast Guard leadership during, 93–94; and congressional hearing support, 95–96; Department of Transportation leadership during, 98–99; and experience at Office of Research and Development, 93; experience gained in, 143; extensive program research required for, 94–95; hard work demanded by, 104; house in Fairfax, 94; mentors, 66; and planning, programming, and budgeting process, 95; as positive experience, 104; programs reviewed, 96–97; responsibilities, 94–95; and shore facilities, difficulty in getting funding for, 97

Programs Division Program Analysts: and Gilbert Study, 101; important work of, 93

Prueher, Joe, 173

Qatar, Commandant Collins' visit to, 299

RCPs. *See* resource change proposals

RDIS. *See* Research Development Information System

RDT&E. *See entries under* Research, Development, Test and Evaluation (RDT&E)

readiness: aging equipment and, 266, 312; effect of budget cuts on, 133–34, 178–79, 209, 234, 235, 312; as essence of Coast Guard mission, 133, 179, 267, 321–22; High Endurance Cutter maintenance issues and, 312; Loy's efforts to restore, 160, 227; multiple dimensions of, 234; as ongoing challenge, 312; partnerships and, 209; in summer of 2001, 234

readiness, Collins focus on: as Commandant, 183, 220, 266, 267; as Commander of 14th District (Hawaii), 158, 178, 179; as Deputy Group Commander St. Petersburg, 80

Rescue 21 program, Collins as Commandant and, 266, 273–74, 316–17

Research, Development, Test and Evaluation (RDT&E) appropriation: defense of, in budget food chain, 73–74; development of, 73; Office of Research and Development role in developing, 71–73

Research, Development, Test and Evaluation (RDT&E) program: functions of, 74–75. *See also* Office of Research and Development

research and development, strategies for defending, 77–78

Research and Development Center, 75; budget of, 76; Collins' visits to, as Office of R&D staff, 76; location of, 76; and oil fingerprinting, 75; and SAR research, 75

Research Development Information System (RDIS), 72

Reserve, Coast Guard: callups of, under Collins as Commandant, 266; Coast Guard budget cuts and, 130; and Hurricane Katrina, 324; Iraq War and, 288–89; and MDZ responsibilities, 161; and Pacific Maritime Defense Zone, 206; role in 14th District, 181–82; role in Group Long Island Sound (GLIS), 114–15; role in Group St. Petersburg, 87–88; September 11th attacks and, 236–37; types of callups, 236

resource change proposals (RCPs), 73, 95

retention: Collins' focus on, as PACAREA Commander, 221; in post-9/11 environment, 221

retirement of Collins: Chinese representatives at ceremony for, 214; and Coast Guard events, 330–31; Collins on, 333; part-time work in, 333; and travel, 255

Ridge, Tom: at CISCO management workshop, 250; at Coast Guard Academy commencement (2003), 291; and Coast Guard move to DHS, 283, 285; Collins' frequent dealings with, 290; and creation of DHS, 264; and HH-65 helicopter engine replacements, 217, 312; and Homeland Security Council (White House), 280; valuing of Coast Guard, 134

Riley, Peggy, 80

risk management: after 9/11, 243–44; importance of, 26, 49; as key to success for COs, 53; prioritization of risk in, 243–44; terrorist threat and, 240

Riutta, Ray, 225

Rivers, L. Mendel, 46–47

Rufe, Roger T., Jr., 158, 159, 176–77

Rush, 164

Russia: Collins' visit to, 301–2; and fisheries law enforcement, 26, 199, 213, 224; and North Pacific Coast Guard Forum, 199, 213, 301–2; and Simas Kudirka incident, 26–27, 50–51

Ryan, John, 86

Rybacki, Richard, 111, 112

Ryzwick, Bill, 162–63

St Petersburg, Florida: Collins' family happiness in, 78, 92. *See also* Group St. Petersburg

San Francisco: Collins' home in, 184, 204, 208, 225; Collins' sadness at departure from, 225; DOD departure from, 204, 208; housing costs in, 208–9; oil spill in harbor of, 196, 222–23; PACAREA headquarters in, 186, 208, 209

SAR. *See* search-and-rescue

Sassafras, 164, 172

Scarborough, Bob, 70, 257

SCIF. *See* Sensitive Compartmented Information Facility

sea marshals, 273

search-and-rescue (SAR): aboard *Cape Morgan*, 38; aboard *Vigilant*, 25–26; in Alaskan Flight 261 crash, 192–95, 222, 290; annual international exercise in Hong Kong, 174–75, 211; and closure for families, 194; Coast Guard research on, 75; Collins as Group Long Island Sound (GLIS) Commander and, 109; communication with families, importance of, 89, 193, 194; exhaustion and, 193–94; in Hurricane Katrina response, 322–28; improvements in response speed, 316–17; and international partnerships, importance of, 175. 199, 176; Korean Air Flight 801 crash and, 178; and North Pacific Coast Guard Forum, 199, 212–13; personnel increases after 9/11, 316; post-9/11 security responsibilities and, 276; public's appreciation of, 194, 320–21; *Selendang Ayu* wreck and, 319–21; and tsunami in Southeast Asia (2004), 321–22; US international leadership in, 174–75

Secretary of Transportation, and Coast Guard budget, 74, 124–25

sector commanders, new, advice for, 116

sectors, reorganization of commands into: Collins' advocacy for, 101, 109–10, 112, 274; completion of, under Collins as Commandant, 266, 273, 274, 306–7; concerns about, 116; efficiency of service delivery as goal of, 266, 274, 306; efforts to win approval for, 112; importance to security regime after 9/11, 273, 274; as integrated services approach, 198; and multi-agency cooperation, 274–75; positive results from, 306–7; study group on, 112

Selendang Ayu wreck and fuel leak, 319–21

Sensitive Compartmented Information Facility (SCIF), addition to Coast Guard ships after 9/11, 151, 241

September 11th terrorist attacks, 235–43; and Coast Guard activity in Port of New York, 241–42; Collins' reaction to, 235–36; and DOD-Coast Guard coordination, 237; evacuation from Battery Park, 241–42; and maritime attacks, expectations for, 240, 307; move to secure maritime system following, 236–38; and Pentagon deaths, 236; and Reserve callups, 236–37; response to, as team effort, 239–40; transformational era following, 305; and uncertainty about further attacks, 236. *See also* port security after 9/11; post-9/11 environment

sequestration, and Coast Guard budgets, 134

service academies, as good value for nation, 10

service delivery to public (tip of the spear): lack of Coast Guard focus on, in Collins' early career, 89; as most important element of Coast Guard work, 89; post-9/11 environment and, 251; preservation of, as priority in budget cuts, 102–3, 122, 123, 125, 128, 132, 133. *See also* efficiency of service delivery

17th District, headquarters, 186

sexual harassment: Collins' efforts to address, 202–3; policies necessary to address, 204

Sharp, Ron, 13

ship wrecks. *See Fiona*, explosion aboard; *New Carissa*; *Selendang Ayu* wreck and fuel leak

ships and planes of Coast Guard: 123-foot patrol boat design problems, 148; optics *vs.* Navy ships, 214

ships and planes of Coast Guard, age of, 29, 103, 150; and Deepwater program for managing older assets, 313; and high cost of maintenance, 122, 129, 140, 150, 151, 153, 235, 275;

and need for replacement, 150; and 123-foot patrol boat as stop-gap measure, 151–52; and readiness problems, 266, 312

shore facilities: and base closings, political difficulty of, 100, 102–3, 318; chronic underfunding of, 97, 317; deferred maintenance of, 97; neglect of, during post-911 buildup, 152–53

Siemens, Abe, 70

Siler, Owen W., 70

Simas Kudirka incident, 26–27, 50–51

Simmons, Rob, 297

Singapore, Coast Guard relationship with, 174, 175

Sirois, Dennis, 170, 236

Skinner, Samuel K., 111

Slater, Rodney, 139, 194, 222, 290

small boat forces, Collins' increase of assets in, 316

SMTC. *See* Special Missions Training Center

Snowe, Olympia, 325, 326

social media, Collins on, 278

Soleto, Lynn, 205

South Korea: and North Pacific Coast Guard Forum, 199; and Pacific Maritime Defense Zone, 206

Southern Command (SOUTHCOM), Coast Guard and, 296

Sovetskaya Litva, 26–27

Special Missions Training Center (SMTC), 294–95

speeches as Commandant, 254, 258–59; on Commandant website, 278; importance of, 258–59; speech writer for, 259

Stabile, Benedict L., 94

staff, advice for management of, 224

State Department: *Cao Yu* 6025 incident and, 172; Capstone course and, 138; and international support for Coast Guard law enforcement efforts, 300; and international support in Marine Environmental Protection, 196–97, 222

State of the Union Addresses, 292

Station McMurdo, 186

Steele, Bob, 60

Stevens, Ted, 128, 153, 249, 281

stewardship, Collins focus on, as Commandant, 183, 220, 267, 275, 311

Stewart, Jim, 70

strategic assessment and planning in Coast Guard: Collins' introduction of, in 14th District, 168–69; Collins' introduction of, in PACAREA, 169, 188–89, 202, 209, 218, 222–24; and national maritime security strategy, 276–77; need for improvement in, 207–8

Sullivan, Mike, 205

Super Typhoon Paka, 178

Swab Summer, 7–10; and Academy attrition, 7–8, 10; advice on surviving, 24; average day in, 8–9; challenges of, 7, 9; Collins' meeting of future wife during, 8, 15; as positive experience, 9, 10; purpose of, 7, 9; relief of finishing, 12; Wilkins as summer ensign at, 32

Tanaka, Brian, 121

teams, deployable: in PACAREA under Collins' command, 187; restructuring into separate commands, 188

teamwork, development of: aboard *Vigilant*, 22, 29–30; on *Barque Eagle* cruises, 17, 68; on *Cape Morgan*, 39; as goal of Coast Guard Academy, 11–12; as goal of Swab Summer, 9; as key to success for COs, 53, 183, 331; at Office of Acquisition under Collins, 154; in PACAREA under Collins, 202; trust and respect in, 22

technology, and efficiency of service delivery, 170, 176, 179, 310–11

terrorist attacks: lack of, during Collins' tenure as Commandant, 330; measures to discourage, 330; as ongoing threat, 240; risk management approach to, 240, 330. *See also* September 11th terrorist attacks

Thompson, Donald "Deese," 79, 94

Thorsen, Howard B., 112, 315–16, 322

Thurmond, Strom, 46–47

Total Quality Management (TQM): and budget cuts, 132; and Collins at 14th District, 118, 121, 169; and Collins' Office of Acquisition procurement reforms, 143

Townsend, Fran, 245

Trainer, Jack, 103

training and qualification processes, reform of, 310

Transportation, Department of: and Coast Guard competition for funding, 74, 99, 283–84; and Secretary's support for Coast Guard budget, 74, 124–25; support for Coast Guard, ebb and flow of, 98–99

Transportation Security Administration (TSA): Loy as head of, 226, 253; move to Department of Homeland Security, 264

tsunami in Southeast Asia (2004), Coast Guard response to, 321–22

TWA Flight 800 crash, 195

Typhoon Paka, Coast Guard response in, 321

Unaccompanied Housing Project, Pataluma, Collins' review of as Program Analyst, 97

United Nations ban on high seas drift nets, 159, 171, 199

University of New Haven MBA, 64

US Customs, and global monitoring of shipping after 9/11, 244

US Interdiction Coordinator (USIC), Commandant as, 296–97

US Pacific Command (USPACOM), and fisheries law enforcement, 159

USPACOM. *See* US Pacific Command

Venuto, Ken, 221, 309

Vessel Monitoring System (VMS), 170

Vessel Traffic Service (VTS), 140–41, 274

Vice Commandant: as flag detailer, 137–38; quarters, move to Bolling AFB, 230–31

Vice Commandant, Collins as: and acting Commandant role, 229; average day, pre 9/11, 229; as Co-Chair of Naval-Coast Guard Board (NAVGUARD Board), 233–34; and Deepwater program, 227, 231–33; and events in Washington DC, 293; flag corps administration duties, 259; guidance from Commandant, 227; innovation as focus of, 255–56; and International Sea Power Symposium, 246; and international visits, protocol for, 201; and Joint Chiefs of Staff meetings, 229–30; and legal issues, addressing of, 228; as liaison to Alumni Association, 233; as liaison to Coast Guard Foundation, 233; living quarters, 227, 230–31; meetings with Commandant, 227–28; and nations' senior leaders, work with, 289–92; office and staff, 227; ops briefs, 228; during period after confirmation as Commandant, 249; and planning and budgeting, 225, 230; plans to retire following, 229; and port security after 9/11, 244–45; responsibilities, 227, 228; selection for, 224–25; and September 11th terrorist attacks, 235–43; transition to post, 226; travel overseas, 298, 299–300; and vetting of issues for Commandant, 228–29; work-related entertaining, 230

Vietnam War: and antiwar protests, 46; Coast Guard service in, 32–33, 35, 47; termination of Coast Guard service before Collins' expected rotation, 47

Vigilant: described, 20, 24; fisheries law enforcement work, 26–27; food and mess staff aboard, 28–29; long period in service, 29; mission of, 24–25; officers aboard, 27, 31; and Simas Kudirka case, 26–27, 50–51; weaponry, 29

Vigilant, Collins aboard: and Academy assignment process, 20; apartment in Mattapoisett, 21, 22; and berths, 31–32; and crew moral, 30; and crew teamwork, development of, 22, 29–30; daily schedule, 28; as deck watch officer, 20, 29; disciplinary problems, 30; effort to listen and learn, 22, 29–30; experience gained, 34; as first assignment, 15; first watch experience, 27; junior officers' comradery, 30; learning of job, 27–28; memorable SAR cases, 25–26; move to command of *Cape Morgan*, 28; pay, 21; qualification as Officer of the Deck, 27, 28; range of ranks and backgrounds aboard, as new experience, 22; responsibilities, 28; and ship discipline, 31

VMS. *See* Vessel Monitoring System

VTS. *See* Vessel Traffic Service

Walker, David, 277

Washington, DC: Coast Guard aircraft stationed near, 303–4; Collins family's happiness in, 78; Collins' life in, as staff at Office of Research and Development, 76–77; Collins' post as Chief of Office of Acquisition as chance to remain in, 137; cost of living in, 76; events in, and Collins as Vice Commandant, 293; events in, Commandant Collins' attendance at, 292–93; housing costs in, 66; traffic in, 77

Watergate scandal, as topic in Collins' Academy classes, 65

weather forecasts, *Cape Morgan* and, 44

Welch, Frank, 261

Welling, Paul, 27, 31

Wells, Ron, 56–57, 59, 62–63

Weslayan University, Collins' post-graduate work at: courses taken, 55, 56, 58; faculty, excellence of, 56, 58; heavy workload, 58; home during, 55–56; other Coast Guard officers at Wesleyan, 55; as positive experience, 58–59; as preparation for faculty post at Academy, 55; return for alumni events, 59; selection for, 47; student responses to, 64–65; thesis, 57

Western Pacific Regional Fisheries Council, 170, 177

Wilkins, Bill, 32–34

Williams, Kent, 103, 125, 139

women in Coast Guard: and childcare issues, 220; and enrichment of diversity, 204; policies necessary to accommodate, 204

working hard, as value learned from family, 1, 20

World War II, Navy's absorption of Coast Guard during, 163

Wurster, Charlie, 205

Y2K preparations, in PACAREA, 216

Yost, Paul, 94, 103, 111, 255, 292

Young, Bill, 303

Zukunft, Paul, 312, 313, 314

Zulu Company: as Collins' company, 7; platoon leaders, 9–10; reputation for toughness, 10

www.ingramcontent.com/pod-product-compliance
Lightning Source LLC
Chambersburg PA
CBHW080621170426
43209CB00007B/1483